The Cognitive Neuroscience of Humor

The Cognitive Neuroscience of Humor

SHELIA M. KENNISON

AMERICAN PSYCHOLOGICAL ASSOCIATION
PUBLISHING

Published by
American Psychological Association
750 First Street, NE
Washington, DC 20002
https://www.apa.org

Order Department
https://www.apa.org/pubs/books
order@apa.org

In the U.K., Europe, Africa, and the Middle East, copies may be ordered from Eurospan
https://www.eurospanbookstore.com/apa
info@eurospangroup.com

Typeset in Meridien and Ortodoxa by Circle Graphics, Inc., Reisterstown, MD

Printer: Sheridan Books, Chelsea, MI
Cover Designer: Naylor Design, Washington, DC

Library of Congress Cataloging-in-Publication Data

Names: Kennison, Shelia M., author.
Title: The cognitive neuroscience of humor / Shelia M. Kennison.
Description: Washington, DC : American Psychological Association, [2020] |
  Includes bibliographical references and index.
Identifiers: LCCN 2020008740 (print) | LCCN 2020008741 (ebook) |
  ISBN 9781433832055 (paperback) | ISBN 9781433832062 (ebook)
Subjects: LCSH: Wit and humor—Physiological aspects. |
  Laughter—Physiological aspects. | Cognitive neuroscience.
Classification: LCC QP430 .K46 2020 (print) | LCC QP430 (ebook) |
  DDC 612.8/233—dc23
LC record available at https://lccn.loc.gov/2020008740
LC ebook record available at https://lccn.loc.gov/2020008741

https://doi.org/10.1037/0000203-000

Printed in the United States of America

10 9 8 7 6 5 4 3 2 1

CONTENTS

LIST OF TABLES AND FIGURES

TABLES

FIGURES

viii   *List of Tables and Figures*

PREFACE

There are no two topics more interesting to me than humor and the brain. The idea for this book grew out of my work teaching an undergraduate course on the psychology of humor. My students and I discovered a vast literature on the topic, which connects to the many subdisciplines within psychology (e.g., cognitive, social, personality, developmental, clinical, biological). Although we found a few books on the science and/or psychology of humor (R. Martin & Ford, 2018; Provine, 2000; Weems, 2014), none were dedicated to the cognitive neuroscience of humor. We found this surprising, given the growing literature on the topic.

The goal of this book is to provide an overview of the research that has been conducted on the cognitive neuroscience of humor. The book was written for those with a background in psychology with some knowledge of the organization and functioning of the brain. Readers may have some expectations about a book on humor and the brain. They may think that because humor is related to fun, it is a trivial part of human behavior and might involve peripheral (vs. central) systems of the brain. The opposite is true. Humor is an exceedingly complex human behavior, which we do not fully understand, and the brain processes involved in our experiences of humor are exceedingly complex and not fully understood. In this book, we learn more about these complexities, consider the multiple possibilities, and think about what future research is needed to make progress in understanding the phenomenon that is humor.

ACKNOWLEDGMENTS

I extend my deepest appreciation and thanks to my American Psychological Association (APA) editors Christopher Kelaher and Beth Hatch, and to everyone at APA Books who helped bring this project to fruition.

I thank my brother Clarence Kennison, Jr., with whom I share a unique sense of humor. Our mutual love of humor and the many hours we have spent laughing together have inspired me to value humor as the powerful human behavior that it is and to believe that some aspects of what we both find funny may be routed in our shared biology.

I thank the students at Oklahoma State University who shared my interest in the psychology of humor and have enrolled in my course over the years. Each semester, a comment or question will lead me to think more deeply about some aspect of humor.

Finally, I thank my husband, Lawrence Liggett, for his continuous encouragement and companionship. I am forever indebted to him for his willingness to proofread multiple versions of chapters and to listen to me talk through ideas before putting them on paper.

The Cognitive Neuroscience of Humor

Introduction

ognitive neuroscience is a relatively young field, beginning only about 50 years ago. The term *cognitive neuroscience* originated on a New York City taxi ride shared by Michael Gazzaniga and George Miller on their way to a meeting of brain scientists (Gazzaniga, 1984; see also Gazzaniga et al., 2013). It combines the term *cognition*, which encompasses all mental processes (e.g., sensory perception, thinking, learning, remembering, using language; see E. B. Goldstein, 2014), with the term *neuroscience*, which is the neural basis of mind and behavior. Gazzaniga and Miller envisioned the new field to be interdisciplinary and include researchers from cognitive psychology and neuroscience as well as medicine, philosophy, linguistics, and computer science (Gazzaniga et al., 2013). The focus of cognitive neuroscience is to understand the functioning of the normal, unimpaired brain (Gazzaniga, 1984). However, case studies of processing that occurs in individuals with atypical brains (i.e., damaged or affected by developmental disorder) provide insight into how such conditions lead to atypical processing.

The aim of this book is to synthesize the numerous cognitive neuroscience studies that have investigated one of the most intriguing and most enjoyable types of cognition: humor. In particular, I summarize research on the cognitive processes involved in humor comprehension. Humor can be defined as any event that leads to an involuntary feeling of amusement (also called "mirth"; R. Martin & Ford, 2018). Consider a popular psychology joke: "How many psychologists does it take to change a lightbulb? Just one, but the lightbulb *really* has to want to change." When did you experience the mirth? Jokes and

https://doi.org/10.1037/0000203-001
The Cognitive Neuroscience of Humor, by S. M. Kennison

cartoons provide opportunities for humor, but the most common occurrences of humor are those spontaneous instances that occur during social interactions (R. A. Martin & Kuiper, 1999).

I begin this book with a basic introduction to the study of cognition, humor, and the brain. Most of the cognitive neuroscience studies of humor have utilized jokes or cartoons as stimuli to understand the mental processes involved in the comprehension of humor, because researchers can create nonhumorous statements and images that serve as a control condition to compare with the humorous condition(s). In Chapter 1, I briefly review the history of brain science, focusing on relevant theories of how the brain controls cognitive processing. This review also includes descriptions of the early methodologies that researchers used to establish links between brain activity and specific aspects of humor processing.

The next four chapters examine different aspects of the cognitive neuroscience of humor, specifically exploring how brain regions contribute to humor processing. In Chapter 2, I focus on how humor processing is affected in individuals who have experienced brain damage or brain degeneration. These studies include patients with a wide variety circumstances, including brain changes due to normal aging, brain injury (e.g., stroke, traumatic brain injury) and brain degeneration (e.g., Alzheimer's disease, Parkinson's disease, Huntington's disease, amyotrophic lateral sclerosis, chronic alcohol addiction). I also discuss case studies of pathological laughter, which is commonly observed in individuals with brain injuries, tumors, or diseases that lead to brain degeneration. These studies provide clues about the locations in the brain that may be involved in typical humor processing.

Chapters 3, 4, and 5 examine the research most directly related to the brain activity occurring during humor processing. In Chapter 3, I review studies that have used electroencephalography (EEG), which involves recording electricity from the scalp (Luck & Kappenman, 2012). In experiments using EEG, electricity is recorded as participants comprehend jokes or cartoons (Amenta & Balconi, 2008; Coulson & Kutas, 2001: Coulson & Lovett, 2004; Coulson & Severens, 2007; Coulson & Williams, 2005; Coulson & Wu, 2005; Derks et al., 1997; Mayerhofer & Schacht, 2015; Svebak, 1982). In Chapter 4, I discuss the brain imaging studies using functional magnetic resonance imaging (fMRI), which involves tracking blood flow in the brain as participants carry out cognitive tasks within a strong magnetic field (Gorgolewski & Poldrack, 2016). The results from the EEG and fMRI studies indicate that humor is processed in multiple stages, which involve activity occurring in different brain regions during these different stages. In Chapter 5, I describe an intriguing body of research that shows that specific brain regions, when directly stimulated with electricity, are associated with laughing, smiling, mirth, the interpretation of comic facial expressions, or the appreciation of humor. These studies have participants who are undergoing brain surgery for the treatment of medical conditions (e.g., epilepsy, Parkinson's disease).

Chapters 6 and 7 examine how humor varies across individuals. In Chapter 6, I explain about how humor develops in typically developing children and how changes in humor processing are related to changes in cognitive and/or brain development. I also explore the research on humor deficits in three developmental disorders in which abnormal brain development occurs: (a) agenesis of the corpus callosum, which is detectable before birth (Penny, 2006); (b) autism spectrum disorder, which is typically diagnosed in children between the ages of 4 years old and 7 years old (Altschuler et al., 2018; Baio et al., 2018; Sheldrick et al., 2017); and (c) schizophrenia, which can emerge before the age of 18 years old (Miettunen et al., 2019). In Chapter 7, I discuss the research conducted with healthy adults, showing that different aspects of humor appreciation and production vary. Some of the variables that have been associated with differences include sex/gender, social status, personality traits, and heredity. Most of these variables have not been investigated in studies of brain processing. The intriguing possibility is that many individual differences in humor appreciation and humor production may stem from brain-based differences, stemming from a combination of genetics and environmental experiences occurring early in development.

In Chapter 8, I review the rapidly growing body of research showing that experiencing humor may have positive health benefits. This research indicates that experiencing humor results in physiological changes in the body, which involves hormones and immune system function. Clinicians are testing the effectiveness of humor-related interventions in improving mental and physical health. Only by fully understanding the nature of the cognitive and neural processes involved in humor can we determine the extent to which humor might play an important role in health and longevity. Future research likely will be able to elucidate how brain-based changes during humor processing set in motion the hormonal changes associated with positive health outcomes.

In Chapter 9, I explore the evolutionary roots of humor and the adaptive value that humor may have had in history. Research suggests that humor in humans can be linked to play behaviors in other species. Smiling and laughing is not unique to humans. A growing number of studies suggest that the tendency for play and engagement in positive emotions can be inherited and may serve specific survival-based functions. I also review studies detailing the development brain systems shown to be involved in humor processing in humans and positive emotions in other species.

In the final chapter, I discuss directions for future research. These include the possibility that researchers could develop a brain-based method for detecting humor in participants. Such an innovation would require researchers to identify a neural signature for humor, which occurs similarly across people and across different types of humor, and to create an algorithm that could detect this signature. I discuss how an algorithm of this type could be useful in research exploring how humor-based interventions could be used to improve mental and physical health. There is also a discussion of how individual differences in humor processing may exist, which would mean that there would likely need to be multiple algorithms to detect humor, each tailored to a specific type of person and/or type of humor. I recommend future research on the effect of humor on cognition, which may yield application in education and workplace training.

It is my hope that this book provides readers with some understanding of the biological basis of humor. Although humor is one of our most pleasurable cognitive processes, it may be one of the most complex. For those readers who are inspired to take up research on the topic, they likely share my view that despite how much we know about the cognitive neuroscience of humor, there is much to be learned. The coming decades will likely yield exciting new research on the topic.

1

Theories and Early Methodologies

The notion that the brain is involved in human abilities and behavior is quite old. The Edwin Smith Papyrus from the 17th century B.C. documents many ailments, including a description of difficulty speaking following a wound to the temple (Minagar et al., 2003). Around 400 B.C., Hippocrates speculated that human intelligence was due to the brain (Bear et al., 2001). Modern understanding of the link between brain processes and human abilities and behavior began in the 1800s. This chapter beings with a review of that work, focusing on competing theories of how the brain controls cognitive processing. Next, some of the early methodologies that cognitive neuroscience researchers use to establish links between brain activity and specific aspects of humor processing are discussed.

THEORETICAL CONSIDERATIONS

Theoretical perspectives in cognitive neuroscience come from the multiple disciplines, including psychology, neuroscience, linguistics, philosophy, computer science, and anthropology (Feinberg & Farah, 2006). For this discussion, the most relevant disciplines to the cognitive neuroscience of humor are philosophy, linguistics, psychology, and neuroscience. The oldest of these disciplines are philosophy (Kenny, 2012; see also Garfield & Edelglass, 2011) and linguistics (Bod, 2014). In philosophy, scholars have focused on questions related to understanding human knowledge, the human mind, and the

https://doi.org/10.1037/0000203-002
The Cognitive Neuroscience of Humor, by S. M. Kennison

relationship between the mind and the body using methods of critical analysis and argumentation (Heil, 2019). In linguistics, scholars meticulously documented the historical origins of language and the similarities among the world's languages (Lehmann, 2013). Considering these similarities in languages along with observations about the similarity of children's language acquisition around the globe, Chomsky (1986) proposed that there is an innate knowledge that equips children to acquire any language that they hear regularly (see also Pinker, 2003). The fields of psychology and neuroscience take a center role in cognitive neuroscience; theories aim to understand how the brain is involved in mental processes that result in behavior and how mental processes occur in real time with the stages of cognitive processing, which might occur one at a time or in parallel (Gazzaniga et al., 2013). Contemporary methods of studying brain activity during processing cannot yet provide a millisecond-by-millisecond record of activity in specific brain regions (Kemmerer, 2015). The following sections review the key theories related to brain functions and behavior and stages of cognitive processing.

Brain Locations and Functions

In the 19th century, Franz Joseph Gall (1758–1828) and Johann Spurzheim (1776–1832) promoted phrenology, which claimed that the patterns of bumps on an individual's head are related to personal characteristics (Parssinen, 1974). The coined expression "get your head checked" originated during the time that phrenology was popular. In the 1790s, Gall proposed that the brain was composed of 35 regions specialized for functions, including benevolence, conscientiousness, and combativeness. The 35 functions are identified on a phrenology head shown in Figure 1.1. Gall believed that bumps on the scalp were indicators of enlarged brain regions within the skull, and these enlarged brain regions were associated with higher levels of the corresponding personal characteristic. The view was widely accepted in the early 19th century, especially among educated and affluent families. Phrenology has long been revealed as a pseudoscience (A. B. Kaufman & Kaufman, 2018), although the idea that specific brain regions may be responsible for specific functions has endured. This view, referred to as the *localization of function view* of the brain, has been supported in numerous studies. The fact that the view has its origins in phrenology (Finger, 2009) may be surprising to some. The localization of function view is widely accepted today (Kolb et al., 2019), but phrenology is not.

In the 19th century, an opposing view of the brain, the *aggregate field theory*, claimed that the entire brain is responsible for the production of all mental functions and behavior (Chakravarthy, 2019). The view is most closely associated with Pierre Flourens (1794–1867), who conducted experiments with birds and rabbits (Boring, 1957). He carried out numerous studies in which he surgically damaged differing amounts of brain tissue in subjects and then observed what the animals could do following the surgery. He found that birds recovered remarkably well following surgery even when the amount

FIGURE 1.1. Phrenology Head

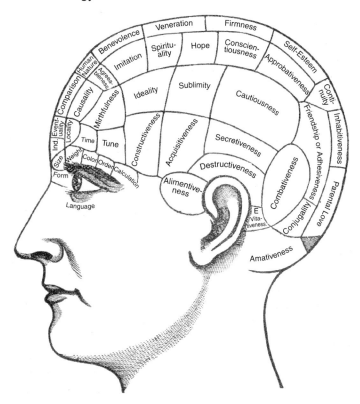

Note. Phrenologists interpreted the pattern of bumps on the scalp with reference to brain regions that were believed to be associated with personal characteristics. From *Phrenological Head* [Illustration first published in Sizer (1882)], by Wellcome Library, n.d., Wellcome Collection (https://wellcomecollection.org/). CC BY 4.0.

of brain damage was high. In the 20th century, the experimental psychologist Karl Lashley (1890–1958) also advocated the aggregate field theory, conducting experiments similar to those by Flourens, but with rats as subjects (Kosslyn & Andersen, 1992). He found that following brain damaging surgeries in which varying amounts of damage was carried out, animals performed reasonably well carrying out experimental tasks involving a variety of behaviors, including maze-learning. He concluded that knowledge/memory is located throughout the brain rather than being located in a single region (Lashley, 1929). Nevertheless, few today regard the aggregate field theory as viable.

Support for Localization of Function

By the end of the 19th century, there were multiple sources of evidence supporting the localization of function view. This evidence came from case studies of individuals who experienced brain damage from trauma or natural causes. The deficits associated with the brain damage provided support for the view that specific brain regions play unique roles in producing behavior. The three most important lines of evidence were the case study of Phineas Gage (1823–1860), Paul Broca's (1824–1880) case studies of patients with language production deficits, and Carl Wernicke's (1848–1905) case studies of patients with deficits in both comprehension and production.

Phineas Gage served as the first case study of the functioning of the frontal lobe. Gage was a Vermont railroad worker who survived being impaled by a metal rod on September 13, 1848 (Harlow, 1848). The rod passed through his skull, entering just below his left cheek, destroying tissue in the frontal lobe. Figure 1.2 displays how the rod might have passed through the skull. The case study described changes in his personality that might have been the result of this damage. His ability to control strong emotional impulses may have been particularly impaired (MacMillan, 2002). Analysis of this case study, along with others, helped researchers understand how a damaged region contributes to

FIGURE 1.2. The Skull of Phineas Gage

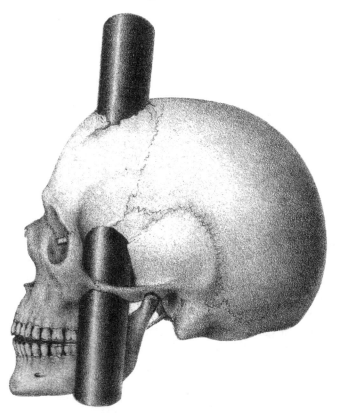

Note. The rod entered Phineas Gage's skull just below the left eye and exited through the top of the head. From "Dr. Harlow's Case of Recovery From the Passage of an Iron Bar through the Head," by H. J. Bigelow, 1850, *American Journal of the Medical Sciences, 20,* frontispiece. In the public domain.

the deficit in the individual under study and typical functioning in individuals with no damage.

Thirteen years after Gage's accident, Paul Broca (Kann, 1950) published his research describing a group of patients who displayed similar problems producing speech and whose brains after postmortem autopsy were found to have damage to a mostly frontal region in the left hemisphere. Using a similar methodology, Carl Wernicke (1874) described a new group of patients displaying a different type of language deficit associated with damage to an area in the left hemisphere that was distinct from the frontal region identified by Broca. These areas are displayed in Figure 1.3. Language problems following brain injury are referred to as aphasia; Broca's and Wernicke's patients are described as having Broca's aphasia and Wernicke's aphasia, respectively (Kemmerer, 2015).

Just a few years before Wernicke published his case studies, the neurologist John Hughlings Jackson (1835–1911) published his ideas about how the brain controls movement, which he developed from observations of the pattern of movement disturbances experienced by individuals having epileptic seizures (Balcells Riba, 1999; York & Steinberg, 2011). He observed that the aberrant movements followed a predictable pattern, starting in one part of the body (often the thumb) on one side of the body and spreading to other locations on that side, then spreading to affect body parts on the opposite side of the body. The pattern would come to be described as "Jackson's march." Now, we know

FIGURE 1.3. Broca's and Wernicke's Areas of the Left Hemisphere

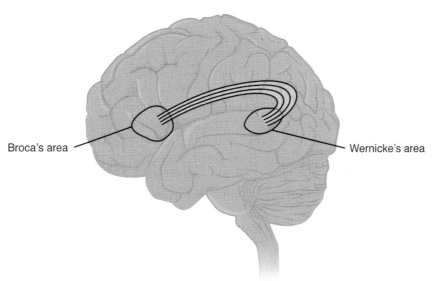

Broca's area

Wernicke's area

Note. From *Anatomy & Physiology*, by OpenStax College, 2013, Connexions (http://cnx.org/content/col11496/1.6/). CC BY 3.0.

that seizures occur because of abnormal electrical activity in the brain, which can spread to affect nearby regions. The predictability of the seizure pattern was due to the fact that the regions of the brain controlling parts of the body affected in sequence during seizures are located close to one another. Decades later, Jackson's theory would be confirmed (Balcells Riba, 1999).

In the early 20th century, the localization of function theory gained additional support and refinement through the work of Wilder Penfield (1891–1976) and colleague Herbert Jasper (1909–1999), who studied the relationship between brain function and behavior in studies in which he stimulated brain tissue directly with a small electrical current (Jasper & Penfield, 1954; Penfield, 1958; Penfield & Roberts, 1959/2014). Using this electrical brain stimulation (EBS) technique, Penfield (1952) demonstrated that stimulating a region could trigger sensory experiences in patients (e.g., hearing music, smelling an aroma), however stimulating the same location at a later time would result in a different experience. In addition, he confirmed that within the region of the brain that controls movement of and sensory input to parts of the body (i.e., the motor cortex), there was a topographical organization, with different subregions controlling specific body locations (Jasper & Penfield, 1954). Figure 1.4 displays the topographical organization of the motor cortex.

Other studies by Penfield and Roberts (1959/2014) demonstrated that language disruption occurred when regions corresponding to Broca's and Wernicke's areas in the left hemisphere were stimulated. This disruption was unlikely to occur when areas in the right hemisphere were stimulated. These observations provided evidence for the modern view that there are two hemispheres of the brain (i.e., left and right) and four major lobes of the brain, which are specialized for different functions. The left hemisphere plays a dominant role in language, logic, and math, and the right hemisphere plays a dominant role in face perception, emotional perception and production, and spatial processing (Kolb et al., 2019). The four lobes include: the occipital lobe, which is involved in visual processing; the temporal lobe, which is involved in hearing and memory; the parietal lobe, which is involved in movement and bodily sensation; and the frontal lobe, which is involved in higher cognitive functions (e.g., planning, organization, emotional regulation; L. J. Rogers & Vallortigara, 2017). Figure 1.5 displays the four major lobes of the brain, which make up the cortex and is distinct from the midbrain and brainstem (Gazzaniga et al., 2013; Kolb et al., 2019).

In the early 20th century, Korbinian Brodmann (1868–1918) identified smaller regions within the four lobes decades before Penfield and colleagues conducted their groundbreaking research (Brodmann, 1909; Garey, 2006; Zilles, 2018). Analyzing the cell structure, Brodmann identified 52 distinct brain regions. Figure 1.6 displays the Brodmann areas of the left and right hemispheres. Broca's area corresponds to Areas 44 and 45, and Wernicke's area corresponds to

FIGURE 1.4. The Topographical Organization of the Motor Cortex

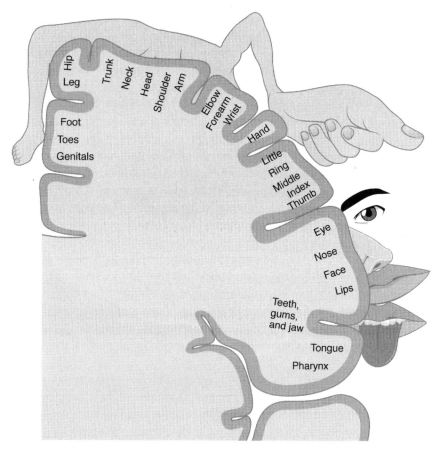

Note. Different parts of the body are controlled by brain regions varying in size. The face and the hands are controlled by larger brain areas than other parts of the body. From *Anatomy & Physiology*, by OpenStax College, 2013, Connexions (http://cnx.org/content/col11496/1.6/). CC BY 3.0.

Area 22 and a portion of Area 39 (Kemmerer, 2015). Within the occipital lobe, there are three areas responsible for visual processing: Area 17 (primary visual cortex), Area 18 (secondary visual cortex), and Area 19 (associative visual cortex). Generally, the Brodmann areas are commonly referenced in contemporary brain imaging research; however, some areas are no longer used (i.e., Areas 12–16, 48–51; Gazzaniga et al., 2013). It remains unclear whether these areas are the best scheme to use as researchers track down their associated functions (Yao et al., 2015). Much remains unknown about the complete role of most brain areas in cognition. Research has shown that most areas are involved in a variety of functions rather than a single function (Kolb et al., 2019).

FIGURE 1.5. The Four Major Lobes of the Brain

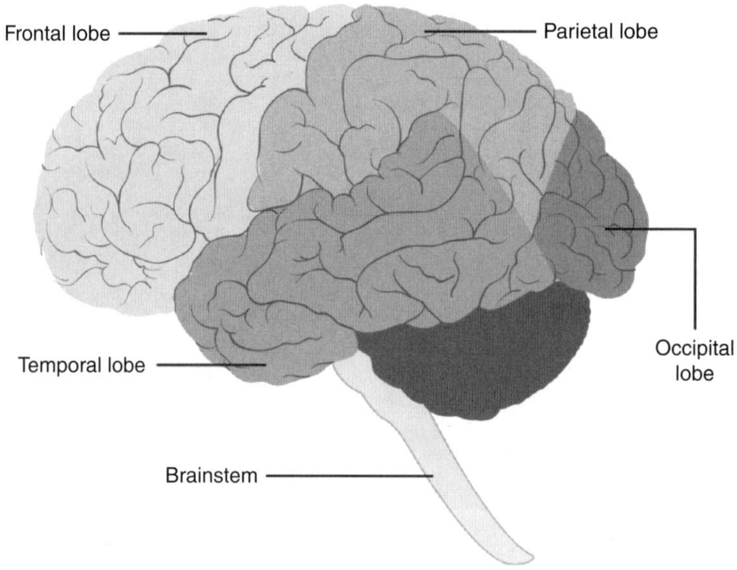

Frontal lobe ——— ——— Parietal lobe

Temporal lobe ———

Occipital lobe

Brainstem ———

Note. Each lobe of the brain is associated with specific functions. From *Diagram Showing the Lobes of the Brain*, by Cancer Research UK, 2016, Wikimedia Commons (https://commons.wikimedia.org/wiki/File:Diagram_showing_the_lobes_of_the_brain_CRUK_308.svg). CC BY 4.0.

Interconnectivity of the Brain Regions

Over the past few decades, we have gained a much more nuanced under-standing of brain functioning, moving beyond a focus on locations toward a focus on the interconnectivity of the brain, specifically on how individual regions are connected to and can communicate with other regions (Bressler & Menon, 2010; Sporns, 2016; Sporns & Betzel, 2016; van den Heuvel et al., 2016). Consider the example of a process people carry out multiple times a day, usually without much conscious effort: recognizing a face. A specific region of the brain is predominantly involved in recognizing faces (i.e., MT region, Brodmann Area 37; see Kanwisher, 2017). In individuals with damage to this area, the ability to recognize faces is lost or impaired, a condition referred to as acquired prosopagnosia (de Renzi et al., 1994). Researchers have identified the brain network involved in recognizing faces, discovering that there are more than 24 regions involved in processing different aspects of the face in functioning individuals (Zhen et al., 2013). In this book, under-standing the relationship between brain activity and how people process a joke or cartoon will involve appreciating the interconnectedness of many brain areas. Rather than a single area of the brain that is solely responsible for humor processing, research suggests that there is a complex network of interconnected brain regions. Chapters 4 and 5 of this volume examine these numerous regions.

FIGURE 1.6. Brodmann Areas of the Brain

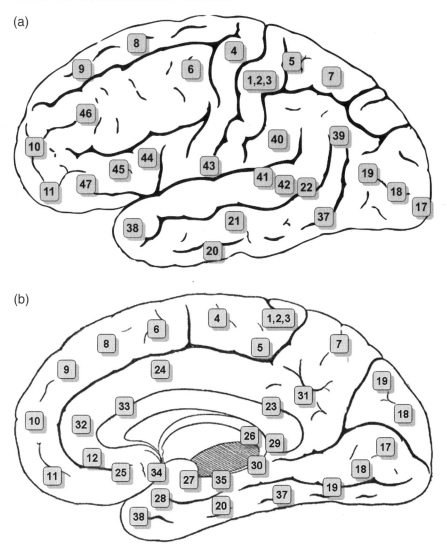

Note. Korbinian Brodmann identified a total of 52 distinct areas in the left (a) and right (b) hemispheres of the brain through visual analysis of the cellular structure of tissue samples. (a) is from *Gray's Anatomy* (Plate 726), by H. Gray, 1918, Bartleby.com. In the public domain. (b) is from *Gray's Anatomy* (Plate 727), by H. Gray, 1918, Bartleby.com. In the public domain.

EARLY METHODOLOGIES IN THE COGNITIVE NEUROSCIENCE OF HUMOR

Researchers in cognitive neuroscience use a variety of methodologies to understand the neural underpinnings of cognitive processes (see Newman, 2019, for a review). The most familiar methodologies used by researchers in cognitive neuroscience are likely those that provide colorful images of brain activity while participants perform cognitive tasks. These methodologies are discussed in more detail in Chapters 3 and 4 of this volume. This section reviews the early methodologies that have been used, and in some cases continue to be used, to understand the cognitive neuroscience of humor, as well as some significant findings associated with each method. These approaches include the philosophical approach; case studies of individuals with brain injury and developmental syndromes; and behavioral studies, which are used to test models empirically, measuring performance in terms of accuracy and reaction time.

The Philosophical Approach

Philosophers typically rely on questioning, reasoning, and argumentation to reach conclusions about phenomena (Haug, 2013). Some of the earliest examples of philosophy date back to around 400 B.C., with Plato (428–348 B.C.) and Aristotle (348–322 B.C.) being the most familiar Greek philosophers of the time. Both reflected on the topic of humor and its role in human interactions (Morreall, 1987). Then, humor was viewed in a negative light. Plato described humor as reflecting malice, pointing out another's shortcomings or misfortunes. Aristotle had a low opinion of individuals who went through life with a humorous nature.

Today, humor is associated with positive emotions, fun, and pleasure. However, this view of humor as a primarily positive behavior has likely evolved over the past century (Wickberg, 1998). In other historical documents, negative aspects of humor are represented more frequently than the positive aspects. There are numerous references to laughter in the Bible, most of which involve laughing individuals holding others in contempt (Koestler, 1964). Documents have survived showing hundreds of jokes and stories about the use of humor in ancient Rome, which provide insight into the role of humor in daily life (Beard, 2014). The jokes of ancient Rome targeted specific types of people for mockery (e.g., foreigners, the highly intelligent, eunuchs, slaves). The term *disparagement humor* is used today to refer to humor that mocks or disparages others because of their sex, ethnicity, or other social category (A. A. Berger, 1993; T. E. Ford & Ferguson, 2004; T. E. Ford et al., 2017; Gockel & Kerr, 2015; Hodson & MacInnis, 2016; Hodson et al., 2010; Saucier et al., 2016). It may be one of the most common and most negative forms of humor.

The topic of humor began to attract the attention of modern scholars around the late 19th and early 20th centuries (e.g., Freud, 1905/1960, 1928; Hall & Allin, 1897; Kline, 1907; Vasey, 1877). At this time, the negative aspects of humor were still emphasized over the positive aspects. Freud (1905/1960, 1928) was among the first scholars to distinguish wit, the negative form of humor, from more positive forms. Early theories focused on different aspects of humor; some researchers viewed humor as a way of conveying superiority over others (Bergson, 1911; Leacock, 1935; Ludovici, 1933; Rapp, 1951), whereas others viewed it as a way to provide relief through the release of tension (Dewey, 1894; Freud, 1905/1960, 1928; Spencer, 1911). Later in the 1970s, researchers came to view most humor as involving a combination of some type of incongruity, such as that introduced by a punchline of a joke and its resolution, which enables the listener or reader to find a way to arrive at the intended humor and subsequent feeling of mirth (Shultz, 1972, 1976; Suls, 1972, 1983).

Case Studies

The earliest attempts to understand the role of the brain in cognitive processing were observations of individuals with acquired impairments, such as Phineas Gage (Harlow, 1848) and the patients of Broca and Wernicke. Cognitive neuroscience researchers have continued to use the case study method to explore the neural underpinnings of many types of cognitive processing, including humor (MacPherson & Della Sala, 2019; Rosenbaum et al., 2014). By linking specific brain regions that have been damaged with specific functions that have been lost following the injury, researchers can test theories about how specific functions are controlled by the brain.

In the 20th century, one of the most famous case studies in all of psychology demonstrated the importance of the hippocampus in memory (Dittrich, 2017; Squire, 2009). In 1953, Henry Molaison (1926–2008), who was known as H. M. to the scientific community, had brain surgery to reduce the severity of epileptic seizures. If the part of the brain that is causing the seizures can be removed, the patient may experience a higher quality of life. Surgeons removed most of Molaison's hippocampus. As he recovered from the surgery, he demonstrated the ability to remember events occurring before the surgery, but he failed to remember events occurring after the surgery. Studies of his memory abilities and memory deficits (also called amnesia) began and continued to the time of his death. These studies supported the conclusion that the hippocampus was responsible for the storage of long-term memories. Without a hippocampus, individuals can hold conversations, read magazines, play games, and carry out other tasks but cannot recall any of those events at a later time. Figure 1.7 displays the location of the hippocampus in the temporal lobes of the brain. Later research confirmed that damage to the hippocampus caused amnesia (Zola-Morgan et al., 1986).

When compared with other methodologies, the case study is viewed as among the weakest in terms of being able to provide support for the cause(s) of an outcome; however, the methodology is still widely used today in a variety of fields as a way of gaining initial, exploratory information on a topic (Goertz, 2017). Despite limitations of case studies, researchers like Broca and Wernicke are often able to identify multiple individuals whose similar types of brain damage result in similar deficits. In other cases, researchers are able to identify individuals with different types of brain damage that appear to result in deficits that reflect different aspects of the same cognitive processing. For example, Caramazza and Hillis (1991) described two case

FIGURE 1.7. Location of the Hippocampus

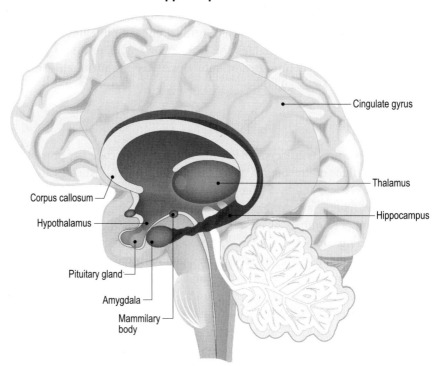

Note. This lateral view of the brain shows the hippocampus, which extends into both the left and right hemispheres. The word "hippocampus" comes from the Greek word *hippo* meaning horse, because of the horseshoe shape of brain organ.

studies of individuals who displayed different deficits in reading and writing nouns and verbs. Following brain injury, one patient could read nouns, but not write them, and could write verbs, but not read them. The opposite pattern was observed in a second patient (i.e., write nouns, but not read them; read verbs, but not write them). The observation supported the view that there is a double dissociation in reading and writing nouns and verbs, indicating that the cognitive processes are independent (i.e., not dependent) of one another and controlled by different parts of the brain.

Case studies of humor deficits date back to the early 20th century (Head, 1926). The cases were typically individuals who had aphasia following a stroke, which occurs when brain cells are damaged because of a reduction of blood flow (National Stroke Association, n.d.-b). Some cases of aphasia involved not only problems with language generally, but problems interpreting humor, specifically. Some of the more intriguing case studies of humor-related processing describe individuals who have experienced brain damage and who are unable to laugh (called *aphonogelia*; Kovarsky et al., 2011; McLeod et al., 2019). The opposite extreme has also been observed in individuals who laugh too much (called *pathological laughter*), which is uncontrollable laughter often occurring in the absence of a triggering humorous experience. Pathological laughter can occur in individuals who have brain injuries, tumors, or diseases that lead to brain degeneration. (Black, 1982, 1984; Dark et al., 1996). The broader term *pseudobulbar affect* refers to disrupted emotional processing, which can include uncontrollable, inappropriate laughing and crying (Parvizi et al., 2009; Poeck, 1985; Schneider & Schneider, 2017; Wortzel et al., 2008). Rare cases of pathological humor (also called *Witzelsucht* or *joking addiction*) have also been observed, where individuals exhibit excessive attempts of humor (J. M. Erickson et al., 2016; Granadillo & Mendez, 2016).

Behavioral Studies

The earliest use of systematic behavioral studies to understand the human mind and behavior occurred in the late 1800s. Wilhelm Wundt (1832–1902) established a laboratory in Leipzig, Germany in 1879 in which he trained numerous students to investigate the structures of the mind (Boring, 1957; Rieber, 2013). Studies involved interactions with participants who were asked to provide detailed reports about various sensory and perceptual processing. These efforts are recognized as the first experiments in psychology. By the end of the 20th century, those interested in understanding the mind referred to themselves as cognitive scientists. Cognitive science involves testing theories about stages of processing involved in a specific type of cognition (e.g., recognizing an object in a picture) in studies with samples of research participants. Participants are asked to carry out tasks during which participants' performance is assessed in terms of accuracy and, often, response time. For example, studies of memory often rely on accuracy. Participants are given an opportunity to process some information and then later given a test to determine how much they remember. There is research on memory and humor suggesting that humorous information is remembered better than nonhumorous information (Carlson, 2011; S. R. Schmidt, 1994, 2002; S. R. Schmidt & Williams, 2001; Summerfelt et al., 2010). S. R. Schmidt (2002) asked participants to view a series of cartoons. Some were humorous, whereas others were not humorous but weird. Still others were neither humorous nor weird. Half of the participants were led to expect a memory test for the cartoons. The other half were asked to recall the cartoons with prior warning. Regardless of whether participants were told about the memory test, participants' memory for the funny cartoons was significantly better than memory for the other two types of cartoons. In the study, R. S. Schmidt also recorded participants' heart rate to explore whether there were physiological differences occurring at the time that the different types of cartoons were first viewed and encoded in memory. He found no significant differences in heart rate at the time participants first viewed the different types of cartoons, ruling out the possibility that participants' physiological arousal differed across the conditions. He suggested humorous material is distinctive and leads to extra processing (compared with the processing of nonhumorous material), which involves connecting the information to related information in memory. This additional processing occurs at the time of encoding and at the time the person tries to retrieve the information from memory. Summerfelt et al. (2010) suggested an alternative explanation for the memory advantage for humorous material. They claim that the humorous material is usually constrained in terms of structure (e.g., set up followed by punchline) and/or in terms of a specific wording that leads to a humorous resolution. In contrast, nonhumorous material is not constrained in either way. The structural and verbal constraints of humorous materials are likely to be encoded in memory and used as memory cues at the time of retrieval.

Other behavior research relies on response time in addition to accuracy to make inferences about the likely stages of processing occurring during the task. The recording of response time in behavioral studies has a long history. Among the earliest to record human response time in research was Sir Francis Galton (1822–1911), who began measuring the time taken to carry out a task for the purposes of comparing individual differences (Jensen, 2006). Later, Franciscus Cornelis Donders (1818–1889) used it to make inferences about cognitive processing involved in visual perception, specifically how people made choices about response types (Donders, 1868/1969; D. E. Meyer et al., 1988). The term *mental chronometry* has been used to describe his approach, which continues to be used by researchers in psychology (Jensen, 2006). Donders measured reaction time in different situations. For example, he measured how quickly someone could make a manual keypress after perceiving some stimulus, such as light. This condition was referred to as simple reaction time. A second condition involved the respondent choosing between two responses depending on what stimulus was detected; if a light was detected on the left, then the respondent was to press the left key, and if a light was detected on the right, then the respondent was to press the right key. He could estimate the time needed for the participant to decide whether to press the correct key by subtracting the reaction time in the simple reaction time condition from the reaction time in the choice reaction time condition. Donders found that this difference was 100 ms.

In the study of cognition generally and humor specifically, the most significant contributions of behavior research are the development of models, which attempted to explain how processing occurs. By the 1970s, researchers viewed cognitive processes as being composed of multiple stages with each stage responsible for a specific aspect of the process (e.g., visual perception of letter features during word recognition; E. B. Goldstein, 2014; R. D. Luce, 1986). Such models were referred to as *process models*. In the early 1970s, multiple researchers described humor processing as involving two stages, one involving the detection of an incongruity (i.e., a violation of expectations) and one involving a resolution of the incongruity (Shultz, 1972, 1976; Suls, 1972, 1983). Suls (1972) proposed a process model for the comprehension of this type of humor, which is shown in Figure 1.8. Despite the fact that there are many aspects of the model that are unspecified (e.g., how are predictions made), the core notion that humor is processed in stages involving

FIGURE 1.8. Suls's Process Model of Humor

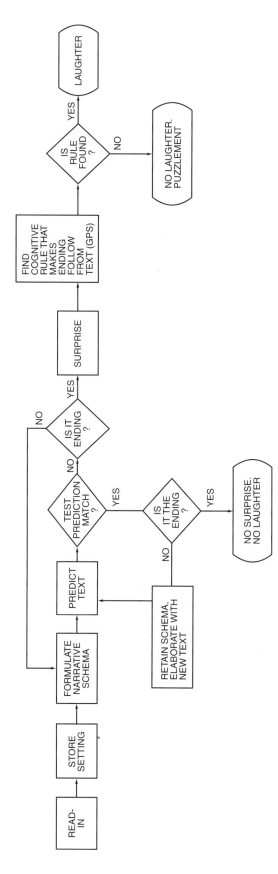

Note. Suls (1972) proposed the stages of humor processing involved in incongruity-resolution humor. GPS = general problem solver. From "A Two-Stage Model for the Appreciation of Jokes and Cartoons: An Information-Processing Analysis," by J. M. Suls, in J. H. Goldstein and P. E. McGhee (Eds.), *The Psychology of Humor: Theoretical Perspectives and Empirical Issues* (p. 85), 1972, Academic Press. Copyright 1972 by Elsevier. Reprinted with permission.

the identification and resolution of incongruity continues to be embraced (see Chapters 3 and 4, this volume). However, the model fails to account for two findings from studies on humor processing: (a) jokes with predictable punchlines are funnier than other types of jokes (Pollio & Mers, 1974), and (b) jokes that are easier to comprehend (i.e., having lower processing difficulty) are rated as funnier by participants (Ayçiçeği-Dinn et al., 2018; Cunningham & Derks, 2005; Derks et al., 1998; Pollio & Mers, 1974). Cunningham and Derks (2005) argued that humor relies on automatic cognitive processing, which occurs rapidly, and involves expert knowledge, which includes language knowledge of word meanings. When automaticity of processing is considered on a continuum, the more automatic the processing of a joke, the funnier it is. Nevertheless, the model has served to be useful to other researchers who have emphasized the role of social context in humor (Wyer & Collins, 1992). Something said in one social context might be perceived as funny but would not be funny when said in a different context.

On the basis of findings from their own work, Cunningham and Derks's (2005) suggestion that linguistic knowledge is used rapidly during humor comprehension is likely correct. Since the 1970s, cognitive psychologists have viewed memory as an interconnected network of information for which the organization is based on relatedness in meaning, following earlier work by Collins and colleagues (Collins & Loftus, 1975; Collins & Quillian, 1969). When a concept is activated in memory (e.g., when it is heard, read, or brought to mind), concepts related in meaning are also activated in proportion to the semantic relatedness. D. E. Meyer and Schvaneveldt (1971) supported this in experiments where participants were shown a series of letter sequences, some words and some nonword foils, and asked to respond quickly whether the letters made up a real word (see also D. E. Meyer et al., 1975). Participants can typically respond to real words within 700 ms. They found that participants responded faster when the immediately preceding word was closely related in meaning (e.g., bread & butter vs. bread & floor). Figure 1.9 displays how semantically related concepts may be connected in memory with shorter distances between strongly related concepts and longer distances between weakly related concepts. For example, the color red is more closely related to fire engines than to sunsets. Memories of words include not only information about their meanings but also all other information that enables people to use them during speaking, listening, reading, and writing. Consequently, when people hear a word and activate it in memory, other words sharing the same sounds can become activated (Goldinger et al., 1989; P. A. Luce et al., 1990). During reading, when an individual activates a word in memory, other words sharing the same letters can become activated (Havens & Foote, 1963). Puns are created when the similar sound of two words is used for comic effect (e.g., The grammar teacher was very logical. He had a lot of comma sense).

A skilled humorist can predict what an audience will find funny. This requires the individual to be aware of what the audience knows and does not know on the topic being discussed. Behavioral studies of humor productions

FIGURE 1.9. Semantically Related Concepts in Memory

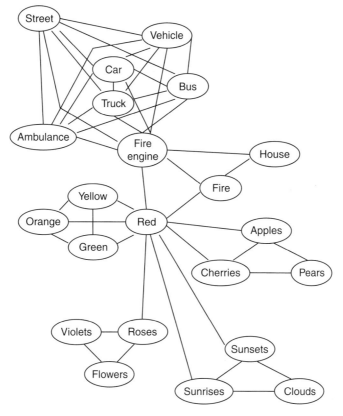

Note. Collins and Loftus (1975) proposed that in memory, the organization of concepts is based on semantic relatedness, with shorter distances between strongly related concepts and longer distances between weakly related concepts. From "A Spreading Activation Theory of Semantic Processing," by A. M. Collins and E. F. Loftus, 1975, *Psychological Review*, *82*(6), p. 412. Copyright 1975 by the American Psychological Association.

often use a cartoon punchline production task (Kohler & Ruch, 1993). Studies have found that some people are more capable of producing funny captions for cartoons than others (Brodzinsky & Rubien, 1976; Kellner & Benedek, 2017; Kohler & Ruch, 1993; Nusbaum et al., 2017; see also Ziv, 1976, 1983). These studies have found that those who score higher in creativity do better on the caption production task. It is possible that creative people can associate concepts in memory more rapidly than others. A popular measure of creativity is the remote associates test, which was created by Mednick (1962, 1968). Participants are shown three words and asked to generate another word that is linked to each. For example, "salts, room, blood" might produce the response "bath." Individuals who are more creative can form links between weakly related concepts that do not become apparent to those who are less creative. These results suggest that as people comprehend humor, they are rapidly associating concepts in memory. When a joke or cartoon directs people to think about a particular group of concepts in a particular way, people rapidly associate these concepts in memory, which leads them to the incongruity or surprise that was intended.

SUMMARY

The historical origins of cognitive neuroscience began with the localization of function view, which claimed that specific brain locations are associated with specific functions. This view began with the phrenologists in the early 1800s, who believed that there were 35 brain regions associated with specific personal characteristics (e.g., conscientiousness, combativeness). Although phrenology was ultimately rejected and determined to be a pseudoscience, the view that specific brain regions are associated with specific functions was supported in subsequent case studies starting in the mid-1800s. These studies included those involving Phineas Gage and the patients of Paul Broca and Carl Wernicke. In the 20th century, Wilder Penfield's EBS studies provided additional support. Later in the 20th century, researchers continued to use case studies to understand the relationship between cognitive processing and the brain. Other approaches included philosophical inquiry and the cognitive approach, which has yielded models of cognitive processing and behavioral studies in which processing is investigated empirically through the measurement of performance accuracy and reaction time.

2

Abnormal Humor Processing Due to Brain Aging, Injury, and Degeneration

Since the 19th century, researchers have relied on case studies of the deficits resulting from brain damage to make inferences about how brain regions are involved in specific functions. For example, Paul Broca (Kann, 1950) and Carl Wernicke (1874) used case studies of on their research of aphasia. In the early 20th century, the first case reports of deficits in humor processing following brain damage were reported among patients who exhibited symptoms of aphasia (Head, 1926; Isserlin, 1936; Luria, 1970). This chapter first reviews studies of brain changes that occur during the aging process that are associated with declines in cognitive ability and impairments in humor processing. Next, the chapter reviews studies documenting deficits in humor comprehension and related processing following brain damage. The third section of this chapter examines similar cognitive deficits leading to impaired humor processing in individuals with disorders that cause gradual degeneration of different brain regions. These disorders include dementia, Parkinson's disease, Huntington's disease, amyotrophic lateral sclerosis (ALS), and chronic alcoholism. In the last section, the chapter reviews studies of individuals whose brain damage or degeneration has led to the unusual condition of pathological laughter, which is uncontrollable laughter in the absence of any triggering event, are reviewed (Dulamea et al., 2015; Forabosco, 1998; Oh et al., 2008; Poeck, 1985; Zeilig et al., 1996). These studies reveal the immense complexity that exists in how laughter and mirth are controlled by the coordination of processing in numerous brain regions.

https://doi.org/10.1037/0000203-003
The Cognitive Neuroscience of Humor, by S. M. Kennison

HUMOR PROCESSING IN OLDER ADULTS

There is now a consensus among researchers that the majority of older adults avoid severe cognitive impairments found in dementia and other diseases (Irwin et al., 2018). Nevertheless, most older adults can expect to experience a gradual decline in working memory, which refers to the type of memory used when making decisions in real time (Bopp & Verhaeghen, 2005). In healthy aging, working memory capacity is reduced in middle and later adulthood and may contribute to increased difficulty in finding words during speaking (also referred to as tip-of-the-tongue states; Burke & MacKay, 1997; Burke et al., 1991, 2000). Reductions in working memory associated with aging appear to contribute to older adults' difficulty with language comprehension (Alloway & Alloway, 2015; de Beni et al., 2007). Research has also shown that older adults may experiences particular declines in humor comprehension and humor appreciation (see Greengross, 2013, for a review). The gradual decreases in memory, language, and humor ability appear to be directly linked to age-related changes that occur in the brain, including shrinkage throughout the brain (Gutchess, 2019).

As the brain ages, numerous changes occur, most notably a reduction in volume (Bajaj et al., 2017; Peters, 2006). Some researchers have suggested the right hemisphere of the brain is more negatively affected by aging than the left hemisphere (Cherry et al., 2005; Dolcos et al., 2002; G. Goldstein & Shelly, 1981). Since the early 20th century, researchers have recognized that the two hemispheres of the brain are specialized for different functions (Penfield & Roberts, 1959/2014; see also Wada, 1949, 1997). For most people, the left hemisphere controls language production and comprehension. Damage to the left hemisphere is more likely to result in aphasia than damage to the right hemisphere (Turkeltaub, 2019). The right hemisphere plays a key role in comprehending emotions (Gainotti, 2019) and recognizing faces (Kanwisher, 2017). Many aspects of processing routinely involve the coordination of both hemispheres, which are connected by a bundle of fibers referred to as the corpus callosum.

The asymmetrical effects of aging may account for why older adults experience greater declines in right hemisphere processing, including emotion recognition (Halberstadt et al., 2011; Prodan et al., 2007) and understanding social interactions (MacPherson et al., 2002; Phillips et al., 2011; Uekermann et al., 2006). An important ability in social interaction is to see a situation from another person's point of view. Individuals vary in their ability to shift perspective. The term *theory of mind* has been used to refer to a person's understanding that others' minds (e.g., thoughts, beliefs, feelings) differ from their own (Baron-Cohen et al., 1985; Conway et al., 2019; Frith & Frith, 1999; Premack & Woodruff, 1978), and the term is used when thinking about the intentions of others. Research has shown that theory of mind processing declines with age (Bischetti et al., 2019; Coolin et al., 2017; Henry et al., 2013) and can be impaired following brain damage (Turkstra et al., 2018).

A number of studies have shown that older adults with no known brain damage are less able to detect social gaffes (i.e., faux pas) than younger adults in laboratory tasks (Stanley et al., 2014; Wang & Su, 2006). Stanley et al. (2014) examined how adults of varying age interpreted social interactions displayed on a video, and some of the scenarios included a social gaffe. One example was a clip from a television comedy show in which the boss reacts negatively when an employee who is overweight expresses a desire to be a cheerleader. Social gaffes were perceived as funny and were viewed with more smiling among younger adults than older adults. The next section examines studies investigating humor deficits following different types of brain damage. Many of these studies confirm the importance of the right hemisphere in understanding the minds of others and comprehending humor, including interpreting sarcasm (Phillips et al., 2014, 2015). Other research with older adults (Uekermann et al., 2008; Westbury & Titone, 2011) has shown that they have difficulty comprehending nonliteral forms of language (i.e., figurative language), which includes idioms ("a stitch in time saves nine") and metaphors ("the discussion between enemies was hand-to-hand combat"). Comprehending figurative language and humor involves the consideration of multiple possible interpretations of phrases or sentences and ultimately arriving at an understanding of the intended meaning.

Since the 1970s, researchers have investigated older adults' ability to process humor (Bischetti et al., 2019; Mak & Carpenter, 2007; R. A. Martin et al., 2003; Ruch et al., 1990; Schaier & Cicirelli, 1976; Shammi & Stuss, 2003; Uekermann et al., 2006). Among the earliest studies was Schaier and Cicirelli's (1976) investigation of humor processing in adults age 50 years old to 80 years old. They found that although comprehension accuracy declined with age, the oldest participants appreciated the humor more than younger ones. The authors suggested that many forms of humor, particularly those involving incongruity, are cognitively complex and challenging for older adults to comprehend fully. In a later study, Shammi and Stuss (2003) investigated how adults age 29 years old to 73 years old comprehended simple jokes. Participants were presented with multiple cartoons and asked to select the funny one. They were also asked to select the funny punchline for a specific cartoon. Their results showed that accuracy was lower for older adults than for younger adults. Researchers also asked participants to rate the humorousness of the stimuli from both tasks. The results showed that older adults consistently provided higher ratings than young adults. Shammi and Stuss concluded that aging negatively affects cognitive processing but does not impair humor appreciation.

More recent studies investigated older adults' comprehension and appreciation of different types of humor (Bischetti et al., 2019; Uekermann et al., 2006). Bischetti et al. (2019) investigated how older adults comprehended humor that did or did not involve theory of mind processing. The humor that did not involve theory of mind processing were those that involved phonological humor (i.e., puns). The humor that involved theory of mind processing involved considering another's state of mind. The results showed that individual differences in theory of mind processing ability in the older adults predicted their ability to

TABLE 2.1. Four Humor Styles as Assessed in the Humor Styles Questionnaire

Type of humor style	Category	Definition
Affiliative	Positive	Uses humor to connect with others
Self-enhancing	Positive	Uses humor to cope in life
Aggressive	Negative	Uses humor to target others
Self-defeating	Negative	Uses humor to put oneself down

Note. Data from R. A. Martin et al. (2003).

find humor in jokes involving theory of mind, but it did not predict how humorous they found the phonological humor.

When examining humor styles across the lifespan in individuals age 14 years old to 87 years old, R. A. Martin et al. (2003) found that older adults used some types of humor less often than younger adults. Their Humor Styles Questionnaire assessed the use of four humor styles (see Table 2.1): *affiliative*, which involves using humor to form connections to others; *self-enhancing*, which involves using humor to cope in daily life; *self-deprecating*, which involves direct negative humor toward oneself; and *aggressive*, which involves targeting others negatively with humor. The affiliative and self-enhancing humor styles are viewed as positive and the self-deprecating and aggressive humor styles as negative. Since its development, the questionnaire has been translated into approximately 30 languages and used to explore humor behavior around the globe (R. Martin & Ford, 2018). Versions have been developed to assess humor styles in children (C. L. Fox et al., 2013) and adolescents (C. L. Fox et al., 2016). Interestingly, recent research conducted with German respondents suggests that there may be as many as nine humor styles (Heintz & Ruch, 2015, 2019; cf. R. A. Martin, 2015).

R. A. Martin et al. (2003) observed that older adults used two of the four humor styles (affiliative and aggressive) less often than did younger adults. In contrast, the self-enhancing humor style was significantly higher for older women than for younger women. No significant relationship was observed between the self-enhancing or self-defeating humor style and men's age. In a more recent study, Stanley et al. (2014) examined differences in younger and older adults' perceptions of social gaffes. They found that younger adults found social gaffes funnier than did older adults, and that older adults used the aggressive humor style less often than did younger adults. In mediation analyses, the researchers found that the relationship between age and social appropriateness ratings of the study stimuli was mediated by use of the aggressive humor style.

HUMOR PROCESSING FOLLOWING BRAIN DAMAGE

Over the last 50 years, researchers have explored the relationship between the location of brain damage and the presence of humor processing deficits using studies in which individuals with brain damage were compared with healthy control participants and which controlled for age, education, and other variables (Mak & Carpenter, 2007; R. A. Martin et al., 2003; Ruch et al., 1990; Schaier & Cicirelli, 1976; Shammi & Stuss, 2003; Stanley et al., 2014). In some cases, performance was also compared with individuals with damage to other regions of the brain, which can show that a function is preserved for some patients but not others.

The majority of studies documenting disruptions in humor processing following brain damage have focused on survivors of stroke (Bihrle et al., 1986; Brownell et al., 1983; Cheang & Pell, 2006; Dagge & Hartje, 1985; Docking et al., 1999; Gardner et al., 1975; Gaudreau et al., 2013, 2015; Gillikin & Derks, 1991; Griffin et al., 2006; Heath & Blonder, 2005; LaPointe et al., 1985; Shammi & Stuss, 1999; Shany-Ur et al., 2012; Wapner et al., 1981) and survivors of closed head trauma (Braun et al., 1989). Stroke occurs when there is a lack of blood flow in a region of the brain, which can lead to the death of cells (National Stroke Association, n.d.-b). Age is a major risk factor for stroke, with risk steadily increasing after age 55, but stroke can affect individuals of any age. Nearly 20% of stroke survivors have some type of aphasia (Mozaffarian et al., 2016), which usually occurs from damage to the left hemisphere regions that control language (Kemmerer, 2015). However, in a small percentage of people, the right hemisphere plays a dominant role in language (Penfield & Roberts, 1959/2014; Wada & Rasmussen, 1960/2007), and for them, damage to the right hemisphere can result in language deficits (de Witte et al., 2008). When aphasia occurs because of damage in the right hemisphere, it is referred to as *crossed aphasia* (de Witte et al., 2008).

Although most individuals with aphasia have damage in the left hemisphere, the majority of studies documenting humor deficits have found that the critical location of damage is in the right hemisphere. For example, Wapner et al. (1981) compared comprehension abilities using humorous and nonhumorous materials with 16 patients with right hemisphere brain damage. The sizes and locations of the right hemisphere damage varied across patients. They were tested on tasks involving language comprehension and humor processing. Their performance was compared with patients with left hemisphere brain damage as well as healthy control participants. During the test of humor processing, participants listened to 16 jokes and were asked to select the punchline that matched the joke from a set of four options. The three foils included three nonfunny continuations of what the participant heard: a sensible, emotionally neutral continuation; a sad continuation; and a non sequitur continuation. They found that those with right-hemisphere damage performed more poorly on comprehension tasks than those with left-hemisphere damage or healthy control participants. The exact materials that were used in the study were not provided in the publication, but Table 2.2 displays an example that was constructed on the basis of the description.

Observing similar results, Bihrle et al. (1986) also asked participants with left or right hemisphere damage to view three cartoon panels and then asked them to choose one of two concluding panels that would serve as the most

TABLE 2.2. Example of Punchline Matching Task Item

I just flew in from Los Angeles.	
a. The flight was delayed for hours.	b. I had been to a funeral.
c. Boy, are my arms tired.	d. The touchdown excited everyone.

Note. Data from Wapner et al. (1981).

humorous concluding panel. Both concluding panels involved an expected resolution, but one was more humorous than the other. The results revealed that accuracy was lower for participants with right-hemisphere damage than for participants with left-hemisphere damage. A second experiment was conducted using text rather than cartoons.

Heath and Blonder (2005) examined humor appreciation in individuals who had experienced stroke, obtaining information from the patient as well as their spouses. Some patients had damage in the left hemisphere and others in the right hemisphere. The results indicated that for those with right-hemisphere damage, there was a perceived reduction in humor appreciation after the stroke as compared with before the stroke. No change in perceived humor appreciation was observed for those with left-hemisphere damage.

Theory of mind processing (i.e., thinking about the mental states of others) can be impaired in healthy older adults (Henry et al., 2013; Moran, 2013; Rakoczy et al., 2012; Wang & Su, 2006). Researchers have also found that theory of mind processing can be impaired in individuals who sustain right-hemisphere brain damage (Baldo et al., 2016; Bibby & McDonald, 2005; Brownell & Stringfellow, 2000; Happé et al., 1999; I. Martin & McDonald, 2006; Weed et al., 2010; Winner et al., 1998; Xi et al., 2013; Yeh et al., 2015; Yeh & Tsai, 2014).

Baldo et al. (2016) examined the social awareness among individuals with brain damage in the left or right hemispheres using a series of cartoons. Each cartoon was presented with a statement. Participants were asked to judge whether they believed that the statement would be something that the character in the cartoon would say or think. Then they were asked to rate the social acceptability of the statement. Individuals with right-hemisphere damage rated statements as less socially acceptable than did those with left-hemisphere damage. Happé et al. (1999) investigated how well individuals with damage to the right hemisphere could infer others' mental states in a story comprehension task compared with healthy control participants. In stories, characters were depicted as holding an accurate belief or false belief about another's mental state. The character later made a joke involving irony or made a statement that could be perceived as a lie. The results indicated that individuals with brain damage performed significantly worse than did healthy control participants. They were particularly poor at detecting and appreciating jokes, and most of the time, they were not able to distinguish jokes from lies.

Deficits in theory of mind processing also were observed by Weed et al. (2010), who investigated how well individuals with right hemisphere damage could infer characters' (e.g., animate triangles) intentions in a series of films. The performance of healthy control participants was also measured. In some conditions, the triangles could be perceived as having mental states related to intention (e.g., the red triangle caught the blue triangle and put it in jail). Participants were asked if the sequences made up a story and were asked to press a button (i.e., yes or no). When they responded "yes," participants were asked to describe the story. The results showed that individuals with right-hemisphere brain damage performed less well than healthy control participants. Performance on the theory of mind tasks (i.e., describing the mental states of the shapes) were the poorest of all.

Using different measures, Xi et al. (2013) investigated theory of mind processing in survivors of stroke who had damage to the right temporal lobe. They measured theory of mind using two tasks: the Reading the Mind in the Eyes test (Baron-Cohen et al., 2001), in which participants are shown photos of the eyes of people and asked to select the correct adjective to describe the person's emotional state, and the faux pas task, in which participants are shown social interactions and asked if any character made a social gaffe. Compared with healthy control participants, patients with right-temporal-lobe damage performed significantly worse in both tasks.

Shamay and colleagues (2002; Shamay-Tsoory et al., 2005) investigated individuals' ability to interpret sarcasm and irony following brain damage. Shamay et al. observed deficits in comprehending sarcasm and ability to empathize in individuals with damage to the prefrontal cortex and compared it with individuals with damage to the posterior cortex. Participants with damage to the right prefrontal cortex performed most poorly. The authors concluded that the ability to empathize is needed to interpret sarcasm. In a later study, Shamay-Tsoory et al. (2005) investigated theory of mind processing in individuals with damage to different subareas of the prefrontal cortex. They tested 26 individuals with damage to either the ventromedial or dorsolateral subareas, 13 individuals with damage to posterior regions of the brain, and 13 healthy control participants on multiple tasks, including comprehending false beliefs, interpreting ironic statements, and detecting socially inappropriate actions. Those with damage to the ventromedial regions of the prefrontal cortex performed more poorly on two of the three tasks (comprehending irony and detecting social faux pas), than did participants in the other two groups. The results documented the important role of these regions of the prefrontal cortex in theory of mind processing.

In a later study, Yeh et al. (2015) examined theory of mind, empathy, and executive functioning (e.g., controlling attention, switching between tasks, as well as other abilities) in eight individuals with damage in the ventromedial prefrontal cortex, 15 individuals with damage in the dorsolateral prefrontal cortex, and 19 healthy control participants of similar age. They found that performance on verbal and nonverbal theory of mind tasks was poorest for the individuals with damage in the dorsolateral prefrontal cortex. All participants also completed the Wisconsin Card Sorting Test-Modified (Schretlen, 2010), which assesses an aspect of executive functioning. Performance on the test predicted performance in the theory of mind tasks for individuals with damage in the dorsolateral prefrontal cortex. The authors concluded that the deficits in theory of mind and empathy can be explained by deficits in executive function. There are a variety of locations in the brain that appear to impair theory of mind processing, comprehension, and humor comprehension when damaged.

HUMOR PROCESSING IN DEGENERATIVE BRAIN DISEASES

Deficits in humor comprehension are observed in individuals with diseases that damage the brain, including different types of dementia, Parkinson's disease, Huntington's disease, ALS, and individuals with a history of chronic alcohol abuse. The affected brain regions differ across the different groups of individuals. As in all cases in which research identifies a link between specific brain areas and behavior functions, it is important to keep in mind that factors other than brain damage may contribute to the observed behavior. This caution is especially relevant to circumstances in which the brain is damaged by a disease process.

Dementia

There are multiple types of dementia, including vascular dementia, frontotemporal dementia, and Alzheimer's dementia (see Burns & Iliffe, 2009, for a review). The most familiar and most frequent form of dementia results from Alzheimer's disease, which accounts for approximately half of all cases of dementia (World Health Organization, 2017). Vascular dementia is the second most common, accounting for approximately 25% of cases. It is caused by the reduction of blood flow in the brain. Among the rarest forms of dementia is frontotemporal dementia, which represent less than 5% of dementia cases. The name reflects the fact that the frontal and the temporal lobes of the brain are particularly affected. Health care providers may have difficulty determining which type of dementia is present in a patient because confirming or disconfirming Alzheimer's dementia is most often done during autopsy (Cure et al., 2014). Imaging the brain with magnetic resonance imaging can provide information about the specific regions of the brain that have atrophied, which may distinguish frontotemporal dementia from Alzheimer's disease, which is associated with loss of volume in the hippocampus in the early stages of the disease (Ferreira et al., 2017).

A relatively small number of studies have documented deficits in humor comprehension in individuals with dementia (C. N. Clark et al., 2015, 2016;

Shany-Ur et al., 2012). C. N. Clark et al. (2015) investigated humor comprehension in 22 individuals with frontotemporal dementia and in 11 individuals with semantic dementia, which is a variant of frontotemporal dementia affecting memory for language. The results showed that both groups of participants processed humor as well as in 21 healthy control participants of similar age. Participants were asked to judge nonverbal cartoons, which were humorous or nonhumorous. Compared with the healthy controls, individuals with dementia performed more poorly in detecting humor in cartoons that involved unfamiliar and familiar situational contexts. Those with frontotemporal dementia performed less well detecting humor in unfamiliar contexts than familiar ones, a difference that was not observed in individuals with semantic dementia.

In a subsequent study, C. N. Clark et al. (2016) interviewed individuals about their humor behavior and preferences. They had a variety of disorders involving brain deterioration, including 15 individuals with frontotemporal dementia, 16 individuals with suspected Alzheimer's disease, seven individuals with semantic dementia, 10 individuals with nonfluent aphasia, and 21 healthy control participants of similar age. The questions in the interview focused particularly on identifying inappropriate humor responses. All patient groups showed greater evidence of altered sense of humor when compared with control participants.

Other studies have found deficits in comprehending sarcasm or irony (Gaudreau et al., 2013; Kipps et al., 2009). Kipps et al. (2009) investigated social processing, including the comprehension of sarcasm, in 9 individuals believed to have Alzheimer's disease, 26 individuals with frontotemporal dementia, and 16 healthy control participants of similar age. Participants answered comprehension questions after watching videos depicting social situations. Those with frontotemporal dementia performed more poorly than the others in comprehending sarcasm and scenarios involving negative emotions. All groups showed good comprehension for sincere statements. In a later study, Gaudreau et al. (2013) investigated the comprehension of irony in a sample of individuals with mild cognitive impairment and who were suspected of having Alzheimer's disease in the early stages. Their performance was compared with that of a sample of healthy control participants of similar age. All participants completed tasks involving theory of mind and distinguishing statements of irony from lies. The results indicated that both theory of mind processing and the comprehension of irony were impaired in the individuals with mild cognitive impairment.

Parkinson's Disease

Parkinson's disease is caused by the degeneration of substantia nigra and the ventral tegmental areas in the basal ganglia. Early symptoms include tremors, muscle spasms, and the increasing inability to control movement (Cudaback et al., 2015). Figure 2.1 displays the structures that make up the basal ganglia. The emergence of Parkinson's disease symptoms is linked to the degeneration

FIGURE 2.1. The Structures of the Basal Ganglia

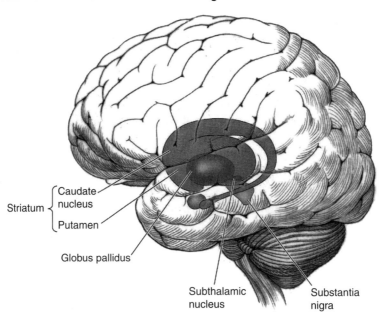

Note. The basal ganglia is located in the middle of the brain and contains multiple subregions. Parkinson's disease occurs from the degeneration of the substantia nigra. Huntington's disease involves the degeneration of the caudate nucleus. From *Biological Psychology: An Introduction to Behavioral, Cognitive, and Clinical Neuroscience* (6th ed., p. 337), by S. M. Breedlove, N. V. Watson, and M. R. Rosenzweig, 2010, Sinauer. Copyright 2010 by Sinauer Associates, Inc. Reprinted with permission.

of cells that produce the neurotransmitter dopamine. Individuals with Parkinson's disease also experience deficits in executive functioning, including planning behavior, inhibiting behavior, carrying out multiple tasks, shifting attention, among others (Benke et al., 1998). Cognitive problems increase as the disease progresses (Dirnberger & Jahanshahi, 2013).

Prior research has established that individuals with Parkinson's disease have deficits in theory of mind (Bodden et al., 2010; M. Freedman & Stuss, 2011; Mengelberg & Siegert, 2003; Poletti et al., 2011; Saltzman et al., 2000; Santangelo et al., 2012; Xi et al., 2015), inferring the emotional states of others from facial expressions (Albuquerque et al., 2016; Marneweck et al., 2014; Wagenbreth et al., 2016) and in the comprehension of speech (Albuquerque et al., 2016). Deficits in humor processing have also been observed (Benke et al., 1998; Monetta et al., 2009; Pell et al., 2015; Thaler et al., 2012). In a study in which individuals with Parkinson's disease and healthy control participants were asked to comprehend stories, Monetta et al. (2009) found that individuals with Parkinson's disease were generally unable to judge whether a concluding statement of a story was a lie (i.e., within the context of the story) or was a joke. Thaler et al. (2012) compared humor appreciation in individuals with Parkinson's disease with healthy control participants. Those with Parkinson's disease gave ratings of humor that were significantly lower than the control group. They also reported lower scores on the sense of humor scale. Pell et al. (2015) assessed abilities of individuals with mild Parkinson's disease symptoms. They aimed to determine patients' abilities to infer the mental states and emotions of others as they watched videotaped social interactions. Patients' performance was compared with that of healthy control participants. Participants responded to questions to determine their ability to determine the intention of a person in the vignette, distinguishing sarcasm and lies from literal statements. Individuals with Parkinson's disease performed less accurately than healthy control participants in interpreting sarcasm and lies but performed similarly in interpreting the emotional states of others from literal statements.

Huntington's Disease

Huntington's disease is an inherited disease that leads to progressive problems controlling movements as well as cognitive deficits (National Institute of Neurological Disorders and Stroke, n.d.). Typically, individuals who carry the mutation on Chromosome 4 develop symptoms between the ages of 40 years old and 50 years old, but in rare cases, symptoms emerge much earlier. The symptoms of the disease appear to be related to the degeneration of the striatum, an area within the basal ganglia, which includes the caudate nucleus and the putamen. These regions are displayed in Figure 2.1. Over the course of several decades, degeneration of the striatum progresses and movement and cognitive symptoms, including apathy, worsen until death (N. E. Fritz et al., 2018). Currently, there is no cure for the disease.

Eddy and Rickards (2015) investigated theory of mind processing in individuals carrying the gene for Huntington's disease before the participants experienced movement problems and in a group of healthy control participants. Individuals with Huntington's disease experience damage to the striatum, which begins before the emergence of movement problems. The movement problems increase as the striatum degenerates. Participants were tested on their comprehension of emotional states depicted in pictures of others' eyes (using the revised version of the Reading the Mind in the Eyes test; Baron-Cohen et al., 2001), perspective taking in familiar situations, detecting social faux pas in videos/stories, and 10 measures of executive function. The results showed that although those in the Huntington's disease sample performed normally for nine of the measures of executive functioning, they performed significantly more poorly on the theory of mind tasks. The results demonstrated the importance of having a healthy striatum in being able to appreciate the mental states of others.

Bora et al. (2016) examined prior studies investigating theory of mind and emotional processing deficits in individuals with Huntington's disease before they had experienced any symptoms. An analysis of the data from these prior studies confirmed that individuals with Huntington's disease performed more poorly than individuals in control groups on theory of mind tasks and on tasks requiring the perception of emotions (especially the negative emotions of disgust, fear, and anger). They also performed more poorly on tasks requiring the comprehension of speech and the comprehension of pictures containing faces. Individuals who had greater disease progression performed more poorly than those with less disease progression. Lagravinese et al. (2017) showed that Huntington's disease patients' deficits in recognizing the emotional states of others using the Reading the Mind in the Eyes test (Baron-Cohen et al., 2001) was unrelated to performance on nonemotional cognitive and visual processing tasks. Baez et al. (2015) suggested that problems with emotion recognition could be useful in evaluating and diagnosing the disease in individuals.

Amyotrophic Lateral Sclerosis

ALS is a degenerative disease affecting motor neurons in the spinal cord and the motor cortex of the brain. The degeneration of motor neurons leads to a progressive loss of control over movement (E. M. Wood, 2015). Figure 2.2 displays the location of the primary motor cortex. Lou Gehrig passed away from the disease in 1941 (Eig, 2005), leading many to refer to ALS as Lou Gehrig's disease. Most cases are viewed as sporadic, having no family history of the disease. The initial symptoms typically occur during the fifth or sixth decade of life, but they can occur in younger adults, particularly when there may be a genetic cause. Renton et al. (2014) suggested that the genetic origins of ALS lie in mutations occurring on multiple genes. The cognitive and social processing deficits observed in the disease have been found to be similar to those observed in frontotemporal dementia (Couratier et al., 2017; Girardi et al., 2011). Machts et al. (2018)

FIGURE 2.2. Location of the Primary Motor Cortex

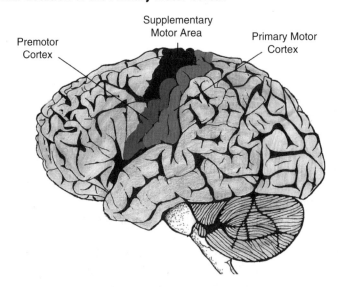

Note. Movement of body parts is controlled by multiple regions of the brains, including the primary motor cortex, the premotor cortex, and the supplementary motor area. From *Motor Cortex Two*, by S. P. Connolly, 2018, Wikimedia Commons (https://commons.wikimedia.org/wiki/File:Motor_Cortex_Two.jpg). CC BY 4.0.

found that patients with ALS showed reduced volume in the prefrontal cortex, specifically in the orbitofrontal region as compared with healthy control participants, providing some explanation for the similarity in the cognitive and social deficits in ALS and frontotemporal dementia.

Staios et al. (2013) demonstrated that individuals with ALS showed deficits in interpreting sarcasm in particular, showing greater success in interpreting literal statements. These results added to studies documenting deficits in social processing in ALS (Crespi et al., 2014; F. Fisher et al., 2017; Girardi et al., 2011; Meier et al., 2010). One of the studies focused specifically on how patients with ALS recognized emotion as compared with healthy control participants. Crespi et al. (2014) had participants judge the emotion in 60 faces. Stimuli depicted fear, anger, sadness, disgust, happiness, and surprise. Individuals with ALS performed more poorly than control participants in recognizing negative emotions.

Chronic Alcoholism

Research has suggested that individuals with a history of chronic alcohol abuse show abnormalities throughout the brain with lower volumes in multiple areas, particularly in the frontal lobe (Harris et al., 2008; Moselhy et al., 2001; Zahr & Pfefferbaum, 2017). Chronic alcohol abuse is observed in approximately 7% of adults (Substance Abuse and Mental Health Services Administration, 2013). Zahr and Pfefferbaum (2017) reviewed numerous studies identifying specific brain regions adversely affected by long-term abuse of alcohol, including, in addition to the frontal lobe, the basal ganglia, hippocampus, and others. Humor deficits have been observed in individuals who .have chronically abused alcohol (Amenta et al., 2013; Cermak et al., 1989; D'Hondt et al., 2014; Kornreich et al., 2016; Uekermann, Channon, et al., 2007; Uekermann, Daum, & Channon, 2007). Cermak et al. (1989) compared performance in a series of tasks that required comprehending emotion, interpreting humor, and comprehending discourses. For each task, participants were required to draw an inference. The experimental group included 20 men with a history of alcohol abuse. Two control groups who had no history of alcohol abuse were also tested, including individuals of similar age to the experimental group (i.e., 45–59 years old) and individuals who were slightly older (i.e., 65–79 years old). For individuals with a history of alcohol abuse, performance was poorer on each of the tasks as compared with those in the control groups who were either younger or slightly older in age. In a similar study by Amenta et al. (2013), men with a history of alcoholism had impairment related to the recognition of emotion, which led to mistakes in comprehending irony. In a recent study, Schermer et al. (2019) found that individuals who met criteria for dependence on alcohol used the aggressive humor style more often than others. Future research might explore whether the use of the aggressive humor style increases over time during the course of the alcohol dependence or can be observed in individuals before the onset of the condition.

PATHOLOGICAL LAUGHTER: WHEN LAUGHTER AND MIRTH OCCUR WITHOUT A TRIGGERING EVENT

Disordered emotional responses, such as pathological laughter, have intrigued medical professionals and researchers for decades (Sher & Brown, 1976). A rare form of epilepsy known as gelastic epilepsy can also cause seizures that involve uncontrollable laughing or crying (Holmes & Goldman, 2012; Shin et al., 2006; Tran et al., 2014). Gelastic epilepsy involving laughter was first described in 1873, as typically accompanying uncontrollable eye movements and body movements with the loss of consciousness (Gascon & Lombroso, 1971). Some individuals who experience gelastic epilepsy have reported the feeling of amusement (mirth) one has during normal laughing (Arroyo et al., 1993); however, many cases occur without a feeling of mirth (Striano et al., 1999; Tasch et al., 1998). The condition has also been observed in newborns, where the possibility of a mirth triggering stimuli is unlikely (Sher & Brown, 1976).

A common cause of gelastic seizures is a benign tumor in the hypothalamus (Khadilkar et al., 2001), which often can be removed successfully during surgery (see Figure 1.7, Chapter 1, this volume for a diagram of the hypothalamus). The hypothalamus is involved in numerous functions, including hormone production, regulation of sleep, hunger, thirst, sleep, temperature, circadian cycles, and sex drive (see Xie & Dorsky, 2017, for a review). It does not appear to be the case that the hypothalamus is the sole controller of laughter in the brain; rather, there appears to be many areas in the brain that are involved in producing laughter and mirth. Researchers know this because studies show that pathological laughter is observed in a variety of conditions, including localized damage to the brain as seen in traumatic brain injury (Engelman et al., 2014; Roy et al., 2015; Zeilig et al., 1996), an enlarging tumor (Herbet et al., 2013), and transient ischemic attacks or ministrokes (Dulamea et al., 2015), which occur when there is a loss of blood supply that damages cells (W. Johnson et al., 2016). In the case of stroke, pathological laughter is common, affecting more than half of stroke survivors (National Stroke Association, n.d.-a). Other conditions in which pathological laughter occurs are related to degeneration of the brain, including Alzheimer's dementia (Y. D. Chang et al., 2016), Parkinson's disease (N. Patel et al., 2018), ALS (Thakore & Pioro, 2017), multiple sclerosis (Hanna et al., 2016; A. Miller, 2006), and narcolepsy (a disorder of excessive sleepiness; Vaudano et al., 2019), as well as other conditions (Brooks et al., 2013). Multiple brain regions are involved in pathological laughter. The evidence has been derived from studies demonstrating that direct stimulation of numerous brain regions by electricity can produce laughter and/or mirth (see Chapter 5, this volume).

SUMMARY

Reductions in humor appreciation have been linked to brain changes related to healthy aging and those related to brain-damaging strokes and disorders, including Alzheimer's disease, frontotemporal dementia, Parkinson's disease, Huntington's disease, ALS, and chronic alcohol abuse. In some individuals with degenerative brain diseases, abnormal emotional states can arise in which there is uncontrollable laughter. Across these conditions in which impairments of humor processing have been observed, there are multiple brain areas involved. In healthy aging, brain changes in both hemispheres, although particularly the right hemisphere, are likely involved in declines in humor processing. Degeneration to the frontal and temporal lobes appear to be related to declines in humor processing in individuals with Alzheimer's disease and frontotemporal dementia (frontal and temporal lobes). Degeneration to subregions of the basal ganglia likely are responsible for declines in humor processing (as well as other physical ability) in individuals with Parkinson's disease (i.e., substantia nigra) and Huntington's disease (i.e., striatum). In ALS, there is degeneration of the motor cortex and motor neurons in the spinal cord, which lead to progressive impairment of movement and cognitive changes that include declines in humor processing. Lastly, the changes in the hippocampus and basal ganglia because of chronic alcoholism lead to cognitive impairments, including declines in humor processing. In sum, these findings support the conclusion that humor processing involves the coordination of multiple regions of the brain and refute the view that there is a single, localized region of the brain responsible for humor processing.

3

Electroencephalography Studies of Humor Comprehension

Since the late 1800s, researchers have recorded electrical activity using electrodes placed on the scalp to study the brain's activity, a technique known as *electroencephalography* (EEG; Coenen et al., 2014; Covey & Carter, 2015; Glickstein, 2014; Swartz, 1998). Early observations included distinct patterns of electrical activity during sleep, dreaming, and different levels of consciousness during awake periods (e.g., drowsiness vs. alertness; Greenfield et al., 2012). In the 20th century, researchers refined the collection and analyses of EEG data to study brain activity during cognitive processing (see Coles & Rugg, 1995, for a review). This chapter reviews the studies that have used EEG to investigate the processes involved in humor comprehension. The discussion begins with some background on the technique, terminology, and the typical experimental set up in studies of comprehension and the most commonly observed patterns of EEG data, which have been linked to different aspects of comprehension (e.g., registering the stimulus, recognizing a stimulus as familiar, integrating the meaning of the stimulus during the task). Next, the early studies of humor comprehension are reviewed. The final section examines recent studies that suggest there are three stages of processing involved in humor comprehension and each is associated with a specific pattern of EEG activity and possibly is associated with activity in a specific region of the brain. Some patterns of EEG data recorded during humor comprehension are similar to patterns recorded during nonhumorous comprehension that involve theory of mind processing.

https://doi.org/10.1037/0000203-004
The Cognitive Neuroscience of Humor, by S. M. Kennison

OVERVIEW OF ELECTROENCEPHALOGRAPHY METHODOLOGY

In EEG studies of comprehension, researchers typically present a stimulus of interest (e.g., word, picture, sentence) and record the subsequent EEG data over several seconds, which enables the researcher to examine the data for any patterns of activity related directly to the processing of the stimulus. This technique of recording EEG data from the point in time that a stimulus is presented is referred to as event-related brain potentials (ERPs; see Luck & Kappenman, 2012, for a review). The event refers to the presentation of a stimulus of interest. EEG data are recorded at each electrode site, and in contemporary studies, hundreds of electrodes may be used. Figure 3.1 displays a participant wearing a typical electrode cap. During comprehension experiments, the participant is equipped with the electrode cap and seated in a comfortable chair where they will either view stimuli on a computer screen or listen to stimuli played over speakers. The participant may experience hundreds of trials of stimuli in one experimental session. Trials representing the same condition (e.g., experimental vs. control, humorous vs. nonhumorous) are averaged and compared with averaged waveforms in other conditions.

The common method of displaying EEG data is to plot the voltage measured over time for each electrode with the y-axis reflecting voltage and the x-axis reflecting time (typically in ms). Some researchers plot waveforms with the negative voltage on top; others, plot them with the positive voltage on top.

FIGURE 3.1. Typical Electrode Cap

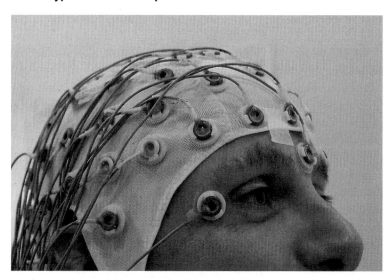

Note. In contemporary EEG/ERP experiments, electrodes are placed on a participant's scalp. Electrode nets are popular because they enable researchers to position electrodes on a participant's scalp more quickly than affixing each electrode one at a time. From *EEG Recording Cap*, by C. Hope, 2012, Wikimedia Commons (https://commons.wikimedia.org/wiki/File:EEG_Recording_Cap.jpg). CC BY 2.0.

FIGURE 3.2. Sample Electroencephalography Waveform

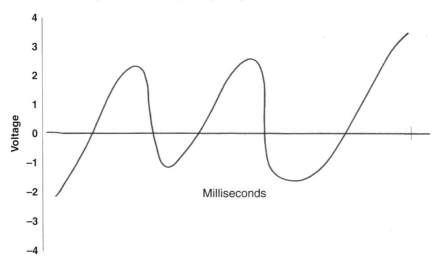

Note. During EEG experiments, data from each electrode are recorded. The data are electrical signals, which can be graphed in terms of voltage level (y-axis) over time (x-axis).

Figure 3.2 displays a sample EEG waveform. The height of the waveform (i.e., amplitude) reflects amount of voltage. When the y-axis plots the negative voltage on top, greater amplitude of a wave reflects higher levels of negative voltage. Depending on the location of the electrode relative to the source of the electrical signal within the brain, the waveform may have a positive or negative polarity (Ham, 2018; Scherg et al., 2019). The extent to which the generator of the electrical source in the brain is playing an inhibitory or excitatory role in the processing may also be a factor in whether a generated waveform is negative or positive. It is important to note that the relationship between brain activity during processing and the polarity of the resulting waveforms is not completely understood (Luck, 2005).

The locations of electrodes on the scalp are commonly coded in terms of left and right of the central axis and in terms of frontal, parietal, or occipital lobe (Murray et al., 2008; Tzovara et al., 2012). Researchers often use terminology from anatomy (e.g., anterior, posterior, lateral, medial) to refer to locations on the scalp where noteworthy EEG results were observed. Table 3.1 provides a list of some of these terms with brief definitions. The terms are also used in Chapters 4 and 5 of this volume. It is important to keep in mind that although EEG provides excellent information about how quickly the brain responds to a stimulus during processing, it does not provide accurate information about the exact location of the source of the electrical signal inside the brain (Kappenman & Luck, 2012; Luck, 2005). There are now multiple techniques that enable researchers to estimate the location(s) of electrical signal generators in the brain (e.g., BESA, n.d.; see Michel & Brunet, 2019, for a review); however, the estimates are interpreted with caution.

TABLE 3.1. Common Anatomical Terms

Term	Definition
Anterior	toward the front
Caudal	toward the tail
Distal	distant from a point of attachment
Dorsal	toward the top
Inferior	lower
Lateral	toward one side, away from the middle
Medial	in the middle
Posterior	toward the back
Proximal	near to a point of attachment
Rostral	toward the nose
Superior	higher
Ventral	toward the bottom or underside

Note. Data from the National Cancer Institute (n.d.).

EEG/ERP studies have limitations other than their poor information about the specific brain locations generating the electrical activity, including the large amount of data collected and the large number of statistical tests that are conducted during the process of data analysis. Researchers aim to detect differences in the voltage levels between experimental (target) trials and control trials at one or more electrodes at a particular time interval following the presentation of the stimulus (i.e., up to 2 seconds). Large differences may prove to be statistically significant, leading the researchers to view the difference between conditions as occurring because of different brain activity. However, as in any research study, as the number of statistical tests a researcher performs increases the chances of observing a significant difference due to randomness alone rather than a true difference in the data (Cohen, 2013). Such findings are called false positives and lead researchers to conclude that there is a difference between conditions when no difference exists (Motulsky, 2015). Luck and Gaspelin (2017) pointed out that EEG/ERP studies are particularly vulnerable to false positive results because of the size of the datasets and the number of statistical tests carried out across multiple possible time intervals (e.g., 0 ms–2,000 ms vs. 0 ms–100 ms, 0 ms–200 ms, 0 ms–300 ms) and multiple electrode sites, which can exceed 200. With these limitations in mind, the most commonly observed patterns of EEG/ERP waveforms (also called ERP components) can be reviewed.

After decades of work with ERP methodology, researchers identified patterns of ERP waveforms linked to particular aspects of stimulus processing (see Kappenman & Luck, 2012, for a review). These are referred to as *ERP components*, and they reflect a distinctive wave pattern that is observed at a particular time interval following the presentation of a stimulus and having a particular polarity (i.e., negative or positive). ERP components have labels to reflect the time interval and the polarity. For example, an N100 is a negative waveform occurring around 100 ms following a stimulus. In cases where the stimulus was presented on a computer screen, the component is observed at the electrodes over the occipital the lobe to a greater degree than at other electrode sites, as the occipital lobe is involved primarily in visual processing. In cases where participants listened to the stimulus, the component is observed at electrodes over the temporal lobes to a greater degree than at other electrode sites, as the temporal lobe is involved primarily in auditory processing.

Other ERP components are P300, N400, P600, and late positive complex, and each has been linked to specific type of cognitive processing during comprehension. The P300 occurs around 300 ms following the presentation of a stimulus in tasks in which participants become more familiar with some stimuli than others (see Polich & Kok, 1995, for a review). Some researchers have suggested that the P300 is composed of two subcomponents: one that reflects participants' experiencing surprise and one that reflects processing the stimulus further in relation to the demands of the task (Polich, 2003). The difference in voltage around 300 ms is larger in amplitude in the positive direction when the stimulus is more surprising (i.e., less frequently experienced). When participants experience "surprise," the P300 is observed most prominently at electrode sites at the center of the scalp and over the frontal lobes. In contrast, when participants are carrying out task-related processing, the P300 is observed most prominently at electrode sites over the parietal lobes. Both aspects of the P300 can be viewed as the participant directing attention to the stimulus.

The N400 occurs around 400 ms following the presentation of a stimulus and is viewed as reflecting processing involved in integrating the meaning of the stimulus (see Kutas & Federmeier, 2011; Swaab et al., 2012, for reviews). For example, in studies in which word pairs are presented to participants, the N400 is typically observed following the presentation of a word that is unrelated in meaning with the preceding word (e.g., "bread" and "moon" vs. "bread" and "butter"; Kutas & Federmeier, 2000). The difference in voltage around 400 ms is larger in amplitude in the negative direction when the stimulus is more dissimilar to a preceding stimulus. N400s have also been observed following the processing of a word occurring within a short sentence context, in which the word does not provide a sensible continuation for the context (e.g., "for breakfast, John ate bacon and *shoes*" vs. "for breakfast, John ate bacon and *eggs*"). The N400 is typically observed at central and parietal electrode sites (Kutas & Federmeier, 2011; Swaab et al., 2012).

The P600 occurs around 600 ms following the processing of a word that is grammatically anomalous within the preceding context (e.g., "when the doorbell rings, the dog *bark*" vs. "when the doorbell rings, the dog *barks*"; see Osterhout & Holcomb, 1992; cf. Leckey & Federmeier, 2019). The P600 occurs when participants comprehend a word within a sentence containing a temporary syntactic ambiguity (also called a *garden path sentence*). The target word signals to the participants that the ambiguity has been continued in an unexpected way (e.g., the word "was" in the sentence "the manager encouraged to cut costs was fired" vs. "the manager who was encouraged to cut costs was fired"). The P600 has also been observed in studies in which participants

TABLE 3.2. Event-Related Brain Potential Components and Associated Cognitive Processes

ERP component	Electrode sites	Cognitive processing
N100	occipital sites for visual stimuli; temporal sites for auditory stimuli	sensory processing of stimulus
P300	central, frontal, and parietal sites	attentional processing of stimulus
N400	central and parietal sites	integrating meaning of stimulus
P600	central, frontal, and parietal sites	detecting structural anomaly
Late positive complex	parietal sites	memory processing

listen to music (A. D. Patel et al., 1998; see also Koelsch & Jentschke, 2008). The P600 is typically observed at central, frontal, and/or parietal sites (Swaab et al., 2012).

Positive waveforms occurring after the P600 are sometimes observed in studies and have been referred to as a *late positive complex* (Paller et al., 1995; Rugg & Curran, 2007). The component is viewed as reflecting memory processing, specifically the integration of the target stimulus with the participants' existing long-term memories. The late positive complex is typically observed at electrode sites over the parietal lobe, but it has been found to occur at different electrode sites, depending on what aspect of the stimulus the task requires participants to remember (Mecklinger, 1998). Table 3.2 lists common ERP components and the cognitive processes associated with each. In ERP studies, these components may overlap in time (Kappenman & Luck, 2012).

EARLY ELECTROENCEPHALOGRAPHY/EVENT-RELATED BRAIN POTENTIAL STUDIES OF HUMOR COMPREHENSION

Since the 1980s, researchers have used ERPs to investigate how people comprehend humor (Amenta & Balconi, 2008; Coulson & Kutas, 2001; Coulson & Lovett, 2004; Coulson & Severens, 2007; Coulson & Williams, 2005; Coulson & Wu, 2005; Derks et al., 1997; Mayerhofer & Schacht, 2015; Svebak, 1982). In the earliest report, Svebak (1982) carried out two studies in which he had participants watch a comedy movie while wearing electrodes over their left and right occipital lobes (i.e., the back of the head). In Experiment 1, he tested 57 right-handed participants (33 men, 24 women). In Experiment 2, he tested 13 right-handed participants (seven men, six women). In both experiments, he observed differences in EEG waveforms for those who laughed during the films and those who did not. He found that there was more coordinated activity in the left and right hemispheres for those who laughed and more discordant activity for those who did not laugh. He concluded that experiencing humor fully (i.e., including a mirth experience) involved processing in both hemispheres.

Fifteen years later, Derks et al. (1997) presented jokes on a computer screen one at a time and recorded ERPs during and after the processing of the punchline of each joke. In addition to recording electrical activity from the scalp, they also recorded electrical activity from the muscles in the face (i.e., electromyography) to monitor participants' smiling and/or laughing. The results were generally consistent with Svebak's (1982) in that humor-related processing corresponded to activity recorded over both hemispheres. They also found that following the comprehension of the punchline, there were P300s and N400s when participants reported experiencing amusement. In a second experiment, they found that N400s were produced only on trials in which the participant laughed.

In the 2000s, Coulson and colleagues (Coulson & Kutas, 2001; Coulson & Lovett, 2004; Coulson & Severens, 2007; Coulson et al., 2006; Coulson & Williams, 2005; Coulson & Wu, 2005) carried out several studies investigating ERPs during the comprehension of humor, in which the recordings of EEG data were tied to the specific word or phrase. Coulson and Kutas (2001) recorded ERPs of 28 right-handed participants (10 men, 18 women) as they comprehended short, one-liner jokes (e.g., "I asked the bartender for something cold and full of rum, and he recommended his wife") and nonjoke controls, which were sensible but not funny. Two types of nonjoke controls were used: supportive contexts that were similar in meaning of the setup of the joke (e.g., something about bars, bartenders, or alcoholic beverages) and nonsupportive contexts that differed in meaning with the setup (e.g., something unrelated to bars, bartenders, or alcoholic beverages). The results showed that all participants produced negative waveforms between 500 ms and 900 ms (i.e., N400s) over the left hemisphere after comprehending the jokes in supportive context. Those participants who tended to get the humor in the jokes in the experiment also showed late occurring positive waveforms between 500 ms and 900 ms over the frontal lobes (i.e., P600s). Coulson and Kutas (2001) suggested that humor is comprehended in two stages, a stage of surprise reflected in an N400 followed by a stage of coherence reflected in a late positive complex. Their view was similar to Suls's (1972, 1983) two-stage model of humor processing that involves incongruity detection followed by incongruity resolution.

In a later study, Coulson and Williams (2005) investigated the relative contributions of the left and right hemispheres in the comprehension of humor. Coulson and Williams recorded ERPs from 16 right-handed participants (nine men, seven women) following the presentation of a word, which ended the joke. The word also served as the first point in the sentence that enabled participants to determine that the sentence was a joke. An example from the study was "I still miss my ex-wife, but I am improving my aim," with the target word "aim" presented either to the left or right hemisphere. Since the 1960s, researchers have presented words or pictures directly to one hemisphere or the other (Gazzaniga et al., 1965). This is possible because of the organization of the visual system. Information viewed at the center of vision is processed by both hemispheres simultaneously, However, when information is viewed to the left of center, it is processed by the right hemisphere, and when it is viewed to the right of the center, it is processed by the left hemisphere. The experimental procedure is referred to as the divided visual field technique (Beaumont, 1982; Bourne, 2006). Coulson and Williams found that when participants viewed the word in the left hemisphere, there was a larger N400 (as compared with the control nonhumorous sentence "I still miss my ex-wife, but I am improving my ego"). When the word was presented to the right hemisphere, N400s were comparable in control and humorous sentences. The authors concluded that the integration of meaning occurs differently in the two hemispheres, and the integration of meaning carried out in the right hemisphere facilitates joke comprehension. Their conclusions were consistent with prior research showing that damage to the right hemisphere can impair humor processing (see Chapter 2, this volume).

Relatively few EEG/ERP studies of humor have investigated individual differences (Y.-T. Chang et al., 2018; Coulson & Lovett, 2004). The studies that have been conducted support the view that humor is processed somewhat differently by different types of people. Coulson and Lovett (2004) compared processing for left-handed and right-handed participants. Left-handers make up only about 10 percent of the population and sometimes have different brain organization (Herron, 2012). Consequently, they are typically excluded from brain imaging studies (Willems, Van der Haegen, Fisher, & Francks, 2014). Coulson and Lovett compared processing for 16 right-handed participants (eight men, eight women) and 16 left-handed participants (eight men, eight women). Their results showed that left-handed participants produced more right-hemisphere activity when comprehending jokes than right-handed participants.

A second, more recent study by Y.-T. Chang et al. (2018) examined ERP differences in men and women. They recorded ERPs from 20 right-handed participants (10 men, 10 women) during the comprehension of incongruity humor, as in "Who goes to the hospital most often? Doctors." Nonhumorous stimuli had the same structure but stated a nonhumorous fact, as in "What do we call the planet we live on? The earth." Men and women produced a late positive complex in humorous trials, but the amplitude of the waveform was larger for women than for men. They concluded that women may engage more of the brain's cognitive and emotional areas during the comprehension of humor than men. These gender differences in comprehending humor are intriguing and may reflect the fact that men and women are affected by humor differently. Chapter 7 of this volume reviews numerous behavioral studies showing that there are gender differences in humor appreciation and production in men and women. One of the directions for future research that is needed is documenting the individual differences of humor in cognitive neuroscience.

Other studies compared processing on different types of humorous stimuli (Y.-T. Chang et al., 2019; Mayerhofer & Schacht, 2015). Y.-T. Chang et al.

(2019) recorded ERPs of 16 right-handed participants (eight men, eight women) as they comprehended puns or jokes involving the integration of meaning of a punchline with a preceding setup sentence. The results showed that following the comprehension of puns, participants produced N400s. In contrast, following the comprehension of semantic jokes participants produced P600s.

In prior research by Coulson and Severens (2007), the processing of puns had been investigated. They measured ERPs from 16 right-handed participants (nine men, seven women) as they listened to puns (e.g., "I used to be a lumberjack, but then I got the axe"). As participants listened, they also were shown probe words, which varied in semantic relatedness to the last word in the pun. The probe word could have been related to the pun (e.g., fired) or to the nonhumorous aspect of the sentence (e.g., chop). They presented probe words using the divided visual field technique. Half of the time, the probe word was presented to the left visual field (i.e., the right hemisphere), and the other half of the time, the probe word was presented to the right visual field (i.e., left hemisphere). The results indicated that N400s and P600s occurred during the processing of the probe words related to the pun at electrode sites above the left and right hemispheres. The authors claimed that the right hemisphere was initially active during the processing of the most relevant meaning of the pun but gained greater access to other meanings after about 500 ms.

Some recent studies have investigated patterns in ERPs during the comprehension of verbal humor that does not involve puns or jokes but rather irony and sarcasm (Amenta & Balconi, 2008; Filik et al., 2014; L. Gibson et al., 2016). *Irony* refers to a statement whose meaning is the opposite of the meaning of the individual words in a statement (e.g., "I love it when the sun is out" said when it is raining). In contrast, *sarcasm* refers to irony that targets a particular person in a negative way (e.g., "you don't say, Einstein" said to someone who has just said something viewed as unintelligent). Irony and sarcasm can be experienced as humorous. Filik et al. (2014) compared waveforms as two groups of participants comprehended ironic and nonironic statements, which varied in familiarity. In the experiment, they tested 32 right-handed participants (eight men, 24 women). Results showed that there were N400s following the comprehension of unfamiliar ironic statements compared with unfamiliar nonironic control statements. In addition, Filik et al. observed late positive complex following the comprehension of ironic statements (familiar and unfamiliar) as compared with nonironic control stimuli. They concluded that the N400 reflects sensitivity to decoding meanings initially, and the late positivity reflects processing related to there being a conflict between the literal and nonliteral meanings. It is noteworthy that an earlier study by Amenta and Balconi (2008) had compared ERPs that were produced as 12 right-handed participants (three men, nine women) listened to examples of sentences with or without ironic content. They found no difference in waveforms in the two conditions.

THE THREE-STAGE MODEL OF HUMOR COMPREHENSION

In a series of ERP studies, Chan and colleagues (Chan et al., 2016; Y. Feng, Chan, & Chen, 2014; Ku et al., 2017; see also Chan, Chou, et al., 2013; Du et al., 2013; Tu et al., 2014) presented data that are consistent with humor being comprehended in three distinct stages, which are associated with different ERP components and activity in different brain regions. This work expanded on Suls's (1972, 1983) two-stage model of humor processing (i.e., incongruity detection followed by resolution), but added a third stage, called *elaboration*, which was inspired by Wyer and Collins's (1992) view that humor involves a stage of comprehension followed by elaboration. In the study by Tu et al. (2014), ERPs were recorded from 16 right-handed participants (eight men, eight women) as they viewed cartoons varying in humorousness. The results showed that the detection of incongruity coincided with an N400 (occurring between 500 ms and 800 ms); the resolution of the incongruity coincided with a P600 (occurring between 800 ms and 1,000 ms); and the elaboration of the incongruity coincided with a much later positivity (occurring between 1,600 ms and 2,000 ms).

Additional studies also supported the three-stage model of humor comprehension (Du et al., 2013; Y. Feng, Chan, & Chen, 2014; Ku et al., 2017). Y. Feng, Chan, and Chen (2014) observed positive waveforms occurring relatively late during the comprehension of humor when they recorded ERPs of 31 right-handed participants (15 men, 16 women) as they comprehended sentences that were either jokes, sensible nonjoke statements, or nonsensical statements. Waveforms in joke and sensible nonjoke conditions differed in the P600 component, which may have reflected processing involved in participants resolving incongruity in the joke condition. There was also a late positive complex between 800 and 1,500 milliseconds in joke conditions, which is consistent with a third stage of humor processing involving the elaboration of the incongruity.

Ku et al. (2017) investigated individual differences in the ERPs produced during humor comprehension. They compared waveforms of 32 right-handed participants (13 men, 19 women) as they read jokes and nonjoke sensible controls and rated the level of funniness, comprehensibility, and surprise. Ku et al. suggested that individual differences in participants' ratings affected processing in each of the three stages of humor processing: incongruity detection (surprise), incongruity evaluation (comprehensibility), and incongruity elaboration (funniness). Ratings were used to identify individuals who showed high versus low levels of surprise, high versus low levels of comprehensibility, and high versus low levels of amusement. They observed differences between humorous and nonhumorous control conditions in the N400 (incongruity detection), the P600 (incongruity evaluation), and late positive complex (elaboration).

Du et al. (2013) measured waveforms of 14 right-handed participants (eight men, six women) as they comprehended stories without their endings, which was either a joke or sensible nonjoke. When they reread the story with the ending, they provided a funniness rating. After the processing of joke and nonjoke endings, N400s were observed at frontal and central electrode sites. Negative waveforms also were observed at 600 ms to 800 ms in the front and central electrode sites. P600s (between 600 ms and 800 ms) were observed over posterior electrode sites. Late positive complexes were observed between 1250 ms and 1400 ms at anterior and posterior electrode sites. The authors used the Brain Electrical Source Analysis (BESA) to estimate the brain locations producing the observed components (see BESA, n.d.). The N400s were localized to two regions in the frontal and temporal lobes in left hemisphere. The P600s were localized to the anterior region of the cingulate cortex, which lies toward the frontal lobe just above the corpus callosum along the midline of the brain (see Figure 1.7, Chapter 1, this volume). The late positive complexes were localized to two regions: the middle frontal gyrus, which is located in the middle of the frontal lobe and the fusiform gyrus, which is located in the ventral part of the temporal lobe below the inferior temporal gyrus. Table 3.3 displays the three stages of humor comprehension and the associated ERP components, which are supported by the results of Tu et al. (2014) and Du et al. (2013).

To fully understand the implications of the three-stage model of humor processing, it is important to consider that the pattern of processing in the three stages can also be observed when participants are comprehending nonhumorous material, specifically material that requires theory of mind and empathy processing. Theory of mind processing involves the ability to perceive and understand others' knowledge and mental states. Empathy is specific to the ability to perceive and understand others' feelings or emotional mental states. Differences in N400s have been observed when participants were required to engage in empathy related processing (Ferguson et al., 2015), and differences in P600s have been observed when participants were required to engage in theory of mind processing related to evaluating false beliefs (Meinhardt et al., 2012; see also Meinhardt et al., 2011).

Empathy related processing was also linked to N400s in studies by Sabbagh and colleagues (2004; Sabbagh & Flynn, 2006) in which they recorded ERPs while participants carried out the Reading the Eyes in the Mind test, which was developed by Baron-Cohen and colleagues (1997, 2001) to assess theory of mind processing. During this test, participants view pictures of the eyes of people and choose an adjective that best describes what the person

TABLE 3.3. Stages of Humor Processing and Associated Event-Related Brain Potential Components

Stage of humor processing	ERP component	Estimated brain locations
Incongruity detection	N400	frontal and temporal lobes
Incongruity resolution	P600	anterior cingulate cortex
Elaboration	P600	medial frontal lobe and fusiform gyrus

Note. Data from Tu et al. (2014) and Du et al. (2013).

is feeling. Four adjectives are provided with each picture. Some researchers have argued that the task is best described as a task requiring participants to judge the emotional states from the pictures of the eyes, which can be viewed as involving perception of nonverbal information, rather than a task that involves participants carrying out only theory of mind processing (Oakley et al., 2016). In Sabbagh et al. (2004), there were 13 right-handed participants (five men, eight women). The results showed that inferring the emotional states of individuals from the pictures of their eyes corresponded to an N400 (270 ms–400 ms) over the right hemisphere (anterior temporal and frontal lobes). Using BESA software to estimate the locations within the brain responsible for the activity, they suggested involvement of two regions: one in the medial temporal lobe and one in the orbitofrontal region. In a later study, Sabbagh and Flynn (2006) recorded EEGs of 23 right-handed women as they performed the Reading the Mind in the Eyes test. The authors found that participants with higher accuracy showed greater activity over the right frontal lobe.

A study by Cao et al. (2012) demonstrated the pattern of empathy-related processing related to N400s and nonemotional theory of mind processing related to P600s within the same study. They recorded ERPs while 13 participants (six men, seven women) whose handedness was not specified viewed pictures depicting an actor who was viewing one of two objects. The actor's facial expression was either unhappy or happy. In the experiment, the instructions were used as manipulation. In half of the conditions, participants were asked to determine the actor's emotion, guess the object that the actor would choose, or determine which object was being viewed by the actor. The results showed that for both the conditions when participants had to consider the actor's mental state, there were early negative waveforms (N200s) at locations over the frontal lobe and early positive waveforms (P300s). The negative waveforms occurred earlier and the positive waveform was more positive for the condition in which participants had to reason about the actor's mental states (i.e., judging which object the actor would choose) than for the condition in which participants had to decode the actor's emotional state.

The three-stage model of humor processing proposed by Chan and colleagues (Chan, Chou, et al., 2013; Chan et al., 2016; Y. Feng, Chan, & Chen, 2014; Ku et al., 2017) is consistent with the results of functional magnetic resonance imaging (fMRI) studies of humor comprehension. In addition, fMRI studies also suggest that brain regions involved in humor processing are also involved in the comprehension of nonhumorous material that requires participants to engage in theory of mind and empathy processing. Ultimately, the fMRI studies and the studies of electrical brain stimulation demonstrate that there is an enormous amount of complexity that is involved in humor processing, involving the coordination of activity across numerous brain regions (see Chapter 5, this volume).

SUMMARY

Over the last 4 decades, researchers have investigated how people comprehend humor in EEG/ERP experiments. The earliest ERP studies showed that the processing of humor leads to electrical activity in both hemispheres of the brain. More recent studies have supported a three-stage model of humor processing with the detection of incongruity related to an N400, the resolution of the incongruity related to a P600, and the elaboration of the incongruity related to later positivity. EEG/ERP studies of theory of mind processing have shown that these components (i.e., N400 and P600) are also produced when participants comprehend nonhumorous stimuli involving judgments about others' mental states. Individual differences in patterns of EEG/ERP data during the comprehension of humor have also been observed comparing men with women and left-handed participants with right-handed participants. More studies are needed to determine the extent to which there are additional individual differences in EEG/ERP responses during humor comprehension.

4

fMRI Studies of Humor

Interest in brain imaging research has increased rapidly over several decades. In that time, there have been numerous studies revealing details of how the brain functions. The majority of these studies have been conducted using functional magnetic resonance imaging (fMRI; Gorgolewski & Poldrack, 2016). fMRI was invented in 1991 and built on the existing technology of magnetic resonance imaging (MRI; Logothetis, 2008), which provides detailed images of anatomical structures of the body, including the brain. As the name suggests, the technology involves exposing the body to a strong magnetic field. MRI is routinely used in hospital settings, to identify problems, such as tumors, broken bones, or torn ligaments. MRI provides excellent information about anatomy, but no information about temporal changes occurring in the body during the scanning. fMRI was invented to do just that. Images generated with fMRI provide information about activity in the body occurring over a time interval (e.g., 6 seconds or more). This chapter begins with an overview of the methodology, followed by a review of early fMRI studies of humor comprehension. The chapter will also review recent fMRI evidence that supports the three-stage model of humor comprehension is also reviewed. Finally, several studies that have used fMRI to investigate the comprehension of humorous forms of irony are also discussed.

https://doi.org/10.1037/0000203-005
The Cognitive Neuroscience of Humor, by S. M. Kennison

OVERVIEW OF THE fMRI METHODOLOGY

fMRI and MRI involve recording the body when it is exposed to a strong magnetic field. Changes in the cells of the body when the magnet is turned on, then off are recorded. During scanning, participants must lie horizontally within a small cylinder for the duration of the study (i.e., 60–120 minutes) as motionless as possible. Movements during scanning can lead to brain response, which may make it harder to detect the relatively small changes in blood flow that are related to cognitive processing during the task of interest (Haller & Bartsch, 2009). The most common form of fMRI uses blood-oxygen-level dependent (BOLD) imaging, which involves sophisticated computer programs to transform the recorded data into images that show the amount of blood in different brain regions (Logothetis, 2008; Mettler & Guiberteau, 2012). Since the work of Angelo Mosso (1846–1910), researchers have recognized that blood flow changes in the brain occur and can be measured (Raichle, 2009). Regions with more blood flow are viewed as more active during processing and viewed as playing a larger role in the processing than in the regions with less blood flow.

Since the introduction of fMRI, researchers have developed multiple procedures for presenting task stimuli to participants during scanning and for creating composite images of the activity occurring during specific periods of time during processing. In early fMRI studies, researchers tested different conditions with participants using a block design (Tie et al., 2009). Participants would experience all instances of one type or condition of stimuli (e.g., nonhumorous cartoons), then rest, and then they would see all instances of a second type or condition of stimuli (e.g., humorous cartoons). With advances in computer software, researchers now have the option to intermix instances of all conditions in the testing session. This type of design is referred to as the event-related design and has been used in most of the studies on humor processing. Some have criticized the event-related design in fMRI studies on statistical grounds, as the measurement of blood flow captured during a single instance of a condition may be unreliable (Buckner, 1998; Rosen et al., 1998). Tie et al. (2009) compared results for the same stimuli using block and event-related designs, finding that the event-related design yielded similar results compared with the block design. It is important to note that neither design provides information about changes in the brain that occur millisecond-by-millisecond (Logothetis, 2008), which would be useful in understanding simple cognitive processes (i.e., recognizing a picture or word). Eye movement research has shown that the recognition of a single word may occur as rapidly as 50 ms (Rayner et al., 2012). For this reason, it is important to remember that fMRI studies provide good information about the brain regions for a complete cognitive process, but they may not provide insight into the activity of brain regions involved in stages of processing that occur along the way. As with EEG/ERP, one would expect that to observe differences in brain responses to stimuli that involve different sensory systems. Processing of visual stimuli would be expected to involve more activity in the occipital lobes (vs. other sensory regions) to a greater extent than processing of auditory stimuli, which would be expected to activity in the temporal lobes (vs. other sensory regions).

Most fMRI studies commonly use comparisons of brain activity when participants carry out tasks involving different cognitive processes. There continues to be debates among fMRI researchers about how the vast amounts of data generated should be analyzed (Ashby, 2011). One such technique is referred to as the subtraction paradigm in which brain activity recorded during a baseline (control) condition is subtracted from brain activity recorded as an experimental condition (Kemmerer, 2015). An alternative approach involves correlating the activity recorded in different brain regions during conditions that vary in complexity (e.g., baseline control condition that does not include the target cognitive process and an experimental condition that does include the target cognitive processing). In the studies that I review later in this chapter, researchers typically have compared processing in a humorous condition (e.g., reading or listening to a joke) with processing in a nonhumorous condition (e.g., reading or listening nonhumorous statements). In some studies, researchers have included multiple types of humorous stimuli (e.g., puns vs. other types of humor). Because puns (e.g., "Reading while sunbathing makes you well red") are likely to involve processing related to the sounds of words in the joke in addition to the meanings, researchers have hypothesized that brain activity occurring during the processing of puns may differ from brain activity occurring during the processing of other types of jokes (Y.-T. Chang et al., 2019; Coulson & Severens, 2007).

In recent years, researchers have attempted to carry out studies in which the excellent temporal information using electroencephalography/event-related brain potential (EEG/ERP) methodology can be recorded along with the excellent location information using fMRI methodology (Huster et al., 2012; Lei et al., 2012). Combining the two methodologies is sometimes not possible, because most researchers use metal electrodes (e.g., stainless steel, silver, tin) that are incompatible with a strong magnetic field. One solution is to have participants perform the cognitive task twice in quick succession, once while fMRI scanning is carried out and once while EEG/ERP recording is carried out. The advantage of this approach is that researchers obtain good temporal and location information about the brain's activity during the cognitive task. The disadvantage is that the repeated testing may lead to participants to carry out the task somewhat differently the second time. Another solution is to use carbon wire electrodes, which enable data collection during fMRI scanning (M. C. Meyer et al., 2020; Negishi et al., 2008). This strategy is used less frequently, perhaps because of the higher cost of carbon wire electrodes. Although none of the studies on humor processing reviewed in this chapter used fMRI with EEG/ERP, this innovation would be the next logical step in understanding more completely how humor is processed.

EARLY fMRI STUDIES OF HUMOR COMPREHENSION

fMRI researchers began reporting studies on humor processing in the 2000s (Bartolo et al., 2006; Goel & Dolan, 2001; Mobbs et al., 2003, 2005; Moran et al., 2004; A. C. Samson et al., 2008; Watson et al., 2007; Wild et al., 2006). In the earliest study, Goel and Dolan (2001) scanned 14 right-handed participants (gender not specified) as they listened to jokes, which were either semantic jokes (e.g., "What do engineers use for birth control? Their personalities") or phonological jokes or puns (e.g., "Why did the golfer wear two sets of pants? He got a hole in one"). They used an event-related design, which allowed them to present the jokes in random order to participants intermixed with nonjoke control items. For each joke, participants heard the setup of the joke, followed by a pause of 1,580 ms, then the punchline. Following each joke or nonjoke control, participants were asked to provide a rating of the item's humorousness using a keypad. The BOLD response was recorded from the midpoint of the presentation of the punchline to the keypress. The results show that during joke comprehension, there was increased blood flow in multiple brain regions: an area in the prefrontal cortex that was ventral and medial (i.e., ventromedial prefrontal cortex) and an area in the posterior region of the middle temporal

FIGURE 4.1. Location of the Prefrontal Cortex and the Middle Temporal Gyrus

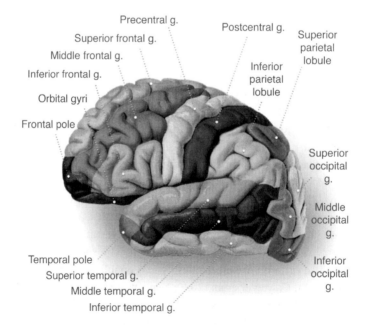

Note. The surface of the brain contains multiple gyri. The major gyri of the left hemisphere are illustrated here. Each of the gyri also occur in the right hemisphere. g. = gyrus. From *Neuroanatomy: Lateral Cortex (Diagrams)*, by F. Gaillard, n.d., Radiopaedia.org (https://radiopaedia.org/cases/neuroanatomy-lateral-cortex-diagrams?lang=us). CC BY 4.0.

gyrus (i.e., posterior medial temporal gyrus). Figure 4.1 displays the location of the prefrontal cortex and the middle temporal gyrus. The results also show that semantic jokes produced more bilateral activity than puns, which produced more left hemisphere than right hemisphere activity. For both types of jokes, increases in blood flow were larger for jokes that participants rated as more humorous. Goel and Dolan suggested that some of the regions are involved in the comprehension aspects of humor processing while others are involved in the emotional aspects of humor processing (i.e., experiencing amusement).

Mobbs et al. (2003) scanned 16 right-handed participants (seven men, nine women) as they viewed cartoons, which were humorous or non-humorous, using an event-related design. Nonhumorous cartoons were created by removing text from the cartoon, which was the source of the humor. They recorded BOLD signals for 6 seconds following the presentation of each cartoon. Their results indicated that there was increased blood flow in four regions in the left hemisphere during comprehension of the cartoon: (a) a region where the occipital lobe borders the temporal lobe (i.e., temporal-occipital junction; see Figure 1.5, Chapter 1, this volume); (b) a region including the inferior frontal gyrus (see Figure 4.1) as well as the most anterior region of the temporal lobe; (c) a region including the supplementary motor area (see Figure 2.2, Chapter 2, this volume) and encompassing the presupplementary motor area and the dorsal anterior cingulate cortex (see Figure 1.7, Chapter 1, this volume); and (d) ventral subregions of the basal ganglia (see Figure 2.1, Chapter 2, this volume), the amygdala, and the hypothalamus (see Figure 1.7, Chapter 1, this volume). Activity in the right hemisphere was observed for the latter group of regions. Mobbs et al. suggested that the observed activity was consistent with Suls's (1972) two-stage model involving incongruity detection followed by resolution. They suggested that increased blood flow in the temporoparietal junction coincided with incongruity detection. Increased blood flow in the inferior temporal gyrus (roughly Broca's area) may have reflected participants' semantic integration during the resolution of the incongruity. Increased blood flow in the regions controlling movement may have coincided with participants' smiling, laughing, and/or feeling of amusement.

Moran et al. (2004) recorded blood flow in the brain as participants watched complete episodes of television comedies, displayed visually while audio was played over headphones. The participants were instructed only to watch and were not required to respond in anyway. In Experiment 1, 12 right-handed participants (five men, seven women) viewed an episode of *Seinfeld*. In Experiment 2, 13 right-handed participants (six men, seven women) viewed an episode of *The Simpsons*. Participants heard the original laugh track of *Seinfeld*, but the researchers created a laugh track for *The Simpsons* by recording the natural laughter of a group of college students who watched the episode. Both experiments used an event-related design. Moran et al. were interested in understanding the brain regions involved in the distinct stages of getting the joke and appreciating the joke. They identified humorous moments (confirmed by independent coders) where laughter occurred in the laugh tracks. BOLD signals were recorded for 2 seconds before the laughter of the humorous moment and also for varying durations following the humorous moment. The results suggested that the cognitive processing involved in the humor processing was related to increased blood flow in the left posterior temporal lobe and the left inferior frontal lobe areas. Moran et al. further linked emotional processes involved in the humor appreciation with increased activity in the amygdala (see Figure 1.7, Chapter 1, this volume) and the insula, which is located in the sulcus of the sylvan fissure (see Figure 4.1). Activity was observed bilaterally in these areas (i.e., in the left and right hemispheres).

Bartolo et al. (2006) compared brain activity as 21 right-handed participants (eight men, 13 women) comprehended pairs of cartoons, which contained no text, but told a single story with the second cartoon containing the elements in which the humor was discovered. Funny cartoon pairs were compared with cartoons pairs that were not funny (as determined by independent raters). The researchers used an event-related design in which humorous and non-humorous cartoon pairs were randomly presented, and BOLD signals were recorded. Each trial involved each cartoon in the pair presented for 3 seconds with a 500 ms blank between them. Brain activity was recorded for 10 seconds following the presentation of the second cartoon. Their results showed that during the processing of humorous cartoons, brain activity was higher in four regions: left cerebellum (see Figure 2.1, Chapter 2, this volume), the left middle temporal gyrus, the left superior temporal gyrus, and the right inferior frontal gyrus (see Figure 4.1). Bartolo et al. also found that there was increased blood flow in the left amygdala when participants comprehended the funniest cartoons, suggesting that these areas are involved in processing the positive emotion that occurs during humorous experiences. The authors suggested that the participants' perception of the humor in the nonverbal cartoon pairs occurred when they considered the intention of a character in the cartoons.

Wild et al. (2006) scanned 13 right-handed men while they comprehended nonverbal cartoons, which were either humorous or nonhumorous. The authors used an event-related design in which the order of cartoons were randomized, and BOLD signals were recorded. Participants were also video-taped to determine on whether smiling occurred. On some trials in which a nonhumorous cartoon was displayed, participants were instructed to smile, a condition that Wild et al. referred to as nonhumorous smiling. The results showed that when participants comprehended the funny cartoons, there was increased blood flow in the left temporal-occipital-parietal junction and the left anterior prefrontal cortex. When cartoons evoked smiling by participants, there was increased blood flow observed in the bottom area of the left and right temporal lobes. When participants smiled as instructed while viewing nonhumorous cartoons, there was increased blood flow in the areas of the motor cortex (see Figure 2.2, Chapter 2, this volume), which controls movement of the face and other body parts. Wild et al. concluded that there are distinct brain regions associated with voluntary, unemotional smiling and the smiling that accompanies the emotional experience of humor. The next chapter will show that this conclusion is supported in studies in which specific brain regions are stimulated directly with electricity.

Only a few fMRI studies have compared brain responses for different types of humorous stimuli within the same experiment (Chan & Lavallee, 2015; A. C. Samson et al., 2008; Watson et al., 2007). For example, Watson et al. (2007) compared changes in blood flow during the comprehension of cartoons that were either language-based cartoons (i.e., the caption was required for the humor) and visual-based cartoons (i.e., the humor stemmed from the drawing itself). They scanned 20 right-handed participants (12 men, eight women) using an event-related design in which the different types of cartoons and nonhumorous control cartoons were presented in random order. At the end of each trial, participants were asked to rate the humorousness of the cartoon. The results showed that different patterns of responses were observed for the two types of stimuli with visual areas in the occipital lobe showing increased blood flow during the comprehension of visual humor and language processing areas (e.g., the inferior temporal gyrus, the superior temporal sulcus, the middle temporal gyrus) showing increased blood flow during the comprehension of language-based jokes. For both types of jokes, there was increased blood flow in the amygdala and regions located in the midbrain, which was viewed as likely related to the experience of amusement, as well as increased blood flow in the anterior cingulate gyrus (see Figure 1.7, Chapter 1, this volume) and the anterior region of the insula, within the sylvan fissure (see Figure 4.1).

A. C. Samson et al. (2008) compared blood flow as participants viewed four types of nonverbal cartoons: semantic cartoons; visual puns, which included ambiguity among visual elements in the cartoon; theory of mind cartoons, which required the perceiver to consider the intention of a character in the cartoon; and cartoons that contained irresolvable incongruity (i.e., there was no clear way to interpret the meaning of the image). A. C. Samson et al. scanned 17 participants (eight men, nine women) using an event-related design as they comprehended each stimulus. After each trial, participants provided a rating of the cartoon's comprehensibility. After the entire session, participants rated the humorousness of the cartoons. The results showed that for all types of humorous stimuli, when participants resolved incongruity, there were increases in blood flow in left hemisphere regions, specifically the ventromedial prefrontal cortex, inferior frontal gyrus, and the border between the temporal and parietal lobes (i.e., the temporoparietal junction). Comprehending visual puns led to increased blood flow in the visual processing area of the occipital lobe (see Figure 1.5, Chapter 1, this volume). When participants comprehended cartoons involving theory of mind processing, there was increased blood flow in three regions in the left and right hemispheres: the temporoparietal junction; the precuneus (see Figure 4.2); and the fusiform gyrus, which is located below the inferior temporal gyrus (see Figure 4.1). When participants viewed cartoons with unresolvable incongruity, there was increased blood flow in a region of the anterior region of the cingulate (see Figure 1.7, Chapter 1, this volume).

FIGURE 4.2. Location of the Precuneus

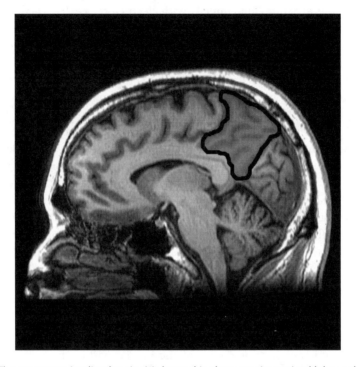

Note. The precuneus (outlined region) is located in the posterior parietal lobe and borders the occipital lobe. Each hemisphere contains a precuneus region. Adapted from *Precuneus*, by G. B. Hall, 2011, Wikimedia Commons (https://commons.wikimedia.org/wiki/File:Precuneus.png). CC0 1.0.

Among the early fMRI studies of humor comprehension, several investigated individual differences, most comparing humor processing in men and women (Azim et al., 2005; Kohn et al., 2011) and one exploring individual differences in personality (Mobbs et al., 2005). Azim et al. (2005) had 20 right-handed participants (10 men, 10 women) view 70 cartoons, which they then rated in terms of funniness. The authors used an event-related design in which humorous and nonhumorous cartoons were presented in random order, and BOLD signals were recorded for 6 seconds as participants viewed the cartoon. The results indicated that for men and women, there was increased blood flow in three brain regions: the inferior frontal gyrus; the temporal pole, which is located at the most anterior location of the temporal lobe; and the temporal-occipital junction. For women, there was greater blood flow than there was for men in regions in the left prefrontal cortex (see Figure 4.1) and the mesolimbic regions, which are located in the ventral region of the basal ganglia. The mesolimbic regions are known to be involved in experiencing pleasure and reward processing from a variety of activities including eating, having sex, and using opioids (Berridge & Kringelbach, 2015).

In a similar study, Kohn et al. (2011) recorded brain activity in 29 right-handed participants (15 men, 14 women) as they comprehended nonverbal cartoons using an event-related design in which humorous and nonhumorous cartoons were presented in random order. Participants were scanned for 7 seconds while viewing each cartoon. Their results observed differences in men and women's brain activity, but in regions different from those studied by Azim et al. (2005). Kohn et al. found that when comprehending humorous cartoons, women had more blood flow than men in three brain regions: the amygdala (see Figure 1.7, Chapter 1, this volume); the insula, which is located in the sulcus of the sylvan fissure; and the anterior region of cingulate cortex, which is located just above the corpus callosum (see Figure 1.7, Chapter 1, this volume).

Mobbs et al. (2005) investigated brain activations with fMRI during humor processing for individuals varying in personality. Individuals reporting higher levels of extraversion produced greater activation during humor processing, specifically in the temporal lobe of the left hemisphere and several right hemisphere regions, including the orbital frontal cortex, the ventrolateral pre-frontal cortex, and the temporal lobe. Individuals reporting higher levels of introversion produced greater activation during humor processing in the left and right amygdalae.

In summary, the early fMRI studies of humor comprehension used multiple types of stimuli (e.g., jokes, cartoons, television shows) and identified a variety of brain areas that became more active during humor comprehension. Two studies observed differences in brain responses during humor processing for men and women with women exhibiting larger responses in the pre-frontal cortex and mesolimbic regions than men. Individual differences in extraversion/introversion were also found to be related to differences in the amount of activation in brain areas during humor processing. A summary of the early fMRI studies of humor processing is provided in Table 4.1.

fMRI EVIDENCE FOR A THREE-STAGE MODEL OF HUMOR COMPREHENSION

A series of fMRI studies by Chan and colleagues (Chan et al., 2012, 2018; Chan, Chou, et al., 2013; Dai et al., 2017) has extended the work of earlier studies, not only confirming the involvement of specific brain areas in humor processing, but also supporting a three-stage model of humor processing. In one of the earliest studies, Chan, Chou, et al. (2013) recorded BOLD signals as 22 right-handed participants (nine men, 13 women) listened to humorous, nonhumorous, and nonsensical stories. They used an event-related design in which the 16 stimuli for each of the three conditions and 16 additional filler nonhumorous stimuli were intermixed. Each story was presented in two parts: the setup for 20 seconds and the ending for 9 seconds, which was a punchline in humorous conditions. Participants provided a rating of the stories' comprehensibility. By comparing brain responses during the processing of different pairs of conditions, they were able to identify brain regions involved incongruity detection, which involves semantic processing by comparing brain

TABLE 4.1. Summary of Early fMRI Studies of Humor Comprehension

Study	Type of stimuli	Brain regions
Goel & Dolan (2001)	Jokes	ventral medial prefrontal cortex posterior middle temporal gyrus
Mobbs et al. (2003)	Cartoons	left temporal-occipital junction Broca's area and other left frontal areas
Moran et al. (2004)	Television comedies	the left inferior frontal lobe left posterior temporal lobe amygdala and insula
Mobbs et al. (2005)	Cartoons	left and right temporal lobe right orbital frontal cortex right ventrolateral prefrontal cortex
Azim et al. (2005)	Cartoons	the inferior frontal gyrus the temporal pole the temporal-occipital junction left prefrontal cortex mesolimbic region
Wild et al. (2006)	Cartoons	left temporal-occipital junction
Bartolo et al. (2006)	Cartoons	the left middle temporal gyrus the left superior temporal gyrus the right inferior frontal gyrus left cerebellum amygdala
Watson et al. (2007)	Jokes and cartoons	anterior insula the anterior cingulate cortex amygdala and midbrain regions
A. C. Samson et al. (2008)	Cartoons	left ventromedial prefrontal cortex left inferior frontal gyrus left temporoparietal junction anterior cingulate cortex
Kohn et al. (2011)	Cartoons	amygdala insula anterior cingulate cortex

activity in nonhumorous conditions versus nonsensical conditions. These regions were the right medial temporal gyrus and right medial frontal gyrus (see Figure 4.1, which displays the corresponding regions in the left hemisphere). Chan, Chou, et al. were able to identify brain regions involved in incongruity resolution by comparing brain activity in humorous and nonsensical conditions. These regions were the left inferior frontal gyrus, the left superior frontal gyrus, and the left inferior parietal lobe (see Figure 4.1). On the basis of their results and results of prior research, Chan, Chou, et al. speculated that the brain regions involved in humor elaboration, which ultimately brings about the feeling of mirth, included the left ventromedial prefrontal cortex, the right anterior cingulate, the left and right amygdalae, and the left and right parahippocampus gyrus. Table 4.2 displays the brain regions associated with the three stages of humor processing.

More recently, Dai et al. (2017) provided a revision to the three-stage model of humor processing. They hypothesized that the processing of incongruity–resolution and nonsense humor may involve different neural regions because nonsense humor involves incongruity that may be unresolvable yet results in humor and amusement. They recorded BOLD signals from 27 right-handed participants (15 men, 12 women) who comprehended short stories that ended a punchline that involved incongruity–resolution humor, nonsense humor, or neutral meaning, which served as the nonhumorous control. For each humorous story, the nonhumorous control was created by changing the punchline to remove the humor. Participants were scanned for 14 seconds as they read the setup of the story and 9 seconds as they read the punchline. After each story, participants provided a humorousness rating. The results showed that for both types of humorous condition, humor comprehension was associated with activity in the middle temporal gyrus and the middle frontal gyrus. However, Dai et al. observed differences in activity for brain regions for the two types of humor. They concluded that incongruity resolution for humor involving an incongruity–resolution structure led to increased blood flow in the temporoparietal junction in the precuneus, which is located in the posterior parietal lobe, including the portion that borders the occipital lobe (see Figure 4.2). Humor elaboration for incongruity–resolution humor led to increased blood flow in the posterior region of the cingulate cortex, which lies just above the corpus callosum (see Figure 1.7, Chapter 1, this volume), the amygdala, and the parahippocampal gyrus, which is a layer of tissue surrounding the hippocampus. In contrast, when participants comprehended nonsense humor, humor comprehension was associated with greater blood

TABLE 4.2. Brain Regions Involved in the Three Stages of Incongruity–Resolution Humor Processing

Stage of humor processing	Type of processing	Brain regions
Incongruity detection	Semantic processing	medial frontal gyrus middle temporal gyrus
Incongruity resolution	Semantic selection and integration	inferior frontal gyrus superior frontal gyrus inferior parietal lobe
Humor elaboration	Emotional response (amusement)	ventromedial prefrontal cortex anterior cingulate cortex amygdala parahippocampal gyrus

Note. From "Towards a Neural Circuit Model of Verbal Humor Processing: An fMRI Study of the Neural Substrates of Incongruity Detection and Resolution," by Y.-C. Chan, T.-L. Chou, H.-C. Chen, Y.-C. Yeh, J.P. Lavallee, K.-C. Liang, and K.-E. Chang, 2013, *NeuroImage, 66,* p. 175 (https://doi.org/10.1016/j.neuroimage.2012.10.019). Copyright 2013 by Elsevier. Adapted with permission.

flow in the inferior frontal gyrus, the superior temporal gyrus, the fusiform gyrus located below the inferior temporal gyrus (see Figure 4.1), and the lingual gyrus (located above the fusiform gyrus extending from the medial temporal lobe into the medial occipital lobe). Figure 4.3 displays Dai et al.'s (2017) three stages of processing for incongruity–resolution and nonsense humor.

Other fMRI studies have observed results that have proven to be largely consistent with a three-stage model of humor processing (Amir et al., 2015; Campbell et al., 2015; S. Feng, Ye, et al., 2014; Franklin & Adams, 2011; Nakamura et al., 2018; Osaka et al., 2015; Shibata et al., 2014; Tian et al., 2017; see also Bekinschtein et al., 2011). Shibata et al. (2014) recorded BOLD signals from 20 participants (five men, 15 women) in an event-related design as they comprehended short discourses composed of three sentences. They were innovative in their construction of materials, as they created humorous and nonhumorous stimuli that had the same first and last sentences. This enabled them to compare processing on the punchline in humorous conditions, which had the same words as the nonhumorous conditions. Their results indicated that in humorous conditions, there was increased blood flow in the right middle temporal gyrus (see Figure 4.1), which was described as incongruity detection, and also in the left inferior frontal gyrus, the left inferior parietal lobe and the left superior frontal gyrus, which corresponded to incongruity resolution. Shibata et al. also noted that participants' brain responses revealed connections between the midbrain, which may be involved in the emotional response to humor (i.e., humor elaboration), and three regions in the cortex:

FIGURE 4.3. The Three-Stage Model of Processing Incongruity–Resolution and Nonsense Humor

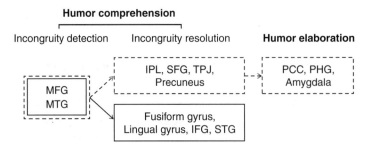

Note. Dai et al. (2017) proposed that there are different brain regions involved in three stages of humor processing for incongruity–resolution humor (boxes with dotted lines) and nonsense humor (boxes with solid lines). MFG = medial frontal gyrus; MTG = medial temporal gyrus; IPL = inferior parietal lobe; SFG= superior frontal gyrus; TPJ = temporo-parietal junction; IFG = inferior frontal gyrus; STG = superior temporal gyrus; PCC = posterior cingulate cortex; PHG = parahippocampal gyrus. From "To Resolve or Not To Resolve, That Is the Question: The Dual-Path Model of Incongruity Resolution and Absurd Verbal Humor by fMRI," by R. H. Dai, H.-C. Chen, Y. C. Chan, C.-L. Wu, P. Li, S. L. Cho, and J.-F. Hu, 2017, *Frontiers in Psychology, 8*(498), p. 11 (https://doi.org/10.3389/fpsyg.2017.00498). CC BY.

the right middle temporal gyrus, the left inferior parietal lobe, and the inferior frontal gyrus.

Osaka et al. (2015) scanned participants as they comprehended a series of four cartoon panels (i.e., Manga style cartoons). They used an event-related design in which each panel was presented for 3 sec with a blank panel in between, which was presented for either 6 seconds or 7.5 seconds. In Experiment 1, 16 participants (nine men, seven women) viewed 24 cartoons that were either presented in the appropriate order (humorous conditions) and 24 cartoons that were presented in a random order (nonhumorous condition). In Experiment 2, 18 participants (14 men, four women) viewed 24 funny Manga cartoons and 24 nonhumorous cartoons. In both experiments, the punchline in humorous conditions occurred in the fourth panel in the sequence. Following the presentation of the fourth panel, participants were asked to rate the humorousness of the four-frame sequence. The results showed that when participants comprehended the second cartoon in the sequence, which provided the setup for the humor, there was increased blood flow in the temporoparietal junction, which Dai et al. (2017) claimed to be involved in incongruity resolution. Further, the results showed that as participants viewed the third cartoon, which provided more information about the setup, there was increased blood flow in the frontal and temporal lobes, which may have reflected additional processing related to incongruity resolution. As participants viewed the final cartoon in the sequence and comprehended the humor, there was increased blood flow in the medial prefrontal cortex (see Figure 4.1) and the cerebellum (see Figure 2.1, Chapter 2, this volume) as compared with conditions in which there was no humor. These results may be consistent with the third stage of humor processing, which involves humor elaboration leading to the feeling of amusement.

Campbell et al. (2015) investigated differences in brain activity that were related to humor comprehension, which occurs early in processing, and humor appreciation, which occurs later in processing and includes the positive emotional response to the humor. They used an event-related design in which 24 right-handed participants (10 men, 14 women) viewed 120 cartoons with captions. Three conditions were compared: cartoons with a high level of humor, cartoons with a low level of humor, and nonhumorous cartoons. Nonhumorous cartoons were created by changing the caption in humorous cartoons to remove the source of the humor. In the fMRI experiment, BOLD signals were recorded for 10.5 seconds as each cartoon was comprehended. At the end of each trial, participants rated the humorousness of the cartoon. Campbell et al. aimed to isolate the brain activity involved in humor appreciation by comparing brain activity occurring during the processing of humorous cartoons with activity occurring during the processing of nonhumorous cartoons. The results showed that humor comprehension was associated with increased activity in the left temporoparietal junction, and humor appreciation was associated with increased activity in the superior frontal gyrus (see Figure 4.1).

Several recent studies have explored individual differences in brain responses during humor processing, each focusing on a different variable, including gender (Chan, 2016), personality (P. Berger et al., 2018a), differences in self-control when comprehending aggressive humor (X. Liu et al., 2019), and differences in humor ability (Amir & Biederman, 2016). In a study of gender differences in humor processing, Chan (2016) scanned 26 right-handed participants (13 men, 13 women) as they read jokes presented in two parts (setup for 12 seconds then punchline for 9 seconds) using an event-related design. Different types of verbal humor were tested: ambiguity jokes, which involve multiple meanings; exaggeration jokes, which involve a meaning that has been exaggerated; and bridging-inference jokes, which require participants to draw an inference between the punchline and the joke setup. For each trial, participants were scanned for 12 seconds as they read the setup and 9 seconds as they read the punchline. They were then asked to provide a humorousness rating. The results showed that overall, there was higher activity in the anterior prefrontal cortex for women than for men, and higher activity in the dorsolateral prefrontal cortex for men than for women. Sex differences were observed in brain activity during the processing of each type of joke. During the processing of ambiguity jokes, there was greater activity in prefrontal cortex and parahippocampal gyrus for men than for women. During the processing of bridging-inference jokes, there was greater activity in orbitofrontal cortex, anterior prefrontal cortex, temporoparietal junction, parahippocampal gyrus, insula, and supplementary motor areas for women than for men.

P. Berger et al. (2018a) investigated individual differences in brain responses during humor comprehension in a study with 19 right-handed participants (nine men, 10 women) who provided self-reports of personality (i.e., Extraversion, Openness to Experience, Agreeableness, Conscientiousness, and Neuroticism; see Widiger, 2017, for a review). They used an event-related design in which humorous and nonhumorous cartoons were presented and participants were scanned for 7 seconds during comprehension. Participants provided a humorous rating for each trial. The results showed that blood flow in the right amygdala and the left insula were related to individual differences in personality, specifically extraversion and neuroticism. However, participants' ratings for the humorousness of the cartoons were not significantly related to personality.

In the only fMRI study that has investigated brain responses during the production of humor, Amir and Biederman (2016) recorded the brain activity of novice and professional improvisational comedians as they generated either humorous or nonhumorous captions for *New Yorker* cartoons. Novice comedians showed increased activation in the medial prefrontal cortex when producing humorous captions. In contrast, professional comedians had increased activation in areas in the temporal lobes but decreased activation in the medial prefrontal cortex and the striatum, a region in the midbrain's basal ganglia.

SUMMARY

Studies using fMRI have revealed numerous brain regions involved in the comprehension of humor. Recent studies have proposed that the pattern of activity across these regions reflect three distinct stages of humor processing: incongruity detection, incongruity resolution, and humor elaboration, which includes the positive emotion associated with mirth. Different brain regions were found to be involved in the resolution of nonsense humor, which presents incongruity that may be more difficult or impossible to resolve than in the resolution of incongruity–resolution humor. Across the studies, these three stages of processing have been captured as participants comprehend humorous cartoons or punchlines preceded by verbal content for a period of time not longer than 11 seconds. When the brain regions identified in fMRI studies are compared, there is some consistency with the brain regions suggested in Du et al.'s (2013) EEG/ERP study. Du et al. identified the anterior cingulate cortex as involved in the second stage of humor processing (i.e., incongruity resolution). This region was also identified in many of the fMRI studies but was associated with humor elaboration in the study by Chan, Chou, et al. (2013). Du et al. identified the medial frontal lobe and the fusiform gyrus as involved in the third stage of humor processing (i.e., humor elaboration), which includes the experience of mirth. These regions were also associated with humor elaboration in the fMRI study by Chan, Chou, et al. (2013). A few regions were linked with humor in only a few studies, suggesting that more research is needed to determine the extent to which those regions are related to humor processing (e.g., cerebellum in Bartolo et al., 2006; insula in Kohn et al., 2011; Moran et al., 2004; Watson et al., 2007). Nevertheless, a limitation of the fMRI studies is the lack of diversity, with studies including a small number of right-handed individuals. It remains unclear whether the observed results will be observed in future studies with larger number of participants and, more important, with different types of participants (i.e., different age groups, education levels, cultural backgrounds, etc.). A few studies have observed individual differences in brain responses to humor for several types of differences (e.g., gender, personality, self-control, humor ability).

5

Brain Stimulation Studies of Laughter, Mirth, and Humor Processing

Among the most compelling studies of humor processing are those in which humor-related behavior (i.e., smiling, laughing, and feelings of mirth) has been elicited by directly stimulating the brain with electricity. Penfield and colleagues used electrical brain stimulation (EBS) to explore the functioning of specific brain regions (Jasper & Penfield, 1954; Penfield, 1958; Penfield & Roberts, 1959/2014; Penfield & Welch, 1951). Then, as now, the procedures were carried out on individuals who required brain surgery (e.g., patients with epilepsy). This chapter reviews how EBS has been used to explore humor processing. The first section focuses on the studies using EBS to explore how specific brain regions are involved in laughter and mirth in patients undergoing brain surgery. The second section reviews studies using a related, but more recently developed technique referred to as *deep brain stimulation* (DBS; see Guillory & Bujarski, 2014, for a review). DBS involves the placement of electrodes deep in the brain for the purposes of controlling an increasing number of brain-based disorders, including Parkinson's disease, severe cases of treatment-resistant depression, and obsessive–compulsive disorder (Miocinovic et al., 2013; Sironi, 2011). Researchers often publish interesting associations that they observe between the stimulation of specific brain areas and the production of specific behaviors. The final section discusses recent studies that have stimulated the brain externally using relatively new transcranial stimulation techniques in which electricity is directed to specific brain locations.

https://doi.org/10.1037/0000203-006
The Cognitive Neuroscience of Humor, by S. M. Kennison

ELECTRICAL BRAIN STIMULATION

The earliest references to using electricity to stimulate the brain are found in ancient Rome, where electric fish were applied to an individual's scalp in an attempt to alleviate headaches and symptoms of depression and epilepsy (Kellaway, 1946). In the 20th century, the methodology of EBS was used by Penfield and colleagues (Penfield, 1958; Penfield & Roberts, 1959/2014) to explore the functions of specific brain locations in patients undergoing brain surgery to treat epilepsy. Jasper and Penfield (1954) carried out numerous brain surgeries to treat epilepsy. Surgery would be performed to remove brain tissue, which caused abnormal activity that led to debilitating seizures. With the abnormal tissue removed, surgeons were able to reduce the severity of symptoms. Patients were placed under local anesthetic, enabling them to be conscious while the surgeon probed into the brain. During the brain stimulation procedure, the patient would be conscious, but felt no pain from the stimulation because of the absence of pain receptors in the brain (see Gazzaniga et al., 2013). Exploratory brain stimulation before surgery is beneficial to the patient, as it enables surgeons to familiarize themselves with the regions of the patient's brain that are involved in functions particularly important to the patient (e.g., language, any special skills related to work or hobbies), which can lead to a higher quality of life for the patient postsurgery (Guillory & Bujarski, 2014). In 2019, Jenna Schardt, a patient from Texas, livestreamed her own brain surgery at Methodist Hospital in Dallas on the social media platform Facebook (DiFurio, 2019). Surgeons were removing a cluster of abnormal blood vessels in her brain. She was alert and describing what was occurring for her audience, which was estimated to be in the tens of thousands.

There are limitations associated with research that uses this technique. First, the research is conducted with patients with existing brain-based disorders, whose results may not generalize to neurotypical individuals (Guillory & Bujarski, 2014). Second, the number of electrodes is not sufficient to test all or most of the brain's surface. Third, and most important, it remains unclear whether the behaviors and experiences that are elicited by directing electricity into the brain are produced in a manner that is the same as when those behaviors and experiences are produced in daily life without EBS. A current of electricity may trigger activity in brain tissue that is unlike activity that would occur during normal functioning. The behaviors that are observed following EBS may appear to be qualitatively the same as behaviors occurring in daily life (e.g., laughter), but the extent to which they are the same remains unclear.

Among the earliest studies to use EBS to investigate humor-related processing was Arroyo et al.'s (1993) study describing three participants who experienced gelastic seizures, one without mirth and two with mirth. For those who experienced gelastic seizures with mirth, electrical stimulation to areas in the temporal lobe—the parahippocampal gyri and fusiform gyrus—produced laughter and mirth. For the patient who experienced gelastic seizures without mirth, electrical stimulation to the left anterior cingulate cortex produced laughter (without mirth). Based on the observation that laughter and mirth can each be experienced without the other, they concluded that the cognitive processing involved in laughter and the experience of mirth are distinct with different brain regions controlling them. Laughter was linked to the left anterior cingulate gyrus (see Figure 1.7, Chapter 1, this volume) and mirth was linked to the temporal lobe (see Figure 1.5, Chapter 1, this volume). In a subsequent study with an 18-month-old boy and a 35-year-old woman, Schmitt et al. (2006) also observed that stimulation near the left superior frontal gyrus repeatedly led to laughter without mirth for the older patient as well as for the child. They identified the area as the anterior portion of the supplementary sensorimotor area, which is also labeled in Figure 2.2 (see Chapter 2, this volume). They concluded that the region is involved in producing the motor aspects of laughter. Lastly, Chassagnon et al. (2008) observed smiling without mirth following the stimulation of the cingulate motor area, which is located in the cingulate gyrus just below the supplementary motor area.

Other studies have found that participants can experience laughter consistently with mirth during EBS (Caruana et al., 2015, 2016; Fernández-Baca Vaca et al., 2011; Fried et al., 1998; Satow et al., 2003; Sperli et al., 2006; Yamao et al., 2015; see also Fish et al., 1993); however, the regions identified have varied across studies. In an early study, Fried et al. (1998) reported a case of stimulated laughter in the prestigious journal *Nature*. It described a case study of a patient who received EBS to the surface of the left hemisphere, which caused laughter and a feeling of mirth. The patient was a 16-year-old girl with epilepsy who was undergoing a procedure to reduce the severity of epileptic seizures. The researchers applied electricity at different times and in different amounts at 85 sites while the patient carried out a variety of tasks, including counting, reading, object naming, and specific changes in body parts dictated by the researchers. Laughter occurred reliably each time an area measuring approximately 2 cm × 2 cm on the left superior frontal gyrus received stimulation. This area is located in the anterior portion of the supplementary motor area (see Figure 2.2, Chapter 2, this volume). The supplementary motor area has been shown to be involved in carrying out movement (Nachev et al., 2008; Penfield & Welch, 1951). The researchers found that the intensity level of the electrical current modulated the behavior with low levels of current appearing to produce smiling in the participant and high levels of current eliciting robust laughter. The researchers noted that the patient reported an environmental trigger for the laughter rather than realizing that the laughter was due to the stimulation of her brain. She commented that the behavior of the research team was amusing to her and that a picture in the room was funny. The research team interpreted her behavior as revealing an experience of mirth caused by the stimulation, which she subsequently tried to attribute the laughter to some external cause.

A subsequent study by Fernández-Baca Vaca et al. (2011) observed laughter with mirth when stimulation occurred in a nearby region in the left hemisphere (i.e., the left inferior frontal gyrus; see Figure 4.1, Chapter 4, this volume), below the regions identified by Fried et al. (1998) and Schmitt et al. (2006). The case study described a woman undergoing surgery to reduce a severe disorder that developed when she was 46 years old. Other brain regions have been associated with producing laughter and/or mirth following electrical stimulation (Caruana et al., 2015; Krolak-Salmon et al., 2006; Satow et al., 2003; Sperli et al., 2006; Yamao et al., 2015). Satow et al. (2003) identified the inferior temporal gyrus in a case study of a 24-year-old woman with epilepsy. Low intensity stimulation to the area elicited mirth without laughter. Krolak-Salmon et al. (2006) reported a case study of a 19-year-old woman with epilepsy who laughed and experienced mirth when they stimulated the presupplementary motor area, which is located anterior to the supplementary motor area. Yamao et al. (2015) described two cases, one in which the patient had a normal hippocampus and one in which the patient did not. For the patient with a normal hippocampus, EBS to the left temporal cortex led to laughter with mirth. In the individual with a damaged hippocampus, EBS to the same area led to mirth without laughter. The researchers noted that the stimulated area was located close to temporal lobe language areas and speculated that the experience of mirth may have some relationship to language.

In a series of recent studies Caruana and colleagues (2015, 2016) explored when laughter and/or mirth occurred during EBS for patients undergoing surgery for epilepsy. Caruana et al. (2015) explored the role of the anterior cingulate cortex (see Figure 1.7, Chapter 1, this volume) in producing laughter in 57 patients who had epilepsy and who had undergone brain stimulation to explore which brain regions contributed to their seizures. The patients had received stimulation to the anterior cingulate cortex during their procedure. The researchers observed that electrical stimulation of a region at the tip of the anterior cingulate cortex (i.e., pregenual anterior cingulate) resulted in laughter with mirth for five patients and resulted in laughter without mirth for five additional patients. They concluded that the region is involved in producing movement and mirth (i.e., an emotional response). The results are consistent with earlier work by Sperli et al. (2006), who reported a case of a patient with epilepsy who laughed without mirth following stimulation to the right cingulate cortex. In a more recent study, Caruana et al. (2016) reported a study involving four patients with epilepsy who smiled and laughed without mirth following stimulation of the left and right frontal operculum, which is an area above the sylvan fissure, but below Broca's area. Table 5.1 displays a summary of the studies that have found that brain stimulation results in laughter with or without mirth.

This body of work supports Arroyo et al.'s (1993) proposal that the brain regions controlling laughter and mirth are distinct. However, because there is variation across studies in the brain regions associated with laughter and mirth, it is not clear how each of these regions participate in these humor-related

TABLE 5.1. Summary of Findings for Electrical Brain Stimulation Studies of Smiling or Laughter and Mirth in Patients With Epilepsy

Study	Year	Stimulated brain region(s)	Observation
Arroyo et al.	1993	left anterior cingulate cortex	laughter without mirth
		parahippocampal gyrus	laughter with mirth
		fusiform gyrus	laughter with mirth
Caruana et al.	2015	pregenual anterior cingulate cortex	with and without mirth
Caruana et al.	2016	left and right frontal operculum	smiles, laughter without mirth
Chassagnon et al.	2008	cingulate motor areas	experienced urge to laugh without mirth
Fernández-Baca Vaca et al.	2011	left inferior frontal gyrus	laughter with mirth
Fried et al.	1993	left superior frontal gyrus	laughter with mirth
Krolak-Salmon et al.	2006	presupplementary motor area	laughter with mirth
Satow et al.	2003	inferior temporal gyrus	mirth without laughter
Schmitt et al.	2006	anterior part of the supplementary sensorimotor area	laughter without mirth
Sperli et al.	2006	right cingulate cortex	laughter without mirth
Yamao et al.	2015	left basal temporal cortex	laughter with mirth when hippocampus normal; mirth without laughter when hippocampus damaged

processes. A reasonable speculation is that laughter is controlled by regions in or near to the supplementary motor area where movement is controlled, and that mirth is controlled by regions in or nearer to the temporal lobe. There is also a possibility that the specific locations controlling laughter and mirth may vary somewhat across individuals because of differences in development, because of differences occurring after the onset of a disorder or because of factors that are yet to be elucidated (Kanai & Rees, 2011).

DEEP BRAIN STIMULATION

Unlike EBS, which involves the temporary stimulation of brain regions with a mild electrical current, DBS is carried out during a process in which surgeons place electrodes deep in the brain for the purposes of providing long-term stimulation (M. H. Rogers & Anderson, 2009; Sironi, 2011). This process is illustrated in Figure 5.1. DBS is being used to treat a widening range of

FIGURE 5.1. The Process of Deep Brain Stimulation

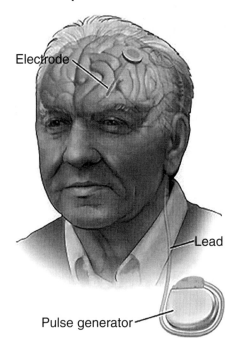

Note. Deep brain stimulation involves the implantation of electrodes in the brain, which can stimulate brain areas with electricity. The electrodes are connected to a controller that is external to the body and can be used to increase or decrease the electrical output of the implanted electrodes. From "Deep Brain Stimulation: A Paradigm Shifting Approach to Treat Parkinson's Disease," by P. Hickey and M. Stacy, 2016, *Frontiers in Neuroscience*, *10*(173), p. 5 (https://doi.org/10.3389/fnins.2016.00173). CC BY.

conditions, including Parkinson's disease (Kuusimäki et al., 2019), major depression that has not responded to other treatments (Crowell et al., 2019), obsessive–compulsive disorder (Rapinesi et al., 2019), and severe forms of treatment-resistant obesity (Halpern et al., 2008). Among its most common use is for patients with Parkinson's disease to control tremors when medications have either failed to control them or have led to severe side effects (Parkinson's Foundation, n.d.). The electrodes are controlled external to the body, with the patient being able to control the intensity of electricity delivered by the electrodes by adjusting a dial/switch. Some have described the treatment as a pacemaker for the brain (Miocinovic et al., 2013). There remains no clear consensus on how DBS leads to the health benefits that it provides (Ashkan et al., 2017).

DBS studies of humor-related behavior (i.e., smiling, laughter, feelings of mirth) have resulted from stimulation to a specific deep brain region during the brain surgery to place electrodes in targeted brain areas. During the implantation procedure, stimulation may be turned on and off, as the surgeons find the ideal location for the placement of the electrode (Ben-Haim &

Falowski, 2018). The position of the electrode may be shifted in an effort to bring about a better response in the participant who is conscious during the procedure and able to report their state of mind as adjustments to the electrodes are made. Some studies using DBS have reported findings similar to those obtained using EBS (i.e., anterior cingulate cortex; Sem-Jacobsen, 1968; cf., Arroyo et al., 1993).

Other studies have identified new locations that appear to be involved in humor-related processing (W. S. Gibson et al., 2017; Haq et al., 2011; Hassler & Riechert, 1961; Krack et al., 2001; Morishita et al., 2015). Among the earliest reports is that of Hassler and Riechert (1961), which observed laughter following the stimulation of the globus pallidus (see Figure 2.1, Chapter 2, this volume) in a patient with Parkinson's disease. Krack et al. (2001) reported two cases of DBS involving patients undergoing electrode placement to treat Parkinson's disease. Laughter with mirth occurred following the stimulation of the subthalamaic nucleus (see Figure 2.1, Chapter 2, this volume). Haq et al. (2011) reported five cases of DBS involving patients undergoing electrode placement to treat obsessive–compulsive disorder. They observed smiling and laughing following stimulation of the nucleus accumbens, which is located within the basal ganglia between the caudate nucleus and the putamen. The nucleus accumbens is well-known as part of the circuit involved in pleasure (i.e., the reward circuit), which is known to be involved in responses to pleasure derived from sexual activity, eating, and taking opioids. Five patients experienced smiling and laughing with mirth when the area was stimulated. Low levels of stimulation resulted in smiling, and laughter occurred following higher levels of stimulation.

Morishita et al. (2015) described a case study involving a woman with post stroke pain who received DBS as treatment. They observed her smiling without mirth following the stimulation of the ventral striatum (see Figure 2.1, Chapter 2, this volume). Similar results were obtained by W. S. Gibson et al. (2017), who described four patients with obsessive–compulsive disorder who smiled with and without mirth following the stimulation of the ventral striatum. In a novel addition to the procedure, W. S. Gibson et al. carried out functional magnetic resonance imaging recording immediately following two stimulations of the area that led to smiling with mirth and also immediately following two stimulations of the area that led to smiling without mirth. The data provided information about the amount of blood flow in brain regions associated with mirth experiences in studies using EBS. The results suggested that the experience of mirth involves a pathway of increased activation between the anterior cingulate (see Figure 1.7, Chapter 1, this volume) and the ventral striatum, as well as a pathway of decreased activation between the thalamus and the ventral striatum. They suggested that activity across multiple regions is coordinated in a loop. This loop involves the anterior cingulate cortex, the ventral striatum, the amygdala, and the medial dorsal thalamus.

In summary, studies of smiling, laughter, and mirth have resulted from the use of DBS as a treatment for a variety of conditions, most often Parkinson's

TABLE 5.2. Summary of Findings for Deep Brain Stimulation Studies of Laughter and Mirth

Study	Year	Stimulated brain region(s)	Observation	Participant condition
W. S. Gibson et al.	2017	ventral striatum	with and without mirth	obsessive–compulsive disorder
Haq et al.	2011	nucleus accumbens	smiles, laughter with mirth	obsessive–compulsive disorder
Hassler & Riechert	1961	globus pallidus	laughter	dystonia, schizophrenia
Krack et al.	2001	subthalamaic nucleus	laughter with mirth	Parkinson's disease
Morishita et al.	2015	ventral striatum	laughter without mirth	poststroke pain
Sem-Jacobsen	1968	anterior cingulate cortex	laughter with mirth	psychosis
		orbitofrontal cortex	laughter with mirth	psychosis

disease. These studies have identified multiple areas involved in humor-related processing, only one that was identified in previous studies using EBS (i.e., the anterior cingulate cortex). The other areas identified include the anterior cingulate cortex and areas within the basal ganglia (i.e., ventral striatum, globus pallidus, subthalamaic nucleus, and nucleus accumbens). A summary is provided in Table 5.2.

TRANSCRANIAL BRAIN STIMULATION

The newest procedures stimulate the brain from outside of the cranium via electrodes on the scalp (Brunyé et al., 2019; Grossman et al., 2019). There are two methods: transcranial direct current stimulation (see Kriotkova et al., 2019, for review) and transcranial magnetic stimulation (see George et al., 2002, for a review), which uses a magnet to create the electrical current. Transcranial direct current stimulation was first used by Giovanni Aldini (1762–1834) in the early 1800s to treat patients with long-term melancholy (Parent, 2004; Sironi, 2011). Today, it is also used as a treatment for major depression (Mondino et al., 2014; Mutz et al., 2019), and has been tested as a possible treatment for other disorders, including schizophrenia (Agarwal et al., 2013; Marzouk et al., 2019), Alzheimer's disease (Rajji, 2019; Vacas et al., 2019), chronic pain (Bayer et al., 2019; Brighina et al., 2019; Galhardoni et al., 2015), addiction (Coles et al., 2018; Ibrahim et al., 2019), and stroke (Bucur & Papagno, 2019). The exact mechanisms involved in its therapeutic benefits remain unknown (Grossman et al., 2019).

Increasingly, transcranial brain stimulation is being used as a research tool to investigate the function of specific brain regions (Brunyé et al., 2019).

In such studies, researchers begin with a hypothesis that a particular brain region is used when an individual performs a particular task. To test the hypothesis, the researchers stimulate the brain region as participants' carry out that task. The hypothesis is supported if the participants' ability to carry out that task is disrupted when the brain region is stimulated. Some have referred to the use of transcranial magnetic stimulation in this way as creating a brief virtual lesion (Pascual-Leone et al., 2000). For example, Pitcher et al. (2011) reviewed multiple studies showing that TMS could disrupt face processing when an area in the occipital lobe hypothesized to be involved in face processing (i.e., occipital face area) was stimulated. An advantage of this technique is that it can be used with healthy participants as well as with participants who have preexisting brain abnormalities.

Three studies have investigated humor processing (Manfredi et al., 2017, 2019; Slaby et al., 2015). Slaby et al. (2015) used transcranial direct current stimulation to stimulate the left temporoparietal junction as participants watched and rated videos varying in humorousness. This area was targeted because it is known to be involved in empathizing with others and theory of mind, which has been shown to play a role in humor processing. The results found significant decreases in humorousness ratings during stimulation, which were also affected by individual differences in participants' humor styles. Slaby et al. concluded that changes in the activity in the temporoparietal junction can influence individuals' appreciation of humor, specifically resulting in aggressive humor being found less humorous.

Manfredi and colleagues (2017, 2019) have reported two studies using transcranial direct current stimulation to explore aspects of humor processing. Manfredi et al. (2019) used direct current stimulation to target the right temporoparietal junction and the medial prefrontal cortex during humor processing, both of which have been identified as involved in theory of mind processing. Participants in the study were asked to comprehend cartoons that were funny or not funny, which served as control stimuli. Those stimuli that were not funny were either being semantically interpretable without humor or semantically anomalous without humor. Manfredi et al. found that stimulation to the medial prefrontal cortex led to participants rating funny cartoons as funnier than when the area was not stimulated. Stimulating the right temporoparietal junction did not affect humor processing in this study. In a study that focused specifically on the processing of comic and noncomic facial expressions in cartoons, Manfredi et al. (2017) showed that stimulating the right superior temporal gyrus led participants to faster reaction times than when there was no stimulation to the area and when the stimulation was directed toward the left superior temporal gyrus. They concluded that the right superior temporal gyrus plays an important role in face processing generally and the processing of comic facial expressions, specifically.

To date, only three studies have investigated humor processing with transcranial brain stimulation methods (transcranial magnetic stimulation or transcranial direct current stimulation). These demonstrated that transcranial

EBS to the temporoparietal junction, the medial frontal cortex, and the right superior temporal gyrus can affect different aspects of humor processing.

SUMMARY

Researchers have studied humor-related behavior (i.e., smiling, laughing and experiencing mirth), as well as humor processing, in studies in which the brain is directly stimulated with electricity. The most commonly used methods have been EBS, DBS, and transcranial stimulation. Multiple areas have been found to be involved in humor-related behavior or processing. A promising proposal is that some, if not all, of these regions function together when we experience humor. The details of how the areas are interconnected, transmitting excitation or inhibition to other areas remain unclear. Research with each of the methodologies is likely to continue long into the future because of the continuing need for patients with epilepsy or Parkinson's disease to receive brain surgeries. The intracranial stimulation techniques stand to provide better information about how stimulation of specific brain regions affect participants' function, as there is better control over where the stimulation is directed in the brain when compared with the transcranial techniques.

6

The Development of Humor in Typical and Atypical Individuals

This chapter reviews how humor develops from birth through adolescence and how changes occurring during development are related to changes in cognitive processing. Children's ability to appreciate and to use humor changes as they age because of changes in brain development and cognitive ability. Relatively few brain imaging studies of humor in children have been conducted. One reason is that brain imaging studies require participants to be as motionless as possible during the session, and children tend to have difficulty minimizing movement during experimental tasks. A second reason is that parents and caregivers have busy schedules and may be unlikely to volunteer for research studies of any type. Future research on the cognitive neuroscience of humor stands to gain a great deal by considering how humor processing changes throughout development. The first two sections of this chapter focus on how humor develops in neurotypical infants and older children, and examine how the development of the brain plays a role in children's changing behaviors and abilities. The third section discusses humor deficits in individuals with developmental disorders, which are usually diagnosed in childhood or early adulthood, including autism spectrum disorder (ASD), agenesis of the corpus callosum (ACC; the bundle of fibers connecting the left and right hemispheres fails to develop), and schizophrenia. Changes in cognitive ability and neurotypical brain development contribute to humor processing in most children and atypical brain development may account for humor processing deficits in others.

https://doi.org/10.1037/0000203-007
The Cognitive Neuroscience of Humor, by S. M. Kennison

MIRTH, SMILING, AND LAUGHING IN INFANTS

The topic of humor in children attracted attention as early as the 1920s (Brackett, 1933; Kenderdine, 1931; McGhee, 1974; Rothbart, 1973; Sherman, 1975; Wolfenstein, 1954; D. Yalisove, 1978; M. Yalisove, 1954; Zigler et al., 1966, 1967). Studies have attempted to understand the extent to which infants' and children's smiling, laughing, and joke-making is influenced by biology and by their experiences with parents, peers, and other people. Researchers who observed laughing and smiling that can occur in gelastic epilepsy pointed out that some smiling, laughing, and even feelings of amusement may be produced by electrical firing occurring during seizures rather than in response to a humorous experience. In the 1970s, cases of gelastic epilepsy in newborns, which caused laughing and smiling during seizure episodes (Sher & Brown, 1976) showed that the ability to laugh and smile is present from birth and likely innate. Later, studies also supported the view that laughing and smiling is innate, showing that children who were blind and deaf from birth produced typical laughter (E. L. Goodenough, 1932; see also Black, 1984) and blind infants produce typical smiles (D. G. Freedman, 1964).

Smiling during social interactions is typically observed earlier in life than laughing (Berk, 2017). Social smiles can occur as early as 2 months old and typically occur regularly by 3 months old. Laughing during social interactions typically begins to emerge in the 3rd and 4th month. Parents and caregivers, as well as researchers, have difficulty determining with certainty what causes these behaviors in young infants. First words do not emerge until around the end of the 1st year, and the ability to produce minisentences with which children could explain what triggered their feelings of happiness or other positive emotions does not typically emerge until sometime between the 2nd and 3rd year (Kennison, 2014).

Over the past decade, K. Kawakami and colleagues (2006, 2007; see also F. Kawakami et al., 2009; F. Kawakami & Yanaihara, 2012) have attempted to understand smiling behavior in infants as well as fetuses. K. Kawakami et al. (2006) observed smiling in newborn infants, finding that the earliest smiles were one-sided. By the time infants were 2 months old, smiles were two-sided. In contrast, laughs were produced in a two-sided fashion from birth. In a longitudinal study in which the smiling of five infants was observed for 15 months, K. Kawakami et al. (2007) found that spontaneous smiles occurred throughout the 15 months, disconfirming the possibility that spontaneous smiles do not occur when infants begin producing social smiles. In a fascinating study, F. Kawakami and Yanaihara (2012) used sonography to image the smiling behavior of fetuses before birth. They observed smiling in infants whose conceptional ages were estimated to be between 156 and 214 days. Although they were unable to determine what might have triggered the smiling behavior in the fetuses, they found that the physical characteristics of the smiling were similar to those observed in newborns in previous studies.

A useful technique for studying the possible reasons infants laugh and smile are laboratory experiments in which infants are exposed to different types of experiences and researchers note their responses (P. M. Miller & Commons, 2007; Parrott & Gleitman, 1989; Snow, 1989; Sroufe & Waters, 1976; Sroufe & Wunsch, 1972). For example, Snow (1989) showed that children in their 2nd year of life are amused when objects are used in unusual ways (e.g., a bowl placed on the head like a hat, a spoon held between the lip and the nose like a mustache).

Parrott and Gleitman (1989) tested the reactions of infants between the ages of 6 months old and 8 months old. The infants were shown a series of trials similar to the game of peek-a-boo. Most trials were similar to the normal peek-a-boo game, where a person's face is visible then is briefly not visible and then becomes visible again. The researchers mixed in several "trick" trials to see whether infants would respond differently to those. For these trials, the face that disappeared at the beginning of the trial was different from the face that appeared at the end of the trial. The results showed that infants showed less positive emotion for the trick trials than for the other trials, and they showed more surprise facial expressions following the trick trials.

Numerous studies have investigated how the presence and/or behavior of a parent or caregiver might influence infants' responses during laboratory sessions to various stimuli (Fogel et al., 1997, 2006; Jones & Raag, 1989; MacDonald & Silverman, 1978; Mireault et al., 2014, 2015, 2018; Mireault, Poutre, et al., 2012; Mireault, Sparrow, et al., 2012; Nwokah et al., 1993, 1994, 1999; Nwokah & Fogel, 1993; Shultz, 1976). In an early study, Jones and Raag (1989) investigated smiling in mother–infant pairs in which the infants were 17 months old or 19 months old. The results showed that smiling occurred for infants and parents when they were paying attention to toys as well as a pleasant stranger. Infants were less likely to smile during times that the mother was not paying attention to them.

Nwokah and colleagues (1993, 1994, 1999; Nwokah & Fogel, 1993; see also Fogel et al., 1997, 2006) carried out a series of longitudinal studies in which mother–infant pairs were observed during play interactions with parents. Recordings were analyzed in terms of the frequency and timing of laughter by infants and parents. Nwokah et al. (1994) studied the laughter of mother–infant pairs over a period of 2 years from the birth of the infants. They focused specifically on the timing of laughter by the infants and the mothers. The results showed that for infants and mothers, most of the laughter was unrelated to the laughter of the other in the pair. Mothers tended to produce laughs that were in response to infants' laughter more often than infants produced laughs in response to mothers' laughter. By the end of the 2nd year, the synchrony of mothers' and infants' laughter increased. Nwokah et al. (1999) found that in mother–infant pairs in which the infants were between 1 month old and 5 months old, mothers' laughter episodes contained infant-directed speech around 50% of the time.

In a series of studies Mireault and colleagues (2014, 2015, 2018; Mireault, Poutre, et al., 2012; Mireault & Reddy, 2016; Mireault, Sparrow, et al., 2012) investigated laughter and smiling in infants. Mireault, Sparrow, and colleagues (2012) investigated how infants' laughter, smiling, and positive affect at between 3 months old and 6 months old changed over several play sessions with a parent and how their responses to play related to their later attachment. Infants who displayed less laughing, smiling, and positive affect at 6 months old were more securely attached at 12 months old. The authors interpreted the results as indicating that infants that display less of a good humor may draw their parents into them, which results in more interaction and more secure attachment later. In a later study, Mireault et al. (2014) investigated parent–infant interactions involving an episode of absurd humor. Infants were either 6 months old or 12 months old. The results showed that parents produced emotional cues that infants might use to evaluate the episode. They also found that parents' responses to the event were more likely to influence children at 12 months old than those at 6 months old, even though both groups looked to parents during the event. Later studies found that even younger infants appeared to be able to evaluate absurd humor. Mireault et al. (2015) observed the behavior in 5-month-old infants, and Mireault et al. (2018) observed the behavior in 4-month-old infants.

Some research has attempted to determine how humorous experiences in infants might be beneficial. Esseily et al. (2016) tested the hypothesis that experiencing humor might facilitate learning a new skill. They tested 53 infants around the age of 18 months old. Half of the infants experienced a humorous interaction and the other half experienced a nonhumorous control condition. In both conditions, infants were able to see an adult use a complex tool to reach and grab a toy placed far away. In the humorous condition, when the toy was obtained, the adult threw it down on the floor. Later, all infants were allowed to explore the tool. The results found that laughter by infants during the humorous condition predicted which infants interacted with the tool in a manner similar to how the adult had used the tool. Such interactions occurred more often in the humorous condition than in the control condition.

HUMOR DEVELOPMENT IN YOUNG CHILDREN

As children develop cognitively, their humorous behavior becomes more complex, as they are able to perceive humor in more complex situations, understand linguistic forms of humor (e.g., riddles, puns, jokes), and do things that make others laugh (Bariaud, 1989). Research has established that in children, as in adults, laughter occurs more often in the presence of others versus when individuals are alone (Addyman et al., 2018; Chapman, 1973, 1975, 1983; Chapman & Wright, 1976). Addyman et al. (2018) investigated whether children's reactions to humorous videos were affected by the presence of peers.

Children were between the ages of 31 months old and 49 months old and watched three videos either alone, with one other child, or with a group of five or seven others. Children laughed significantly more when they were with one or more others (i.e., 8 times more laughter and 3 times more smiling). There was no significant difference in the amount of laughing in the pair or group conditions. Other research has shown that children also produce laughter in situations that are not strictly humorous, such as when they are afraid (Romanova, 2014) and sometimes after performing an act that they perceive as misbehaving.

Researchers have observed age differences and sex differences in laughing and smiling (Bainum et al., 1984; DeSantis et al., 2005; Fabrizi & Pollio, 1987). Bainum et al. (1984) investigated laughing and smiling of boys and girls between the ages of 3 years and 5 years. They found that older children laughed more often and smiled less often than younger children. Overall, 95% of smiling and laughing was produced during exchanges with others. There were no statistical differences in the amount of laughing and smiling by boys and girls. DeSantis et al. (2005) investigated smiling among boys and girls and men and women. They found no difference in smiling between boys and girls, but in adolescence and adulthood, women smile more than men.

Understanding how children's appreciation of humor develops in childhood has been guided by McGhee's (1979; see also McGhee, 2014) early work on the topic. He described the development of humor appreciation as occurring in four stages, which are displayed in Table 6.1. In all but the first stage, children's ability to produce and comprehend language is related to their humor behavior. Research from the 1960s pointed out that children as young as 3 years old play with speech sounds and words for the purpose of amusing themselves (Helmers, 1965). Purposeful word play appears to emerge around the age of 4 years. By the age of 5 years, children begin to be amused by jokes told by other people. As their language develops, their ability to appreciate riddles, puns, and jokes also develops.

Early research by Shultz and colleagues (Shultz, 1972, 1974a, 1974b; Shultz & Horibe, 1974; Shultz & Robillard, 1980; Shultz & Scott, 1974) investigated the ability of young children to understand verbal humor. For example, Shultz and Horibe (1974) presented jokes to first, third, fifth, and seventh graders and asked them to judge the funniness of incongruity–resolution jokes (e.g., "Person A says, 'Call me a taxi.' Person B replies, 'You're a taxi'") and versions of the jokes with either the resolution eliminated (e.g., "Person A says,

TABLE 6.1. The Four Stages of Humor Development

Stage	Age	Amused by
1	18–24 months old	objects used in unusual ways
2	24–36 months old	using wrong words to refer to objects
3	3–7 years old	toilet humor, simple jokes, riddles
4	7–11 years old	teasing, jokes, puns

Note. Data from McGhee (1979).

'Call a taxi for me.' Person B replies, 'You're a taxi'") or the incongruity elimi-nated ("Person A says, 'Call me a taxi.' Person B replies, 'Yes, right away'"). The results showed that all but the first graders found the original versions of the jokes funnier than the variations. Other studies have found that young children can comprehend incongruity–resolution jokes and find them funny, if the jokes are easy to comprehend (Pien & Rothbart, 1976). Nevertheless, other research has found that riddles and jokes that are amusing to young children differ from those that are amusing to older children (Bever, 1968; Whitt & Prentice, 1977; Yalisove, 1978). Bever (1968) found that 5-year-old children found sentences containing a grammatical ambiguity humorous (e.g., "Why can't you starve in the desert? Because of the sand witches there"). In contrast, 10-year-old children found jokes containing a semantic ambiguity humorous (e.g., "Why can you jump higher than the Empire State Building? Because it can't jump at all").

Researchers have shown that the ability to comprehend irony, a form of verbal humor, develops during childhood (Creusere, 2000; de Groot et al., 1995; Dews et al., 1996; Glenwright et al., 2014; González Fuente et al., 2016; Nicholson et al., 2013; Winner, 1997). These studies did not examine irony comprehension in relation to children's ability to reason about others' minds or to empathize with others. As discussed in prior chapters, theory of mind processing is involved in the comprehension of many forms of humor by adults (Vrticka, Black, & Reiss, 2013). In children, awareness of the minds of others and being able to consider the mental states of others develops between the ages of 2 years and 5 years during the period when children are also developing language ability (Ebert, 2015; Milligan et al., 2007). Others have shown that in typically developing individuals, the ability to reason about others' minds continues to develop into adolescence (Im-Bolter et al., 2016; S. A. Miller, 2012) and may not develop fully in some individuals with ASD (Baron-Cohen, 1990, 2009).

Numerous studies have investigated the relationship between theory of mind ability and children's appreciation or comprehension of humor (Angeleri & Airenti, 2014; Bosacki, 2013; Kielar-Turska & Białecka-Pikul, 2009; Puche-Navarro, 2004, 2009; Sullivan et al., 1995). Sullivan et al. (1995) showed that children's theory of mind was related to their ability to distinguish jokes from lies. Participants were between the ages of 5 years and 8.4 years. Angeleri and Airenti (2014) investigated how children between the ages of 3 years and 6.5 years comprehended ironic statements in interactions with a puppet. The results suggested that even the youngest children understood the jokes but may not have always comprehended the ironic statements.

Hoicka and colleagues (Hoicka, 2016; Hoicka & Akhtar, 2011, 2012; Hoicka & Butcher, 2016; Hoicka et al., 2017; Hoicka & Gattis, 2008; Hoicka & Martin, 2016) investigated how young children evaluated humor in others, showing that they made sophisticated appraisals of others' intentions. For example, Hoicka and Akhtar (2011) investigated English-speaking preschoolers' reactions to jokes that were told by foreigners or nonforeigners. Children between the ages of 30 months old and 36 months old were asked to label joke tellers as "foreign" or "nonforeign" (i.e., English speakers) and to judge joke tellers' utterances as humorous or nonhumorous (i.e., sincere). Children were less likely to repeat a humorous action if the joke teller was foreign, suggesting that humor was more easily inferred when the speaker was perceived as nonforeign. Hoicka et al. (2017) showed that children between the ages of 3 years and 5 years considered another person's intention when carrying out a task in which they had to determine whether to trust another's statements.

Hoicka and Akhtar (2012) investigated the humor productions of children between the ages of 2 years and 3 years while they were with their parents. Some parents were surveyed, and others were observed interacting with their child. The results of both studies indicated that children regularly create humor that is novel, rather than merely repeating or imitating the behavior of another (e.g., using an object in a humorous way, like underwear as a hat). Hoicka and Martin (2016) demonstrated that children as young as 2 years old could distinguish pretending and joking. Hoicka and Butcher (2016) showed that parents produce explicit cues that help toddlers between 16 months old and 24 months old to distinguish joking and pretending. Hoicka (2016) examined parents' interactions with toddlers during pretending and joking, finding that parents altered their speech to children during joking, specifically exaggerating the parentese features (e.g., exaggerated pitch in voice intonation, increased positive emotion). Children also smiled and looked more in the humorous condition as compared with the nonhumorous and pretending conditions.

Children's brains undergo substantial development throughout childhood, increasing not only in overall volume but also in terms of the white matter, which functions to connect brain regions (Blakemore, 2012). For example, the corpus callosum is a bundle of white matter fibers connecting the brain's hemispheres. The corpus callosum is not fully myelinated until around the age of 4 years (Gazzaniga, 1974); for the child's early years, their hemispheres function with little or no communication from one another. It is not until around the age of 12 years that the volume of the parietal and frontal lobes reaches adult levels; the temporal lobes continue to increase in volume until around the age of 17 years (Blakemore, 2012). Other developmental changes continue into the mid-20s (Arain et al., 2013).

The temporoparietal junction was found to be involved in theory of mind processing and in the processing of some forms of humor (see Chapter 5, this volume). A small number of studies have examined brain responses during humor processing by children (Neely et al., 2012; Vrticka, Black, Neely, et al., 2013). Using functional magnetic resonance imaging (fMRI), Neely et al. (2012) showed that the temporoparietal junction is also involved in the processing of humor by children between the ages of 6 years and 12 years. In the study, the children were scanned as they viewed humorous stimuli, nonhumorous stimuli that were emotionally positive, and emotionally neutral stimuli. Interestingly, for the youngest children, blood flow was higher in the inferior frontal gyrus (see Figure 4.1, Chapter 4, this volume) and nucleus accumbens, which is located within the basal ganglia between the caudate nucleus and the putamen (see Figure 2.1, Chapter 2, this volume) than for older children. These results suggested that brain responses during humor processing vary across development.

HUMOR IN ATYPICAL DEVELOPMENT

Over the last 50 years, much has been learned about typical and atypical development (Berk, 2017). For parents and caregivers, understanding the milestones of typical development is helpful in identifying a child whose abilities and/or behavior may be different. Such cases are likely to receive increased attention from pediatricians to determine what may be the cause of the unusual circumstances. Increasingly, humor ability is being recognized as reflecting typical development and problems with humor processing as reflecting atypical development. Three syndromes in which there are deficits in humor processing are examined next: ASD, ACC, and schizophrenia.

Autism Spectrum Disorder

ASD is a developmental disorder characterized by problems in communication and social interactions (Lerner et al., 2018). Individuals with ASD have problems noticing and interpreting social cues and also with social behavior. Individuals typically are diagnosed between the ages of 4 years and 7 years (Altschuler et al., 2018; Baio et al., 2018; Sheldrick et al., 2017). Earlier diagnosis is beneficial, as behavioral interventions may be more effective if started as early as possible. Over the last several decades, there has been increased awareness of the earliest behaviors characteristic of ASD (e.g., delays in cooing and laughter; Gallagher et al., 1983). The causes of ASD remain unclear. Studies support the roles of genetics (Caronna et al., 2008), environmental factors, maternal health during pregnancy (E. Fox et al., 2012), epigenetic changes in the baby because of maternal stress (Miyake et al., 2012), and maternal exposure to pollution during pregnancy (Flores-Pajot et al., 2016; Weisskopf et al., 2015). A growing number of brain imaging studies have documented differences in the brains of individuals with ASD and individuals having typical development (Picci et al., 2016; Vogan et al., 2016).

Since the 1990s, researchers have noted that individuals with ASD often have deficits in theory of mind (Baron-Cohen, 1990, 2009; see also Altschuler et al., 2018; Peterson, 2014, for reviews). The term *mind blindness* has been used to describe the condition an individual has when there is no or limited theory of mind (Baron-Cohen, 1990, 2009). Individuals with ASD may not develop theory of mind completely or at all. Problems with theory of mind processing may underlie the problems with humor processing observed in individuals with ASD. Humor deficits in individuals with ASD have been noted going back several decades (Lyons & Fitzgerald, 2004;

Pexman et al., 2011; Silva et al., 2017; St. James & Tager-Flusberg, 1994). For example, St. James and Tager-Flusberg (1994) investigated how 6-year-old children with ASD or Down syndrome responded during hour long naturalistic humorous interactions with their mothers, which were repeated once per month for a year. The children in the two groups were closely matched on language ability. The results indicated that in both groups, children produced humorous responses, but rarely. Joke-telling was observed only in two children with Down syndrome. In a more recent study, Pexman et al. (2011) investigated irony comprehension in a group of individuals with high-functioning autism and compared their performance with two control groups, one matched in age and the other matched in language ability. Although interpretations of ironic statements were comparable with all groups, analyses of reaction time, eye movement behavior, and evaluations of the humor suggested that the children with ASD arrived at the interpretations using different strategies than children in the other group.

Silva et al. (2017) investigated the comprehension of explicit and implicit forms of humor in individuals diagnosed with ASD, comparing their performance with a group of typically developing participants. They found that on explicit forms of humor, individuals with ASD performed as well as the typically developing group. In contrast, on implicit forms of humor individuals with ASD performed as well as typically developing individuals when the humor did not involve social content, but performed less well, when the humor involved social content. The authors concluded that individuals with ASD are able to appreciate humor, especially those forms without social content. Consequently, humor, as a social reward, appears to be possible for individuals with ASD.

Some individuals diagnosed with ASD have less severe symptoms, which results in their being able to function at a higher level. In the past, Asperger syndrome was used to identify this type of individual. Researchers sometimes use the term *high-functioning autism*. Samson and colleagues (A. C. Samson, 2012; A. C. Samson & Antonelli, 2013; A. C. Samson & Hegenloh, 2010; A. C. Samson et al., 2012, 2013), as well as other researchers (Eriksson, 2013; Nagase & Tanaka, 2015; Weiss et al., 2013), showed that individuals with high-functioning autism performed significantly more poorly on humor processing than did individuals without ASD. For example, A. C. Samson et al. (2013) compared the trait seriousness, trait cheerfulness, and humor styles of individuals with ASD and control participants without ASD of similar age. They found that those with ASD scored higher in trait seriousness and lower in trait cheerfulness. They also reported using affiliative, self-enhancing, and aggressive humor styles less often and the self-defeating humor style more often than those in the control group. Similarly, Eriksson (2013) investigated humor styles in individuals with high-functioning autism. He found that individuals scoring high on a common ASD assessment used positive humor styles less often that did individuals without ASD. Further examination of the subcomponents of the ASD assessment measure revealed that individuals with low scores on the mind-reading component tended to use negative humor styles more often than individuals with high scores on the mind-reading component.

Agenesis of the Corpus Callosum

Some individuals are born without a corpus callosum. The condition is rare, occurring in seven out of every 10,000 births (T. J. Edwards et al., 2014; Glass et al., 2008). In populations where there is routine use of prenatal ultrasound examinations, ACC may be detected in the last trimester of pregnancy (Penny, 2006). For some individuals, ACC is diagnosed during adulthood when a brain scan is ordered for an unrelated reason. For those individuals who have received diagnosis during adulthood, it is sometimes the case that they have completed high school and even college.

Early research shows that in individual with ACC, cognitive ability (Chiarello, 1980; Sauerwein et al., 1994) and language ability are in the normal range (Liederman et al., 1985; Sauerwein et al., 1994; Temple et al., 1989, 1990), but in fine-grained analyses, deficits occur in comprehending figurative language and comprehending the emotional content of speech, also referred to as prosody (W. S. Brown et al., 2005) as well as inferring meaning from context (Banich & Brown, 2000; W. S. Brown et al., 2005; Huber-Okrainec et al., 2005; Paul et al., 2003). Studies have found that memory is impaired for verbal information (R. L. Erickson et al., 2014) and visual information (Paul et al., 2016). Marco et al. (2012) concluded that lower levels of executive functioning (e.g., planning, coordinating behaviors, regulating emotions) in ACC may be due to the fact that general cognitive processes take longer to complete than in neurotypical individuals. Those with ACC may have underdeveloped conversation skills and reduced ability to express their emotional experiences verbally (O'Brien, 1994) and lower levels of interpersonal skills (also called emotional intelligence) than individuals without ACC (L. B. Anderson et al., 2017).

Some researchers have concluded that the impairments observed in ACC are comparable with those observed in individuals with ASD (Y. C. Lau et al., 2013; Paul et al., 2003, 2014; Romaniello et al., 2017; Symington et al., 2010; Turk et al., 2010). Y. C. Lau et al. (2013) investigated the prevalence of ASD traits in individuals with ACC. In a sample of 106 individuals, they found that many met criteria for an ASD diagnosis (i.e., 18% of adults, 35% of adolescents, and 45% of children). Paul et al. (2014) compared a sample of 26 individuals with ACC with IQs in the normal range with a group of 28 individuals diagnosed with ASD. The results indicated that among those in the group with ACC, 30% met criteria for an ASD diagnosis.

Other research has found that individuals with ACC may also have deficits in theory of mind processing (W. S. Brown et al., 2005; Brownell et al., 1983; Lábadi & Beke, 2017). Lábadi and Beke (2017) compared children with ACC between the ages of 6 years and 8 years with age- and IQ-matched control participants and found impairment related to theory of mind and recognizing emotions. W. S. Brown et al. (2005) investigated humor processing in adults with ACC. They administered narrative joke and cartoon sections of Brownell et al.'s (1983) test for humor to 16 individuals with ACC and 31 control participants similar in age and IQ. The results showed that individuals with ACC performed more poorly than control participants on the narrative jokes but performed comparable with control participants comprehending cartoons. Further analyses suggested that individual differences in figurative language processing predicted performance understanding narrative jokes.

Schizophrenia Spectrum Disorder

Schizophrenia is among the most severe mental health disorders, and its symptoms include difficulties distinguishing reality from fantasy (Kurtz et al., 2016; National Institute of Mental Health, n.d.). Some individuals diagnosed with schizophrenia may experience hallucinations and/or delusions. Schizophrenia can be considered a developmental disorder, because its onset occurs during the teenage years or later (van Os & Kapur, 2009). The prevalence is quite low, observed in less than 1% of the population (van Os & Kapur, 2009). Men and women are affected at similar rates, but the age of onset tends to be earlier for men (McGrath et al., 2008). There are different types of the disorder, varying in average age of onset and also in predominant symptoms. The most common type is associated with symptoms emerging between the ages of 16 years and 30 years. Symptoms are described as positive (e.g., unusual body movements, hallucinations, delusions, paranoia) or negative (e.g., lack of emotion, apathy, problems finishing tasks, difficulty beginning tasks). The causes of the disorder are not fully understood. There appears to be roles for genetic and environmental contributors (Kurtz et al., 2016).

Differences in brain composition have been detected in individuals prior to the onset of symptoms and diagnosis (Lewis & Levitt, 2002). In an fMRI study, Palaniyappan et al. (2013) showed that the language regions in individuals with schizophrenia differed from healthy control participants initially after diagnosis and also 24 months later. Unlike the brains of healthy control participants, which showed asymmetry larger in the left than right hemispheres, brains of individuals with schizophrenia initially showed smaller asymmetry. Over time, the asymmetry increased in healthy brains, but decreased in individuals with schizophrenia. Close family members of individuals with schizophrenia have also been found to have atypical patterns of brain activity in word processing tasks (Thermenos et al., 2013). Over the last decade, some researchers have suggested that schizophrenia is a language disorder that occurs because of abnormal processing of concepts in semantic memory (M. Brown & Kuperberg, 2015; Ditman et al., 2011; Hinzen & Rosselló, 2015; Kuperberg, 2010a, 2010b). This view contrasts with the traditional view of schizophrenia as a thought disorder (Jablensky, 2010).

Multiple studies have documented theory of mind deficits in individuals with schizophrenia (Kantrowitz et al., 2014; see Mothersill et al., 2016, for a review).

Kantrowitz et al. (2014) showed that deficits of theory of mind processing in individuals with schizophrenia are due to deficits in auditory processing, at least in part. These auditory deficits can also lead to problems interpreting sarcasm. Other studies have documented deficits in individuals with schizophrenia in the recognition of emotional facial expressions (Tsoi et al., 2008). Tsoi et al. (2008) found that individuals with schizophrenia are less able to recognize happy facial expressions. Happy faces were found to be interpreted as sad or fearful. Some have suggested that the deficit in recognizing emotion could be useful as a diagnostic criterion (C. M. Corcoran et al., 2015).

A growing number of studies have shown that individuals with schizophrenia may exhibit an inability to appreciate humor (Adamczyk et al., 2018; P. Berger et al., 2018b; R. Corcoran et al., 1997; Daren et al., 2019; Ivanova et al., 2014; Pawełczyk et al., 2018; Polimeni et al., 2010; Rapp et al., 2014; Varga et al., 2013). R. Corcoran et al. (1997) compared the comprehension of different types of cartoons in a sample of individuals with schizophrenia and a group of control participants without schizophrenia. Half of the cartoons required the participant to consider the point of view of an individual in the cartoon. The remainder could be interpreted without mentalizing (i.e., the humor involved physical or semantic aspects of a scenario). Individuals with schizophrenia performed more poorly on the mentalizing group of cartoons compared with the control group. Performance was poorest among those individuals with schizophrenia who were experiencing symptoms during the session. Individuals with schizophrenia who were asymptomatic at the session performed as well as those in the control group.

Using fMRI, Adamczyk et al. (2017) investigated humor comprehension in a group of individuals with schizophrenia and a control group without schizophrenia who were matched for education level, age, and sex. Participants comprehended 60 short discourses, which were either humorous, nonhumorous but sensical, or nonsensical. Following each discourse, they were asked to judge whether the story made sense and to rate its humorousness. The results showed that individuals with schizophrenia rated humorous conditions as less funny than individuals in the control group. Differences were also observed in brain responses during comprehension. Individuals with schizophrenia had lower increases in blood flow in the frontal and temporal regions as compared with individuals in the control group. When comprehending nonsensical stimuli, there were lower increases in blood flow in the right posterior superior temporal gyrus (see Figure 4.1, Chapter 4, this volume). When comprehending humorous conditions, there were lower increases in blood flow in the dorsomedial middle and superior frontal gyrus (see Figure 4.1, Chapter 4, this volume) and the interhemispheric dorsal anterior cingulate cortex (see Figure 1.7, Chapter 1, this volume). P. Berger et al. (2018b) carried out a similar study and found similar results. In addition to observing differences in the blood flow of the anterior superior frontal gyrus, middle frontal gyrus, and cingulate cortex in individuals with schizophrenia versus individuals in the control group, they also observed differences in the blood flow to the putamen and caudate nucleus (see Figure 2.1, Chapter 2, this volume) when individuals rated the humorousness of stimuli.

In an fMRI study in which scanning was conducted using the event-related methodology, Varga et al. (2013) compared brain responses during irony comprehension for a group of individuals with schizophrenia who were in remission in terms of symptoms and a control group of individuals without schizophrenia. Individuals with schizophrenia comprehended irony less well than individuals in the control group. Further, patterns of blood flow during the comprehension task differed for individuals with schizophrenia, who showed increased blood flow in the frontal and parietal lobes, and for individuals in the control group, who showed increased blood flow in the temporal, frontal, and parietal areas.

Several studies have found that close biological relatives of individuals with schizophrenia show atypical patterns of brain responses during processing (Herold et al., 2018; Marjoram et al., 2006). For example, Herold et al. (2018) examined the processing of irony among individuals with schizophrenia, individuals who had a close family member diagnosed with schizophrenia (first-degree relative), and a control group of individuals without schizophrenia. The materials contained an ironic statement preceded by a short context. Comprehension of irony was better for the control group and the first-degree relative group than for individuals with schizophrenia. Brain activity during processing differed for all three groups. In the control group, there were higher levels of processing in the right inferior frontal gyrus (see Figure 4.1, Chapter 4, this volume) and in the left dorsomedial prefrontal cortex during the processing of the statement containing irony as compared with the first-degree relative group. In the first-degree relative group, there were higher levels of processing during the contextual information before the ironic statement in the left dorsolateral prefrontal cortex as compared with the control group. In the group of individuals with schizophrenia, the patterns of brain activity differed from the control group and first-degree relative groups during the processing of the context and the ironic statement.

Individuals who do not have a diagnosis of schizophrenia but who score high in traits associated with schizophrenia have been shown to comprehend irony differently than others. In an fMRI study, Rapp et al. (2010) scanned individuals with no known history of schizophrenia who completed a questionnaire assessing schizotypal personality. During scanning participants read short discourses, which ended with an ironic or literal statement. During the reading of ironic statements as compared with literal statements, higher levels of schizotypical personality traits was related to decreased blood flow in the left and right middle temporal gyri (see Figure 4.1, Chapter 4, this volume), increased blood flow in the left inferior frontal gyrus, and abnormal processing in the left temporal lobe.

SUMMARY

Research has focused on investigating smiling and laughing in infants and humor production and comprehension in young children. Children's ability to comprehend verbal humor is linked to their theory of mind processing, which emerges between the 2nd and 5th year and continues to develop throughout childhood. The brain continues to develop in volume and connectivity until individuals are in their 20s. fMRI studies have shown that different brain areas respond during humor processing in children than in adults, suggesting that as the brain matures, there are changes in how processing occurs. In cases of atypical development, as in ASD, ACC, and schizophrenia, deficits in theory of mind, perception of emotion, and humor processing have been observed.

7

Individual Differences in Humor

Previous chapters in this volume examined studies that shed light on how the brain is involved in humor processing and how changes in brain development may be related to why children's ability to produce and understand humor changes during childhood. Future research is needed to determine whether those studies provide accurate predictions about how humor is processed by most people. There is a large literature demonstrating that there are individual differences in the use of humor and perceptions of humor. Understanding thoroughly how humor processing occurs in most people can inform future behavioral as well as brain-imaging studies of humor. A fascinating question is to what extent can individual differences in humor ability and humor processing be directly linked to differences in brain responses during humorous experiences. This chapter examines a portion of the large literature focusing on individual differences in adults' use and perception of humor. It begins with a review of the research showing the differences in men's and women's humor behavior (i.e., being humorous as well as responding to humor). Second, it discusses how differences in social status appear to be related to producing and appreciating humor. Next, studies are reviewed that show how individual differences in personality traits are related to humor appreciation. Research comparing the characteristics of professional comedians with the general public, usually college undergraduates, is also discussed. The last section of this chapter examines studies suggesting that genetics plays a role in individual differences in humor behavior.

https://doi.org/10.1037/0000203-008
The Cognitive Neuroscience of Humor, by S. M. Kennison

GENDER DIFFERENCES

A common view is that men are funnier than women (Greer, 2009; Shlesinger, 2017). This view has been famously promoted by powerful men (Getlen, 2012; Hitchens, 2007) and rebutted by professional comediennes and female comedy writers (MacFarlane, 2014). In the scientific literature, numerous studies have shown that men are generally perceived as more humorous than women (see Greengross et al., 2020; R. A. Martin, 2014, for reviews), but women are perceived to be more receptive to humor than men (Chapell et al., 2002; M. Crawford, 1989, 1992, 2003; M. Crawford & Gressley, 1991; K. R. Edwards & Martin, 2010; Hay, 2000; Lampert, 1996; R. A. Martin & Kuiper, 1999; Myers et al., 1997; Provine & Yong, 1991; Robinson & Smith-Lovin, 2001; Thorson & Powell, 1996). In studies of naturalistic interactions, Provine (2000) found that men tend to tell more jokes and women tend to laugh more (see also Provine & Yong, 1991). Greengross et al. (2020) suggested that the gender differences observed in humor production can be explained by sociocultural and evolutionary theories. Studies from the evolutionary perspective are discussed in Chapter 9 of this volume. The social factors that contribute to humor differences in men and women are considered next.

Additional support for the view that men produce more humor than women comes from R. A. Martin and colleagues' (2003) research on humor styles. Their humor styles questionnaire is one of the most popular measures of individual differences in humor usage. The questionnaire assesses four humor styles: two positive (affiliative and self-enhancing) and two negative (aggressive and self-defeating). R. A. Martin et al.'s results showed that men reported using each of the four humor styles more often than women; however, the largest differences were observed for the two negative humor styles, which men used much more often than women. Correlations with participants' self-reported masculinity and femininity were also observed. More masculine individuals used the negative humor styles more often, and more feminine individuals used the negative humor styles less often (see also Abel & Flick, 2012). Research by Wu et al. (2016) showed that gender differences in the use of the four humor styles were mediated by individual differences in other traits, including empathy (aggressive humor style) and perspective taking (affiliative, self-enhancing, and self-defeating humor styles). Higher levels of empathy predicted less frequent use of the aggressive humor style and more frequent use of the affiliative and self-enhancing humor styles.

Research also suggests that men's and women's tastes in humor (i.e., what they find funny) may also differ (Engelthaler & Hills, 2018; A. M. Johnson, 1992; Swani et al., 2013). For example, A. M. Johnson (1992) found that men appreciated aggressive humor more than women, and women appreciated nonsense humor more than men. In a later study, Swani et al. (2013) examined gender differences in the persuasiveness of humor in advertisements. Their results showed that humor coupled with higher levels of violence was more effective in influencing men than women. Recently, Engelthaler and Hills

(2018) explored gender differences in humor in a study in which 4,997 English words were rated for their humorousness. Overall, the results showed that the mean ratings provided by men and women did not differ significantly; however, there were specific words for which men's and women's ratings varied. For example, men rated "orgy" and "buzzard" as more humorous than women, and women rated "giggle" and "burp" as more humorous than men. Chapter 9 of this volume discusses men's and women's different participation in humorous situations that may be related to how individuals consider humor in the evaluation of others as prospective mates.

Laboratory studies have compared men's and women's ability to produce humor, such as generating a funny caption for a cartoon (Greengross & Miller, 2011; Hooper et al., 2016; Mickes et al., 2012). Others are asked to rate the humorousness of the captions. Some of these studies have shown those rating the humorousness fall prey to memory bias, which leads to a tendency to believe that the funniest material was produced by men rather than women (Hooper et al., 2016; Mickes et al., 2012). For example, Hooper et al. (2016) investigated memory bias in humor perception in college students in three English speaking countries (Canada, Australia, and England). Participants rated the humorousness of captions to cartoons without information about the gender of the author of the caption. They were asked to guess the author's gender. When asked, they endorsed the view that men were funnier than women. The results were consistent with the view that raters were vulnerable to the bias of attributing male authorship to the funniest captions and female authorship to the least funny captions. Consequently, in daily life, our perception that men may be funnier than women may stem from our tendencies to misremember humor as being produced by men more often than women.

Other research has shown that individual differences in the ability to produce funny captions for cartoons are related to other variables, including intelligence (Christensen et al., 2018; Greengross et al., 2012b, 2020; Kellner & Benedek, 2017) and creativity (Brodzinsky & Rubien, 1976; Kellner & Benedek, 2017; Kohler & Ruch, 1993; Nusbaum et al., 2017; see also Ziv, 1976, 1983). *The New Yorker* magazine holds a weekly caption contest in which readers can submit entries. After a few attempts, most readers are likely to find that creating a funny caption is a difficult task. Individual differences in social status are related to producing and responding to humor, and social variables and personal characteristics (e.g., sex, gender, intelligence) are also correlated, which leads to difficulty in determining the underlying causal relationships. The effect of practice cannot be overlooked. Those who have spent more time attempting to make others laugh are likely to have learned more ways of being successful at it than others who have not.

DIFFERENCES IN SOCIAL STATUS

Throughout history, humor has appeared to be used by high-status individuals to target individuals of lower status (Beard, 2014; Billig, 2005). The gender differences observed in humor production and appreciation can also be viewed as resulting, at least in part, because of differences in social status between men and women. In many cultures, men have higher status (i.e., financial, political, and social status) than women (Paxton & Hughes, 2017). There are several studies suggesting that the gender difference observed for humor may also be related to the differences in social status between men and women (Cantor, 1976; Evans et al., 2019; Gambacorta & Ketelaar, 2013). For example, Cantor (1976) investigated how men and women perceived humor in cartoons depicting a character directing humor at another character who was either a man or woman. The results showed that men and women rated jokes as more humorous when the joke included a targeted woman versus jokes with a targeted man. In addition, Gambacorta and Ketelaar (2013) investigated the use of humor and other creative behavior (e.g., storytelling) by lower status men in a setting where there was an attractive woman and a higher status man. The results showed that in these circumstances, subordinate men were less likely to use humor and to tell stories.

Additional support for the view that individuals who differ in social status participate in humorous interactions differently has come from studies conducted in workplaces (Evans et al., 2019), undergraduates' social organizations (Oveis et al., 2016), and conversational groups created for research purposes (Bitterly et al., 2017; Robinson & Smith-Lovin, 2001). In an early study, Robinson and Smith-Lovin (2001) recorded interactions among individuals in 29 groups. After they considered the differences in amount of engagement across participants, they found that those who used humor most often were also more likely to have interrupted others, which conveyed higher status than those who were interrupted. The authors suggested that some individuals might have used humor as a strategy to be perceived as high status. The results showed that when groups contained men and women, men produced more attempts at humor than women, and women were more likely to respond to the humor by laughing than men.

Bitterly et al. (2017) reported eight studies on the perception of users of humor. They concluded that how individuals use humor strongly influences how others perceive their status within a group's hierarchy. Those who use humor unsuccessfully (e.g., telling jokes that are viewed as inappropriate) are perceived as low status. Those who use humor successfully are perceived as higher status. This is true for new and established relationships. Furthermore, any use of humor leads to the user being perceived as confident. It is also true that an individual's status can be harmed when one displays high confidence but produces humor that is unsuccessful.

Social status has also been found to be related to how men use humor with one another in college fraternity settings. In two studies of teasing and laughter among men in a college fraternity, Oveis et al. (2016) examined the relationship between individuals' social status and their laughter. In one of the studies, a group of naive raters viewed interactions among fraternity members and evaluated the status of the individuals and the dominance/submissiveness of their laughter. The results showed that those who exhibited dominant laughter were perceived as higher status than those who exhibited submissive laughter, even when the individual was perceived as low status overall. Oveis et al. built on prior research showing that the teasing between high- and low-status members in a fraternity differed with the teasing of low-status members being more affiliative and the teasing of high-status members being more aggressive (Keltner et al., 1998).

Evans et al. (2019) investigated how humor is perceived in the workplace when used by men and women. Their results indicated that humor by women was viewed as less useful and more disruptive than humor by men. Among men, those who were viewed as humorous were also viewed as higher status than nonhumorous men; however, among women, humorous women were viewed as lower status than nonhumorous women. The authors suggested that their results indicate that the ramifications of being funny in the workplace may differ for men and women, with more negative outcomes occurring for women.

The use of humor by high-status individuals to disparage low-status individuals has a long history (see Chapter 1, this volume). Disparagement humor used by men often targets women. Recent research has examined how disparagement humor targeting women is perceived (T. E. Ford et al., 2015; O'Connor et al., 2017; Thomae & Pina, 2015; Thomas & Esses, 2004). Thomae and Pina (2015) studied women's and men's perceptions of sexist humor, concluding that the primary function of disparagement humor is to increase feelings of membership within a group by targeting another group. O'Connor et al. (2017) found that men who scored higher on measures of precarious manhood (e.g., a form of insecurity about one's own masculinity) judged sexist and antigay humor to be more humorous than other men.

The effect of teasing and/or ridicule on individuals has been investigated in several studies (Bryant et al., 1981; Janes & Olson, 2000). Janes and Olson (2000) showed that when participants watched others being the target of ridicule, their own behavior changed. They experienced greater fear of failing, greater inhibition, greater tendency to conform, and reduced tendency for risky behavior (see also Janes & Olson, 2015). Some researchers have shown that a common form of sexual harassment is the use of sexist jokes (Duncan et al., 1990; Fitzgerald et al., 1988; T. E. Ford et al., 2015; Pryor, 1995a, 1995b). T. E. Ford et al. (2015) investigated how sexist humor affects women and men. They showed participants short film clips of sexist humor. The results of two experiments showed that after women experience sexist humor, they have higher levels of body surveillance and self-objectification, but men did not. Mallett et al. (2016) investigated the effects of sexist humor, showing participants short film clips. Like T. E. Ford et al., Mallett et al. found that after women experienced sexist humor, they had higher levels of body surveillance (i.e., feeling concerned about one's appearance) and self-objectification (i.e., viewing oneself as an object), but men did not.

There are gender differences in the production and appreciation of humor. Men tend to produce more humor than women; however, higher status individuals tend to use humor more often than lower status individuals, which may account for the gender difference in humor production because women are generally viewed as lower status than men in society. Women may also find themselves targeted by humor more often than men. Future research is needed to determine whether individuals' comfort level in producing humor is related to their prior experiences being targeted by humor. The next section examines studies that link individual differences in humor with personality traits.

PERSONALITY DIFFERENCES

Numerous studies have investigated the relationships between personality traits and humor appreciation and production. Four categories of personality traits have received attention by researchers: (a) sensation-seeking personality traits, which include individuals' who tend to seek out thrills and adventures, tend to seek out new experiences, enjoy feeling out of control (i.e., disinhibition), and tend to grow bored easily (i.e., boredom susceptibility); (b) Big Five personality traits (i.e., Openness to Experience, Conscientiousness, Agreeableness, Extraversion, and Neuroticism; McCrae & John, 1992; Widiger, 2017); (c) the Dark Triad (i.e., Machiavellianism, narcissism, and psychopathy; Furnham et al., 2013; Muris et al., 2017); and (d) trait cheerfulness, which refers to individual differences in having a consistently positive mood (Ruch & Carrell, 1998; Ruch et al., 2019).

Sensation-Seeking Personality Traits

Zuckerman and colleagues (1978, 1964; Horvath & Zuckerman, 1993; Zuckerman, 1994) examined individual differences in sensation seeking personality traits. The results indicated that individuals describing themselves has having high levels of sensation seeking took risks more often than others, including heavy drinking (Zuckerman, 1987), smoking tobacco (Zuckerman et al., 1990), illegal drug use (Zuckerman, 1983), and having a greater number of sex partners (Zuckerman et al., 1976). Individual differences in disinhibition and experience seeking appear to be related to biology. For example, Zuckerman (1984, 1985) found that in individuals with higher sensation-seeking traits, there were lower levels of monoamine oxidase, an enzyme in the mitochondria of cells. Later work revealed that individuals' levels of sensation-seeking traits were related to neurotransmitter systems in the brain (Gerra et al., 1999; Netter et al., 1996).

Numerous studies have observed relationships between sensation-seeking and humor (Carretero-Dios & Ruch, 2010; Forabosco & Ruch, 1994; Galloway, 2009; Galloway & Chirico, 2008; Gerber & Routh, 1975; Kennison & Messer, 2019; Lourey & McLachlan, 2003; Ruch, 1988). For example, Deckers and Ruch (1992) investigated the relationship between sensation-seeking traits and responses on R. A. Martin and Lefcourt's (1984) Situational Humor Response

Questionnaire. The questionnaire was designed to assess the frequency in which one has outward expressions of amusement (e.g., smiling and laughing). For each of the 18 items describing situations that might evoke positive or negative emotion, participants provided a rating of their likely level of amusement in that situation. They found that those who reported more frequent amusement also reported higher levels of sensation seeking. Specifically, higher levels of boredom susceptibility and higher levels of thrill and adventure seeking.

Lourey and McLachlan (2003) suggested that individuals high in sensation seeking may use humor as a novel source of stimulation (see also Galloway, 2009). The suggestion that there is a link between arousal and humor is consistent with Kennison and Messer's (2019) study of cursing and humor. They explored the relationships among sensation seeking, humor styles, and cursing, a verbal behavior shown to occur more frequently in those higher in sensation seeking (Kennison & Messer, 2019). Kennison and Messer's results showed that men and women higher in sensation seeking and who cursed more frequently also used the aggressive humor style more often. For men, but not women, higher levels of sensation-seeking was related to both using the affiliative humor style more often and cursing more often. The authors concluded that using humor and using curse words is a form of social risk-taking, as there is uncertainty in how others will be affected. There is always a possibility that the listener will be offended. There is also the possibility that cursing in some individuals is a form of self-stimulation, serving to raise the level of arousal.

Some researchers have concluded that sensation-seeking traits can be inherited (Stoel et al., 2006). Stoel et al. (2006) conducted a twin study, which is the traditional approach used by researchers to estimate how genetics and environment contribute to a particular personal characteristic. Other twin studies exploring the extent to which individual differences in humor may be determined from genetics are discussed later in this chapter. Despite the impressive body of research demonstrating the role of genetics in humor, these studies come with the usual limitations associated with twin studies. Genes and environmental factors may be correlated (Plomin et al., 1977), which may occur when families with genetics predisposing them to being humorous live in environments in which humor is promoted. In addition, twins reared apart because of adoption may end up in family environments similar in terms of socioeconomic state and/or culture.

Big Five Personality Traits

Among personality researchers, the Big Five personality traits (Extraversion, Conscientiousness, Agreeableness, Openness to Experience, and Neuroticism) have come to be regarded as the most useful approach to understand individual differences in personality (McCrae & John, 1992; Widiger, 2017). In numerous studies, relationships between the four humor styles and the Big Five have been investigated (Cann & Calhoun, 2001; Galloway, 2010; R. A. Martin et al., 2003; Mendiburo-Seguel et al., 2015; Schermer et al., 2013; Vernon, Martin, Schermer, & Mackie, 2008; see Plessen et al., 2020, for a review). Participants in a study by McCrae and John (1992) associated being less Conscientious and Neurotic but more Extraverted and Agreeable with having a good sense of humor. Nusbaum et al. (2017) investigated the relationship between the Big Five and individual differences in the ability to produce humor. Their results also showed that those with higher levels of Openness to Experience had greater ability to produce humor.

Vernon, Martin, Schermer, and Mackie (2008) investigated the relationship between humor styles and the Big Five personality traits. The results showed that the use of the affiliative humor style occurred more often in individuals higher in Openness to Experience, Extraversion and Agreeableness, and the use of the aggressive humor style occurred more often in individuals higher in Neuroticism, Extraversion, and Openness to Experience and lower in Agreeableness and Conscientiousness. They also found that the use of the self-enhancing humor style occurred less often in individuals higher in Neuroticism and more often in individuals higher in Openness to Experience, Extraversion, Agreeableness, and Conscientiousness. The use of the self-defeating humor style occurred more often in individuals higher in Neuroticism and Openness to Experience and occurred less often in individuals higher in Conscientiousness and Agreeableness. Later, this chapter reviews research from twin studies showing that Big Five personality traits are also heritable.

The Dark Triad

The Dark Triad refers to three malevolent personality types: (a) Machiavellianism, which is associated with the manipulation of others for personal gain; (b) narcissism, which is associated with arrogance, vanity, and exaggerated positive self-regard; and (c) psychopathy, which is associated with lack of empathy and engaging in antisocial behaviors without remorse (see Furnham et al., 2013; Muris et al., 2017, for reviews). Three studies have examined humor in relation to Dark Triad traits (R. A. Martin et al., 2012; Veselka, Schermer, Martin, & Vernon, 2010; E. E. Wood et al., 2019). Veselka, Schermer, Martin, and Vernon (2010) surveyed 114 sets of twins, recruited in North America. They assessed the Dark Triad traits as well as humor styles using R. A. Martin et al.'s (2003) humor styles questionnaire. Their results indicated that those reporting higher levels of narcissism reported using the positive humor styles (affiliative and self-enhancing) more often than the negative humor styles (self-deprecating and aggressive). In contrast, those reporting higher levels of Machiavellianism and psychopathy reported using negative humor style more often than positive humor styles. In a later study by R. A. Martin et al. (2012), these results were replicated with a sample of college undergraduates. In a recent study also involving undergraduate participants, E. E. Wood et al. (2019) observed similar results, also finding that individuals reporting higher levels of Machiavellianism and psychopathy reported using negative humor styles more often than positive humor styles and also engaging in negative verbal behaviors more often (e.g., using curse words, lying, exaggerating) than others. Individuals reporting higher levels of narcissism also reported using positive humor styles more often than negative ones and also reported enjoying talking generally more than others.

Trait Cheerfulness

Ruch and colleagues (Ruch, 1988; Ruch & Carrell, 1998; Ruch et al., 1996) have proposed that individuals vary in terms of cheerfulness and that the cheerfulness trait may be part of an individual's genetic makeup and heritable from parents (see also Leventhal & Safer, 1977). Ruch et al. (1996) developed the State-Trait Cheerfulness Inventory to assess three factors: cheerfulness, bad mood, and seriousness. Studies conducted with the inventory have shown that individuals with high levels of trait cheerfulness smile and laugh more frequently than others when exposed to humor and can be brought to experience amusement more easily than others. Yip and Martin (2006) found that higher levels of trait cheerfulness, as well as greater use of positive humor styles (affiliative and self-enhancing), were related to higher levels of social competence. The State-Trait Cheerfulness Inventory has been translated and tested in numerous countries (see Hofmann et al., 2018; López-Benítez et al., 2017, 2019). There is convincing research showing that there are mental and physical health benefits of humor (see Chapter 8, this volume). Some of these studies have suggested that individuals who are high in trait cheerfulness enjoy better health and longer lifespans than others.

ABILITY: PROFESSIONAL VERSUS NOVICE COMEDIANS

Since the 1970s, researchers have attempted to identify the factors related to humor ability by studying the funniest individuals in society: professional comedians and comedy writers (Janus, 1975; Janus et al., 1978). Janus and colleagues (Janus, 1975; Janus et al., 1978) studied professional comedians (55 men, 14 women) who were interviewed extensively about their family background, experience and childhood aspirations. They were also given intelligence tests. The research painted a bleak portrait, as participants were described as unhappy, angry, depressed, and suspicious. The authors speculated that participants had these characteristics because of their self-reported feelings of isolation early in life. In addition, the researchers found that the comedians were intelligent. In the 1980s, these conclusions were supported in a large study relying primarily on psychoanalytical methods, which many think rely too heavily on subjective interpretation (S. Fisher & Fisher, 1981).

In a more recent study, Schwehm et al. (2015) assessed personality traits and humor styles of professional male and female comedians with those of a control group of undergraduate students. They aimed to determine whether personality traits, humor styles and sex across participants could accurately predict individuals' status as being a comedian versus a noncomedian. The results of a logistic regression showed that 83% of individuals were correctly classified. Although humor styles and personality traits were significant predictors, sex was not. Professional comedians (men and women) scored higher on all four levels of the humor styles questionnaire and had higher scores on Openness to Experience and Extraversion than did undergraduates. Female comedians reported higher levels of Neuroticism than male comedians.

In a series of studies by Greengross and colleagues (Greengross et al., 2012b; Greengross & Miller, 2009) explored the characteristics of those working in the comedy profession. Greengross et al. (2012a) examined the possibility that the early childhood experiences (relationships with parents and peers) of professional comedians differed from a control group of undergraduate students. They concluded that the early life experiences of professional comedians did not differ significantly from those of the control group. Greengross et al. (2012b) examined differences in the humor styles (i.e., affiliative, self-enhancing, self-deprecating, and aggressive) between professional comedians and undergraduates. Professional comedians were asked to provide information about their personal use of humor, rather than humor used for performing. The results showed that professional comedians had higher levels of each of the four humor styles than undergraduates. Greengross and Miller (2009) investigated the Big Five personality traits of professional comedians, writers of comedy who were not performers, and undergraduate students. The results showed that comedy writers and professional comedians reported higher levels of Openness to Experience than did undergraduates, and interestingly, the highest levels were observed for comedy writers. Professional comedians had the lowest levels of Extraversion, Agreeableness, and Conscientiousness. The observation that Openness to Experience is generally high among the funniest people in society is consistent with prior research suggesting that there are links between openness and creativity, which is generally defined as having original ideas or approaches that are useful in solving a problem or achieving an outcome (Conner & Silvia, 2015; Crabtree & Green, 2016) and openness and some aspects of intelligence (DeYoung et al., 2014; Ziegler et al., 2012).

Increasingly, there are health care providers and volunteers who work as hospital clowns. The American Patch Adams has been credited with being the first clown doctor in the 1970s. His story was depicted in the film *Patch Adams* starring Robin Williams (Shadyac, 1999). Over the last 50 years, interest in using humor to supplement standard medical treatment has increased, and programs to train medical personnel to use clowning have been created around the world. A recent study of clown doctors in Italy by Dionigi (2016) compared Big Five personality traits of clown doctors with national norms. They found that clown doctors had higher levels of Openness to Experience, but also higher levels of Extraversion, Conscientiousness, and Agreeableness and lower levels of Neuroticism. Those that worked exclusively as clown doctors had lower Agreeableness than volunteer clown doctors.

Ando et al. (2014) explored the relationship between humor ability and psychotic traits related to some severe mental health disorders (e.g., bipolar disorder, schizophrenia). They compared the levels of traits associated with psychotic personality traits observed in some mental health disorders (e.g., bipolar disorder, schizophrenia) in a group of professional comedians and a group of actors who described themselves as noncomedic. Participants completed the Oxford–Liverpool Inventory of Feelings and Experiences (Mason et al., 2005), which assesses cognitive organization/disorganization (e.g., ability to focus, distractibility), impulsive nonconformity (e.g., poor self-regulation of mood, resulting in antisocial behavior), introvertive anhedonia (e.g., intimacy avoidance, low levels of experiencing pleasure), and unusual experiences (e.g., delusional thinking, strange beliefs, unusual perceptual experiences, including hallucinations). Professional comedians had higher levels of these four traits than noncomedic actors or the general population, on the basis of preexisting norms.

HUMOR AND HEREDITY

Humor is a personal characteristic that may appear to be common among members of the same family. Sometimes, a witty person may comment that they share their particular sense of humor with a parent or grandparent. Since the 1970s, the role of genetics in humor ability has attracted attention from researchers (Atkinson et al., 2015; Baughman et al., 2012; Cherkas et al., 2000; Haase et al., 2015; Manke, 1998; Nias & Wilson, 1977; Rushton et al., 2009; Vernon, Martin, Schermer, Cherkas, & Spector, 2008; Vernon, Martin, Schermer, & Mackie, 2008; Vernon et al., 2009; Veselka, Schermer, Martin, & Vernon, 2010; Weber et al., 2014; Wilson et al., 1977). In an early study, Manke (1998) examined the similarities in the use of humor in relationships in a sample of biological siblings (who share half their genes) or adopted siblings (who share none of their genes) raised within the same family since birth. Shared genes accounted for humor used in their relationships with their mothers, but not in their relationships with friends. Nonshared environment accounted for over 50% of the variance in the humor used with all relationships (i.e., mothers, siblings, and friends), indicating that sharing the same family environment did not lead to siblings having similar use of humor in relationships. The authors concluded that individual differences in humor was influenced by genetics and the environment.

A study by Cherkas et al. (2000) failed to find evidence for the role of genetics in the humor of 56 fraternal and 71 identical female twins between the ages of 20 years and 75 years. Identical twins have greater genetic similarity than fraternal twins. In the study, the researchers assessed their humor appreciation on a scale from 0 to 10 (0 = *not funny*, 10 = *very funny*) for five cartoons from the same cartoonist (i.e., Gary Larsen's *Far Side* series). The results indicated that participants' humorousness ratings for the cartoons were best explained by environmental similarity rather than genetic similarity. The limitations of the study included the relatively narrow range of humor tested in the study.

Subsequent studies have avoided this methodological limitation and have tested larger numbers of twin participants. These studies by Vernon and colleagues (Atkinson et al., 2015; Vernon, Martin, Schermer, Cherkas, & Spector, 2008; Vernon, Martin, Schermer, & Mackie, 2008; Veselka, Schermer, Martin, & Vernon, 2010) have successfully obtained support for a role of genetics in humor. The studies tested over a thousand twins from the United Kingdom and found that all four humor styles were explained by genetic similarity to a greater degree than by shared environment. In a sample conducted with twins from North America, Vernon, Martin, Schermer, and Mackie (2008) found a role for genetics in the positive humor styles (affiliative and self-enhancing) but not for the negative humor styles (aggressive and self-deprecating). In a more recent study by Baughman et al. (2012), a role for genetics was observed for all four humor styles (cf. Vernon, Martin, Schermer, & Mackie, 2008). Atkinson et al. (2015) investigated the relationships among alexithymia and the four humor styles among identical and fraternal twins. They found higher levels of alexithymia were related to higher levels of the positive humor styles (affiliative and self-enhancing) and lower levels of the negative humor styles (self-deprecating and aggressive). The relationships were shown to be related to shared genetic make-up and not environmental influences.

SUMMARY

Across individuals, there are numerous differences in humor-related behavior (e.g., appreciation, production, use). Men are perceived to be funnier than women, and humorous statements tend to be remembered as produced by men, even when they were not. Higher status individuals use humor more often than others. Directing humor at others who are perceived as lower status is a long-standing use of humor. The term disparagement humor is now used to refer to humor that targets and derogates one or more characteristics of others (e.g., gender, sexual orientation, ethnicity, national origin). Research has shown that those higher in sensation-seeking personality traits appreciate humor more than others. Big Five personality traits also predict humor appreciation with higher levels of Extraversion and Agreeableness predicting higher levels of humor appreciation. Dark Triad traits (i.e., Machiavellianism, narcissism, and psychopathy) show different tendencies in humor use with positive humor styles being used more often than negative humor styles by those reporting higher levels of narcissism and the opposite pattern for those reporting higher levels of Machiavellianism and psychopathy. Trait cheerfulness has been found to be related to use of positive humor styles more often than negative humor styles. Studies of professional comedians confirm the findings about the role of Big Five personality traits and intelligence in humor. In addition, professional comedians may score higher on measures of psychotic personality traits. A growing number of studies suggest that genetics play a role in determining humor styles.

8

The Effects of Humor on the Mind and Body

Previous chapters reviewed how humor is influenced by many different factors. In contrast, this chapter examines how humor influences other factors, including an individual's health and well-being. A growing body of research shows that experiencing humor and other forms of positive mood influence the body and the mind for the better. The majority of these studies reflect a subfield within psychology known as positive psychology. This relatively young field of psychology is focused on investigating aspects of normal and extraordinary functioning, which contrasts with the focus on atypical functioning in mainstream psychology (Maslow, 1954; Seligman & Csikszentmihalyi, 2000). Without the growing number of scientific studies on the topic, we might mistakenly conclude that the idea that humor benefits health is too good to be true. This chapter reviews studies showing links between humor and health and discusses studies that detail humor's multiple effects on the body. Last, the chapter takes a look at studies that have attempted to demonstrate that brief humor interventions produce measurable improvements in health.

HUMOR AND HEALTH

Over the last several decades, a consensus has emerged that there are links between humor and health (Allport, 1961; Carroll, 1990; Carroll & Shmidt, 1992; Cousins, 1985; Dillon & Totten, 1989; Dyck & Holtzman, 2013;

https://doi.org/10.1037/0000203-009
The Cognitive Neuroscience of Humor, by S. M. Kennison

P. S. Fry, 1995; J. H. Goldstein, 1982; Pressman & Cohen, 2005; Ruch & Köhler, 1999; Stewart & Thompson, 2015; Walsh, 1928). Nevertheless, the research on the topic has yielded conflicting results. In studies examining the relationship between humor and measures of physical health, some studies have failed to find that higher levels of sense of humor are related to better health (A. Clark et al., 2001; Kerkkänen et al., 2004) or have found significant trends in which humor explained only a small amount of the overall variance in outcome variables (Svebak et al., 2004). L. R. Martin et al. (2002) found evidence that trait cheerfulness was significantly related to longevity. However, in a study in which the biographies of professional comics were examined, Rotton (1992) found no support for the possibility that they lived longer than others.

In the largest study of its kind, Svebak et al. (2004) investigated the relationship between sense of humor and health. They surveyed over 65,000 Norwegians, asking them questions about their sense of humor, health status, health satisfaction, health complaints, body mass index, and blood pressure. Overall, higher health satisfaction was found among those who rated their own sense of humor as high. Those with higher senses of humor had lower blood pressure. In statistical analyses that controlled for age of the respondents, Svebak et al. found that these significant correlations ultimately explained a relatively small amount of the variance in blood pressure and health satisfaction scores. They concluded that the results were fairly weak in supporting a link between sense of humor and health.

More recent studies using similar methods produced stronger evidence for the link between humor and health (Romundstad et al., 2016; Svebak et al., 2006, 2010). Svebak et al. (2006) examined possible health benefits from individual differences in sense of humor among a sample of patients diagnosed with kidney failure who received regular dialysis. The study was carried out over 2 years. After controlling for sex, age, education, and disease severity measures, sense of humor was found to significantly predict quality of life and likelihood of survival from the beginning of the study to the end of the study. In a larger study, Svebak et al. (2010) investigated the relationship between sense of humor and mortality among a sample of adults in Norway. They included measures of sense of humor in a public health survey of over 50,000 respondents. The results showed that the likelihood of living to retirement age increased with self-reported sense of humor even when self-reported health status was controlled. The relationship was similar for men and women. Romundstad et al. (2016) investigated the relationship between humor and mortality in a large population-based study involving 53,556 individuals living in Norway with a follow up after 15 years. Multiple facets of individuals' sense of humor (i.e., affective, social, and cognitive) were assessed. The cognitive facet of sense of humor predicted overall mortality, cardiovascular deaths, and deaths caused by chronic obstructive pulmonary disease (COPD), cancer, and infections.

The benefits of humor on well-being and/or mental health have been demonstrated in a growing number of studies, many of them documenting the positive relationship between humor and measures of well-being (Doosje et al., 2010, 2012; Lockwood & Yoshimura, 2014), life satisfaction (Lockwood & Yoshimura, 2014; Peterson et al., 2007; Ruch et al., 2010), purpose in life (Mak & Sörensen, 2018), zest for life (Celso et al., 2003), and greater morale (Simon, 1990). There is a fairly large literature demonstrating that humor may be useful to those coping with stress (Bizi et al., 1988; Kuiper et al., 1993, 1998; R. A. Martin et al., 1993; Marziali et al., 2008). Other studies have shown that higher levels of humor predict lower levels of depression (C. A. Anderson & Arnoult, 1989; Nezu et al., 1988; Overholser, 1992; Porterfield, 1987; Safranek & Schill, 1982; Thorson & Powell, 1994; Thorson et al., 1997). However, other studies have failed to find benefits of humor among patients with serious physical illness (Merz et al., 2009) and psychiatric disorders (Freiheit et al., 1998).

There have been studies exploring the relationship between the use of positive and negative humor styles and depression in adults (Frewen et al., 2008; Schneider et al., 2018) and adolescents (C. L. Fox et al., 2016). For example, Frewen et al. (2008) found that individuals who reported greater use of the self-defeating humor style and less use of the affiliative and self-enhancing humor styles reported more depression than others. Dyck and Holtzman (2013) showed that there were links between positive humor styles and well-being related to perceived increases in social support. Similar results have been observed by Sirigatti et al. (2016). In a meta-analysis that examined 37 studies in which humor styles were correlated with mental health variables (e.g., depression, life satisfaction, optimism, self-esteem), Schneider et al. (2018) found that the use of the self-defeating humor style predicted lower levels of mental health. However, the strength of the relationship appeared to vary by sex and by geographical region of the United States in which participants were residing.

Research also shows that greater use of positive humor styles (i.e., affiliative and self-enhancing) and less use of negative humor styles (i.e., aggressive and self-defeating) may facilitate social relationships (Yip & Martin, 2006). Supportive social relationships have been shown to be related to better health (Holt-Lunstad & Uchino, 2015). Boyle and Joss-Reid (2004) examined the relationships between humor and health in college students, adults from the community with no health issues, and adults with a health issue. The results indicated that individuals reporting higher levels of humor reported better health.

Tucker, Judah, et al. (2013) investigated whether humor styles would moderate the relationship between anxiety and depression, and found that two of the humor styles (affiliative and self-defeating) confirmed this theory. In a follow up study, Tucker, Wingate, et al. (2013) explored how humor styles were related to factors known to predict suicidal ideation (e.g., perceived burdensome and thwarted belongingness). Interestingly, they found that when participants' level of depression was considered, self-defeating and affiliative humor styles moderated the relationship between these factors and suicidal ideation.

PHYSIOLOGICAL EFFECTS OF HUMOR

Over the last 100 years, researchers have documented how experiencing humor affects our bodies. This section reviews the evidence that experiencing humor leads to increased arousal in the sympathetic nervous system (Ulrich-Lai & Herman, 2009), activating the adrenal glands and processing in the brainstem. Second, the chapter reviews evidence that humor leads to activation of the hypothalamic–pituitary–adrenocortical (HPA) axis, which is involved in our responses to stress. Last, the chapter covers the growing body of research documenting humor's effects on the immune system and the research on humor's effects on pain perception, which appear to be related to increases in the release of endorphins in the brain during humorous experiences.

Activation of the Sympathetic Nervous System

The sympathetic nervous system (e.g., the "fight-or-flight" system; Sapolsky, 1994) is activated during episodes of anger or fear, as well as amusement, which leads to changes in breathing, muscle tone, heart rate, and skin conductance (e.g., increased physiological arousal; Mauss & Robinson, 2010) and changes in the levels of some hormones (e.g., epinephrine, norepinephrine). Among the earliest observations about the effects of humor on bodily function related to the expansion of the lungs and increases in breathing that occurs during laughter (W. F. Fry, 1992, 1994; W. F. Fry & Rader, 1977; W. F. Fry & Stoft, 1971; Lackner et al., 2013, 2014; Lloyd, 1938; Svebak, 1975). Lloyd (1938) pointed out that during laughter, there is an initial strong exhalation that is followed by smaller ones, often accompanied by a sequence of vocalizations (e.g., *ha ha*). Because the exhalations during laughter empty a majority of the air in the lungs, there is increased breathing immediately following the laughter. The increase in breathing is estimated to be over twice the level of normal breathing. The increased exhalation is brought about by muscle contractions in the body's trunk, which do not occur during normal breathing (Ruch & Ekman, 2001). W. F. Fry and Stoft (1971) found that levels of oxygen in the blood were higher following a humor experience. W. F. Fry (1994) compared vigorous laughter with a brief session of aerobic exercise (see also Szabo, 2003; Szabo et al., 2005).

Muscles are also acutely affected during experiences leading to mirth and laughter. In some languages, a common descriptor of people having a good time is that they were "weak with laughter" (Overeem et al., 1999). Research suggests that the expression has a basis in fact. As early as the 1930s, there was evidence supporting the link between mirth and muscle weakness during laughter (Paskind, 1932; Prerost & Ruma, 1987; Wagner et al., 2014). Recent studies have shown that there is reduced muscle tone during mirth and laughing (Overeem et al., 1999, 2004), specifically the Hoffman's reflex, which was produced in participants by nerve stimulation using electromyography. Participants experiencing humor or mirth showed a nearly 90% reduction in muscle response. Overeem et al. (2004) examined whether the muscle effects were due to mirth only or the breathing and movement occurring during the mirth response. Their results confirmed that the cause was mirth alone. Reductions in Hoffman's reflex can also be observed when pressure is applied to a muscle, as in manual massage (Goldberg et al., 1992).

Changes in blood pressure during and following humor have been examined (W. F. Fry & Savin, 1988; Lefcourt et al., 1997; White & Camarena, 1989). W. F. Fry and Savin (1988) observed increases in blood pressure following a bout of laughter accompanied by mirth, which were rapidly followed by reductions in blood pressure that were lower than individuals' baseline blood pressure level. In contrast, White and Camarena (1989) found no evidence for significant changes in blood pressure following a humor experiment. They randomly assigned participants to one of three groups: a relaxation training group, a laughter group, or a control group. Each group met weekly over 6 weeks for 90 minutes. Compared with the control group, the laughter group showed lower levels of self-reported stress but did not differ in physiological measures (i.e., heart rate and blood pressure).

Numerous studies have examined possible changes in heart rate as the result of experiencing humor (Averill, 1969; Fiacconi & Owen, 2015; Foster et al., 2002; Giuliani et al., 2008; Godkewitsch, 1974, 1976; J. H. Goldstein et al., 1975; Herring et al., 2011; Hubert & de Jong-Meyer, 1990, 1991; J. M. Jones & Harris, 1971; Lackner et al., 2013, 2014; Langevin & Day, 1972; Marci et al., 2004). Averill (1969) showed that humor processing was associated with increases in heart rate and skin conductance. The results suggest that humor processing involves an increase in arousal within the sympathetic nervous system. Langevin and Day (1972) demonstrated that the increases in heart rate and skin conductance were greater when participants rated the stimuli as more humorous. Godkewitsch (1974, 1976) measured heart rate and skin conductance as participants comprehended simple jokes with punchlines. He found that during the processing of the setup of the joke and the punchline, skin conductance increased as rated humorousness increased. There was an increase in heart rate related to the humorousness of jokes during the processing of the punchlines.

Giuliani et al. (2008) investigated the effects of brief movie clips involving amusement. Participants were randomly assigned to one of three groups. The first group was asked to watch the clips with no further instruction. The second group was instructed to try to increase the amusement that they experienced by watching the film by using cognitive reappraisal. The third group was instructed to try to decrease their amusement also using cognitive reappraisal. Compared with the no-instructions group, participants' physiological responses to the film clips differed as a function of the instructions that they were given. Physiological responses (i.e., heart rate, respiration, sympathetic nervous system activation) were higher in the condition in which participants were instructed to increase amusement and lower in the condition in which participants were instructed to decrease amusement.

Foster et al. (2002) examined participants' physiological responses while experiencing humor, imagining a humorous scenario, or recalling a humorous scenario. Interestingly, imagined and recalled humor resulted in greater physiological changes (i.e., heart rate and galvanic skin response) than experiencing humor in the moment. In addition, they found that the increased arousal occurs even when an individual does not laugh in response to funny material, rather experiences only the feeling of mirth. The greater the mirth experience, the higher the level of arousal.

More recently, Lackner and colleagues (2013, 2014) examined participants' cardiovascular responses as they watched humorous and emotionally neutral film clips. Lackner et al. (2013) asked participants to press a button as soon as they understood a humorous film's meaning. The results indicated that cardiac changes (i.e., cardiac output and heart rate) occurred approximately 500 ms before participants pressed the button to confirm their comprehension of the humorous clip. The researchers suggested that the changes in heart functioning were temporally linked to the participants' "moment of insight" involved in understanding the humor of each clip (see also Fiacconi & Owen, 2015). Lackner et al. (2014) also had participants watch comedy films and emotionally neutral films while their cardiovascular responses were recorded. They found evidence for increased arousal of the sympathetic nervous system when amusement levels were high. They were able to rule out the possibility that the observed changes were due to changes in breathing during the humor experience. Experiencing humor was not found to lead to changes of the parasympathetic nervous system.

Activation of the Hypothalamic–Pituitary–Adrenocorticol Axis

The processing of humor also activates the human stress responses (e.g., HPA axis; Acevedo-Rodriguez et al., 2018), resulting in the release of the stress hormone cortisol. Following the experience of a stressor, the hypothalamus releases hormones that act on the pituitary gland (see Figure 1.7, Chapter 1, this volume) and the adrenal glands, which are located near the kidneys. The pituitary gland and adrenal glands also produce hormones. The most studied stress-related hormone is cortisol (Heim et al., 2000). Long-term stress leading to elevated levels of cortisol over a long period has been associated with negative health outcomes. There have been cases in which individuals report using humor to cope with extreme circumstances involving long-term stress (C. V. Ford & Spaulding, 1973). The term "black humor" or "gallows humor" refers to humor that arises in adverse situations (Obrdlik, 1942). Some studies have measured the levels of cortisol, which can be measured in saliva and in blood, and found increased levels of cortisol after watching comedy films (Hubert & de Jong-Meyer, 1990, 1991; Hubert et al., 1993; Lai et al., 2010). Hubert and de Jong-Meyer (1990) found that watching 90 minutes of a comedy film resulted in significant increases in salivary cortisol levels in participants, whereas watching a shorter film lasting 9 minutes did not. Hubert et al. (1993)

observed increased cortisol in about half of the participants tested when measurements were taken 1 hour after participants began viewing a comedy film. Interestingly, their results showed that higher levels of humorousness resulted in higher levels of cortisol.

Other research has shown that experiencing humor is associated with lower levels of cortisol (Berk, Tan, Fry, et al., 1989; Lai et al., 2010). Lai et al. (2010) found evidence that higher levels of humor in daily life was related to lower cortisol levels in a sample of older men between the ages of 64 years old and 86 years old. Still another study observed a more complex relationship between positive emotions and cortisol. Human et al. (2015) investigated the relationship between individual differences in positive emotions across days (Study 1) or weeks (Study 2) and cortisol levels. The results of both studies revealed that those reporting the lowest and the highest levels of positive emotions had higher cortisol levels.

Effects on the Immune System

The immune system functions to defend the body from foreign substances (e.g., parasites, viruses, bacteria; Kusnecov & Anisman, 2014). The immune system can be weakened through malnutrition, prolonged exposure to illness, long-term stress, and the normal aging process. In studies investigating the effect of humor and immune system function, researchers have measured salivary secretory-IgA (also called S-IgA), which has been shown to reflect the body's immune system response to minor infections (e.g., colds, flu) and has been shown to increase during short-term stress and decrease in response to long-term stress (Neale & Stone, 1989).

Dillon et al. (1986) compared salivary S-IgA collected from participants who had watched a comedy video or a video with neutral context. They found that levels of S-IgA were significantly higher for those who had viewed comedy. Similar results have been observed in several other studies (Dillon & Totten, 1989; Harrison et al., 2000; Hucklebridge et al., 2000; Lambert & Lambert, 1995; Lefcourt et al., 1990; McClelland & Cheriff, 1997; Perera et al., 1998). Inconsistent findings have been reported in at least three studies (Harrison et al., 2000; Labott et al., 1990; Njus et al., 1996).

R. A. Martin and Dobbin (1989) investigated the effect of humor on immune system function. Participants provided information about their daily hassles and their sense of humor, and a saliva sample from which levels of S-IgA was obtained. The results showed that those who reported more hassles had lower levels of S-IgA in their saliva. For three of the four aspects of sense of humor, there were significant moderations of this relationship with sense of humor functioning as a buffer against the negative effects of hassles on the immune system. In contrast, Hucklebridge et al. (2000) found that S-IgA was increased in individuals following negative moods states as well as positive mood states.

Others have examined blood samples in search of support for the view that experiencing humor has positive effects on the immune system (Bennett et al., 2003; Berk et al., 1984, 1988, 2001; Berk, Tan, Napier, & Eby, 1989; Itami et al., 1994; Kamei et al., 1997; Locke et al., 1984; Mittwoch-Jaffe et al., 1995; Yoshino et al., 1996; cf. Kamei et al., 1997). For example, Berk et al. (2001) had 52 men who reported being in good health watch a comedy film for an hour. Blood was sampled before the film, after the film had been played 30 minutes, and 12 hours after the film ended. Blood was analyzed for numerous immune system markers. Significant increases were observed for many of these markers, including natural killer cell activity, immunoglobulins, and activated T-cells, as well as others. Several markers were significantly higher 12 hours following the film. In a similar study with 33 women, Bennett et al. (2003) found that participants who watched a comedy film were later found to have lower levels of stress and higher levels of natural killer cells than those in the control group. Participants who scored higher on a humor appreciation measure showed the largest reduction in stress and largest increases in natural killer cells.

In multiple studies, Kimata (2001, 2004a, 2004b) showed that experiencing humor reduced allergic responses to an allergen. In the earliest study, Kimata (2001) investigated how individuals with dermatitis responded to skin prick test in which they were exposed to multiple allergens. Exposure to the allergens occurred after participants either watched a humorous film or nonhumorous documentary film. The results showed that allergic reactions were less severe when performed after the humorous film. In follow up studies, Kimata (2004a, 2004b) demonstrated similar reductions in allergic reactions following humor experiences in participants with allergic conjunctivitis and bronchial asthma. The results suggest that experiencing humor reduces the likelihood of an overreaction by the immune system. In other research by Atsumi et al. (2004), blood samples of participants had higher levels of antioxidant-like substances that served to reduce free radicals after they had watched humorous videos as compared with blood samples taken before they had watched the videos.

Increased Pain Tolerance

Numerous studies have shown that humor experiences (including play states) can increase pain tolerance (Cogan et al., 1987; Dunbar et al., 2012; H. L. Fritz et al., 2017; Mitchell et al., 2006; Nevo et al., 1993; Panksepp, 1993, 1998; Weaver & Zillmann, 1994; Weisenberg et al., 1995; Zillmann et al., 1993, 1996; Zweyer et al., 2004). Cogan et al. (1987) measured pain thresholds for participants who listened to audiotapes containing humorous, relaxing, or dull content. Pain thresholds were measured using pressure-induced discomfort in which participants who could tolerate higher levels of pressure on an arm were viewed as having higher pain threshold. The results showed that pain thresholds were higher when participants listened to humorous or relaxing content than when they listened to dull content. A second experiment showed that pain thresholds were higher when participants experienced humor versus doing a short math activity.

A number of studies have induced pain in participants using a cold pressor task, in which participants are asked to keep a hand or arm submerged in ice water (Nevo et al., 1993; Zweyer et al., 2004). Participants who can keep their hand in cold water the longest are viewed as having a higher pain tolerance (MacLachlan et al., 2016; Patanwala et al., 2019). Nevo et al. (1993) investigated to what extent experiencing humor reduced pain in college students. Participants were instructed to hold their hands in cold water while watching either a humorous film or a nonhumorous documentary film. Participants in both groups spent more time in the cold water than participants in a "no film" control group. In the humor group, individual differences in participants' sense of humor and ability to produce humor were related to task performance with higher levels of humor ability related to more pain tolerance. In a later study Zweyer et al. (2004) showed that experiencing humor increased participants' pain tolerance in a laboratory task. Participants (all women) watched a humorous film and carried out the cold pressor task before the film, immediately following the film, and 20 min after the film ended.

In a study of different types of laughter, Dunbar et al. (2012) investigated pain reduction following unforced laughter using two methods for inducing pain: exposing participants to intense cold using a frozen wine cooler sleeve that was −16 degrees Celsius or exposing participants to a maximally inflated cuff used to measure blood pressure. Dunbar et al. claimed that unforced laughter is spontaneously produced in response to a stimulus and is associated with positive emotion. In their study, they examined the pain-reducing effects of unforced laughter in naturalistic and laboratory experiments. Participants either viewed humorous or emotionally neutral videos or stage performance and then carried out a pain tolerance task. The results showed that there was increased pain tolerance in the humorous condition. They concluded that the reduction of pain following laughter stems from the effects of endorphins, which are released during social laughter.

In at least one study, the effect of humor on pain was suggested to be related to endorphin levels in the brain. Manninen et al. (2017) used positron emission tomography to measure the activation of opioid release following laughter. Participants sat alone in a room for 30 minutes after which a baseline scan was obtained. Then, they had participants watch a 30-minute comedy film with others, after which a second scan was obtained. The scan taken after the comedy film revealed that there was release of endogenous opioid in multiple brain areas (i.e., anterior insula, caudate nucleus, and thalamus). The results suggest that humor may be a useful therapeutic intervention for individuals who have health conditions causing debilitating pain. H. L. Fritz et al. (2017) surveyed individuals with fibromyalgia, a condition that can cause widespread body pain. They found that participants reporting higher levels of humor appreciation reported lower levels of pain in daily life. The next section reviews numerous studies investigating the use of humor-based therapies to improve a variety of medical conditions.

It is important to remember that there are other studies that have not shown that humor affects pain (Bruehl et al., 1993; Dixey et al., 2008; Rotton & Shats, 1996). Research with children investigated whether humor could reduce pain during injections (Dixey et al., 2008; B. Goodenough & Ford, 2005). B. Goodenough and Ford (2005) found that children who described themselves as appreciating humor were better able to cope with the unpleasantness of pain. No relationship was found between humor and the intensity of the pain. In a compelling application of these results, Dixey et al. (2008) investigated whether children between the ages of 3 years old and 5 years old who received an injection would experience less discomfort when the injection was preceded by a humorous cartoon sticker (versus no sticker). Unfortunately, the results failed to show a decrease in reported pain in the humorous sticker condition.

THE EFFECTIVENESS OF HUMOR INTERVENTIONS

Given the impressive number of research studies documenting the positive effects of humor on physical and mental health, it is not surprising that some researchers have begun developing and testing the extent to which short-term humor interventions improve mental and physical health outcomes. Calls for this type of research are decades old (McGhee, 1999; Salameh & Fry, 2001). Before discussing the studies that have yielded encouraging results, it should be noted that there are studies in which interventions involving humor have not produced significant outcomes (Adams & McGuire, 1986; Gelkopf et al., 1993; Ko & Youn, 2011; Lapierre et al., 2019; Low et al., 2013; Walter et al., 2007; White & Camarena, 1989).

Among the studies that have demonstrated significant outcomes, the targeted populations include middle-age women (Cha & Hong, 2015), older adults living in care facilities (Boyd & McGuire, 1996; B. Goodenough et al., 2012; Houston et al., 1998; Hsieh et al., 2015; Kuru & Kublay, 2017), older adults living independently (Ghodsbin et al., 2015; Ko & Youn, 2011; Mathieu, 2008; Morse et al., 2018; Prerost, 1993; Proyer et al., 2013; Tse et al., 2010; Yoshikawa et al., 2019), older adults with depression (Konradt et al., 2013), patients with dementia (Brodaty et al., 2014; Kontos et al., 2016; Takeda et al., 2010; Walter et al., 2007), individuals with Parkinson's disease (Bega et al., 2017), adults with schizophrenia (Cai et al., 2014; Rosenheim et al., 1989; Witztum et al., 1999), adults with Type 2 diabetes (Hirosaki et al., 2013), adults with mental illness (Rosenheim & Golan, 1986; Rudnick et al., 2014), women following childbirth (Ryu et al., 2015), patients with cancer (S. H. Kim et al., 2015), individuals with COPD (Lebowitz et al., 2011), hospitalized children (Sánchez et al., 2017), and college undergraduates (Foley et al., 2002; Neuhoff & Schaefer, 2002).

McGhee (1999, 2010) developed a humor regime for the purposes of promoting health in daily life. He referred to it as the Seven Humor Habits

Program, which was later expanded to include eight habits (McGhee, 1999; see Figure 8.1). The effectiveness of training people to use the eight habits for the purposes of well-being has been examined in two studies (S. A. Crawford & Caltabiano, 2011; Falkenberg et al., 2011). Falkenberg et al. (2011) reported a pilot study involving six adults hospitalized with a diagnosis of major depression. There was no control group. At weekly sessions, participants were introduced to one of the habits. Measures of mood and general functioning were administered before and after the introduction of the humor program. Significant improvement was observed in the majority of measures.

In a larger study involving participants recruited from a community, S. A. Crawford and Caltabiano (2011), compared three groups of individuals over a period of 8 weeks. The humor group learned how to use the eight humor habits. A second social group met weekly and engaged in conversation but did not receive any humor training. A third group served as the control group, completing the same measures as the other two groups after 8 weeks and also 3 months following the completion of the study, but did not receive any additional training or contact. A variety of measures were used to assess well-being, emotions, and self-efficacy. The same questions were asked at the end of the program as well as 3 months after participants completed the program. Participants in the humor group experienced decreased stress, anxiety, and depression and increased optimism, positive affect, perceptions of control, and self-efficacy. Outcomes for the social and control groups were similar and did not show the patterns of the humor group.

Recently, the Second City Comedy Troup based in Chicago, which is well known for producing many professional comedians, has developed partnerships with researchers to develop interventions for populations who might benefit in terms of mental and/or physical functioning (Bega et al., 2017; Morse et al., 2018). In a qualitative study, Morse et al. (2018) investigated the effectiveness of a humor intervention associated with Second City for adults over age 55 years. Among the benefits of the program described by participants were increase levels of comfort, positivity, self-awareness, and feelings of acceptance by others in the group. Participants also indicated that following the intervention, they experienced improvements in social functioning and ability to solve problems. In a similar study, Bega et al. (2017) tested 22 individuals

FIGURE 8.1. The Eight Humor Habits

Humor Habit	Expected Level of Difficulty
1. Adopting a playful attitude	Easiest
2. Laughing more often	
3. Laughing more heartily	
4. Cultivating joke-telling skills	
5. Creating verbal humor	
6. Looking for humor in everyday life	
7. Laughing at yourself	
8. Finding humor in the midst of stress	Hardest

Note. Data from McGhee (1999)

with Parkinson's disease who met once a week for 12 weeks with a member of the Second City faculty. The results indicated that participants enjoyed the intervention, all participants completed it, and most participants attended at least 80% of the meetings. Measures of daily functioning in terms of Parkinson's symptoms were taken before and after the program. On average, participants' scores reflected significance improvement.

Wellenzohn and colleagues (2016a, 2016b) tested the effectiveness of a brief online humor intervention. Wellenzohn et al. (2016b) tested the benefits five humor activities: focusing on three funny things; counting funny things from the day; collecting funny things, which involved selecting the funniest experience in their life and writing it down in as much detail as possible; applying humor during the day; and considering how humor could have reduced stress during a prior event. For each activity, there was a placebo control group in which participants were asked to reflect on early childhood memories. The results showed that participants reported lower levels of depression and higher levels of happiness. Three of the interventions led to higher happiness 6 months later. Further, Wellenzohn et al. found that some individuals liked the intervention more than others and that the benefits of the intervention may have been higher for those who liked the program more.

Wellenzohn et al. (2016a) tested the effectiveness of the three funny things humor-based intervention. Participants were randomly assigned to one of three intervention conditions or to a condition that served as a placebo control. For 1 week, participants were instructed to write about three funny things with either a past, present, or future focus. In the control condition, participants wrote about memories from early childhood. Participants completed pretest and posttest measures of depression and happiness. Increased happiness and decreased levels of depression were observed in all three humor conditions.

Using a similar approach, Maiolino and Kuiper (2016) investigated whether participants writing briefly (for 5 minutes) about their own positive experiences after a couple weeks would increase well-being. Participants in another group were asked to write about things that made them feel grateful or examples of positive life experiences that they savored. Participants in a control group wrote about daily life experiences. Participants in all groups reported their well-being in a variety of measures before and after the writing exercise. Writing about humor, experiences leading to gratitude, and savored positive life experiences lead to increased well-being, but writing about daily life experiences did not. Overall, individuals reported using affiliative and self-enhancing humor types more often in daily life had higher levels of well-being. In addition, those who reported using self-defeating and aggressive humor styles more often had lower levels of well-being.

Researchers have begun to demonstrate that humor-related interventions can produce benefits for individuals with a range of health statuses. Relatively few of these studies have used the most rigorous of methods, which involves randomly assigning participants to an intervention or a control condition. Randomized clinical trials of humor-based interventions are rare, as there are multiple obstacles in conducting them, including cost, availability of capable staff, and research volunteers (Djurisic et al., 2017). In one of the few studies using a randomized clinical trial design, S. H. Kim et al. (2015) investigated the effect of a laughter intervention for a group of patients treated for breast cancer. There were four sessions in the intervention, which were completed by 31 participants. Twenty-nine additional participants were included in the control group. Both groups completed assessments of stress, anxiety, and depression at the start of the study and after each session. Participants in the intervention group showed significant reductions in all three measures following the intervention, with significant reductions observed as soon as after the first session. Those in the control group showed no significant change.

Among the most compelling research on the benefits of humor interventions on health are those involving individuals with Type 2 diabetes. (Hayashi et al., 2006; Hirosaki et al., 2013). Hirosaki et al. (2013) found that laughing after eating resulted in lower glucose levels in a group of healthy older adults. Two groups, which assigned randomly, were given an exercise program involving laughter. Hayashi et al. (2006) investigated whether positive emotion expressed through laughter affected changes in individuals' gene expression. They collected blood samples of individuals with Type 2 diabetes. One group had heard a humorous story, and the control group had listened to a nonhumorous lecture. They analyzed the expression of over 18,000 genes from blood leukocytes, which are cells that participate in the human immune response. The results showed that the expression of 23 genes differed in the humor intervention group. Hayashi et al. urged caution in interpreting the results, suggesting that the study merely showed that there may be a link between positive emotion and gene expression.

Among the most impressive studies is the Sydney Multisite Intervention of LaughterBosses and ElderClowns study (Brodaty et al., 2014; B. Goodenough et al., 2012; Low et al., 2013), which was conducted across multiple healthcare settings in Australia. Low et al. (2013) reported results from 418 participants from 35 nursing homes regarding the effectiveness of a humor intervention in reducing depression, quality of life, or social engagement. The results showed that there was a greater reduction in participants' levels of agitation for those receiving the humor intervention as compared with participants who did not receive the humor intervention. Brodaty et al. (2014) analyzed the data for those individuals who received the humor interventions (i.e., 189 participants from 17 nursing homes) as well as responses from staff at the facilities, finding the higher commitment by the staff predicted higher engagement on the part of the participants. Further, when participants' engagement was high, there were lower levels of depression, agitation, and neuropsychiatric symptoms.

Not every study has found benefits to humor-based interventions. In some cases, humor-related interventions may not be ideal, as in cases where it may lead to adverse side effects. At least one study has demonstrated that humor therapy inducing laughter may not be ideal for some patient groups.

For example, Lebowitz et al. (2011) investigated the effects of a humor intervention on a group of patients diagnosed with COPD. They found that when patients laughed, they experienced hyperinflation of their lungs, which severely reduces breathing ability. For other populations, which have been shown to have deficits in comprehending humor, there may be little or no benefits of therapeutic uses of humor, such as with individuals with schizophrenia (Gelkopf et al., 1993; Gelkopf & Sigal, 1995).

SUMMARY

This chapter reviewed the large and growing literature on the topic of the effects of humor on the body and mind. Correlational studies have found some evidence that higher levels of sense of humor are related to better physical and mental health. Large studies from Norway provide some of the strongest evidence for the link between humor and better physical health. Greater use of the positive humor styles (i.e., self-enhancing and affiliative) has been found to be related to lower levels of depression and higher levels of well-being. The health benefits of humor may stem from the effects of humor experiences on the body, including activation of the sympathetic nervous system affecting breathing, heart rate, the release of hormones (e.g., epinephrine, norepinephrine, cortisol), and the production of endorphins in the brain. Studies have also found that experiencing humor leads to increases in immune functioning, as indicated by increases in immune markers in saliva and blood. A growing number of clinicians have tested the feasibility and effectiveness of humor interventions for a variety of target populations. Many of these studies show that humor interventions can produce positive outcomes in healthy individuals and those dealing with illness. One study showed that laughter therapy may produce adverse outcomes for individuals with COPD. The benefit of humor-related interventions in populations that have been found to have deficits in comprehending humor (e.g., individuals with schizophrenia) may be smaller than with other populations.

9

Evolutionary Perspectives on Humor

The previous chapters of this book examined the biological basis of humor in humans and the possibility that experiencing humor may have benefits for health. The role of biology in humor leads directly to the question of how humor evolved in human history and whether it provided a survival advantage. Numerous researchers in the field of evolutionary psychology have suggested ways in which humor may have provided advantages for human survival (Dixon, 1980; Gervais & Wilson, 2005; Greengross & Miller, 2011; Howrigan & MacDonald, 2008; O'Connell, 1960; Provine, 2017; H. E. Schmidt & Williams, 1971; Viana, 2017; Weisfeld, 1993, 2006). These approaches emphasize the biological origins of humor-related behaviors (i.e., laughing, smiling, and playing), which are observed in other species too (Gamble, 2001; Preuschoft & Van-Hooff, 1997). This chapter reviews studies exploring the evolutionary roots of humor in humans, beginning with a discussion of how humor and humor-related behavior (i.e., smiling and laughing) are related to play and play-related behaviors in nonhuman species (Bateson, 2005; Bateson & Martin, 2013; Fagen, 1981). The second section reviews the possible ways in which humor may have provided a survival advantage during the evolution of humans. The final section looks at how the regions of the brain involved in producing and comprehending humor may have evolved in humans.

https://doi.org/10.1037/0000203-010
The Cognitive Neuroscience of Humor, by S. M. Kennison

SMILING, LAUGHING, AND PLAYING ACROSS SPECIES

Smiling and laughing occur in all human cultures and reflect the experience of positive emotion (Apte, 1985; Lefcourt, 2001). In the 19th century, Darwin (1872/2007) commented about the likely universality of emotion in humans. In the 1970s, Ekman and Friesen (1971, 1978) documented the universality of emotions in facial expressions in a study in which individuals from different cultures were asked to identify emotions in photographs of faces. These emotions included anger, fear, disgust, sadness, happiness, and surprise. The authentic or natural human smile involves not only the broad, open mouth revealing the teeth but also the contraction of muscles around the eyes (Ekman et al., 1990). The natural smile is commonly referred to as the "Duchenne smile" after the French neurologist Guillaume Duchenne de Boulogne, who described it in the 1800s (Duchenne de Boulogne, 1990). Natural smiles can be easily distinguished from nonnatural smiles (Gunnery & Ruben, 2016). Three types of smiles with distinct functions have been identified: maintaining or welcoming social interaction, rewarding desirable behavior on the part of others, and communicating dominance in a group with a hierarchical dominance structure (see J. Martin et al., 2017, for a review).

The human smile has been compared with facial displays in chimpanzees, including the silent bared teeth display and the relaxed open mouth display. On the basis of behavior, Waller and Dunbar (2005) concluded that chimpanzees communicate affinity with silent displays of bared teeth. In contrast, when chimpanzees are engaged in play, they used the relaxed open mouth display. Similar results have been observed in subsequent studies of chimpanzees (Cordoni & Palagi, 2011; Waller et al., 2007; Waller & Dunbar, 2005), lemurs (Palagi et al., 2014), captive capuchin monkeys (Visalberghi et al., 2006), macaques (Pellis et al., 2011), bonobos (Palagi, 2008), and wild gorillas (Palagi et al., 2007; Waller & Cherry, 2012). In observations of captive capuchin monkeys, Visalberghi et al. (2006) noted that facial expressions resembling smiling (i.e., relaxed open mouth and silent bared teeth) were used during courtship among adults and also to signal submissiveness among juveniles. Waller and Dunbar concluded that in chimpanzees the silent bare teeth and the relaxed open mouth displays are used in different contexts. The latter is used during play, and the former is often followed by positive affiliative behaviors. A. M. Samson and Waller (2010) concluded that the bare teeth display signals to others unambiguously that the individual's intent is not aggressive.

During play, laughter is sometimes the result of tickling. Among the earliest insights into human responses during tickling was Darwin (1872/2007), who observed that "[it] seems primarily to be the expression of mere joy or happiness" (p. 196). He also noted that individuals cannot tickle themselves; that some parts of the body are more likely to be tickled than others; and that in terms of social norms, tickling is only appropriate within close relationships. The topic of tickling continues to interest researchers (Blakemore et al., 1998; Provine, 2004). Provine (2004) discussed the fact that tickling in humans provides as example of social play observed across mammals. During tickling, an individual experiences an increase in positive emotion and mirth. On the other hand, Provine noted that tickling was also used as a form of torture during the Middle Ages. Blakemore et al. (1998) explained that some individuals can experience mirth from tickling themselves because of neural processing that occurs during self-produced movements. Movements that are produced in the body set in motion brain responses that set up expectations of sensory experiences resulting from the movements. The researchers found that individuals with schizophrenia could, in fact, tickle themselves and experience the mirthful result because of a disruption in the neural pathways involved in triggering sensory expectations during self-produced movements.

Since the 1980s, researchers have recognized that nonhuman species engage in play (Adang, 1984, 1986; Bateson, 2005; Bateson & Martin, 2013; Burghardt, 2005; Butovskaya & Kozintsev, 1996; Fagen, 1981; Gamble, 2001; Gomez & Martin-Andrade, 2005; Matsusaka, 2004; McGhee, 2018; Panksepp, 2000; Panksepp & Burgdorf, 2000, 2003; Smith, 1982; Smith & Pelligrini, 2005). Adang (1984, 1986) reported teasing-like behavior in young chimpanzees and suggested that the behaviors facilitate social learning, particularly of the acceptability of some behaviors over others. Butovskaya and Kozintsev (1996) reported instances of mock aggression occurring between chimpanzees, which were carried out with facial expressions similar to the human smile.

Researchers have noted similarities between human laughter and vocalizations in other primates (for reviews, see Burling et al., 1993; Caron, 2002; Davila-Ross et al., 2009, 2011; Devereux & Ginsburg, 2001; Todt & Vettin, 2005; see also Polimeni & Reiss, 2006; Provine, 2016; Simonet, 2004). Todt and Vettin (2005) examined the acoustic characteristics of vocalizations made during tickling. Samples from humans, chimpanzees and macaques were compared. The acoustic characteristics of human laughter during tickling are similar to the vocalizations produced by chimpanzees and macaques. Davila-Ross et al. (2009) carried out a similar study comparing the vocalizations produced during tickling in human infants and juvenile and infant bonobos, chimpanzees, gorillas, and orangutans. They found similarities in these vocalizations across species. Davila-Ross et al. (2011) examined the naturally occurring laughter among chimpanzees and identified spontaneous laughter and a laughter that was elicited by another's laughter. The latter type of laughter appeared to function to maintain play with a partner. The authors concluded that laughter in humans has its origins in a vocal signal of play.

In a series of studies with rats, Panksepp and colleagues (Knutson et al., 1998; Panksepp, 2000, 2005, 2007; Panksepp & Burgdorf, 2000, 2003; Popik et al., 2012; Siviy & Panksepp, 2011) demonstrated that rats produce vocalizations that are analogous to human laughter. The vocalizations occur when they are tickled by humans and also when they are engaging in play with other rats. The frequency of the sounds cannot be detected by the unaided human ear but can be perceived by rats and other animals. Kisko et al. (2015) carried out a series of studies from which they concluded that adult rats emit a 50 kHz vocalization during play in which there is the possibility that play will evolve into aggression.

The well-known neurologist Ramachandran (1998) presented a compelling speculation about the origins of laughter, suggesting that it functioned as a false alarm call. Many animal species have vocalizations that serve as alarm calls to indicate the presence of a nearby predator. For example, prairie dogs have alarm calls for hawks, for coyotes, for domesticated dogs, and for humans (Slobodchikoff et al., 2009). Ramachandran's speculation is that the laugh originated as a vocalization produced when an individual perceived a threat, but subsequently determined that there was no threat (e.g., perceiving a movement in the brush thought to be a predator but found to be kin).

An alternative possibility is that laughter is a vocalization linked with the emotion of surprise, which occurs when expectations are violated. Surprise was one of the basic emotions that was found to be universally recognized across cultures (Ekman & Friesen, 1971, 1978). Some researchers who have examined the neurological nature of surprise suggesting that surprise is an inherently negative emotional state (Noordewier & Breugelmans, 2013). Others have argued that surprise is emotionally neutral (Russell, 2003), and still others have suggested that it is emotionally positive (Fontaine et al., 2007). Recent approaches to the study of emotions rejects the view that they are innate and invariant across situations (Barrett, 2017). This approach provides a way of characterizing humor as a surprise experience that is particularly positive. Support for this view has been observed in studies in which participants were asked to compare the weight of objects in a weight comparison task (Deckers, 1993; Deckers et al., 1977; Gerber & Routh, 1975; Nerhardt, 1970, 1976). In such studies, participants were told that they were participating in a study about physiological processes related to weight comparisons. They were shown weights, which were similar in appearance. The initial comparisons involved objects that were similar in weight. A subsequent comparison involved an object that was very different in weight from the standard. The results showed that participants produced more smiling and laughter when there was a greater incongruity between a standard weight and a test weight (Deckers, 1993; Deckers et al., 1977).

EVOLUTIONARY ADVANTAGES OF HUMOR

Researchers have identified multiple ways in which humor may have increased survival of individuals. There have been numerous suggestions for the ways in which humor may have supported survival. This section reviews some of these possibilities. Play across species appears to function to diffuse conflict (Bateson, 2005; Bateson & Martin, 2013), which can lead to avoiding injury and/or death. Humor also acts to form and strengthen social bonding, which can lead to avoiding early death by having the physical support of others (Curry & Dunbar, 2013). Finally, humor serves as a signal of good genes during mate selection, which can lead to the trait humor becoming more common with each generation (Bressler & Balshine, 2006; Bressler et al., 2006; Greengross, 2014; S. B. Kaufman et al., 2008; Lippa, 2007; G. F. Miller, 1997, 2000).

Diffusing Conflict

The link between humor and aggression has been discussed by many researchers (Epstein & Smith, 1956; Gruner, 1978; Gutman & Priest, 1969; McCauley et al., 1983; McGhee, 1979; Palmer, 1993; Shuster, 2012; Singer et al., 1967; Sinnott & Ross, 1976; Weinstein et al., 2011). In the 1970s, Gruner (1978) proposed that laughter began as a form of vocal triumph in situations following conflict. In humans, as well as in other species, males are typically involved in responding when there is conflict between groups (Geary, 2005). Males tend to engage in conflict with other males when protecting territory and resources and also in competing for access to mates. In contrast, females tend to care for offspring and forge social bonds with others, who may be helpful in securing resources and caring for offspring (Taylor et al., 2000; see also Geary & Flinn, 2002).

There is ample evidence that aggressive humor is used more often by men than women (Greengross & Miller, 2008), and men use the negative humor styles (aggressive and self-deprecating) more often (R. A. Martin et al., 2003). Greengross and Miller (2008) examined sex and personality differences in the use of other-deprecating and self-deprecating humor and found that men use other-deprecating humor more than women and its use decreases with age. Palmer (1993) observed interactions among hockey players, who frequently engaged in intense physical competition and in aggressive humor. Players smiled and laughed more during aggressive competition with friends than nonfriends. Shuster (2012) analyzed the responses of people when they viewed a unicyclist. They found that men, but not women, produced aggressive humor.

Humorous individuals, particularly men, are viewed as higher status than others (Oveis et al., 2016; see also Chapter 6, this volume). Other research shows that as men evaluate other men as potential friends, they attend to the presence of humor as well as low pitch of the voice, signaling dominance (Cowan et al., 2016). In a study of adolescents, Bowker and Etkin (2014) found that those who used more relational aggression, including teasing, were the most popular. Norrick and Spitz (2008) suggested that humor functions to diffuse conflict among groups. Support for this view was found in two studies by Nir and Halperin (2018). In the first study, they asked Palestinian Israelis to review a message described as being written by an "Israeli representative" that provided a description of the Palestinian–Israeli conflict. The message either did or did not contain three instances of humor targeting Jewish Israelis. In the condition in which the message contained humor, participants were later more likely to express a willingness to take steps to resolve the conflict. In a second study, participants were Jewish Israelis who were tested with similar conditions. In the message with humor, there were three stories targeting Palestinian Israelis. The results again showed that when participants read the humorous message, they were later more likely to take steps to resolve the conflict.

Gray (2009, 2013, 2014) described that among modern hunter–gatherers, play is an important cultural activity. Hunter–gather groups are known to be nonautocratic and egalitarian, with movement of individuals between bands that are known to each other. Cooperation between individuals and bands is important for survival. He observed that playfulness and humor are used frequently, particularly to diffuse tension arising when there is conflict, but also during religious ceremonies, hunting, gathering, and other daily activities.

Forming and Strengthening Social Bonds

In human history, humor may have served to facilitate social bonding among group members and to distance those who were considered in an outgroup (Alexander, 1986). Humor can be used positively to facilitate social relations and strengthen social bonds (Cowan & Little, 2013; Curry & Dunbar, 2013; Kashdan et al., 2014; Storey, 2003; Treger et al., 2013), which may increase cooperation (Jung, 2003). Kashdan et al. (2014) investigated whether sharing laughter with someone else affected future interactions. They carried out a diary study over a period of 2 weeks in which participants made daily entries. The results showed that laughing with someone else predicted their future level of enjoyment when interacting with that person.

Curran et al. (2018) investigated how humor and laughter facilitates bonding and cohesion within a group. Two views were compared: laughter that serves to convey information about the speakers' intentional and/or emotional state and laughter that serves to influence others in the context where other influencing factors may be present. The latter approach suggests that laughter itself is inherently ambiguous and its meaning dependent on the context. In an experiment in which participants listened to recordings of social interactions containing laughter, Curran et al. found support for this view. Other research found that when individuals hear a joke that they believe is being told by someone within their group rather than a member of an outgroup, they experience more amusement and more smiling (Morisseau et al., 2017).

Treger et al. (2013) showed that the use of humor was associated with liking for men and women across all types of relationships. Cowan and Little (2013) found that for long-term relationships, affiliative humor style was rated as more attractive in a relationship than aggressive humor style. Affiliative humor style was perceived as related to behaviors associated with positive relationship interactions (e.g., cooperation). Curry and Dunbar (2013) found that when individuals provided information about their relationships, sharing a sense of humor was a significant predictor of their emotional closeness and also their likelihood of acting altruistically toward the friend. The notion that humor serves to reduce conflict and foster closeness in romantic relationships has been supported in several studies (Butzer & Kuiper, 2008; Campbell et al., 2008; de Koning & Weiss, 2002).

Research on the acoustical properties of laughter has also shown that the way humans laugh with friends differs from the way we laugh with strangers. Smoski and Bachorowski (2003) recorded laughter produced during interactions with friends and strangers. The acoustic properties of laughter differed for the two situations. More antiphonal laughter was produced when people laughed with friends than with strangers. Consequently, one may use information about the acoustical properties of the laughter shared by others to judge how well individuals know one another (see also McGettigan et al., 2015; Scott et al., 2014; A. Wood et al., 2017).

Selecting a Mate

There is a consensus among evolutionary psychologists that human males, as well as males from other species, engage in behaviors designed to attract female mates (Buss, 2003; Buss & Schmitt, 1993). Females typically prefer mates with greater physical strength, greater intelligence, and greater access to resources. Females select mates who possess characteristics signaling good genes, which would likely lead to greater overall mating success (e.g., producing healthy offspring). Attracting mates is a high stakes enterprise; as many as 40% of men fail to contribute genes to the next generation (Dunbar, 1996). Because the cost of creating viable offspring differs for males and females, females tend to invest more than males physical and emotional resources in their offspring. Both sexes prefer mates with good genes (e.g., physical attractiveness), which has been related to greater symmetry of features and fewer biological abnormalities in development (Feingold, 1992). In addition, females may also prefer mates who invest in ways that maintain long-term relationships, which are likely to facilitate investment in offspring (Buss, 2016).

In romantic relationships, women prefer men who are funny (Bressler & Balshine, 2006; Bressler et al., 2006; Daniel et al., 1985; DiDonato et al., 2013; Goodwin, 1990; Guéguen, 2010; Hone et al., 2015; Lippa, 2007; Wilbur & Campbell, 2011; see also Chapter 6, this volume). For example, Bressler et al. (2006) investigated sex differences in the role of humor in romantic relationships and found that women preferred men who were humorous, and men preferred women who found them humorous. Hone et al. (2015) replicated these results using an improved methodology. When considering long-term relationships, men rated a mate's receptivity to their humor as necessary, but a mate's production of humor as unnecessary (i.e., a luxury). Women showed the opposite pattern, rating a mate's production of humor as a necessity and a mate's receptivity of humor as a luxury.

A growing number of researchers suggest that humor may serve as a fitness indicator in males (Greengross et al., 2012a; G. F. Miller, 1997, 2000). Research supports the claim that those who are the funniest are likely to be the most intelligent (Christensen et al., 2018; Greengross et al., 2012a; S. B. Kaufman et al., 2008). Greengross et al. (2012a) tested the hypothesis that individuals who are more humorous are also higher in intelligence and mating success (as assessed by a sexual behavior questionnaire). They assessed intelligence, mating success, and humor production in 400 college students. The results showed that higher intelligence predicted greater humor production, which was positively correlated with mating success.

Of the few studies that have been conducted examining the relationship between intelligence and humor, a consensus has emerged—those who are the most humorous appear to be higher in intelligence than others (Christensen et al., 2018; Feingold & Mazzella, 1991; Howrigan & MacDonald, 2008; Janus, 1975; Janus et al., 1978; Kellner & Benedek, 2017; Weisfeld et al., 2011). Howrigan and MacDonald (2008) examined the relationship between the Big Five personality traits, intelligence, and ability to produce humor in a laboratory study. Participants' attempts at humor were evaluated for their humorousness by a group of raters. The results indicated that for men and women, the most intelligent and the most extraverted participants were the most humorous. Among the more recent studies, Christensen et al. (2018) assessed three aspects of intelligence (i.e., vocabulary knowledge, fluid reasoning, and retrieval ability) and asked participants to generate humor in a series of tasks. The humorousness of those productions were judged by others. The results showed that those judged to be the most humorous had higher vocabulary knowledge and faster retrieval ability, but not higher levels of fluid reasoning. Kellner and Benedek (2017) investigated the relationship between IQ and individual differences in the ability to produce humor. They had participants view six cartoons and asked them to produce a funny caption for each. The captions were rated for humorousness by others. The results showed that the most humorous captions were produced by the most intelligent, who also showed higher levels of creativity and divergent thinking.

Hendrie and Brewer (2012) suggested that the appearance of teeth, which occurs during social interactions, may serve as an indicator of fitness (good genes). When men interact with women producing humor, smiling and laughing likely occur a great deal, allowing the teeth to be seen. As one ages, however, the teeth become more discolored. In their study, Hendrie and Brewer presented digitally manipulated images of teeth to participants who rated attractiveness. The spacing and color of the teeth were varied. The results showed lower attractiveness ratings by men and women when teeth had extra spacing and/or discoloration in photographs of men and women. Larger declines in attractiveness were observed for photographs of women. The pattern was not influenced by the sex of the rater.

There are links between humor and physical and mental health. There is a growing literature documenting this, which includes a link between individual differences in intelligence and mortality (Gottfredson & Deary, 2004) and humor and mortality (L. R. Martin et al., 2002). For example, L. R. Martin et al. (2002) found that individuals who describe themselves as higher in trait cheerfulness appear to have longer lifespans than others. When considering data of this type, it is important to consider the possibility that women find humor a useful criterion when they select mates because they are, albeit unconsciously, preferring mates who may provide their future offspring the best possible chance for survival.

EVOLUTIONARY CHANGES IN HUMOR-RELATED BRAIN REGIONS

Multiple regions of the brain appear to be involved in humor processing (e.g., parietal, temporal, and frontal lobes; areas involved in reward processing like the striatum in the basal ganglia and amygdala). Most of the regions are located in the neocortex, which is often referred to as the mammalian brain and the region of the brain that has evolved most recently (Kaas, 2013; Loonen & Ivanova, 2018; MacLean, 1990; see also Cory, 2002). MacLean (1990) proposed a model of brain evolution for vertebrates, distinguishing the evolutionarily oldest brain systems (i.e., brain stem and cerebellum) from the more recently evolved limbic system (i.e., the hippocampus, hypothalamus, and amygdala) and the neocortex. Some researchers have described MacLean's view as a fantasy or a myth (Barrett & Satpute, 2017; Striedter, 2006; Sutton, 2017). For our purposes, it is a useful way to discuss the most recently evolved brain regions (i.e., the neocortex) from the areas of the brain shared by other species.

The neocortex of nonhuman primates varies in size compared with the neocortex of humans (Kaas, 2013). Dunbar (Dunbar, 1993, 1998, 2017; Dunbar & Shultz, 2007) argued that the demanding social lives of primates led to increases in neocortex size. The view has been referred to as the *social brain hypothesis* (Dunbar, 1998). Dunbar showed that the average group size across primates, including humans, predicted neocortex size with those having the largest groups also having the largest neocortex sizes. Living in large groups successfully required more individual interactions to be peacefully maintained. Dunbar (1992) estimated the average group size for humans to be between 150 and 250 individuals. He derived his estimate from analyses of historical data and estimates from prehistory, including information about the sizes of towns and villages in England. In later research, the estimate has been supported in studies quantifying individuals' Christmas card lists (Hill & Dunbar, 2003) and social networks (MacCarron et al., 2016). Other research showed that brain size differences in mammals and birds also relates to social differences with pair-bonding in mating occurring among those with the largest neocortices (Dunbar, 1992).

Other researchers have suggested that factors related to the environment in which animals lived and what the animals ate, rather than social factors, led to increases in brain size. Research has shown that the diets of nonhuman primates vary in terms of fruit and nonfruit vegetation (Milton, 2003). Fruits are considered a higher quality food source compared with other lower energy vegetation sources, such as leaves and vines. Others have pointed out the percentage of fruits in the diet of nonhuman primates appears to be correlated with brain volume with more fruit eating predicting bigger brains

(Kolb et al., 2019). Kolb et al. (2019) pointed out that foraging for fruits skillfully requires sophisticated visual and spatial ability. Strategies for fruit hunting could be a skill taught to juveniles by experienced adults.

Nonhuman primates spend up to 50% of their day foraging for food (Milton, 2003). In human history, the innovation of cooking has been viewed as having a profound development, as it made foods, particularly meats, easier to digest (Carmody et al., 2011; Carmody & Wrangham, 2009; Fonseca-Azevedo & Herculano-Houzel, 2012; Wrangham, 2009). Humans' cooking of food and later slicing of food with stone tools reduced the time needed to chew (Zink & Lieberman, 2016), which likely led to less time required for food gathering and food preparation and possibly more leisure time that could have involved socializing with others. In a recent study, González-Forero and Gardner (2018) used mathematical modeling to find the best set of predictors of body size and brain size among primates. Their results suggested that the ecological factors accounted for most of the variable (e.g., 60%) with social factors explaining about 40% (i.e., 30% of within-group cooperation and 10% of between-group competition). The authors acknowledged that social factors may have played a role in aiding the maintenance of food-related behaviors in the group (e.g., adults assisting juveniles in learning critical skills).

One of the abilities that likely became increasingly important as humans lived in larger groups and also critically important in comprehending humor is theory of mind. Without theory of mind, individuals living in large groups may misunderstand one another more often, which may lead to conflict and possibly death if the conflict is not diffused. For nonhuman primates, the evidence for theory of mind is sparse with some studies showing evidence for only basic perspective taking (Kennison, 2019). The lack of robust theory of mind ability in nonhuman primates may stem, at least in part, from lower levels of connectivity in the brain as compared with the brains of humans. Ardesch et al. (2019) compared the white matter connections in brains of humans and chimpanzees, finding that human brains had many more connections between multimodal association areas, which receive input from all of the senses, and the lateral parietal, temporal, and inferior frontal lobes. Human brains have more connections between left hemisphere language regions and the temporal lobe, the inferior frontal gyrus, and the supramarginal/angular gyrus. Lastly, human brains have fewer interhemispheric connections and more intrahemispheric connections than chimpanzee brains, as well as larger corpus callosa (i.e., the bundle of fibers connecting the hemispheres).

Kumar et al. (2016) compared the connectivity in the brains of humans and rhesus monkeys, focusing specifically on the laryngeal motor cortex, which controls speech in humans. They found that in many respects, the regions were similar in humans and rhesus monkeys; however, differences in the connections between the area and other brain regions were observed. In human brains, there were as many as seven times the number of connections in human brains than in the brains of rhesus monkeys between the laryngeal motor cortex and the inferior parietal lobes and the laryngeal motor cortex and the somatosensory areas. In humans, the laryngeal motor cortex is not responsible for the production of all vocalizations; laughter and other emotional vocalizations are produced via the emotional motor system, which includes the mesencephalic periaqueductal gray (Holstege & Subramanian, 2016). Nonhuman species also produce emotional vocalizations via this emotional motor system. In humans, there are connections between the mesencephalic periaqueductal gray and areas that have been identified in humor processing (i.e., the orbitofrontal cortices, insula, and the anterior cingulate). This research is consistent with Provine's (2017) observation that laughter during conversations occurs at the ends of utterances, rather than within them. Much remains unknown about why the human brain differs so much from the brains of other primates. The brain differences are likely to account for differences in complex cognitive and social behavior that is observed. I believe that humor may be the most complex behavior of them all.

SUMMARY

Humor behavior in humans, like play behaviors in other species, are very likely to have been determined through natural selection. Behaviors similar to smiling and laughing are observed across species. In humans, humor may have played multiple roles aiding the survival of the species. These include diffusing conflict, creating and maintaining social groups, and playing a role in the selection of mates with humor possibly signaling good genes. Support for this view shows that humor ability is related to intelligence. The regions of the human brain that have been shown to be involved in humor processing are found in the most recently evolved regions of the brain (i.e., the limbic system and the neocortex). Comparisons of human and nonhuman primate brains show that the human brain contains many more connections between the brain areas involved in language, theory of mind, and laughter.

10

Future Directions

This journey through the literature on the cognitive neuroscience of humor shows that, despite how much has been learned on the topic, there is still much more to know. This final chapter focuses on three areas of possible future research. The possibility is considered that the understanding of the neural processes involved in humor might, one day, be so complete as to enable researchers to recognize a neural signature of a humorous experience from a functional magnetic resonance imagining (fMRI) scan. How such an algorithm can be used in the area of health care is also discussed. Next, the chapter reviews known cross-cultural differences in humor and suggests that future research on this topic may reveal how different types of people can benefit from humor. The last section considers potential ways in which research identifying a neural signature of humor could be used to address practical problems in the area of education and training.

A NEURAL SIGNATURE OF HUMOR

The research presented in Chapters 3, 4, and 5 of this volume identified numerous brain regions involved in humor-related behavior (i.e., smiling, laughing, and mirthful feelings). Optimists could predict that in the not-so-distant future, researchers will have developed algorithms to analyze electroencephalography/event-related brain potential data and/or fMRI data with the capability of distinguishing humorous experiences from nonhumorous

https://doi.org/10.1037/0000203-011
The Cognitive Neuroscience of Humor, by S. M. Kennison

ones. A brain-based mirth-detecting algorithm would work to identify a neural signature that occurs during humorous processing but does not occur during nonhumorous processing. The neural signature of mirth (should it be found) would not likely be a simple pattern of activity in one brain region; rather, it would be a complex pattern of activity across numerous brain regions. Dai et al.'s (2017) three-stage model of processing incongruity–resolution humor included no fewer than nine brain regions. Multiple versions of the algorithm would likely be needed for different types of humor (e.g., incongruity–resolution humor, absurd humor). Although Dai et al. identified two brain regions that were involved in the processing of incongruity–resolution humor and absurd humor, they noted four brain regions that were involved in the processing of absurd humor that were not involved in the processing of incongruity–resolution humor. When considering the possible duration of a neural signature of humor, most fMRI studies can be considered, in which participants were scanned as they read punchlines for between 3 and 12 seconds. Electroencephalography/event-related brain potential studies can also be considered, in which the three stages of processing reflected in N400s, P600s, and late positive complexes were observed within 3 seconds of participants processing punchlines. A brain-based mirth-detecting algorithm could sample data for 5 seconds while a participant processes a punchline, and then rapidly generate a probability that the participant had experienced humor.

Considering the numerous brain regions identified in humor processing studies, identifying a single neural signature of humor may be difficult. The three-stage model of humor processing has been linked with processing in specific brain regions (see Chapter 4, this volume), but not all of fMRI studies of humor processing observed processing in the same regions. Across the studies that identified the same regions, there was variation in which part of the region was involved in processing (i.e., anterior vs. posterior, left vs. right). Some of the same areas produced smiling, laughter, and/or mirth when stimulated with electricity (see Chapter 5). It is also unclear to what extent the regions involved in the processing are directly related to the type of humor stimuli (e.g., jokes, nonverbal cartoons, verbal cartoons). Future research is needed to determine how the responses in brain regions involved in experiencing mirth from a humor experience differ from other experiences producing high levels of positive emotion, like thinking of something that makes the participant very happy (e.g., viewing pictures of loved ones, viewing pictures of cute animals, thinking of happy memories). It would be critical to develop an algorithm that detected signature brain responses to humor and not merely brain responses to positive emotional experiences.

If a mirth-detecting algorithm could be developed, it may first be used in the field of entertainment. Comedians could use it with their friends and family to test the quality of their jokes when making selections for a future performance. A kind friend might claim they liked a joke, when they did not. A mirth-detecting algorithm could detect a lack of candor in these situations and may be able to detect large mirth responses from smaller mirth responses.

Entertainment companies could use the algorithm with focus groups brought together to view the latest comedy movie. Audience members would not have to describe their thoughts about the funny parts of the film; rather, their recorded brain responses would reveal it all. Ultimately, the cost to use the algorithm will determine whether it comes to replace the contemporary self-report techniques that are used to survey audiences. However, a brain-based mirth-detecting algorithm also could be used in other areas of research, including health care, cross-cultural differences in humor attitudes and appreciation, and education and training.

FUTURE DIRECTIONS IN HEALTH RESEARCH

A mirth-detecting algorithm could make contributions to three possible areas of health care. First, such a technology could assist in the diagnosis of individuals who are suspected to have brain conditions that can result in humor deficits. The studies reviewed in Chapter 2 focused on humor impairments in a variety of conditions, some of which progressed over time. A mirth-detecting algorithm could be used to track changes in humor appreciation over time, identifying significant decrements for further exploration. Significant reductions in humor appreciation could be an indicator of cognitive changes not readily apparent in other examinations.

Second, a mirth-detecting algorithm could be used by researchers conducting humor-based interventions of the type described in Chapter 8. Researchers could use the algorithm with patients to find the type of humor that produces the strongest humor response. By tailoring the humor used in the intervention to the patient's personal taste, researchers may be able to boost the amount of benefit produced by the intervention. The optimal material to use in a humor-based intervention may prove to be specific to the health condition. Demjén (2016) analyzed the humor within an online support forum for individuals dealing with cancer. There appeared to be multiple functions of humor among the forum interactions, including coping with aspects of the illness and/or treatment (see also Branney et al., 2014; Roaldsen et al., 2015), creating a sense of group affiliation, reducing feelings of loneliness and isolation, and increasing personal empowerment. The jokes that patients find the funniest may strike family and friends as inappropriate (Mapes, 2015). Although researchers may avoid using humorous material that addresses the illness affecting their participants, research suggests that this is a missed opportunity, as individuals dealing with illness may seek out and actively engage in creating humor related to their daily life.

Future studies of humor-based interventions on health could benefit from the incorporation of brain imaging data. Comparisons of brain activity before, during, and after the intervention could produce insight into how humor experiences affect health. Currently, it is not known which specific changes in the brain are related to changes in well-being (e.g., mood, optimism) and/or changes in levels of cortisol and biomarkers related to immune system functioning. Studies have demonstrated that experiencing humor activates the sympathetic nervous system and the hypothalamus–pituitary–adrenal axis (see Chapter 7). Future brain imaging studies may be able to demonstrate that the physiological changes following the experience of humor (e.g., changes in hormone, neurotransmitters, immune system markers) are related to changes in brain regions (see Ulrich-Lai & Herman, 2009). Studies that use brain imaging data provide information about individual differences in the responses and nonresponses to humor interventions that may be useful in fine-tuning the delivery of future interventions. Such data would be helpful in determining what types of individuals are most likely and least likely to benefit from this type of intervention.

FUTURE DIRECTIONS IN CROSS-CULTURAL DIFFERENCES RESEARCH

The biggest hurdle that will need to be overcome in the effort to identify a neural signature of humor is the individual differences in response to humor. It remains to be determined whether the brain regions shown to be involved in the three stages of humor processing in fMRI studies are the same for most people. As stated in Chapters 3 and 4 of this volume, there have been relatively few brain imaging studies exploring individual differences, so any future study on the topic would be valuable. The studies that have been conducted so far have involved a relatively small number of right-handed participants from a relatively small number of countries. Humor is universal, occurring in all cultures (Apte, 1985); however, there are likely differences in how individuals create humor in daily life that are related to differences in language and cultural and social norms, which would lead to different expectations in individuals. Existing humor-related research on cross-cultural differences and differences related to language are reviewed next.

More research is needed to investigate how what individuals find funny varies across cultures. The more we understand each other, the less likely we are to land in conflict with others because of a poorly conceived attempt at humor. With the exception of an early study by Ruch and colleagues (1991), which compared the humor in samples from France and Germany, most of the research on humor has been conducted in the United States, other English-speaking countries, and Germany (Sinkeviciute & Dynel, 2017). Among the studies conducted so far, some observed differences in humor for people from different English-speaking countries (G. N. Martin & Sullivan, 2013) and some compared an English-speaking population with one or more other groups in countries in which English is not the dominant language (Jiang et al., 2019; Kalliny et al., 2006; Tosun et al., 2018). G. N. Martin and Sullivan (2013) explored differences in humor perceptions and use among people in three English speaking countries (the United States, the United Kingdom, and Australia). The results showed that respondents from the United Kingdom reported the most negative perceptions of humor and the lowest use of humor in social interactions. A recent study found that Australians may be particularly appreciative of mock aggression (Béal & Mullan, 2017). Tosun et al. (2018) compared the concept of an ideal sense of humor in samples from three countries (the United States, Turkey, and Iran). Across samples, they found that participants' notion of an ideal humorous person was a man. American respondents indicated that an ideal sense of humor involved creativity, sarcasm/hostility, and caring. Respondents from other countries also emphasized creativity. Those from Iran had the lowest endorsements of caring and sarcasm/hostility. In a similar study, Kalliny et al. (2006) examined the different humor styles of individuals from Arab countries and those from the United States. They observed that Arabs used self-enhancing and self-defeating humor styles less often than Americans.

A few studies have compared humor among those in Western countries with humor among those in Eastern countries (Krys et al., 2016; Nevo et al., 2001; Yue et al., 2016). Others have compared perceptions of humor in individualistic versus collectivistic cultures (Hatzithomas et al., 2011). For example, Nevo et al. (2001) investigated the use of humor by adults in Singapore, comparing the trends with those previously reported in the United States and Israel. Humor was used less often for coping in Singapore than in the United States or Israel. More aggressive humor and less sexual humor were also observed in Singapore. Men and women viewed men as being more humorous than women. In a later study, Yue et al. (2016) compared beliefs about the importance of humor for Canadian and Chinese individuals. The former group placed a higher value on humor, and the latter group viewed humor a specialized skill developed by comedians. Krys et al. (2016) explored individuals' reactions to humor from three cultures: Poland, in which honor is important; China, in which preserving face is important; and Canada, in which dignity is important.

A small number of studies have examined humor produced spontaneously in other cultures, including Denmark (Lundquist, 2014), China (Yue, 2011, 2018; Yue et al., 2014), Jordan (Al-Khatib, 1999), Korea (H. S. Kim & Plester, 2019; Roesch et al., 2006), and Lebanon (Kazarian et al., 2009). For example, Lundquist (2014) described the use of humor in the workplace by individuals from Denmark who live in an equalitarian culture where workplaces typically have horizontal power structures. Humor is encouraged, particularly laughing at oneself. The research found that Danes, compared with others, had a lower level of gelotophobia (i.e., fear of being laughed at).

The most rapidly growing line of humor research that has compared results across cultures is on the topic of gelotophobia. The term was first used by Titze in his dissertation research (Ruch & Titze, 1998; see also Titze, 2009), which produced a measure of gelotophobia, containing 46 items. A shorter version of measure with only 15 items has been shown to have good reliability (Proyer et al., 2009). Studies have been conducted with participants in Austria

(Papousek et al., 2014), Austria and Switzerland (Proyer et al., 2012), Germany (Platt et al., 2010; Ruch et al., 2015), India (Kamble et al., 2014), and Taiwan (Chan, Chen, & Lavallee, 2013; C.-H. Liu et al., 2016; Wu et al., 2016). The topic has likely attracted attention from researchers from many countries because of its relevance to clinical practice, as some cases of extreme geloto-phobia may be debilitating (Forabosco et al., 2009). Recent research supports including gelotophobia as a criterion for avoidant personality disorder and social anxiety disorder (Havranek et al., 2017).

Individual differences in scores on the gelotophobia measures have been found to be related to happiness and life satisfaction (Proyer et al., 2012). Proyer et al. (2012) compared these relationships in samples in China, Austria, and Switzerland. They found that the percentage of those meeting the cutoff for gelotophobia was below 8% in each sample (e.g., 7.3% in China, 5.8% in Austria, and 7.2% in Switzerland). Across samples, those with higher levels of gelotophobia had lower levels of life satisfaction and the life engagement aspect of happiness.

Age differences in gelotophobia have also been observed (Platt et al., 2010; Wu et al., 2016). Platt et al. (2010) investigated the prevalence of geloto-phobia across age groups. They found that it peaks during adolescence, declines into middle adulthood and remains at the same level thereafter. In a study with a large sample, Wu et al. (2016) compared sex differences in cognitions related to laughing and laughter across age groups (age 11 years–66 years), specifically enjoying laughing (i.e., gelotophilia), fearing of being on the receiving end of laughter (i.e., gelotophobia) and enjoying laughing at others (i.e., katagelasticism). The results showed that the relationship between sex and these categories varied across the age groups, likely because of the relative high levels of gelotophobia and katagelasticim reported by adolescent boys.

In the coming decades, research illuminating the similarities and differences in humor across cultures is likely to produce results that will be useful in promoting greater understanding and tolerance among people from different cultural groups. There are obstacles to conducting this type of research. F. F. Chen (2008) pointed out that translating questionnaires into different languages can result in subtle differences in how participants interpret questions that lead to a cross-cultural difference being found when there is none. Some researchers have begun the arduous task of developing and validating mea-sures in multiple languages to reduce the likelihood of such false positive results (Heintz et al., 2018; Proyer et al., 2009). Proyer et al. (2009) assessed gelotophobia in 73 countries, having translated the measure into 42 languages. They showed that the measure was reliable across samples. Using the 12-item measure of positive types of humor (Ruch, 2012), Heintz et al. (2018) compared samples of respondents from 22 nations. The measure distinguished benevo-lent humor, which targets human weakness with humorous acceptance, from corrective humor, which targets some undesirable aspect of the world or people with a desire to change it. In the groups, participants responded to the 12-item questionnaire that was translated into 13 languages.

Other research has documented differences in humor for individuals living within the same country but belonging to different cultural groups (C. Lau et al., 2019; Nevo, 1984, 1985, 1986; Niwa & Maruno, 2009; Yue, 2011). In a series of studies, Nevo (1984, 1985, 1986) compared the use of humor by Jewish and Arab individuals living in Israel. In these studies, which used different methods, she found that Jewish individuals used aggressive humor more often than Arab individuals. Niwa and Maruno (2009) compared the appreciation of self-deprecating humor among two cultural groups within Japan (one associated with longstanding merchants in Osaka and one in Tokyo), finding that individuals from Osaka engaged in self-deprecating humor more than individuals from Tokyo. Yue (2011) investigated the proposal that in Chinese culture, there is an ambivalence regarding humor. He surveyed college students in Hong Kong and a city in the Mongolian region of North China (i.e., Huhehot). The results indicated that although participants indicated that they believed humor to be important, they did not believe themselves to be very humorous. Men viewed themselves as more humorous than did women. In addition, respondents reported characteristics most associated with the Chinese personality, which were not associated with humor.

Future studies involving bilingual participants may lead to more studies investigating the different ways in which people create humor with language. Puns and other forms of word play are likely to occur across languages (Attardo, 2017; Vaid, 2006). Vaid (2006) described how bilingual speakers often create puns whose resolution requires information from both of the bilinguals' languages. A familiar example is: "Why do the French only eat one egg for breakfast? Because one egg is *un oeuf*" (which sounds like the English word *enough*). Across languages, speakers create humor in numerous ways that exploit grammatical or other characteristics of the language (Cisneros et al., 2006; Jaroenkiatboworn, 2007; Takanashi, 2007). Future studies with multilingual individuals should consider the possibility that the language in which one is tested may influence the results (S. X. Chen & Bond, 2010; Ervin, 1964; Hull, 1996; Ramírez-Esparza et al., 2006). For example, Ramírez-Esparza et al. (2006) investigated the possibility that when considering their own personality, bilinguals engage in cultural frame switching, which refers to switching between cultural mindsets depending on the cultural cues in the context (Hong et al., 1997). Ramírez-Esparza et al. showed that when Spanish–English bilinguals reported their personality on an English-language version of the measure, they rated their extraversion and agreeableness as higher and their neuroticism as lower than those who reported their personality on a Spanish-language version of the measure.

Within a culture, attitudes toward humor and humor behavior can change over time. Some researchers (Lamm & Meeks, 2009; Strauss & Howe, 1991; Twenge, 2014; Twenge & Campbell, 2008) have suggested that it is useful to consider generational cohorts as different cultural groups (e.g., baby boomers, millennials, Generation X, Generation Z). Perceptions of humor have changed over history. This view of humor as a primarily positive behavior evolved over the last century (Wickberg, 1998). Throughout history, negative aspects of humor have been emphasized. For example, Plato (428–348 B.C.) described humor as reflecting malice, pointing out another's shortcomings or misfortunes (Morreall, 1987). Aristotle (348–322 B.C.) also had a low opinion of individuals who went through life with a humorous nature. One can find numerous references to laughter in the Bible, most of which involve the laughing individuals holding others in contempt (Koestler, 1964). Much has been written about humor in ancient Rome, as it played an important role in daily life (Beard, 2014). Hundreds of jokes and stories about the use of humor from that era have survived. The jokes of ancient Romans targeted specific types of people for mockery (e.g., foreigners, the highly intelligent, eunuchs, slaves). Disparagement humor is used today to refer to humor to mock or disparage others because of their sex, ethnicity, or other social category (A. A. Berger, 1993; Ford & Ferguson, 2004; Ford et al., 2017; Gockel & Kerr, 2015; Hodson & MacInnis, 2016; Hodson et al., 2010; Saucier et al., 2016). Today, humor is associated with positive emotions, fun, and pleasure.

Prior studies provide evidence that differences in humor appreciation and attitudes about humor exist across cultures. It is possible that cross-cultural differences in humor processing may be reflected in brain responses, which would mean that a neural signature of humor would be culture specific. Different algorithms would be needed to detect brain-based mirth responses in each cultural group and may need to consider the language involved in the humor and whether the participant knows multiple languages.

FUTURE DIRECTIONS IN RESEARCH ON EDUCATION AND TRAINING

A promising avenue of future research is exploring how experiencing humor affects subsequent cognitive processing, like memory and problem solving. The notion that humor can spark creativity is a relatively old view (Freud, 1905/1960; Koestler, 1964). More recently, scholars have suggested that experiencing humor may change patterns of thinking (Dixon, 1980; R. A. Martin & Lefcourt, 1983; O'Connell, 1976). There is already strong evidence supporting the predicted link between humor and creativity (Brodzinsky & Rubien, 1976; Huang et al., 2015; Isen et al., 1985, 1987; Kellner & Benedek, 2017; Kohler & Ruch, 1993; Miron-Spektor et al., 2011; Nusbaum et al., 2017; see also Chapter 1, this volume). In laboratory studies, those who score high in creativity produce the funniest captions for cartoons (Brodzinsky & Rubien, 1976; Kellner & Benedek, 2017; Kohler & Ruch, 1993; Nusbaum et al., 2017). Other studies have shown that experiencing sarcasm can lead to increases in creativity (Huang et al., 2015; Miron-Spektor et al., 2011). One study with 18-month-old children showed that those exposed to a humorous event were more likely to use a tool in a manner similar to how it was used by an adult than were children who were not exposed to a humorous event (Esseily et al., 2016).

Is this type of learning categorized as a change in thinking patterns or an increase in creativity? Although it is not clear, it remains an intriguing possibility.

Research on humor and memory suggests that there is a memory advantage for humorous information (Carlson, 2011; S. R. Schmidt, 1994, 2002; S. R. Schmidt & Williams, 2001; Summerfelt et al., 2010). S. R. Schmidt (2002) asked participants to view a series of cartoons. Some were humorous, others were not humorous but weird, and some were not humorous nor weird. Half of the participants were led to expect a memory test for the cartoons. The other half later were asked to recall the cartoons with prior warning. Regardless of whether participants were told about the memory test, participants' memory for the funny cartoons was significantly better than memory for the other two types of cartoons. In the study, S. R. Schmidt (2002) also recorded participants' heart rate to explore whether there were physiological differences occurring at the time that the different types of cartoons were viewed and encoded in memory. He found no significant differences in heart rate at the time participants first viewed the different types of cartoons, ruling out the possibility that participants' physiological arousal differed across the conditions. He suggested that humorous material is distinctive and leads to elaboration, which occurs at the time of encoding and at the time of retrieval. Summerfelt et al. (2010) suggested an alternative explanation for the memory advantage for humorous material. They claimed that the humorous material is usually constrained in terms of structure (e.g., setup followed by punchline) and/or in terms of a specific wording that leads to a humorous resolution. In contrast, nonhumorous material is not constrained in either way. The structural and verbal constraints of humorous materials are likely to be encoded in memory and to be used as memory cues at the time of retrieval.

Summerfelt et al. (2010) investigated memory for sentences that did or did not contain a pun. Memory was better for sentences containing puns. The memory advantage was shown not to be caused by incidental rehearsal of stimuli, but rather how much contextual constraint was present leading up to the pun or nonpun. In the studies that have tested the benefits of humor on learning in academic settings, conflicting results have emerged (Kaplan & Pascoe, 1977; LoSchiavo & Shatz, 2005; Ziv, 1988). Some studies have found that students participate more in classes containing humor and report increased interest in the material, but a memory advantage for the material was not observed. Future research is needed to determine whether there are memory advantages for classroom material that is directly tied to a humorous event (as compared with the same material presented in an emotionally neutral situation). Anecdotal evidence from my own teaching provides preliminary support. The topic being covered was one of the driest and most difficult of the course (i.e., categorical perception). I had found it to be challenging for students, especially during exams where only about 50% of students answering a short question on the subject were able to answer correctly. During one lecture in a 3-hour/day summer class, I made an unfortunate and unintentional slip of the tongue, which caused the entire class to erupt in laughter. The slip of the tongue was directly related to the concept of how our knowledge of the sounds /p/ and /b/, which is stored in memory and is used during speech perception. On the later exam, everyone who was in attendance that day answered the question correctly.

Educational applications for the memory advantage of humor are worth pursuing because of research by Greeley and Seidler (2017) that showed general learning is enhanced for some individuals when positive emotional states are induced. They hypothesized that individuals lower in working memory capacity may be affected by positive affect during learning more than those higher in working memory capacity, because positive affect leads to increased release of dopamine in the brain. In a study of individuals with Parkinson's disease, those with lower working memory capacity had been shown to have lower levels of dopamine synthesis in the striatum than those with higher working memory capacity (Cools et al., 2008). Greeley and Seidler tested the effect of positive affect in a reaction-time learning task, finding support for their hypothesis. Positive affect led to increased learning only for those with lower working memory capacity.

In the future, research investigating the effect of humor/positive mood on learning and memory could use a brain-based mirth-detecting algorithm to confirm that participants have experienced positive mood. If studies can establish a causal link between the induction of positive mood and learning, then future applications of this type of research could include scanning students or employees before a learning session to increase the likelihood that maximal learning will occur.

CLOSING REMARKS

This book has examined the cognitive neuroscience of humor, finding that the topic is more than frivolous fun and games; rather, humor is a core human ability, whose processing involves many regions of the brain. These regions are the most recently evolved (e.g., neocortex and midbrain). In the coming decades, new research is likely to show that adding humor in lives where it may be lacking may lead to benefits to mental and physical health. Many questions remain on the topic of the cognitive neuroscience of humor. This chapter discussed only possible lines of future research, including health care, specifically humor-based interventions; cross-cultural studies of humor attitudes, humor appreciation, and humor processing; and studies on the use of humor to improve learning in schools and workplaces. It is my hope that this book will lead people to include more humor in their daily lives and to reflect on how humor is one of our most mysterious and important behaviors.

GLOSSARY

absurd humor A less common type of humor that presents an incongruous element in the context, which may be unresolvable or difficult to resolve, but still leads to amusement.

adrenaline See *epinephrine*.

affiliative humor style A type of humor that involves the use of humor to connect or bond with others.

agenesis of the corpus callosum A disorder that involves the *corpus callosum* not being formed at all or not being formed properly during prenatal development.

aggressive humor style A type of humor that involves targeting others, ranging from mild teasing to extreme bullying.

agreeableness A trait in the Big Five personality inventory, which is characterized by being sympathetic, kind, and warm.

Alzheimer's dementia A progressive brain degeneration in adults, resulting in progressive memory loss and cognitive dysfunction.

amnesia Memory loss following brain injury or brain degeneration.

amygdala An almond-shaped part of the brain located in each hemisphere that is involved in emotional processing, including the *mirth* experienced during humor processing.

amyotrophic lateral sclerosis (ALS) A degenerative disease affecting motor neurons, leading to a progressive loss of control over movement.

anterior An anatomical term used to describe a location that is toward the front.

aphasia A deficit or disruption to language processing following a brain injury.

autism spectrum disorder A group of disorders characterized by social and language deficits that are present early childhood and vary widely in severity across individuals.

autonomic nervous system The system of the brain that controls involuntary processes involved in respiration, heart functions, and digestion, as well as others.

basal ganglia A group of regions at the base of the brain that have pathways to the *thalamus*; this group is involved in numerous functions, including the control of movement.

brainstem The region of the brain that includes the pons and medulla oblongata, connects with the spine, and controls basic functions, including the regulation of blood pressure, breathing, consciousness, and others.

Broca's aphasia A type of *aphasia* characterized by difficulty articulating speech and having speech that is telegraphic in nature (e.g., "go store milk" for "let's go to the store for milk"); it is caused by damage to *Broca's Area*.

Broca's area Area of the brain located in the prefrontal region of the left hemisphere, in the *inferior* temporal gyrus, roughly near the left temple.

Brodmann areas 52 brain regions identified in terms of their cell structure by Korbinian Brodmann.

case study method A method used to explore a research topic by focusing on a single individual or event; conclusions about causation cannot be drawn from this method.

caudal An anatomical term used to refer to a location toward the tail of an animal, when considering locations from head to tail.

caudate nucleus A brain region with the *basal ganglia*, which is involved in many behaviors, including movement. Individuals with *Huntington's disease* experience degeneration of this region.

central sulcus A major landmark of the brain, it is the deep groove between the *frontal lobe* and *parietal lobe*.

cerebellum The brain region at the back of the skull, which involves many behaviors, including planning and controlling movement.

cingulate cortex A region of the brain that is located above the *corpus callosum*. The *anterior* region is involved in numerous aspects of human behavior, such as controlling and modulating emotions and making decisions. The *posterior* region has been found to be involved in the *mirth* experience during humor processing.

cold pressor test A task that involves a participant keeping a hand in ice-cold water as long as possible. It is used as stress or pain manipulation, but also can be used to test heart and respiratory responses.

conscientiousness A trait in the Big Five personality inventory, which is characterized by being organized, efficient, and careful.

corpus callosum The part of the brain that connects the two hemispheres and enables information to be passed in both directions.

cortex The most outer layers of the brain, which makes up the four major lobes.

cortisol A hormone produced by the body during stressful experiences.

creativity Having original ideas or approaches that are useful in solving a problem or achieving an outcome.

crossed aphasia Instances in which brain injury or disease in the right hemisphere results in language deficits or dysfunction.

deep brain stimulation A procedure that involves placing one or more electrodes in the brain connected to wires through which electrical stimulation can be delivered. It has been used to treat *Parkinson's disease* and major depression.

distal An anatomical term used to refer to a location that is far away from a point of attachment (e.g., the wrist is distal to the shoulder).

divided visual field (DVF) paradigm A procedure that involves the researcher presenting a visual stimulus to the left or right hemisphere for processing by ensuring that the stimulus is located in the right visual field or left visual field, respectively, while the participant is looking straight ahead at a computer screen.

dopamine A neurotransmitter expressed in the brain during pleasurable experiences that is also involved in the production and control of movements. *Parkinson's disease* occurs when neurons producing dopamine in the *substantia nigra* within the *basal ganglia* degenerate.

dorsal An anatomical term used to refer to a location toward the top.

Down syndrome A developmental disorder due to a chromosomal copying error occurring during development. Individuals have extra copies of Chromosome 21, which results in severe intellectual impairment, abnormal organ development, and abnormal physical features of body parts.

Duchenne smile An instance of genuine smiling (vs. smiling with feigned positive emotion). It involves the tensing of muscles at both the corners of the mouth and also the corners of the eyes.

electrical brain stimulation A procedure that involves directing an electrical current into brain tissue for the purposes of determining what functions are carried out or controlled by that part of the brain.

electroencephalogram (EEG) A measure of the electrical activity on the head, using electrodes placed on the scalp.

electromyography A measure of the electrical activity in muscles, using electrodes placed on the skin.

endorphins A neurotransmitter that when released in the brain causes a reduction of pain and increases in feelings of well-being similar to that produced by opiates.

epilepsy A disorder characterized by recurrent seizures brought about by abnormal electrical activity in the brain.

epinephrine A hormone which is released at times of stress, facilitating breathing, blood flow, metabolism of carbohydrates, and use of muscles, as well as others.

event-related potential (ERP) A procedure that involves measuring an *electro-encephalogram* following the presentation of a stimulus to the participant.

executive functioning The processes involved in the control of cognition, attention, and emotion involved in planning and completing tasks in daily life.

extraversion A trait in the Big Five personality inventory, which is characterized by sociability, boldness, and talkativeness.

false positive results Results that occur when a researcher finds a statistical difference between conditions that is due to randomness alone.

frontal lobe One of the four major lobes of the brain located at the front of the head just behind the forehead. Its major functions include planning, decision making, and emotional regulation, as well as others.

frontotemporal dementia A form of dementia that occurs due to the shrinkage of the *frontal* and *temporal lobes*.

functional magnetic resonance imaging (fMRI) A brain imaging methodology that measures the activity of brain regions by tracking the blood flow in brain areas when the participant's body is exposed to a strong magnetic field during a specific interval of time during which the participant is performing a cognitive task.

fusiform gyrus A region located at the junction of the *occipital* and *temporal lobes* and is involved in face recognition and word reading, as well as others.

gelastic seizures An uncontrolled electrical disturbance in the brain characterized by intense laughing or crying due to internal brain processes having no relationship with an environmental stimulus.

gelotophobia The fear of being the target of laughter.

globus pallidus A subregion within the *basal ganglia* in the brain.

gray matter The tissue of the brain composed of cell bodies.

gyrus The ridge in the *cortex*; the opposite of a *sulcus*.

hippocampus The horseshoe-shaped region of the brain located in the *limbic system* and known to be involved in memory processing, specifically the creation of new, conscious long-term memories.

Humor Styles Questionnaire (HSQ) An inventory developed by Martin and colleagues (1993) to assess individual differences in humor styles; the questionnaire assesses four styles, including affiliative, self-enhancing, self-defeating, and aggressive.

Huntington's disease An inherited disorder causing the individual to experience worsening involuntary body movements and cognitive impairment. Core symptoms are related to the gradual degeneration of the *caudate nucleus*.

hypothalamic–pituitary–adrenocortical (HPA) system A brain network that is activated during the human stress response, leading to an increase in *cortisol*.

hypothalamus The region in both hemispheres of the brain located below the *thalamus*, which is involved in numerous processes including coordinating pituitary activity and the *autonomic nervous system*, sleep, hunger, thirst, temperature control, and emotional experiences.

incongruity-resolution humor A common type of humor (e.g., most *jokes* and some cartoons) that involves an element that is surprising or unexpected in the context, but when resolved, leads to humor.

inferior An anatomical term used to refer to a location that is lower.

insula A region of the brain located deep in the *sylvan fissure* and involved in a variety of processes including humor, consciousness, and responses in social interactions.

irony A statement whose literal meaning is the opposite of the meaning intended by the speaker.

jokes Structured statements or stories that end with a humorous twist or punchline.

laryngeal motor cortex A subregion within the *primary motor cortex* that is involved in controlling the movement of the larynx.

late positive complex Waveforms observed in *event-related potential* studies, characterized by positive waveforms occurring relatively late in processing, usually longer than 600 ms following the presentation of a stimulus, and observed at electrode sites over the *parietal lobes*.

lateral An anatomical term used to refer to a location away from the midline, toward one side.

lateral fissure See *sylvan fissure*.

lesions Areas within organs, including the brain, which have been damaged due to surgery, accidental injury, or disease.

limbic system A brain system containing regions involved in memory (*hippocampus*) and emotion (*amygdala*) as well as other functions.

lingual gyrus A brain region located above the *fusiform gyrus*, extending from the *medial* occipital lobe into the *medial* temporal lobe and has been found to be involved in the comprehension of *absurd humor*.

literal language Language that is interpreted incrementally through the identification of the meaning of each word and combining word meanings to reach an overall meaning of the phrase or sentence.

magnetic resonance imaging (MRI) A methodology that is used to scan the body for injury or disease at a single point in time.

medial An anatomical term used to refer to a location toward the middle.

mesencephalic periaqueductal gray A subregion within the tegmentum area of the *midbrain*, which is involved in a variety of behaviors, including responding to fear-provoking stimuli.

mesolimbic areas Areas of the brain located in the *ventral* region of the *basal ganglia* in each hemisphere; they are known to be involved in experiencing pleasure from a variety of activities including eating, sex, and using opioids.

meta-analysis A method that involves examining the results of numerous studies that have investigated the same question; it pools the results of many studies with the aim of assessing the statistical significance of one or more effects.

midbrain A region of the brain located above the brain stem and includes multiple sub-regions involved in arousal, temperature regulation, vision, hearing, and other functions.

middle frontal gyrus A region of the brain located in the *medial* portion of the *frontal lobes*, which has been found to be active during humor comprehension.

middle temporal gyrus A region of the brain located in the *medial* portion of the *temporal lobes*, which has been found to be active during humor comprehension.

mirth Amusement, particularly that involving laughter.

N400 A component observed using *electroencephalogram*; it is a negative waveform occurring approximately 400 ms following the presentation of a stimulus.

narcolepsy A neurological condition characterized by excessive sleepiness and/or sudden sleep onset at inappropriate times.

neuroticism A trait in the Big Five personality inventory, which is characterized by nervousness, jealousy, and negative affect.

nonsense humor See *absurd humor*.

nucleus accumbens A region of the brain known as the pleasure center, which releases *dopamine* during pleasurable experiences; it is part of the *limbic system*.

occipital lobe One of four major lobes of the brain located at the back of the skull involved predominantly in visual processing.

openness A trait in the Big Five personality inventory, which is characterized by *creativity*, intellectual interests, and having a well-developed imagination.

orbital frontal cortex A region of the brain in the *frontal lobe*, located directly behind each eye in the left and right hemisphere.

P300 A component observed using *electroencephalogram*; it is a positive waveform occurring approximately 300 ms following the presentation of a stimulus.

P600 A component observed using *electroencephalogram*; it is a positive waveform occurring approximately 600 ms following the presentation of a stimulus.

parahippocampal gyrus A layer of tissue that surrounds the *hippocampus* in both hemispheres; it has been found to be involved in the feeling of amusement during humor processing.

parietal lobe One of the four major lobes of the brain located on the top of the head, behind the *frontal lobe* and above the *temporal lobe* in each hemisphere.

Parkinson's disease A disorder characterized by worsening involuntary tremors and body movements and cognitive impairment, related to the degeneration of the *substantia nigra* in the *basal ganglia*.

pathological humor (*witzelsucht*) A condition that involves excessive joking in individuals without other symptoms of *pseudobulbar affect*.

pathological laughter A condition that involves laughter with or without *mirth* without a trigger event (e.g., joke or amusing experience). The condition is observed in patients who have experienced brain damage or have a degenerative brain disease.

Phineas Gage A railroad worker who survived having a metal rod pass through his skull, damaging his *frontal lobes*. He experienced personality changes following the accident, which were reported as the first case study of *frontal lobe* functioning.

phrenology A pseudoscience popular in the 19th century that claimed specific brain regions were responsible for specific human personal characteristics and abilities.

positive psychology The branch of psychology involved in investigating aspects of normal and extraordinary functioning, contrasting with the focus on atypical functioning usually taken in mainstream psychology.

posterior An anatomical term used to refer to locations toward the back.

posterior cingulate cortex The part of the *cingulate cortex* that is located toward the back of the brain; it has been shown to be active during the feelings of amusement during humor processing.

postmortem autopsy An in-depth examination of the body after death. Researchers interested in neuropsychology used the technique prior to the 1900s to link specific brain areas appearing damaged and behavioral deficits in the individual before death.

precuneus A region on the surface of the *parietal lobe* located medially within in each hemisphere.

prefrontal cortex A part of the *frontal lobe* located at the most *anterior* location that is believed to be involved in numerous processes, including decision making, planning, emotional regulation, and personality.

premotor cortex A part of the *frontal lobe*, *anterior* to the *primary motor cortex*.

primary motor cortex A part of the *frontal lobe* located in the *posterior* region that is involved in the control of movement.

prosody The melodic nature of spoken language contained in its patterns of stress, rhythm, and intonation.

proximal An anatomical term used to refer to a location that is close to a point of attachment (e.g., the bicep is proximal to the shoulder).

pseudobulbar affect A condition occurring secondary to brain injury or diseases; it involves neural degeneration in which an individual experiences uncontrollable emotions, including laughing or crying.

punchlines The concluding portion of a joke, which when processed leads to amusement.

puns A form of humor created through manipulation of the words often involving the sounds of words.

relaxed open mouth display A facial behavior in nonhuman species produced during play sessions; it is believed to be related to smiling in humans.

remote associates test An assessment that measures *creativity*; participants receive a series of groups of three words and are asked to generate a fourth word that is related in some way to each of the three words.

reward processing The experience of pleasure from a variety of activities including eating, sex, and using opioids.

rostral An anatomical term used to refer to a location toward the nose of an animal, when considering locations from head to tail.

sarcasm A form of humor that targets an individual in an aggressive way.

schizophrenia A mental illness usually beginning during adolescence or early adulthood, which is characterized by a range of symptoms that can vary across individuals, including confusion of reality from imagination, false beliefs, paranoia, and hallucinations.

secretory-IgA (S-IgA) An antibody produced by the immune system and is found in mucous, saliva, and tears.

self-deprecating humor style A type of humor targeting oneself by highlighting a physical characteristic or some other flaw.

self-enhancing humor style A type of humor used to cope with challenging events in daily life.

striatum A region within the *basal ganglia* of the brain, which deteriorates in individuals with *Parkinson's disease* and *Huntington's disease* and is believed to be involved in language processing.

stroke A reduction in blood flow in the brain, often due to blockage; it can lead to individuals experiencing a loss of function.

substantia nigra A region in the *basal ganglia* that produces *dopamine*; it is the region that degenerates in *Parkinson's disease*.

sulcus A groove in the *cortex*; it is the opposite of a *gyrus*.

superior An anatomical term used to refer to a location that is higher.

superior frontal gyrus A subregion within the *frontal lobe* that can produce laughter when stimulated electrically.

supplementary motor area A region in the *frontal lobe* located *anterior* to the *primary motor cortex*; it is involved in the control of movement.

sylvan fissure A major landmark in the *cortex*, a *sulcus* that corresponds to the horizontal border between the *temporal lobe* and the *frontal lobe*, also bordering the *parietal lobe*.

sympathetic nervous system The system of the brain that controls the body's fight-or-flight responses.

temporal lobe One of the four major lobes of the brain located on the side of the head; it is involved in numerous processes, including hearing and memory.

temporal–occipital junction The region of the brain where the *temporal lobe* borders the occipital lobe.

temporal–occipital–parietal junction The region of the brain where the temporal and occipital lobes meet and border the *parietal lobe*.

temporal pole The tip of the *temporal lobe*, which is located at the most *anterior* point of the lobe.

temporoparietal junction The region of the brain where the temporal and *parietal lobes* meet; it receives information from many brain areas including the sensory areas, *limbic system*, and *thalamus*.

thalamus The brain region located in both hemispheres that is involved in numerous processes, including the sensation of pain and interpreting sound.

theory of mind The awareness that other individuals may possess knowledge and/or have perspectives different from one's own.

trait cheerfulness A personality characteristic that varies across individuals, defined in terms of three personality traits: cheerfulness, seriousness, and bad mood.

transcranial magnetic stimulation (TMS) A procedure that stimulates brain cells noninvasively by directing a magnetic field toward the head. It is used in research to investigate cognitive processing and to treat depression and other mental illnesses.

traumatic brain injury An injury to the brain caused by either a penetrating wound or closed head trauma (e.g., a blow to the head).

trial An event in an experiment in which participants experience stimuli and sometimes are asked to make a response.

ventral An anatomical term used to refer to a location near the underside.

ventral striatum An area of the brain located in the *basal ganglia* that contains the *nucleus accumbens* and the olfactory tubercle; it is involved in decision making and reinforced behaviors, as well as others.

virtual lesion A disruption to the processing of a brain region using transcranial electrical stimulation.

voltage A unit of measurement of electricity recorded in *electroencephalogram* and *event-related potential* studies of cognitive processing.

Wernicke's aphasia A type of *aphasia* characterized by fluent speech that in non-sensical, lacking content words (e.g., nouns, verbs) and sometimes containing suffixes and prefixes joined to root words inappropriately; it is caused by damage to *Wernicke's area*.

Wernicke's area An area of the brain located in the back of the left hemisphere, roughly behind the ear.

white matter The tissue in the brain that is composed of axons, which are involved in the communication between cell bodies.

working memory The mental blackboard in short-term memory that individuals use to carry out tasks in the present; information held in working memory is available for approximately 2–3 minutes, if not updated.

REFERENCES

Abel, M. H., & Flick, J. (2012). Mediation and moderation in ratings of hostile jokes by men and women. *Humor: International Journal of Humor Research, 25*(1), 41–58. https://doi.org/10.1515/humor-2012-0003

Acevedo-Rodriguez, A., Kauffman, A. S., Cherrington, B. D., Borges, C. S., Roepke, T. A., & Laconi, M. (2018). Emerging insights into hypothalamic-pituitary-gonadal axis regulation and interaction with stress signalling. *Journal of Neuroendocrinology, 30*(10), e12590. https://doi.org/10.1111/jne.12590

Adamczyk, P., Wyczesany, M., Domagalik, A., Cepuch, K., Daren, A., & Marek, T. (2018). Diminished activation of the right inferior parietal lobule as a neural substrate of impaired cartoon-jokes comprehension in schizophrenia outpatients. *Schizophrenia Research, 197*, 593–595. https://doi.org/10.1016/j.schres.2018.01.004

Adamczyk, P., Wyczesany, M., Domagalik, A., Daren, A., Cepuch, K., Błądziński, P., Cechnicki, A., & Marek, T. (2017). Neural circuit of verbal humor comprehension in schizophrenia—An fMRI study. *NeuroImage: Clinical, 15*, 525–540. https://doi.org/10.1016/j.nicl.2017.06.005

Adams, E. R., & McGuire, F. A. (1986). Is laughter the best medicine? A study of the effects of humor on perceived pain and affect. *Activities, Adaptation and Aging, 8*(3–4), 157–175. https://doi.org/10.1300/J016v08n03_17

Adang, O. M. (1984). Teasing in young chimpanzees. *Behaviour, 88*(1/2), 98–121. http://www.jstor.org/stable/4534319

Adang, O. M. (1986). Exploring the social environment: A developmental study of teasing in chimpanzees. *Ethology, 73*(2), 136–160. https://doi.org/10.1111/j.1439-0310.1986.tb01005.x

Addyman, C., Fogelquist, C., Levakova, L., & Rees, S. (2018). Social facilitation of laughter and smiles in preschool children. *Frontiers in Psychology, 9*, 1048. https://doi.org/10.3389/fpsyg.2018.01048

Agarwal, S. M., Shivakumar, V., Bose, A., Subramaniam, A., Nawani, H., Chhabra, H., Kalmady, S. V., Narayanaswamy, J. C., & Venkatasubramanian, G. (2013). Transcranial direct current stimulation in schizophrenia. *Clinical Psychopharmacology and Neuroscience, 11*(3), 118–125. https://doi.org/10.9758/cpn.2013.11.3.118

Albuquerque, L., Martins, M., Coelho, M., Guedes, L., Ferreira, J. J., Rosa, M., & Martins, I. P. (2016). Advanced Parkinson disease patients have impairment in prosody processing. *Journal of Clinical and Experimental Neuropsychology, 38*(2), 208–216. https://doi.org/10.1080/13803395.2015.1100279

Alexander, R. D. (1986). Ostracism and indirect reciprocity: The reproductive significance of humor. *Ethology and Sociobiology, 7*(3–4), 253–270. https://doi.org/10.1016/0162-3095(86)90052-X

Al-Khatib, M. A. (1999). Joke-telling in Jordanian society: A sociolinguistic perspective. *Humor: International Journal of Humor Research, 12*(3), 261–288. https://doi.org/10.1515/humr.1999.12.3.261

Alloway, R. G., & Alloway, T. P. (2015). The working memory benefits of proprioceptively demanding training: A pilot study. *Perceptual and Motor Skills, 120*(3), 766–775. https://doi.org/10.2466/22.PMS.120v18x1

Allport, G. W. (1961). *Pattern and growth in personality.* Holt, Reinhart & Winston.

Altschuler, M., Sideridis, G., Kala, S., Warshawsky, M., Gilbert, R., Carroll, D., Burger-Caplan, R., & Faja, S. (2018). Measuring individual differences in cognitive, affective, and spontaneous theory of mind among school-aged children with autism spectrum disorder. *Journal of Autism and Developmental Disorders, 48*(11), 3945–3957. https://doi.org/10.1007/s10803-018-3663-1

Amenta, S., & Balconi, M. (2008). Understanding irony: An ERP analysis on the elaboration of acoustic ironic statements. *Neuropsychological Trends, 3*, 7–27.

Amenta, S., Noël, X., Verbanck, P., & Campanella, S. (2013). Decoding of emotional components in complex communicative situations (irony) and its relation to empathic abilities in male chronic alcoholics: An issue for treatment. *Alcoholism, Clinical and Experimental Research, 37*(2), 339–347. https://doi.org/10.1111/j.1530-0277.2012.01909.x

Amir, O., & Biederman, I. (2016). The neural correlates of humor creativity. *Frontiers in Human Neuroscience, 10*, 597–608. https://doi.org/10.3389/fnhum.2016.00597

Amir, O., Biederman, I., Wang, Z., & Xu, X. (2015). Ha ha! Versus aha! A direct comparison of humor to nonhumorous insight for determining the neural correlates of mirth. *Cerebral Cortex, 25*(5), 1405–1413. https://doi.org/10.1093/cercor/bht343

Anderson, C. A., & Arnoult, L. H. (1989). An examination of perceived control, humor, irrational beliefs, and positive stress as moderators of the relation between negative stress and health. *Basic and Applied Social Psychology, 10*(2), 101–117. https://doi.org/10.1207/s15324834basp1002_1

Anderson, L. B., Paul, L. K., & Brown, W. S. (2017). Emotional intelligence in agenesis of the corpus callosum. *Archives of Clinical Neuropsychology, 32*(3), 267–279. https://doi.org/10.1093/arclin/acx001

Ando, V., Claridge, G., & Clark, K. (2014). Psychotic traits in comedians. *The British Journal of Psychiatry, 204*(5), 341–345. https://doi.org/10.1192/bjp.bp.113.134569

Angeleri, R., & Airenti, G. (2014). The development of joke and irony understanding: A study with 3- to 6-year-old children. *Canadian Journal of Experimental*

Psychology/Revue Canadienne De Psychologie Expérimentale, 68(2), 133–146. https://doi.org/10.1037/cep0000011

Apte, M. L. (1985). *Humor and laughter: An anthropological approach.* Cornell University Press.

Arain, M., Haque, M., Johal, L., Mathur, P., Nel, W., Rais, A., Sandhu, R., & Sharma, S. (2013). Maturation of the adolescent brain. *Neuropsychiatric Disease and Treatment, 9,* 449–461. https://doi.org/10.2147/NDT.S39776

Ardesch, D. J., Scholtens, L. H., Li, L., Preuss, T. M., Rilling, J. K., & van den Heuvel, M. P. (2019). Evolutionary expansion of connectivity between multimodal association areas in the human brain compared with chimpanzees. *PNAS: Proceedings of the National Academy of Sciences of the United States of America, 116*(14), 7101–7106. https://doi.org/10.1073/pnas.1818512116

Arroyo, S., Lesser, R. P., Gordon, B., Uematsu, S., Hart, J., Schwerdt, P., Andreasson, K., & Fisher, R. S. (1993). Mirth, laughter and gelastic seizures. *Brain: A Journal of Neurology, 116*(4), 757–780. https://doi.org/10.1093/brain/116.4.757

Ashby, F. G. (2011). *Statistical analysis of fMRI data.* MIT Press. https://doi.org/10.7551/mitpress/8764.001.0001

Ashkan, K., Rogers, P., Bergman, H., & Ughratdar, I. (2017). Insights into the mechanisms of deep brain stimulation. *Nature Reviews. Neurology, 13*(9), 548–554. https://doi.org/10.1038/nrneurol.2017.105

Atkinson, B. E., Lipton, D., Baughman, H. M., Schermer, J. A., Harris, J., & Vernon, P. A. (2015). How do emotional restrictions affect the use of humor? A behavior genetic analysis of alexithymia and humor styles. *Twin Research and Human Genetics, 18*(2), 138–141. https://doi.org/10.1017/thg.2014.89

Atsumi, T., Fujisawa, S., Nakabayashi, Y., Kawarai, T., Yasui, T., & Tonosaki, K. (2004). Pleasant feeling from watching a comical video enhances free radical-scavenging capacity in human whole saliva. *Journal of Psychosomatic Research, 56*(3), 377–379. https://doi.org/10.1016/S0022-3999(03)00064-3

Attardo, S. (Ed.). (2017). *Routledge handbook on language and humor.* Routledge. https://doi.org/10.4324/9781315731162

Averill, J. R. (1969). Autonomic response patterns during sadness and mirth. *Psychophysiology, 5*(4), 399–414. https://doi.org/10.1111/j.1469-8986.1969.tb02840.x

Ayçiçeği-Dinn, A., Şişman-Bal, S., & Caldwell-Harris, C. L. (2018). Are jokes funnier in one's native language? *Humor: International Journal of Humor Research, 31*(1), 5–37. https://doi.org/10.1515/humor-2017-0112

Azim, E., Mobbs, D., Jo, B., Menon, V., & Reiss, A. L. (2005). Sex differences in brain activation elicited by humor. *PNAS: Proceedings of the National Academy of Sciences of the United States of America, 102*(45), 16496–16501. https://doi.org/10.1073/pnas.0408456102

Baez, S., Herrera, E., Gershanik, O., Garcia, A. M., Bocanegra, Y., Kargieman, L., Manes, F., & Ibanez, A. (2015). Impairments in negative emotion recognition and empathy for pain in Huntington's disease families. *Neuropsychologia, 68,* 158–167. https://doi.org/10.1016/j.neuropsychologia.2015.01.012

Bainum, C. K., Lounsbury, K. R., & Pollio, H. R. (1984). The development of laughing and smiling in nursery school children. *Child Development, 55*(5), 1946–1957. https://doi.org/10.2307/1129941

Baio, J., Wiggins, L., Christensen, D. L., Maenner, M. J., Daniels, J., Warren, Z., Kurzius-Spencer, M., Zahorodny, W., Robinson Rosenberg, C., White, T.,

Durkin, M. S., Imm, P., Nikolaou, L., Yeargin-Allsopp, M., Lee, L. C., Harrington, R., Lopez, M., Fitzgerald, R. T., Hewitt, A., . . . Dowling, N. F. (2018). Prevalence of autism spectrum disorder among children aged 8 years— Autism and Developmental Disabilities Monitoring Network, 11 Sites, United States, 2014. *MMWR Surveillance Summaries, 67*(6), 1–23. https://doi.org/ 10.15585/mmwr.ss6706a1

Bajaj, S., Alkozei, A., Dailey, N. S., & Killgore, W. D. S. (2017). Brain aging: Uncovering cortical characteristics of healthy aging in young adults. *Frontiers in Aging Neuroscience, 9*, 412. https://doi.org/10.3389/fnagi.2017.00412

Balcells Riba, M. (1999). Aportación de John Hughlings Jackson al conocimiento de la epilepsia [Contribution of John Hughlings Jackson to the understanding of epilepsy]. *Neurologia (Barcelona, Spain), 14*(1), 23–28.

Baldo, J. V., Kacinik, N. A., Moncrief, A., Beghin, F., & Dronkers, N. F. (2016). You may now kiss the bride: Interpretation of social situations by individuals with right or left hemisphere injury. *Neuropsychologia, 80*, 133–141. https://doi.org/ 10.1016/j.neuropsychologia.2015.11.001

Banich, M. T., & Brown, W. S. (2000). A life-span perspective on interaction between the cerebral hemispheres. *Developmental Neuropsychology, 18*(1), 1–10. https://doi.org/10.1207/S15326942DN1801_1

Bariaud, F. (1989). Age differences in children's humor. *Journal of Children in Contemporary Society, 20*(1–2), 15–45. https://doi.org/10.1300/J274v20n01_03

Baron-Cohen, S. (1990). Autism: A specific cognitive disorder of mind-blindness. *International Review of Psychiatry, 2*(1), 81–90. https://doi.org/10.3109/ 09540269009028274

Baron-Cohen, S. (2009). Autism: The empathizing-systemizing (E-S) theory. *Annals of the New York Academy of Sciences, 1156*(1), 68–80. https://doi.org/ 10.1111/j.1749-6632.2009.04467.x

Baron-Cohen, S., Jolliffe, T., Mortimore, C., & Robertson, M. (1997). Another advanced test of theory of mind: Evidence from very high functioning adults with autism or Asperger syndrome. *Journal of Child Psychology and Psychiatry, and Allied Disciplines, 38*(7), 813–822. https://doi.org/10.1111/j.1469-7610.1997. tb01599.x

Baron-Cohen, S., Leslie, A., & Frith, U. (1985). Does the autistic child have a theory of mind? *Cognition, 21*(1), 37–46. https://doi.org/10.1016/0010- 0277(85)90022-8

Baron-Cohen, S., Wheelwright, S., Hill, J., Raste, Y., & Plumb, I. (2001). The "Reading the Mind in the Eyes" test revised version: A study with normal adults, and adults with Asperger syndrome or high-functioning autism. *Journal of Child Psychology and Psychiatry, and Allied Disciplines, 42*(2), 241–251. https:// doi.org/10.1111/1469-7610.00715

Barrett, L. F. (2017). *How emotions are made: The secret life of the brain.* Houghton Mifflin Harcourt.

Barrett, L. F., & Satpute, A. B. (2017). Historical pitfalls and new directions in the neuroscience of emotion. *Neuroscience Letters, 693*, 9–18. https://doi.org/ 10.1016/j.neulet.2017.07.045

Bartolo, A., Benuzzi, F., Nocetti, L., Baraldi, P., & Nichelli, P. (2006). Humor comprehension and appreciation: An FMRI study. *Journal of Cognitive Neuro- science, 18*, 1789–1798. https://doi.org/10.1162/jocn.2006.18.11.1789

Bateson, P. (2005). The role of play in the evolution of great apes and humans. In A. D. Pellegrini & P. K. Smith (Eds.), *The nature of play: Great apes and humans* (pp. 13–24). Guilford Press.

Bateson, P., & Martin, P. (2013). *Play, playfulness, creativity and innovation.* Cambridge University Press. https://doi.org/10.1017/CBO9781139057691

Baughman, H. M., Giammarco, E. A., Veselka, L., Schermer, J. A., Martin, N. G., Lynskey, M., & Vernon, P. A. (2012). A behavioral genetic study of humor styles in an Australian sample. *Twin Research and Human Genetics, 15*(5), 663–667. https://doi.org/10.1017/thg.2012.23

Bayer, K. E., Neeb, L., Bayer, A., Wiese, J. J., Siegmund, B., & Prüß, M. S. (2019). Reduction of intra-abdominal pain through transcranial direct current stimulation. *Medicine, 98*(39), e17017. Advance online publication. https://doi.org/10.1097/MD.0000000000017017

Béal, C., & Mullan, K. (2017). The pragmatics of conversational humour in social visits: French and Australian English. *Language & Communication, 55,* 24–40. https://doi.org/10.1016/j.langcom.2016.09.004

Bear, M. F., Connors, B. W., & Paradiso, M. A. (2001). *Neuroscience: Exploring the brain.* Lippincott.

Beard, M. (2014). *Laughter in ancient Rome: On joking, tickling, and cracking up.* University of California Press.

Beaumont, J. G. (1982). *Divided visual field studies of cerebral organisation.* Academic Press.

Bega, D., Palmentera, P., Wagner, A., Hovde, M., Barish, B., Kwasny, M. J., & Simuni, T. (2017). Laughter is the best medicine: The Second City improvisation as an intervention for Parkinson's disease. *Parkinsonism & Related Disorders, 34,* 62–65. https://doi.org/10.1016/j.parkreldis.2016.11.001

Bekinschtein, T. A., Davis, M. H., Rodd, J. M., & Owen, A. M. (2011). Why clowns taste funny: The relationship between humor and semantic ambiguity. *The Journal of Neuroscience: The Official Journal of the Society for Neuroscience, 31*(26), 9665–9671. https://doi.org/10.1523/JNEUROSCI.5058-10.2011

Ben-Haim, S., & Falowski, S. M. (2018). Evaluation of patient perspectives toward awake, frame-based deep-brain stimulation surgery. *World Neurosurgery, 111,* e601–e607. https://doi.org/10.1016/j.wneu.2017.12.122

Benke, T., Bösch, S., & Andree, B. (1998). A study of emotional processing in Parkinson's disease. *Brain and Cognition, 38*(1), 36–52. https://doi.org/10.1006/brcg.1998.1013

Bennett, M. P., Zeller, J. M., Rosenberg, L., & McCann, J. (2003). The effect of mirthful laughter on stress and natural killer cell activity. *Alternative Therapies in Health and Medicine, 9*(2), 38–45.

Berger, A. A. (1993). *An anatomy of humor.* Transaction.

Berger, P., Bitsch, F., Nagels, A., Straube, B., & Falkenberg, I. (2018a). Frontal hypoactivation and alterations in the reward-system during humor processing in patients with schizophrenia spectrum disorders. *Schizophrenia Research, 202,* 149–157. Advance online publication. https://doi.org/10.1016/j.schres.2018.06.053

Berger, P., Bitsch, F., Nagels, A., Straube, B., & Falkenberg, I. (2018b). Personality modulates amygdala and insula connectivity during humor appreciation: An event-related fMRI study. *Social Neuroscience, 13*(6), 756–768. https://doi.org/10.1080/17470919.2017.1403375

Bergson, H. (1911). *Laughter: An essay on the meaning of the comic.* Macmillan. https://doi.org/10.1037/13772-000

Berk, L. (2017). *Child development* (7th ed.). Pearson.

Berk, L. S., Felten, D. L., Tan, S. A., Bittman, B. B., & Westengard, J. (2001). Modulation of neuroimmune parameters during the eustress of humor-associated mirthful laughter. *The Alternative Therapies in Health and Medicine, 7*(2), 62–72, 74–76.

Berk, L. S., Tan, S. A., Eby, W. C., Carmona, M., & Vorce, D. (1984). Modulation of human natural killer cells by catecholamines. *Clinical Research, 32,* 38A.

Berk, L. S., Tan, S. A., Fry, W. F., Jr., Napier, B. J., Lee, J. W., Hubbard, R. W., Lewis, J. E., & Eby, W. C. (1989). Neuroendocrine and stress hormone changes during mirthful laughter. *The American Journal of the Medical Sciences, 298*(6), 390–396. https://doi.org/10.1097/00000441-198912000-00006

Berk, L. S., Tan, S. A., Napier, B. J., & Eby, W. C. (1989). Eustress of mirthful laughter modifies natural killer cell activity. *Clinical Research, 37,* 115A.

Berk, L. S., Tan, S. A., Nehlsen-Cannarella, S., Napier, B. J., Lewis, J. E., Lee, J. W., & Eby, W. C. (1988). Humor associated laughter decreases cortisol and increases spontaneous lymphocyte blastogenesis. *Clinical Research, 36,* 435A.

Berridge, K. C., & Kringelbach, M. L. (2015). Pleasure systems in the brain. *Neuron, 86*(3), 646–664. https://doi.org/10.1016/j.neuron.2015.02.018

BESA. (n.d.). *BESA research 7.0: Overview.* Retrieved May 8, 2019 from http://www.besa.de/products/besa-research/besa-research-overview/

Bever, T. G. (1968). Associations to stimulus-response theories of language. In T. R. Dixon & D. L. Horton (Eds.), *Verbal behavior and general behavior theory* (pp. 418–494). Prentice Hall.

Bibby, H., & McDonald, S. (2005). Theory of mind after traumatic brain injury. *Neuropsychologia, 43*(1), 99–114. https://doi.org/10.1016/j.neuropsychologia.2004.04.027

Bigelow, H. J. (1850). Dr. Harlow's case of recovery from the passage of an iron bar through the head. *American Journal of the Medical Sciences, 20,* 13–22.

Bihrle, A. M., Brownell, H. H., Powelson, J. A., & Gardner, H. (1986). Comprehension of humorous and nonhumorous materials by left and right brain-damaged patients. *Brain and Cognition, 5*(4), 399–411. https://doi.org/10.1016/0278-2626(86)90042-4

Billig, M. (2005). *Laughter and ridicule: Towards a social critique of humor.* Sage.

Bischetti, L., Ceccato, I., Lecce, S., Cavallini, E., & Bambini, V. (2019). Pragmatics and theory of mind in older adults' humor comprehension. *Current Psychology.* Advance online publication. https://doi.org/10.1007/s12144-019-00295-w

Bitterly, T. B., Brooks, A. W., & Schweitzer, M. E. (2017). Risky business: When humor increases and decreases status. *Journal of Personality and Social Psychology, 112*(3), 431–455. https://doi.org/10.1037/pspi0000079

Bizi, S., Keinan, G., & Beit-Hallahmi, B. (1988). Humor and coping with stress: A test under real-life conditions. *Personality and Individual Differences, 9*(6), 951–956. https://doi.org/10.1016/0191-8869(88)90128-6

Black, D. W. (1982). Pathological laughter. *Journal of Nervous and Mental Disease, 170*(2), 67–71. https://doi.org/10.1097/00005053-198202000-00001

Black, D. W. (1984). Laughter. *JAMA, 252*(21), 2995–2998. https://doi.org/10.1001/jama.1984.03350210043027

Blakemore, S. J. (2012). Imaging brain development: The adolescent brain. *NeuroImage, 61*(2), 397–406. https://doi.org/10.1016/j.neuroimage.2011.11.080

Blakemore, S. J., Wolpert, D. M., & Frith, C. D. (1998). Central cancellation of self-produced tickle sensation. *Nature Neuroscience, 1*(7), 635–640.

Bod, R. (2014). *A new history of the humanities: The search for principles and patterns from antiquity to the present.* Oxford University Press.

Bodden, M. E., Mollenhauer, B., Trenkwalder, C., Cabanel, N., Eggert, K. M., Unger, M. M., Oertel, W. H., Kessler, J., Dodel, R., & Kalbe, E. (2010). Affective and cognitive theory of mind in patients with Parkinson's disease. *Parkinsonism & Related Disorders, 16,* 466–470. https://doi.org/10.1016/j.parkreldis.2010.04.014

Bopp, K. L., & Verhaeghen, P. (2005). Aging and verbal memory span: A meta-analysis. *The Journals of Gerontology. Series B, Psychological Sciences and Social Sciences, 60*(5), 223–233. https://doi.org/10.1093/geronb/60.5.P223

Bora, E., Velakoulis, D., & Walterfang, M. (2016). Social cognition in Huntington's disease: A meta-analysis. *Behavioural Brain Research, 297,* 131–140. https://doi.org/10.1016/j.bbr.2015.10.001

Boring, E. G. (1957). *A history of experimental psychology.* Prentice Hall.

Bosacki, S. L. (2013). A longitudinal study of children's theory of mind, self-concept, and perceptions of humor in self and other. *Social Behavior and Personality, 41*(4), 663–673. https://doi.org/10.2224/sbp.2013.41.4.663

Bourne, V. J. (2006). The divided visual field paradigm: Methodological considerations. *Laterality, 11*(4), 373–393. https://doi.org/10.1080/13576500600633982

Bowker, J. C., & Etkin, R. G. (2014). Does humor explain why relationally aggressive adolescents are popular? *Journal of Youth and Adolescence, 43*(8), 1322–1332. https://doi.org/10.1007/s10964-013-0031-5

Boyd, R., & McGuire, F. (1996). The efficacy of humor in improving psychological well-being of residents of long-term care facilities. *Journal of Leisurability, 23,* 1–15.

Boyle, G. J., & Joss-Reid, J. M. (2004). Relationship of humour to health: A psychometric investigation. *British Journal of Health Psychology, 9*(1), 51–66. https://doi.org/10.1348/135910704322778722

Brackett, C. W. (1933). Laughing and crying of preschool children. *Journal of Experimental Education, 2*(2), 119–126. https://doi.org/10.1080/00220973.1933.11009932

Branney, P., Witty, K., Braybrook, D., Bullen, K., White, A., & Eardley, I. (2014). Masculinities, humour and care for penile cancer: A qualitative study. *Journal of Advanced Nursing, 70*(9), 2051–2060. https://doi.org/10.1111/jan.12363

Braun, C. M., Lussier, F., Baribeau, J. M., & Ethier, M. (1989). Does severe traumatic closed head injury impair sense of humour? *Brain Injury, 3*(4), 345–354. https://doi.org/10.3109/02699058909004559

Bressler, E. R., & Balshine, S. (2006). The influence of humor on desirability. *Evolution and Human Behavior, 27*(1), 29–39. https://doi.org/10.1016/j.evolhumbehav.2005.06.002

Bressler, E. R., Martin, R. A., & Balshine, S. (2006). Production and appreciation of humor as sexually selected traits. *Evolution and Human Behavior, 27*(2), 121–130. https://doi.org/10.1016/j.evolhumbehav.2005.09.001

Bressler, S. L., & Menon, V. (2010). Large-scale brain networks in cognition: Emerging methods and principles. *Trends in Cognitive Sciences, 14*(6), 277–290. https://doi.org/10.1016/j.tics.2010.04.004

Brighina, F., Curatolo, M., Cosentino, G., De Tommaso, M., Battaglia, G., Sarzi-Puttini, P. C., Guggino, G., & Fierro, B. (2019). Brain modulation by electric currents in fibromyalgia: A structured review on non-invasive approach with transcranial electrical stimulation. *Frontiers in Human Neuroscience, 13*, 40. https://doi.org/10.3389/fnhum.2019.00040

Brodaty, H., Low, L.-F., Liu, Z., Fletcher, J., Roast, J., Goodenough, B., & Chenoweth, L. (2014). Successful ingredients in the SMILE study: Resident, staff, and management factors influence the effects of humor therapy in residential aged care. *The American Journal of Geriatric Psychiatry, 22*(12), 1427–1437. https://doi.org/10.1016/j.jagp.2013.08.005

Brodmann, K. (1909). *Vergleichende Lokalisationslehre der Grosshirnrinde* [Comparative localization theory of the cerebral cortex]. Johann Ambrosius Barth.

Brodzinsky, D. M., & Rubien, J. (1976). Humor production as a function of sex of subject, creativity, and cartoon content. *Journal of Consulting and Clinical Psychology, 44*(4), 597–600. https://doi.org/10.1037/0022-006X.44.4.597

Brooks, B. R., Crumpacker, D., Fellus, J., Kantor, D., & Kaye, R. E. (2013). PRISM: A novel research tool to assess the prevalence of pseudobulbar affect symptoms across neurological conditions. *PLOS ONE, 8*(8), e72232. Advance online publication. https://doi.org/10.1371/journal.pone.0072232

Brown, M., & Kuperberg, G. R. (2015). A hierarchical generative framework of language processing: Linking language perception, interpretation, and production abnormalities in schizophrenia. *Frontiers in Human Neuroscience, 9*, 643. https://doi.org/10.3389/fnhum.2015.00643

Brown, W. S., Paul, L. K., Symington, M., & Dietrich, R. (2005). Comprehension of humor in primary agenesis of the corpus callosum. *Neuropsychologia, 43*(6), 906–916. https://doi.org/10.1016/j.neuropsychologia.2004.09.008

Brownell, H. H., Michel, D., Powelson, J., & Gardner, H. (1983). Surprise but not coherence: Sensitivity to verbal humor in right-hemisphere patients. *Brain and Language, 18*(1), 20–27. https://doi.org/10.1016/0093-934X(83)90002-0

Brownell, H. H., & Stringfellow, A. (2000). Cognitive perspectives on humor comprehension after brain injury. In L. T. Connor & L. K. Obler (Eds.), *Neurobehavior of language and cognition: Studies of normal aging and brain damage* (pp. 241–258). Kluwer Academic.

Bruehl, S., Carlson, C. R., & McCubbin, J. A. (1993). Two brief interventions for acute pain. *Pain, 54*(1), 29–36. https://doi.org/10.1016/0304-3959(93)90096-8

Brunyé, T. T., Hussey, E. K., Fontes, E. B., & Ward, N. (2019). Modulating applied task performance via transcranial electrical stimulation. *Frontiers in Human Neuroscience, 13*, 140. https://doi.org/10.3389/fnhum.2019.00140

Bryant, J., Brown, D., & Parks, S. L. (1981). Ridicule as an educational corrective. *Journal of Educational Psychology, 73*(5), 722–727. https://doi.org/10.1037/0022-0663.73.5.722

Buckner, R. L. (1998). Event-related fMRI and the hemodynamic response. *Human Brain Mapping, 6*, 373–377. https://doi.org/10.1002/(SICI)1097-0193(1998)6:5/6<373::AID-HBM8>3.0.CO;2-P

Bucur, M., & Papagno, C. (2019). Are transcranial brain stimulation effects long-lasting in post-stroke aphasia? A comparative systematic review and meta-analysis on naming performance. *Neuroscience and Biobehavioral Reviews, 102*, 264–289. https://doi.org/10.1016/j.neubiorev.2019.04.019

Burghardt, G. M. (2005). *The genesis of animal play*. MIT Press. https://doi.org/10.7551/mitpress/3229.001.0001

Burke, D. M., & MacKay, D. G. (1997). Memory, language, and ageing. *Philosophical Transactions of the Royal Society of London. Series B, Biological Sciences, 352*, 1845–1856. https://doi.org/10.1098/rstb.1997.0170

Burke, D. M., MacKay, D. G., & James, L. E. (2000). Theoretical approaches to language and aging. In T. Perfect & E. Maylor (Eds.), *Models of cognitive aging* (pp. 204–237). Oxford University Press.

Burke, D. M., MacKay, D. G., Worthley, J. S., & Wade, E. (1991). On the tip of the tongue: What causes word finding failures in young and older adults? *Journal of Memory and Language, 30*(5), 542–579. https://doi.org/10.1016/0749-596X (91)90026-G

Burling, R., Armstrong, D. F., Blount, B. G., Callaghan, C. A., Foster, M. L., King, B. J., Parker, S. T., Sakura, O., Stokoe, W. C., Wallace, R., Wallman, J., Whiten, A., Wilcox, S., & Wynn, T. (1993). Primate calls, human language, and nonverbal communication. *Current Anthropology, 34*(1), 25–53. https://doi.org/10.1086/ 204132

Burns, A., & Iliffe, S. (2009). Dementia. *BMJ, 338*, b75. https://doi.org/10.1136/ bmj.b75

Buss, D. M. (2003). *The evolution of desire: Strategies of human mating.* Basic Books.

Buss, D. M. (2016). *Evolutionary psychology: The new science of mind.* Routledge.

Buss, D. M., & Schmitt, D. P. (1993). Sexual strategies theory: An evolutionary perspective on human mating. *Psychological Review, 100*(2), 204–232. https:// doi.org/10.1037/0033-295X.100.2.204

Butovskaya, M. L., & Kozintsev, A. G. (1996). A neglected form of quasi-aggression in apes: Possible relevance for the origins of humor. *Current Anthropology, 37*(4), 716–717. https://doi.org/10.1086/204548

Butzer, B., & Kuiper, N. A. (2008). Humor use in romantic relationships: The effects of relationship satisfaction and pleasant versus conflict situations. *The Journal of Psychology, 142*(3), 245–260. https://doi.org/10.3200/JRLP.142.3.245-260

Cai, C., Yu, L., Rong, L., & Zhong, H. (2014). Effectiveness of humor intervention for patients with schizophrenia: A randomized controlled trial. *Journal of Psychiatric Research, 59*, 174–178. https://doi.org/10.1016/j.jpsychires.2014.09.010

Campbell, D. W., Wallace, M. G., Modirrousta, M., Polimeni, J. O., McKeen, N. A., & Reiss, J. P. (2015). The neural basis of humour comprehension and humour appreciation: The roles of the temporoparietal junction and superior frontal gyrus. *Neuropsychologia, 79*(Part A), 10–20. https://doi.org/10.1016/ j.neuropsychologia.2015.10.013

Campbell, L., Martin, R. A., & Ward, J. R. (2008). An observational study of humor use while resolving conflict in dating couples. *Personal Relationships, 15*(1), 41–55.

Cancer Research UK. (2016, January 12). *Diagram showing the lobes of the brain.* Wikimedia Commons. https://commons.wikimedia.org/wiki/File:Diagram_showing_ the_lobes_of_the_brain_CRUK_308.svg

Cann, A., & Calhoun, L. G. (2001). Perceived personality associations with differences in sense of humor: Stereotypes of hypothetical others with high or low senses of humor. *Humor: International Journal of Humor Research, 14*, 117–130. https://doi.org/10.1515/humr.14.2.117

Cantor, J. R. (1976). What is funny to whom? The role of gender. *Journal of Communication, 26*(3), 164–172. https://doi.org/10.1111/j.1460-2466.1976. tb01920.x

Cao, B., Li, Y., Li, F., & Li, H. (2012). Electrophysiological difference between mental state decoding and mental state reasoning. *Brain Research, 1464*, 53–60. https://doi.org/10.1016/j.brainres.2012.05.009

Caramazza, A., & Hillis, A. E. (1991). Lexical organization of nouns and verbs in the brain. *Nature, 349*(6312), 788–790. https://doi.org/10.1038/349788a0

Carlson, K. A. (2011). The impact of humor on memory: Is the humor effect about humor? *Humor: International Journal of Humor Research, 24*(1), 21–41. https://doi.org/10.1515/humr.2011.002

Carmody, R. N., Weintraub, G. S., & Wrangham, R. W. (2011). Energetic consequences of thermal and nonthermal food processing. *PNAS: Proceedings of the National Academy of Sciences of the United States of America, 108,* 19199–19203. https://doi.org/10.1073/pnas.1112128108

Carmody, R. N., & Wrangham, R. W. (2009). The energetic significance of cooking. *Journal of Human Evolution, 57,* 379–391. https://doi.org/10.1016/j.jhevol.2009.02.011

Caron, J. E. (2002). From ethology to aesthetics: Evolution as a theoretical paradigm for research on laughter, humor, and other comic phenomena. *Humor: International Journal of Humor Research, 15*(3), 245–281. https://doi.org/10.1515/humr.2002.015

Caronna, E. B., Milunsky, J. M., & Tager-Flusberg, H. (2008). Autism spectrum disorders: Clinical and research frontiers. *Archives of Disease in Childhood, 93*(6), 518–523. https://doi.org/10.1136/adc.2006.115337

Carretero-Dios, H., & Ruch, W. (2010). Humor appreciation and sensation seeking: Invariance of findings across culture and assessment instrument? *Humor: International Journal of Humor Research, 23*(4), 427–445. https://doi.org/10.1515/humr.2010.020

Carroll, J. L. (1990). The relationship between humor appreciation and perceived physical health. *Psychology: A Journal of Human Behavior, 27*(2), 34–37.

Carroll, J. L., & Shmidt, J. L., Jr. (1992). Correlation between humorous coping style and health. *Psychological Reports, 70*(2), 402. https://doi.org/10.2466/pr0.1992.70.2.402

Caruana, F., Avanzini, P., Gozzo, F., Francione, S., Cardinale, F., & Rizzolatti, G. (2015). Mirth and laughter elicited by electrical stimulation of the human anterior cingulate cortex. *Cortex, 71,* 323–331. https://doi.org/10.1016/j.cortex.2015.07.024

Caruana, F., Gozzo, F., Pelliccia, V., Cossu, M., & Avanzini, P. (2016). Smile and laughter elicited by electrical stimulation of the frontal operculum. *Neuropsychologia, 89,* 364–370. https://doi.org/10.1016/j.neuropsychologia.2016.07.001

Celso, B. G., Ebener, D. J., & Burkhead, E. J. (2003). Humor coping, health status, and life satisfaction among older adults residing in assisted living facilities. *Aging & Mental Health, 7*(6), 438–445. https://doi.org/10.1080/13607860310001594691

Cermak, L. S., Verfaellie, M., Letourneau, L., Blackford, S., Weiss, S., & Numan, B. (1989). Verbal and nonverbal right hemisphere processing by chronic alcoholics. *Alcoholism, Clinical and Experimental Research, 13*(5), 611–617. https://doi.org/10.1111/j.1530-0277.1989.tb00391.x

Cha, M. Y., & Hong, H. S. (2015). Effect and path analysis of laughter therapy on serotonin, depression and quality of life in middle-aged women. *Journal of Korean Academy of Nursing, 45*(2), 221–230. https://doi.org/10.4040/jkan.2015.45.2.221

Chakravarthy, V. S. (2019). *Demystifying the brain.* Springer. https://doi.org/10.1007/978-981-13-3320-0

Chan, Y.-C. (2016). Neural correlates of sex/gender differences in humor processing for different joke types. *Frontiers in Psychology, 7*, 536. https://doi.org/10.3389/fpsyg.2016.00536

Chan, Y.-C., Chen, H.-C., & Lavallee, J. (2013). The impact of gelotophobia, gelotophilia, and katagelasticism on creativity. *Humor: International Journal of Humor Research, 26*(4), 609–628. https://doi.org/10.1515/humor-2013-0037

Chan, Y.-C., Chou, T.-L., Chen, H.-C., & Liang, K.-C. (2012). Segregating the comprehension and elaboration processing of verbal jokes: An fMRI study. *NeuroImage, 61*, 899–906. https://doi.org/10.1016/j.neuroimage.2012.03.052

Chan, Y.-C., Chou, T.-L., Chen, H.-C., Yeh, Y.-C., Lavallee, J. P., Liang, K.-C., & Chang, K.-E. (2013). Towards a neural circuit model of verbal humor processing: An fMRI study of the neural substrates of incongruity detection and resolution. *NeuroImage, 66*, 169–176. https://doi.org/10.1016/j.neuroimage.2012.10.019

Chan, Y.-C., Hsu, W.-C., Liao, Y.-J., Chen, H.-C., Tu, C.-H., & Wu, C.-L. (2018). Appreciation of different styles of humor: An fMRI study. *Scientific Reports, 8*(1), 15649. https://doi.org/10.1038/s41598-018-33715-1

Chan, Y.-C., & Lavallee, J. P. (2015). Temporo-parietal and fronto-parietal lobe contributions to theory of mind and executive control: An fMRI study of verbal jokes. *Frontiers in Psychology, 6*, 1285. https://doi.org/10.3389/fpsyg.2015.01285

Chan, Y.-C., Liao, Y.-J., Tu, C.-H., & Chen, H.-C. (2016). Neural correlates of hostile jokes: Cognitive and motivational processes in humor appreciation. *Frontiers in Human Neuroscience, 10*, 527. https://doi.org/10.3389/fnhum.2016.00527

Chang, Y. D., Davis, M. P., Smith, J., & Gutgsell, T. (2016). Pseudobulbar affect or depression in dementia? *Journal of Pain and Symptom Management, 51*(5), 954–958. https://doi.org/10.1016/j.jpainsymman.2015.12.321

Chang, Y.-T., Ku, L.-C., & Chen, H.-C. (2018). Sex differences in humor processing: An event-related potential study. *Brain and Cognition, 120*, 34–42. https://doi.org/10.1016/j.bandc.2017.11.002

Chang, Y.-T., Ku, L.-C., Wu, C.-L., & Chen, H.-C. (2019). Event-related potential (ERP) evidence for the differential cognitive processing of semantic jokes and pun jokes. *Journal of Cognitive Psychology, 31*(2), 131–144. https://doi.org/10.1080/20445911.2019.1583241

Chapell, M., Batten, M., Brown, J., Gonzalez, E., Herquet, G., Massar, C., & Pedroche, B. (2002). Frequency of public laughter in relation to sex, age, ethnicity, and social context. *Perceptual and Motor Skills, 95*(3), 746. https://doi.org/10.2466/pms.2002.95.3.746

Chapman, A. J. (1973). Social facilitation of laughter in children. *Journal of Experimental Social Psychology, 9*(6), 528–541. https://doi.org/10.1016/0022-1031(73)90035-8

Chapman, A. J. (1975). Humorous laughter in children. *Journal of Personality and Social Psychology, 31*(1), 42–49. https://doi.org/10.1037/h0076235

Chapman, A. J. (1983). Humor and laughter in social interaction and some implications for humor research. In J. H. Goldstein & P. E. McGhee (Eds.), *Handbook of humor research* (pp. 135–158). Springer Verlag. https://doi.org/10.1007/978-1-4612-5572-7_7

Chapman, A. J., & Wright, D. S. (1976). Social enhancement of laughter: An experimental analysis of some companion variables. *Journal of Experimental Child Psychology, 21*, 201–218. https://doi.org/10.1016/0022-0965(76)90034-5

Chassagnon, S., Minotti, L., Kremer, S., Hoffmann, D., & Kahane, P. (2008). Somatosensory, motor, and reaching/grasping responses to direct electrical stimulation of the human cingulate motor areas. *Journal of Neurosurgery, 109*, 593–604. https://doi.org/10.3171/JNS/2008/109/10/0593

Cheang, H. S., & Pell, M. D. (2006). A study of humour and communicative intention following right hemisphere stroke. *Clinical Linguistics & Phonetics, 20*(6), 447–462. https://doi.org/10.1080/02699200500135684

Chen, F. F. (2008). What happens if we compare chopsticks with forks? The impact of making inappropriate comparisons in cross-cultural research. *Journal of Personality and Social Psychology, 95*(5), 1005–1018. https://doi.org/10.1037/a0013193

Chen, S. X., & Bond, M. H. (2010). Two languages, two personalities? Examining language effects on the expression of personality in a bilingual context. *Personality and Social Psychology Bulletin, 36*(11), 1514–1528.

Cherkas, L., Hochberg, F., MacGregor, A. J., Snieder, H., & Spector, T. D. (2000). Happy families: A twin study of humour. *Twin Research, 3*(1), 17–22. https://doi.org/10.1375/twin.3.1.17

Cherry, B. J., Adamson, M., Duclos, A., & Hellige, J. B. (2005). Aging and individual variation in interhemispheric collaboration and hemispheric asymmetry. *Aging, Neuropsychology, and Cognition, 12*(4), 316–339. https://doi.org/10.1080/17444128.2005.10367004

Chiarello, C. (1980). A house divided? Cognitive functioning with callosal agenesis. *Brain and Language, 11*(1), 128–158. https://doi.org/10.1016/0093-934X(80)90116-9

Chomsky, N. (1986). *Knowledge of language: Its nature, origin, and use.* Praeger.

Christensen, A. P., Silvia, P. J., Nusbaum, E. C., & Beaty, R. E. (2018). Clever people: Intelligence and humor production ability. *Psychology of Aesthetics, Creativity, and the Arts, 12*(2), 136–143. https://doi.org/10.1037/aca0000109

Cisneros, R. E., Alexanian, J., Begay, J., & Goldberg, M. (2006). The language of humor: Navajo. In L. Harper (Ed.), *Santa Barbara papers in linguistics, Vol. 18: Proceedings from the ninth workshop on American indigenous languages.* University of California.

Clark, A., Seidler, A., & Miller, M. (2001). Inverse association between sense of humor and coronary heart disease. *International Journal of Cardiology, 80*, 87–88. https://doi.org/10.1016/S0167-5273(01)00470-3

Clark, C. N., Nicholas, J. M., Gordon, E., Golden, H. L., Cohen, M. H., Woodward, F. J., Macpherson, K., Slattery, C. F., Mummery, C. J., Schott, J. M., Rohrer, J. D., & Warren, J. D. (2016). Altered sense of humor in dementia. *Journal of Alzheimer's Disease, 49*(1), 111–119. https://doi.org/10.3233/JAD-150413

Clark, C. N., Nicholas, J. M., Henley, S. M., Downey, L. E., Woollacott, I. O., Golden, H. L., Fletcher, P. D., Mummery, C. J., Schott, J. M., Rohrer, J. D., Crutch, S. J., & Warren, J. D. (2015). Humour processing in frontotemporal lobar degeneration: A behavioural and neuroanatomical analysis. *Cortex, 69*, 47–59. https://doi.org/10.1016/j.cortex.2015.03.024

Coenen, A., Fine, E., & Zayachkivska, O. (2014). Adolf Beck: A forgotten pioneer in electroencephalography. *Journal of the History of the Neurosciences, 23*(3), 276–286. https://doi.org/10.1080/0964704X.2013.867600

Cogan, R., Cogan, D., Waltz, W., & McCue, M. (1987). Effects of laughter and relaxation on discomfort thresholds. *Journal of Behavioral Medicine, 10*(2), 139–144. https://doi.org/10.1007/BF00846422

Cohen, B. H. (2013). *Explaining psychological statistics* (3rd ed.). John Wiley & Sons.

Coles, A. S., Kozak, K., & George, T. P. (2018). A review of brain stimulation methods to treat substance use disorders. *The American Journal on Addictions*, 27(2), 71–91. https://doi.org/10.1111/ajad.12674

Coles, M. G. H., & Rugg, M. D. (1995). Event-related brain potentials: An introduction. In M. D. Rugg & M. G. H. Coles (Eds.), *Oxford psychology series, No. 25. Electrophysiology of mind: Event-related brain potentials and cognition* (pp. 1–26). Oxford University Press.

Collins, A. M., & Loftus, E. F. (1975). A spreading activation theory of semantic processing. *Psychological Review*, 82, 407–428. https://doi.org/10.1037/0033-295X.82.6.407

Collins, A. M., & Quillian, M. R. (1969). Retrieval time from semantic memory. *Journal of Verbal Learning and Verbal Behavior*, 8(2), 240–247. https://doi.org/10.1016/S0022-5371(69)80069-1

Conner, T. S., & Silvia, P. J. (2015). Creative days: A daily diary study of emotion, personality, and everyday creativity. *Psychology of Aesthetics, Creativity, and the Arts*, 9(4), 463–470. https://doi.org/10.1037/aca0000022

Connolly, S. P. (2018, June 6). *Motor cortex two*. Wikimedia Commons. https://commons.wikimedia.org/wiki/File:Motor_Cortex_Two.jpg

Conway, J. R., Catmur, C., & Bird, G. (2019). Understanding individual differences in theory of mind via representation of minds, not mental states. *Psychonomic Bulletin & Review*, 26, 798–812. https://doi.org/10.3758/s13423-018-1559-x

Coolin, A., Fischer, A. L., Aßfalg, A., Thornton, W. L., & Loken, W. (2017). Decomposing false-belief performance across the life span. In J. A. Sommerville & J. Decety (Eds.), *Social cognition: Development across the life span* (pp. 280–302). Routledge/Taylor & Francis.

Cools, R., Gibbs, S. E., Miyakawa, A., Jagust, W., & D'Esposito, M. (2008). Working memory capacity predicts dopamine synthesis capacity in the human striatum. *Journal of Neuroscience*, 28(5), 1208–1212.

Corcoran, C. M., Keilp, J. G., Kayser, J., Klim, C., Butler, P. D., Bruder, G. E., Gur, R. C., & Javitt, D. C. (2015). Emotion recognition deficits as predictors of transition in individuals at clinical high risk for schizophrenia: A neurodevelopmental perspective. *Psychological Medicine*, 45(14), 2959–2973. https://doi.org/10.1017/S0033291715000902

Corcoran, R., Cahill, C., & Frith, C. D. (1997). The appreciation of visual jokes in people with schizophrenia: A study of "mentalizing" ability. *Schizophrenia Research*, 24(3), 319–327. https://doi.org/10.1016/S0920-9964(96)00117-X

Cordoni, G., & Palagi, E. (2011). Ontogenetic trajectories of chimpanzee social play: Similarities with humans. *PLoS ONE*, 6(11), e27344. Advance online publication. https://doi.org/10.1371/journal.pone.0027344

Cory, G. A., Jr. (2002). Reappraising MacLean's triune brain concept. In G. A. Cory, Jr., & R. Gardner, Jr. (Eds.), *The evolutionary neuroethology of Paul MacLean: Convergences and frontiers* (pp. 9–27). Praeger/Greenwood.

Coulson, S., & Kutas, M. (2001). Getting it: Human event-related brain response to jokes in good and poor comprehenders. *Neuroscience Letters*, 316, 71–74. https://doi.org/10.1016/S0304-3940(01)02387-4

Coulson, S., & Lovett, C. (2004). Handedness, hemispheric asymmetries, and joke comprehension. *Cognitive Brain Research*, 19, 275–288. https://doi.org/10.1016/j.cogbrainres.2003.11.015

Coulson, S., & Severens, E. (2007). Hemispheric asymmetry and pun comprehension: When cowboys have sore calves. *Brain and Language*, 100, 172–187. https://doi.org/10.1016/j.bandl.2005.08.009

Coulson, S., Urbach, T. P., & Kutas, M. (2006). Looking back: Joke comprehension and the space structuring model. *Humor: International Journal of Humor Research*, *19*(3), 229–250. https://doi.org/10.1515/HUMOR.2006.013

Coulson, S., & Williams, R. F. (2005). Hemispheric asymmetries and joke comprehension. *Neuropsychologia, 43*(1), 128–141. https://doi.org/10.1016/j.neuropsychologia.2004.03.015

Coulson, S., & Wu, Y. C. (2005). Right hemisphere activation of joke-related information: An event-related brain potential study. *Journal of Cognitive Neuroscience, 17*(3), 494–506. https://doi.org/10.1162/0898929053279568

Couratier, P., Corcia, P., Lautrette, G., Nicol, M., & Marin, B. (2017). ALS and frontotemporal dementia belong to a common disease spectrum. *Revue Neurologique, 173*(5), 273–279. https://doi.org/10.1016/j.neurol.2017.04.001

Cousins, N. (1985). Therapeutic value of laughter. *Integrative Psychiatry, 3*(2), 112.

Covey, E., & Carter, M. (Eds.). (2015). *Basic electrophysiological methods*. Oxford University Press.

Cowan, M. L., & Little, A. C. (2013). The attractiveness of humour types in personal advertisements: Affiliative and aggressive humour are differentially preferred in long-term versus short-term partners. *Journal of Evolutionary Psychology, 11*(4), 159–170. https://doi.org/10.1556/JEP.11.2013.4.1

Cowan, M. L., Watkins, C. D., Fraccaro, P. J., Feinberg, D. R., & Little, A. C. (2016). It's the way he tells them (and who is listening): Men's dominance is positively correlated with their preference for jokes told by dominant-sounding men. *Evolution and Human Behavior, 37*(2), 97–104. https://doi.org/10.1016/j.evolhumbehav.2015.09.002

Crabtree, J., & Green, M. J. (2016). Creative cognition and psychosis vulnerability: What's the difference? *Creativity Research Journal, 28*(1), 24–32. https://doi.org/10.1080/10400419.2015.1030305

Crawford, M. (1989). Humor in conversational context: Beyond biases in the study of gender and humor. In R. K. Unger (Ed.), *Representations: Social constructions of gender* (pp. 155–166). Baywood.

Crawford, M. (1992). Just kidding: Gender and conversational humor. In R. Barreca (Ed.), *New perspectives on women and comedy* (pp. 23–37). Gordon and Breach.

Crawford, M. (2003). Gender and humor in social context. *Journal of Pragmatics, 35*(9), 1413–1430. https://doi.org/10.1016/S0378-2166(02)00183-2

Crawford, M., & Gressley, D. (1991). Creativity, caring, and context: Women's and men's accounts of humor preferences and practices. *Psychology of Women Quarterly, 15*(2), 217–231. https://doi.org/10.1111/j.1471-6402.1991.tb00793.x

Crawford, S. A., & Caltabiano, N. J. (2011). Promoting emotional well-being through the use of humour. *The Journal of Positive Psychology, 6*(3), 237–252.

Crespi, C., Cerami, C., Dodich, A., Canessa, N., Arpone, M., Iannaccone, S., Corbo, M., Lunetta, C., Scola, E., Falini, A., & Cappa, S. F. (2014). Microstructural white matter correlates of emotion recognition impairment in amyotrophic lateral sclerosis. *Cortex, 53*, 1–8. https://doi.org/10.1016/j.cortex.2014.01.002

Creusere, M. A. (2000). A developmental test of theoretical perspectives on the understanding of verbal irony: Children's recognition of allusion and pragmatic insincerity. *Metaphor and Symbol, 15*(1–2), 29–45. https://doi.org/10.1080/10926488.2000.9678863

Crowell, A. L., Riva-Posse, P., Holtzheimer, P. E., Garlow, S. J., Kelley, M. E., Gross, R. E., Denison, L., Quinn, S., & Mayberg, H. S. (2019). Long-term outcomes of subcallosal cingulate deep brain stimulation for treatment-resistant depression. *The American Journal of Psychiatry, 176*(11), 949–956. https://doi.org/10.1176/appi.ajp.2019.18121427

Cudaback, E., Cholerton, B. A., Montine, K. S., & Montine, T. J. (2015). Neuropathology, biomarkers, and cognition in Parkinson's disease. In A. I. Tröster (Ed.), *Clinical neuropsychology and cognitive neurology of Parkinson's disease and other movement disorders* (pp. 129–147). Oxford University Press.

Cunningham, W. A., & Derks, P. (2005). Humor appreciation and latency of comprehension. *Humor: International Journal of Humor Research, 18*(4), 389–403. https://doi.org/10.1515/humr.2005.18.4.389

Cure, S., Abrams, K., Belger, M., Dell'agnello, G., & Happich, M. (2014). Systematic literature review and meta-analysis of diagnostic test accuracy in Alzheimer's disease and other dementia using autopsy as standard of truth. *Journal of Alzheimer's Disease, 42*(1), 169–182. https://doi.org/10.3233/JAD-131559

Curran, W., McKeown, G. J., Rychlowska, M., André, E., Wagner, J., & Lingenfelser, F. (2018). Social context disambiguates the interpretation of laughter. *Frontiers in Psychology, 8*, 2342.

Curry, O. S., & Dunbar, R. I. M. (2013). Sharing a joke: The effects of a similar sense of humor on affiliation and altruism. *Evolution and Human Behavior, 34*(2), 125–129. https://doi.org/10.1016/j.evolhumbehav.2012.11.003

Dagge, M., & Hartje, W. (1985). Influence of contextual complexity on the processing of cartoons by patients with unilateral lesions. *Cortex, 21*(4), 607–616. https://doi.org/10.1016/S0010-9452(58)80008-8

Dai, R. H., Chen, H.-C., Chan, Y. C., Wu, C.-L, Li, P., Cho, S. L., & Hu, J.-F. (2017). To resolve or not to resolve, that is the question: The dual-path model of incongruity resolution and absurd verbal humor by fMRI. *Frontiers in Psychology, 8*, 498. https://doi.org/10.3389/fpsyg.2017.00498

Daniel, H. J., O'Brien, K. E., McCabe, R. B., & Quinter, V. E. (1985). Values in mate selection: A 1984 campus survey. *College Student Journal, 19*(1), 44–50.

Daren, A., Adamczyk, P., Błądziński, P., & Cechnicki, A. (2019). Humor perception in schizophrenia appears to be related to disorganization syndrome. *Comprehensive Psychiatry, 96*, 152149. https://doi.org/10.1016/j.comppsych.2019.152149

Dark, F. L., McGrath, J. J., & Ron, M. A. (1996). Pathological laughing and crying. *The Australian and New Zealand Journal of Psychiatry, 30*(4), 472–479. https://doi.org/10.3109/00048679609065020

Darwin, C. (2007). *The expression of the emotions in man and animals*. Filiquarian. (Original work published 1872)

Davila-Ross, M., Allcock, B., Thomas, C., & Bard, K. A. (2011). Aping expressions? Chimpanzees produce distinct laugh types when responding to laughter of others. *Emotion, 11*(5), 1013–1020. https://doi.org/10.1037/a0022594

Davila-Ross, M., Owren, M. J., & Zimmermann, E. (2009). Reconstructing the evolution of laughter in great apes and humans. *Current Biology, 19*(13), 1106–1111. https://doi.org/10.1016/j.cub.2009.05.028

de Beni, R., Borella, E., & Carretti, B. (2007). Reading comprehension in aging: The role of working memory and metacomprehension. *Aging, Neuropsychology, and Cognition, 14*(2), 189–212. https://doi.org/10.1080/13825580500229213

Deckers, L. (1993). On the validity of a weight-judging paradigm for the study of humor. *Humor: International Journal of Humor Research, 6*(1), 43–56. https://doi.org/10.1515/humr.1993.6.1.43

Deckers, L., Jenkins, S., & Gladfelter, E. (1977). Incongruity versus tension relief: Hypotheses of humor. *Motivation and Emotion, 1,* 261–272. https://doi.org/10.1007/BF00998864

Deckers, L., & Ruch, W. (1992). Sensation seeking and the situational humour response questionnaire (SHRQ): Its relationship in American and German samples. *Personality and Individual Differences, 13*(9), 1051–1054. https://doi.org/10.1016/0191-8869(92)90138-F

de Groot, A., Kaplan, J., Rosenblatt, E., Dews, S., & Winner, E. (1995). Understanding versus discriminating nonliteral utterances: Evidence for a dissociation. *Metaphor and Symbol, 10*(4), 255–273. https://doi.org/10.1207/s15327868ms1004_2

de Koning, E., & Weiss, R. L. (2002). The relational humor inventory: Functions of humor in close relationships. *The American Journal of Family Therapy, 30*(1), 1–18. https://doi.org/10.1080/019261802753455615

Demjén, Z. (2016). Laughing at cancer: Humour, empowerment, solidarity and coping online. *Journal of Pragmatics, 101,* 18–30. https://doi.org/10.1016/j.pragma.2016.05.010

de Renzi, E., Perani, D., Carlesimo, G. A., Silveri, M. C., & Fazio, F. (1994). Prosopagnosia can be associated with damage confined to the right hemisphere—An MRI and PET study and a review of the literature. *Neuropsychologia, 32*(8), 893–902. https://doi.org/10.1016/0028-3932(94)90041-8

Derks, P., Gillikin, L. S., Bartolome-Rull, D. S., & Bogart, E. H. (1997). Laughter and electroencephalographic activity. *Humor: International Journal of Humor Research, 10*(3), 285–300. https://doi.org/10.1515/humr.1997.10.3.285

Derks, P., Staley, R. E., & Haselton, M. G. (1998). "Sense" of humor: Perception, intelligence, or expertise? In W. Ruch (Ed.), *The sense of humor: Explorations of a personality characteristic* (pp. 143–158). Walter de Gruyter & Co. https://doi.org/10.1515/9783110804607.143

DeSantis, M., Mohan, P. J., & Steinhorst, R. K. (2005). Smiling in photographs: Childhood similarities between sexes become differences constant in adulthood. *Psychological Reports, 97*(2), 651–665. https://doi.org/10.2466/pr0.97.2.651-665

Devereux, P. G., & Ginsburg, G. P. (2001). Sociality effects on the production of laughter. *The Journal of General Psychology, 128,* 227–240. https://doi.org/10.1080/00221300109598910

Dewey, J. (1894). The theory of emotion: I. Emotional attitudes. *Psychological Review, 1,* 553–569. https://doi.org/10.1037/h0069054

de Witte, L., Verhoeven, J., Engelborghs, S., De Deyn, P. P., & Mariën, P. (2008). Crossed aphasia and visuo-spatial neglect following a right thalamic stroke: A case study and review of the literature. *Behavioural Neurology, 19*(4), 177–194. https://doi.org/10.1155/2008/905187

Dews, S., Winner, E., Kaplan, J., Rosenblatt, E., Hunt, M., Lim, K., McGovern, A., Qualter, A., & Smarsh, B. (1996). Children's understanding of the meaning and functions of verbal irony. *Child Development, 67*(6), 3071–3085. https://doi.org/10.2307/1131767

DeYoung, C. G., Quilty, L. C., Peterson, J. B., & Gray, J. R. (2014). Openness to experience, intellect, and cognitive ability. *Journal of Personality Assessment, 96*(1), 46–52. https://doi.org/10.1080/00223891.2013.806327

D'Hondt, F., Campanella, S., Kornreich, C., Philippot, P., & Maurage, P. (2014). Below and beyond the recognition of emotional facial expressions in alcohol dependence: From basic perception to social cognition. *Neuropsychiatric Disease and Treatment, 10,* 2177–2182. https://doi.org/10.2147/NDT.S74963

DiDonato, T. E., Bedminster, M. C., & Machel, J. J. (2013). My funny valentine: How humor styles affect romantic interest. *Personal Relationships, 20*(2), 374–390. https://doi.org/10.1111/j.1475-6811.2012.01410.x

DiFurio, D. (2019, October 28). Tens of thousands watch Allen woman stream her brain surgery on Facebook while awake. *Dallas Morning News.* https://www.dallasnews.com/business/health-care/2019/10/28/a-dallas-woman-is-streaming-her-brain-surgery-on-facebook-while-awake/

Dillon, K. M., Minchoff, B., & Baker, K. H. (1986). Positive emotional states and enhancement of the immune system. *International Journal of Psychiatry in Medicine, 15*(1), 13–18. https://doi.org/10.2190/R7FD-URN9-PQ7F-A6J7

Dillon, K. M., & Totten, M. C. (1989). Psychological factors, immunocompetence, and health of breast-feeding mothers and their infants. *The Journal of Genetic Psychology, 150*(2), 155–162. https://doi.org/10.1080/00221325.1989.9914587

Dionigi, A. (2016). Personality of clown doctors: An exploratory study. *Journal of Individual Differences, 37*(1), 49–55. https://doi.org/10.1027/1614-0001/a000187

Dirnberger, G., & Jahanshahi, M. (2013). Executive dysfunction in Parkinson's disease: A review. *Journal of Neuropsychology, 7*(2), 193–224. https://doi.org/10.1111/jnp.12028

Ditman, T., Goff, D., & Kuperberg, G. R. (2011). Slow and steady: Sustained effects of lexico-semantic associations can mediate referential impairments in schizophrenia. *Cognitive, Affective & Behavioral Neuroscience, 11*, 245–258. https://doi.org/10.3758/s13415-011-0020-7

Dittrich, L. (2017). *Patient HM: A story of memory, madness, and family secrets.* Random House.

Dixey, P., Seiler, J., Woodie, J. A., Grantham, C. H., & Carmon, M. C. (2008). Do cartoon stickers given after a hemoglobin finger stick influence preschoolers' pain perception? *Journal of Pediatric Health Care, 22*(6), 378–382. https://doi.org/10.1016/j.pedhc.2008.04.014

Dixon, N. E. (1980). Humor: A cognitive alternative to stress? In I. G. Sarason & C. D. Spielberger (Eds.), *Stress and anxiety* (Vol. 7, pp. 281–289). Hemisphere.

Djurisic, S., Rath, A., Gaber, S., Garattini, S., Bertele, V., Ngwabyt, S. N., Hivert, V., Neugebauer, E. A. M., Laville, M., Hiesmayr, M., Demotes-Mainard, J., Kubiak, C., Jakobsen, J. C., & Gluud, C. (2017). Barriers to the conduct of randomised clinical trials within all disease areas. *Trials, 18*(1), 360. https://doi.org/10.1186/s13063-017-2099-9

Docking, K., Jordan, F. M., & Murdoch, B. E. (1999). Interpretation and comprehension of linguistic humour by adolescents with head injury: A case-by-case analysis. *Brain Injury, 13*(12), 953–972. https://doi.org/10.1080/026990599120972

Dolcos, F., Rice, H. J., & Cabeza, R. (2002). Hemispheric asymmetry and aging: Right hemisphere decline or asymmetry reduction. *Neuroscience and Biobehavioral Reviews, 26*, 819–825. https://doi.org/10.1016/S0149-7634(02)00068-4

Donders, F. C. (1969). On the speed of mental processes. *Acta Psychologica: Attention and Performance II, 30*, 412–431. https://doi.org/10.1016/0001-6918(69)90065-1. (Original work published 1868)

Doosje, S., de Goede, M., van Doornen, L., & Goldstein, J. (2010). Measurement of occupational humorous coping. *Humor: International Journal of Humor Research, 23*(3), 275–305. https://doi.org/10.1515/humr.2010.013

Doosje, S., Landsheer, J. A., de Goede, M. P. M., & van Doornen, L. J. P. (2012). Humorous coping scales and their fit to a stress and coping framework. *Quality & Quantity: International Journal of Methodology, 46*(1), 267–279. https://doi.org/10.1007/s11135-010-9348-2

Du, X., Qin, Y., Tu, S., Yin, H., Wang, T., Yu, C., & Qiu, J. (2013). Differentiation of stages in joke comprehension: Evidence from an ERP study. *International Journal of Psychology, 48*(2), 149–157. https://doi.org/10.1080/00207594.2012.665162

Duchenne de Boulogne, G.-B. (1990). *The mechanism of human facial expression* (A. R. Cuthbertson, Trans.). Cambridge University Press. https://doi.org/10.1017/CBO9780511752841

Dulamea, A. O., Matei, C., Mindruta, I., & Ionescu, V. (2015). Pathological laughter as prodromal manifestation of transient ischemic attacks—Case report and brief review. *BMC Neurology, 15*, 196. https://doi.org/10.1186/s12883-015-0457-3

Dunbar, R. I. M. (1992). Neocortex size as a constraint on group size in primates. *Journal of Human Evolution, 22*(6), 469–493. https://doi.org/10.1016/0047-2484(92)90081-J

Dunbar, R. I. M. (1993). Coevolution of neocortical size, group size and language in humans. *Behavioral and Brain Sciences, 16*(4), 681–694.

Dunbar, R. I. M. (1996). *Grooming, gossip, and the evolution of language*. Faber and Faber.

Dunbar, R. I. M. (1998). The social brain hypothesis. *Evolutionary Anthropology, 6*, 178–190. https://doi.org/10.1002/(SICI)1520-6505(1998)6:5<178::AID-EVAN5>3.0.CO;2-8

Dunbar, R. I. M. (2017). Group size, vocal grooming and the origins of language. *Psychonomic Bulletin & Review, 24*(1), 209–212. https://doi.org/10.3758/s13423-016-1122-6

Dunbar, R. I. M., Baron, R., Frangou, A., Pearce, E., van Leeuwen, E. J. C., Stow, J., Partridge, G., MacDonald, I., Barra, V., & van Vugt, M. (2012). Social laughter is correlated with an elevated pain threshold. *Proceedings of the Royal Society B: Biological Sciences, 279*(1731), 1161–1167. https://doi.org/10.1098/rspb.2011.1373

Dunbar, R. I. M., & Shultz, S. (2007). Understanding primate brain evolution. *Philosophical Transactions of the Royal Society of London. Series B: Biological Sciences, 362*(1480), 649–658. https://doi.org/10.1098/rstb.2006.2001

Duncan, W. J., Smeltzer, L. R., & Leap, T. L. (1990). Humor and work: Applications of joking behavior to management. *Journal of Management, 16*(2), 255–278. https://doi.org/10.1177/014920639001600203

Dyck, K. H., & Holtzman, S. (2013). Understanding humor styles and well-being: The importance of social relationships and gender. *Personality and Individual Differences, 55*(1), 53–58. https://doi.org/10.1016/j.paid.2013.01.023

Ebert, S. (2015). Longitudinal relations between theory of mind and metacognition and the impact of language. *Journal of Cognition and Development, 16*(4), 559–586. https://doi.org/10.1080/15248372.2014.926272

Eddy, C. M., & Rickards, H. E. (2015). Theory of mind can be impaired prior to motor onset in Huntington's disease. *Neuropsychology, 29*(5), 792–798. https://doi.org/10.1037/neu0000190

Edwards, K. R., & Martin, R. A. (2010). Humor creation ability and mental health: Are funny people more psychologically healthy? *Europe's Journal of Psychology, 6*(3), 196–212. https://doi.org/10.5964/ejop.v6i3.213

Edwards, T. J., Sherr, E. H., Barkovich, A. J., & Richards, L. J. (2014). Clinical, genetic and imaging findings identify new causes for corpus callosum development syndromes. *Brain: A Journal of Neurology, 137*(6), 1579–1613. https://doi.org/10.1093/brain/awt358

Eig, J. (2005). *Luckiest man: The life and death of Lou Gehrig.* Simon & Schuster.

Ekman, P., Davidson, R. J., & Friesen, W. V. (1990). The Duchenne smile: Emotional expression and brain physiology. II. *Journal of Personality and Social Psychology, 58*(2), 342–353. https://doi.org/10.1037/0022-3514.58.2.342

Ekman, P., & Friesen, W. V. (1971). Constants across cultures in the face and emotion. *Journal of Personality and Social Psychology, 17,* 124–129. https://doi.org/10.1037/h0030377

Ekman, P., & Friesen, W. V. (1978). *Facial action coding system.* Consulting Psychologists Press.

Engelman, W., Hammond, F. M., & Malec, J. F. (2014). Diagnosing pseudobulbar affect in traumatic brain injury. *Neuropsychiatric Disease and Treatment, 10,* 1903–1910. https://doi.org/10.2147/NDT.S63304

Engelthaler, T., & Hills, T. T. (2018). Humor norms for 4,997 English words. *Behavior Research Methods, 50*(3), 1116–1124. https://doi.org/10.3758/s13428-017-0930-6

Epstein, S., & Smith, R. (1956). Repression and insight as related to reaction to cartoons. *Journal of Consulting Psychology, 20,* 391–395.

Erickson, J. M., Quinn, D. K., & Shorter, E. (2016). Moria revisited: Translation of Moritz Jastrowitz's description of pathologic giddiness. *The Journal of Neuropsychiatry and Clinical Neurosciences, 28*(2), 74–76. https://doi.org/10.1176/appi.neuropsych.15080205

Erickson, R. L., Paul, L. K., & Brown, W. S. (2014). Verbal learning and memory in agenesis of the corpus callosum. *Neuropsychologia, 60,* 121–130. https://doi.org/10.1016/j.neuropsychologia.2014.06.003

Eriksson, K. (2013). Autism-spectrum traits predict humor styles in the general population. *Humor: International Journal of Humor Research, 26*(3), 461–475. https://doi.org/10.1515/humor-2013-0030

Ervin, S. M. (1964). Language and TAT content in bilinguals. *Journal of Abnormal Psychology, 68,* 500–507. https://doi.org/10.1037/h0044803

Esseily, R., Rat-Fischer, L., Somogyi, E., O'Regan, K. J., & Fagard, J. (2016). Humour production may enhance observational learning of a new tool-use action in 18-month-old infants. *Cognition and Emotion, 30*(4), 817–825. https://doi.org/10.1080/02699931.2015.1036840

Evans, J. B., Slaughter, J. E., Ellis, A. P. J., & Rivin, J. M. (2019). Gender and the evaluation of humor at work. *Journal of Applied Psychology, 104*(8), 1077–1087. https://doi.org/10.1037/apl0000395

Fabrizi, M. S., & Pollio, H. R. (1987). A naturalistic study of humorous activity in a third, seventh, and eleventh grade classroom. *Merrill-Palmer Quarterly, 33*(1), 107–128. https://www.jstor.org/stable/23086149

Fagen, R. (1981). *Animal play behavior.* Oxford University Press.

Falkenberg, I., Jarmuzek, J., Bartels, M., & Wild, B. (2011). Do depressed patients lose their sense of humor? *Psychopathology, 44*(2), 98–105. https://doi.org/10.1159/000317778

Feinberg, T. E., & Farah, M. J. (2006). A historical perspective on cognitive neuroscience. In M. J. Farah & T. E. Feinberg (Eds.), *Patient based approaches to cognitive neuroscience* (2nd ed., 3–20). MIT Press.

Feingold, A. (1992). Gender differences in mate selection preferences: A test of the parental investment model. *Psychological Bulletin, 112*, 125–139. https://doi.org/10.1037/0033-2909.112.1.125

Feingold, A., & Mazzella, R. (1991). Psychometric intelligence and verbal humor ability. *Personality and Individual Differences, 12*(5), 427–435. https://doi.org/10.1016/0191-8869(91)90060-O

Feng, S., Ye, X., Mao, L., & Yue, X. (2014). The activation of theory of mind network differentiates between point-to-self and point-to-other verbal jokes: An fMRI study. *Neuroscience Letters, 564*, 32–36. https://doi.org/10.1016/j.neulet.2014.01.059

Feng, Y., Chan, Y., & Chen, H. (2014). Specialization of neural mechanisms underlying the three-stage model in humor processing: An ERP study. *Journal of Neurolinguistics, 32*, 59–70. https://doi.org/10.1016/j.jneuroling.2014.08.007

Ferguson, H. J., Cane, J. E., Douchkov, M., & Wright, D. (2015). Empathy predicts false belief reasoning ability: Evidence from the N400. *Social Cognitive and Affective Neuroscience, 10*(6), 848–855. https://doi.org/10.1093/scan/nsu131

Fernández-Baca Vaca, G., Lüders, H. O., Basha, M. M., & Miller, J. P. (2011). Mirth and laughter elicited during brain stimulation. *Epileptic Disorders, 13*(4), 435–440. https://doi.org/10.1684/epd.2011.0480

Ferreira, D., Verhagen, C., Hernández-Cabrera, J. A., Cavallin, L., Guo, C. J., Ekman, U., Muehlboeck, J. S., Simmons, A., Barroso, J., Wahlund, L. O., & Westman, E. (2017). Distinct subtypes of Alzheimer's disease based on patterns of brain atrophy: Longitudinal trajectories and clinical applications. *Scientific Reports, 7*, 46263. https://doi.org/10.1038/srep46263

Fiacconi, C. M., & Owen, A. M. (2015). Using psychophysiological measures to examine the temporal profile of verbal humor elicitation. *PLoS ONE, 10*(9), e0135902. Advance online publication. https://doi.org/10.1371/journal.pone.0135902

Filik, R., Leuthold, H., Wallington, K., & Page, J. (2014). Testing theories of irony processing using eye-tracking and ERPs. *Journal of Experimental Psychology: Learning, Memory, and Cognition, 40*(3), 811–828. https://doi.org/10.1037/a0035658

Finger, S. (2009). The birth of localization theory. In M. Aminoff, F. Boller, & D. Swaab (Eds.), *Handbook of clinical neurology: Vol. 95* (pp. 117–128). Elsevier. https://doi.org/10.1016/S0072-9752(08)02110-6

Fish, D. R., Gloor, P., Quesney, F. L., & Oliver, A. (1993). Clinical responses to electrical brain stimulation of the temporal and frontal lobes in patients with epilepsy. *Brain: A Journal of Neurology, 116*, 397–414. https://doi.org/10.1093/brain/116.2.397

Fisher, F., Philpott, A., Andrews, S. C., Maule, R., & Douglas, J. (2017). Characterizing social communication changes in amyotrophic lateral sclerosis. *International Journal of Language & Communication Disorders, 52*(2), 137–142. https://doi.org/10.1111/1460-6984.12267

Fisher, S., & Fisher, R. L. (1981). *Pretend the world is funny and forever: A psychological analysis of comedians, clowns, and actors.* Lawrence Erlbaum.

Fitzgerald, L. F., Shullman, S. L., Bailey, N., Richards, M., Swecker, J., Gold, Y., Ormerod, M., & Weitzman, L. (1988). The incidence and dimensions of sexual harassment in academia and the workplace. *Journal of Vocational Behavior, 32*(2), 152–175. https://doi.org/10.1016/0001-8791(88)90012-7

Flores-Pajot, M. C., Ofner, M., Do, M. T., Lavigne, E., & Villeneuve, P. J. (2016). Childhood autism spectrum disorders and exposure to nitrogen dioxide, and particulate matter air pollution: A review and meta-analysis. *Environmental Research, 151,* 763–776. https://doi.org/10.1016/j.envres.2016.07.030

Fogel, A., Dickson, K. L., Hsu, H.-C., Messinger, D., Nelson-Goens, G. C., & Nwokah, E. E. (1997). Communication of smiling and laughter in mother–infant play: Research on emotion from a dynamic systems perspective. In K. C. Barrett (Ed.), *The communication of emotion: Current research from diverse perspectives* (pp. 5–24). Jossey-Bass.

Fogel, A., Hsu, H. C., Shapiro, A. F., Nelson-Goens, G. C., & Secrist, C. (2006). Effects of normal and perturbed social play on the duration and amplitude of different types of infant smiles. *Developmental Psychology, 42*(3), 459–473. https://doi.org/10.1037/0012-1649.42.3.459

Foley, E., Matheis, R., & Schaefer, C. (2002). Effect of forced laughter on mood. *Psychological Reports, 90*(1), 184. https://doi.org/10.2466/pr0.2002.90.1.184

Fonseca-Azevedo, K., & Herculano-Houzel, S. (2012). Metabolic constraint imposes tradeoff between body size and number of brain neurons in human evolution. *PNAS: Proceedings of the National Academy of Sciences, 109*(45), 18571–18576.

Fontaine, J. R. J., Scherer, K. R., Roesch, E. B., & Ellsworth, P. C. (2007). The world of emotions is not two-dimensional. *Psychological Science, 18,* 1050–1057. https://doi.org/10.1111/j.1467-9280.2007.02024.x

Forabosco, G. (1998). The ill side of humor: Pathological conditions and sense of humor. In W. Ruch (Ed.), *The sense of humor: Explorations of a personality characteristic* (pp. 271–292). Walter de Gruyter. https://doi.org/10.1515/9783110804607.271

Forabosco, G., & Ruch, W. (1994). Sensation seeking, social attitudes and humor appreciation in Italy. *Personality and Individual Differences, 16*(4), 515–528. https://doi.org/10.1016/0191-8869(94)90179-1

Forabosco, G., Ruch, W., & Nucera, P. (2009). The fear of being laughed at among psychiatric patients. *Humor: International Journal of Humor Research, 22*(1–2), 233–251. https://doi.org/10.1515/HUMR.2009.011

Ford, C. V., & Spaulding, R. C. (1973). The Pueblo incident: A comparison of factors related to coping with extreme stress. *Archives of General Psychiatry, 29*(3), 340–343. https://doi.org/10.1001/archpsyc.1973.04200030038005

Ford, T. E., & Ferguson, M. A. (2004). Social consequences of disparagement humor: A prejudiced norm theory. *Personality and Social Psychology Review, 8*(1), 79–94. https://doi.org/10.1207/S15327957PSPR0801_4

Ford, T. E., Teeter, S. R., Richardson, K., & Woodzicka, J. A. (2017). Putting the brakes on prejudice rebound effects: An ironic effect of disparagement humor. *The Journal of Social Psychology, 157*(4), 458–473. https://doi.org/10.1080/00224545.2016.1229254

Ford, T. E., Woodzicka, J. A., Petit, W. E., Richardson, K., & Lappi, S. K. (2015). Sexist humor as a trigger of state self-objectification in women. *Humor: International Journal of Humor Research, 28*(2), 253–269. https://doi.org/10.1515/humor-2015-0018

Foster, P. S., Webster, D. G., & Williamson, J. (2002). The psychophysiological differentiation of actual, imagined, and recollected mirth. *Imagination, Cognition and Personality, 22*(2), 163–180. https://doi.org/10.2190/KL08-1P9C-K9BE-K8VA

Fox, C. L., Dean, S., & Lyford, K. (2013). Development of a Humor Styles Question-naire for children. *Humor: International Journal of Humor Research, 26*(2), 295–319. https://doi.org/10.1515/humor-2013-0018

Fox, C. L., Hunter, S. C., & Jones, S. E. (2016). Children's humor types and psychosocial adjustment. *Personality and Individual Differences, 89*, 86–91. https://doi.org/10.1016/j.paid.2015.09.047

Fox, E., Amaral, D., & Van de Water, J. (2012). Maternal and fetal antibrain anti-bodies in development and disease. *Developmental Neurobiology, 72*, 1327–1334. https://doi.org/10.1002/dneu.22052

Franklin, R. G., Jr., & Adams, R. B., Jr. (2011). The reward of a good joke: Neural correlates of viewing dynamic displays of stand-up comedy. *Cognitive, Affective & Behavioral Neuroscience, 11*(4), 508–515. https://doi.org/10.3758/s13415-011-0049-7

Freedman, D. G. (1964). Smiling in blind infants and the issue of innate vs. acquired. *Journal of Child Psychology and Psychiatry, 5*(3–4), 171–184. https://doi.org/10.1111/j.1469-7610.1964.tb02139.x

Freedman, M., & Stuss, D. T. (2011). Theory of mind in Parkinson's disease. *Journal of the Neurological Sciences, 310*(1–2), 225–227. https://doi.org/10.1016/j.jns.2011.06.004

Freiheit, S. R., Overholser, J. C., & Lehnert, K. L. (1998). The association between humor and depression in adolescent psychiatric inpatients and high school students. *Journal of Adolescent Research, 13*(1), 32–48. https://doi.org/10.1177/0743554898131003

Freud, S. (1928). Humour. *The International Journal of Psycho-Analysis, 9*, 1–6.

Freud, S. (1960). *Jokes and their relation to the unconscious.* Norton. (Original work published 1905)

Frewen, P., Brinker, J., Martin, R., & Dozois, D. (2008). Humor styles and personality-vulnerability to depression. *Humor: International Journal of Humor Research, 2*(21), 179–195.

Fried, I., Wilson, C. L., MacDonald, K. A., & Behnke, E. J. (1998). Electric current stimulates laughter. *Nature, 391*, 650. https://doi.org/10.1038/35536

Frith, C. D., & Frith, U. (1999, November). Interacting minds—A biological basis. *Science, 286*(5445), 1692–1695. https://doi.org/10.1126/science.286.5445.1692

Fritz, H. L., Russek, L. N., & Dillon, M. M. (2017). Humor use moderates the relation of stressful life events with psychological distress. *Personality and Social Psychology Bulletin, 43*(6), 845–859. https://doi.org/10.1177/0146167217699583

Fritz, N. E., Boileau, N. R., Stout, J. C., Ready, R., Perlmutter, J. S., Paulsen, J. S., Quaid, K., Barton, S., McCormack, M. K., Perlman, S. L., Carlozzi, N. E., (2018). Relationships among apathy, health-related quality of life, and func-tion in Huntington's disease. *The Journal of Neuropsychiatry and Clinical Neuro-sciences, 30*(3), 194–201. https://doi.org/10.1176/appi.neuropsych.17080173

Fry, P. S. (1995). Perfectionism, humor, and optimism as moderators of health outcomes and determinants of coping styles of women executives. *Genetic, Social, and General Psychology Monographs, 121*(2), 211–245.

Fry, W. F., Jr. (1992). The physiologic effects of humor, mirth, and laughter. *JAMA, 267*(13), 1857–1858. https://doi.org/10.1001/jama.267.13.1857

Fry, W. F., Jr. (1994). The biology of humor. *Humor: International Journal of Humor Research, 7*(2), 111–126. https://doi.org/10.1515/humr.1994.7.2.111

Fry, W. F., Jr., & Rader, C. (1977). The respiratory components of mirthful laughter. *Journal of Biological Psychology, 19*(2), 39–50.

Fry, W. F., Jr., & Savin, W. M. (1988). Mirthful laughter and blood pressure. *Humor: International Journal of Humor Research, 1*(1), 49–62. https://doi.org/10.1515/humr.1988.1.1.49

Fry, W. F., Jr., & Stoft, P. E. (1971). Mirth and oxygen saturation levels of peripheral blood. *Psychotherapy and Psychosomatics, 19*, 76–84. https://doi.org/10.1159/000286308

Furnham, A., Richards, S. C., & Paulhus, D. L. (2013). The Dark Triad of personality: A 10-year review. *Social and Personality Psychology Compass, 7*(3), 199–216. https://doi.org/10.1111/spc3.12018

Gaillard, F. (n.d.). *Neuroanatomy: Lateral cortex (diagrams)*. Radiopaedia.org. https://radiopaedia.org/cases/neuroanatomy-lateral-cortex-diagrams?lang=us

Gainotti, G. (2019). Emotions and the right hemisphere: Can new data clarify old models? *The Neuroscientist, 25*(3), 258–270. https://doi.org/10.1177/1073858418785342

Galhardoni, R., Correia, G. S., Araujo, H., Yeng, L. T., Fernandes, D. T., Kaziyama, H. H., Marcolin, M. A., Bouhassira, D., Teixeira, M. J., & de Andrade, D. C. (2015). Repetitive transcranial magnetic stimulation in chronic pain: A review of the literature. *Archives of Physical Medicine and Rehabilitation, 96*(4, Suppl.), 156–172. https://doi.org/10.1016/j.apmr.2014.11.010

Gallagher, R., Jens, K., & O'Donnell, K. (1983). The effect of physical status on the affective expression of handicapped infants. *Infant Behavior and Development, 6*(1), 73–77. https://doi.org/10.1016/S0163-6383(83)80009-5

Galloway, G. (2009). Humor and ad liking: Evidence that sensation seeking moderates the effects of incongruity-resolution humor. *Psychology and Marketing, 26*(9), 779–792. https://doi.org/10.1002/mar.20299

Galloway, G. (2010). Individual differences in personal humor styles: Identification of prominent patterns and their associates. *Personality and Individual Differences, 48*(5), 563–567. https://doi.org/10.1016/j.paid.2009.12.007

Galloway, G., & Chirico, D. (2008). Personality and humor appreciation: Evidence of an association between trait neuroticism and preferences for structural features of humor. *Humor: International Journal of Humor Research, 21*(2), 129–142. https://doi.org/10.1515/HUMOR.2008.006

Gambacorta, D., & Ketelaar, T. (2013). Dominance and deference: Men inhibit creative displays during mate competition when their competitor is strong. *Evolution and Human Behavior, 34*(5), 330–333. https://doi.org/10.1016/j.evolhumbehav.2013.05.003

Gamble, J. (2001). Humor in apes. *Humor: International Journal of Humor Research, 14*(2), 163–179. https://doi.org/10.1515/humr.14.2.163

Gardner, H., Ling, P. K., Flamm, L., & Silverman, J. (1975). Comprehension and appreciation of humorous material following brain damage. *Brain: A Journal of Neurology, 98*(3), 399–412. https://doi.org/10.1093/brain/98.3.399

Garey, L. J. (2006). *Brodmann's localisation in the cerebral cortex*. Springer.

Garfield, J. L., & Edelglass, W. (Eds.). (2011). *The Oxford handbook of world philosophy*. Oxford University Press.

Gascon, G. G., & Lombroso, C. T. (1971). Epileptic (gelastic) laughter. *Epilepsia, 12*, 63–76. https://doi.org/10.1111/j.1528-1157.1971.tb03916.x

Gaudreau, G., Monetta, L., Macoir, J., Laforce, R., Jr., Poulin, S., & Hudon, C. (2013). Verbal irony comprehension in older adults with amnestic mild cognitive impairment. *Neuropsychology, 27*(6), 702–712. https://doi.org/10.1037/a0034655

Gaudreau, G., Monetta, L., Macoir, J., Poulin, S., Laforce, R., Jr., & Hudon, C. (2015). Mental state inferences abilities contribution to verbal irony comprehension in older adults with mild cognitive impairment. *Behavioural Neurology, 2015,* 685613. Advance online publication. https://doi.org/10.1155/2015/685613

Gazzaniga, M. (1974). Cerebral dominance viewed as a decisions system. In S. Dimond & J. Beaumont (Eds.), *Hemisphere function in the human brain* (pp. 367–382). John Wiley & Sons.

Gazzaniga, M. (Ed.). (1984). *Handbook of cognitive neuroscience.* Plenum Press. https://doi.org/10.1007/978-1-4899-2177-2

Gazzaniga, M. S., Bogen, J. E., & Sperry, R. W. (1965). Observations on visual perception after disconnexion of the cerebral hemispheres in man. *Brain: A Journal of Neurology, 88,* 221–236. https://doi.org/10.1093/brain/88.2.221

Gazzaniga, M. S., Ivry, R. B., & Mangun, G. R. (2013). *Cognitive neuroscience: The biology of the mind* (4th ed.). W. W. Norton.

Geary, D. C. (2005). *The origin of mind: Evolution of brain, cognition, and general intelligence.* American Psychological Association. https://doi.org/10.1037/10871-000

Geary, D. C., & Flinn, M. V. (2002). Sex differences in behavioral and hormonal response to social threat: Commentary on Taylor et al. (2000). *Psychological Review, 109*(4), 745–750. https://doi.org/10.1037/0033-295X.109.4.745

Gelkopf, M., Kreitler, S., & Sigal, M. (1993). Laughter in a psychiatric ward. Somatic, emotional, social, and clinical influences on schizophrenic patients. *Journal of Nervous and Mental Disease, 181*(5), 283–289. https://doi.org/10.1097/00005053-199305000-00002

Gelkopf, M., & Sigal, M. (1995). It is not enough to have them laugh: Hostility, anger, and humor-coping in schizophrenic patients. *Humor: International Journal of Humor Research, 8*(3), 273–284. https://doi.org/10.1515/humr.1995.8.3.273

George, M. S., Nahas, Z., Kozel, F. A., Li, X., Denslow, S., Yamanaka, K., Mishory, A., Foust, M. J., & Bohning, D. E. (2002). Mechanisms and state of the art of transcranial magnetic stimulation. *The Journal of ECT, 18*(4), 170–181. https://doi.org/10.1097/00124509-200212000-00002

Gerber, W. S., & Routh, D. K. (1975). Humor response as related to violation of expectancies and to stimulus intensity in a weight-judgment task. *Perceptual and Motor Skills, 41*(2), 673–674. https://doi.org/10.2466/pms.1975.41.2.673

Gerra, G., Avanzini, P., Zaimovic, A., Sartori, R., Bocchi, C., Timpano, M., Zambelli, U., Delsignore, R., Gardini, F., Talarico, E., & Brambilla, F. (1999). Neurotransmitters, neuroendocrine correlates of sensation-seeking temperament in normal humans. *Neuropsychobiology, 39,* 207–213. https://doi.org/10.1159/000026586

Gervais, M., & Wilson, D. S. (2005). The evolution and functions of laughter and humor: A synthetic approach. *The Quarterly Review of Biology, 80*(4), 395–430. https://doi.org/10.1086/498281

Getlen, L. (2012, June 17). The man's man. *New York Post.* https://nypost.com/2012/06/17/the-mans-man/

Ghodsbin, F., Sharif Ahmadi, Z., Jahanbin, I., & Sharif, F. (2015). The effects of laughter therapy on general health of elderly people referring to Jahandidegan community center in Shiraz, Iran, 2014: A randomized controlled trial. *International Journal of Community Based Nursing and Midwifery, 3*(1), 31–38.

Gibson, L., Atchley, R. A., Voyer, D., Diener, U. S., & Gregersen, S. (2016). Detection of sarcastic speech: The role of the right hemisphere in ambiguity resolution. *Laterality, 21*(4–6), 549–567. https://doi.org/10.1080/1357650X.2015.1105246

Gibson, W. S., Cho, S., Abulseoud, O. A., Gorny, K. R., Felmlee, J. P., Welker, K. M., Klassen, B. T., Min, H. K., & Lee, K. H. (2017). The impact of mirth-inducing ventral striatal deep brain stimulation on functional and effective connectivity. *Cerebral Cortex, 27*(3), 2183–2194. https://doi.org/10.1093/cercor/bhw074

Gillikin, L. S., & Derks, P. L. (1991). Humor appreciation and mood in stroke patients. *Cognitive Rehabilitation, 9*(5), 30–35.

Girardi, A., MacPherson, S. E., & Abrahams, S. (2011). Deficits in emotional and social cognition in amyotrophic lateral sclerosis. *Neuropsychology, 25*(1), 53–65. https://doi.org/10.1037/a0020357

Giuliani, N. R., McRae, K., & Gross, J. J. (2008). The up- and down-regulation of amusement: Experiential, behavioral, and autonomic consequences. *Emotion, 8*(5), 714–719.

Glass, H. C., Shaw, G. M., Ma, C., & Sherr, E. H. (2008). Agenesis of the corpus callosum in California 1983–2003: A population-based study. *American Journal of Medical Genetics: Part A, 146A*, 2495–2500. https://doi.org/10.1002/ajmg.a.32418

Glenwright, M., Parackel, J. M., Cheung, K. R., & Nilsen, E. S. (2014). Intonation influences how children and adults interpret sarcasm. *Journal of Child Language, 41*(2), 472–484. https://doi.org/10.1017/S0305000912000773

Glickstein, M. (2014). *Neuroscience: A historical introduction.* MIT Press. https://doi.org/10.2307/j.ctt19qgfcm

Gockel, C., & Kerr, N. L. (2015). Put-down humor directed at outgroup members increases perceived—But not experienced—Cohesion in groups. *Humor: International Journal of Humor Research, 28*(2), 205–228. https://doi.org/10.1515/humor-2015-0020

Godkewitsch, M. (1974). Correlates of humor: Verbal and nonverbal aesthetic reactions as functions of semantic distance within adjective-noun pairs. In D. E. Berlyne (Ed.), *Studies in the new experimental aesthetics: Steps towards an objective psychology of aesthetic appreciation* (pp. 279–304). Hemisphere.

Godkewitsch, M. (1976). Physiological and verbal indices of arousal in rated humour. In A. J. Chapman & H. C. Foot (Eds.), *Humor and laughter: Theory, research, and applications* (pp. 117–138). John Wiley & Sons.

Goel, V., & Dolan, R. J. (2001). The functional anatomy of humor: Segregating cognitive and affective components. *Nature Neuroscience, 4*, 237–238. https://doi.org/10.1038/85076

Goertz, G. (2017). *Multimethod research, causal mechanisms, and case studies: An integrated approach.* Princeton University Press.

Goldberg, J., Sullivan, S. J., & Seaborne, D. E. (1992). The effect of two intensities of massage on H-reflex amplitude. *Physical Therapy, 72*(6), 449–457. https://doi.org/10.1093/ptj/72.6.449

Goldinger, S. D., Luce, P. A., & Pisoni, D. B. (1989). Priming lexical neighbors of spoken words: Effects of competition and inhibition. *Journal of Memory and Language, 28*(5), 501–518. https://doi.org/10.1016/0749-596X(89)90009-0

Goldstein, E. B. (2014). *Cognitive psychology: Connecting mind, research and everyday experience.* Cengage.

Goldstein, G., & Shelly, C. (1981). Does the right hemisphere age more rapidly than the left? *Journal of Clinical Neuropsychology, 3*(1), 65–78. https://doi.org/10.1080/01688638108403114

Goldstein, J. H. (1982). A laugh a day: Can mirth keep disease at bay? *The Sciences, 22*(6), 21–25. https://doi.org/10.1002/j.2326-1951.1982.tb02088.x

Goldstein, J. H., Harman, J., McGhee, P. E., & Karasik, R. (1975). Test of an information-processing model of humor: Physiological response changes during problem- and riddle-solving. *The Journal of General Psychology, 92*(1), 59–68. https://doi.org/10.1080/00221309.1975.9711328

Gomez, J.-C., & Martin-Andrade, B. (2005). Fantasy play in apes. In A. D. Pellegrini & P. K. Smith (Eds.), *The nature of play: Great apes and humans* (pp. 139–172). Guilford Press.

González-Forero, M., & Gardner, A. (2018). Inference of ecological and social drivers of human brain-size evolution. *Nature, 557*(7706), 554–557. https://doi.org/10.1038/s41586-018-0127-x

González Fuente, S., Prieto Vives, P., & Noveck, I. A. (2016, May 31–June 3). *A fine-grained analysis of the acoustic cues involved in verbal irony recognition in French* [Paper presentation]. Speech Prosody 2016, Boston, MA, United States.

Goodenough, B., & Ford, J. (2005). Self-reported use of humor by hospitalized pre-adolescent children to cope with pain-related distress from a medical intervention. *Humor: International Journal of Humor Research, 18*(3), 279–298. https://doi.org/10.1515/humr.2005.18.3.279

Goodenough, B., Low, L.-F., Casey, A.-N., Chenoweth, L., Fleming, R., Spitzer, P., Bell, J. P., & Brodaty, H. (2012). Study protocol for a randomized controlled trial of humor therapy in residential care: The Sydney Multisite Intervention of LaughterBosses and ElderClowns (SMILE). *International Psychogeriatrics, 24*(12), 2037–2044. https://doi.org/10.1017/S1041610212000683

Goodenough, E. L. (1932). Expression of the emotions in a blind-deaf child. *Journal of Abnormal and Social Psychology, 27*(3), 328–333. https://doi.org/10.1037/h0076099

Goodwin, R. (1990). Sex differences among partner preferences: Are the sexes really very similar? *Sex Roles, 23*, 501–513. https://doi.org/10.1007/BF00289765

Gorgolewski, K. J., & Poldrack, R. A. (2016). A practical guide for improving transparency and reproducibility in neuroimaging research. *PLOS Biology, 14*(7), e1002506. https://doi.org/10.1371/journal.pbio.1002506

Gottfredson, L. S., & Deary, I. J. (2004). Intelligence predicts health and longevity, but why? *Current Directions in Psychological Science, 13*(1), 1–4.

Granadillo, E. D., & Mendez, M. F. (2016). Pathological joking or *Witzelsucht* revisited. *The Journal of Neuropsychiatry and Clinical Neurosciences, 28*(3), 162–167. https://doi.org/10.1176/appi.neuropsych.15090238

Gray, H. (1918). *Gray's anatomy.* Bartleby.com. https://www.bartleby.com/107/indextn18.html

Gray, P. (2009). Play as a foundation for hunter–gatherer social existence. *American Journal of Play, 1*(4), 476.

Gray, P. (2013). The value of a play-filled childhood in development of the hunter–gatherer individual. In D. Narvaez, J. Panksepp, A. N. Schore, & T. R. Gleason (Eds.), *Evolution, early experience and human development: From research to practice and policy* (pp. 352–370). Oxford University Press.

Gray, P. (2014). Play theory of hunter-gatherer egalitarianism. In D. Narvaez, K. Valentino, A. Fuentes, J. J. McKenna, & P. Gray (Eds.), *Ancestral landscapes in human evolution: Culture, childrearing and social wellbeing* (pp. 192–215). Oxford University Press. https://doi.org/10.1093/acprof:oso/9780199964253.003.0014

Greeley, B., & Seidler, R. D. (2017). Mood induction effects on motor sequence learning and stop signal reaction time. *Experimental Brain Research, 235*(1), 41–56. https://doi.org/10.1007/s00221-016-4764-8

Greenfield, L. J., Geyer, J. D., & Carney, P. R. (2012). *Reading EEGs: A practical approach.* Lippincott Williams & Wilkins.

Greengross, G. (2013). Humor and aging—A mini-review. *Gerontology, 59*(5), 448–453. https://doi.org/10.1159/000351005

Greengross, G. (2014). Male production of humor produced by sexually selected psychological adaptations. In V. A. Weekes-Shackelford & T. K. Shackelford (Eds.), *Evolutionary perspectives on human sexual psychology and behavior* (pp. 173–196). Springer Science + Business Media. https://doi.org/10.1007/978-1-4939-0314-6_9

Greengross, G., Martin, R. A., & Miller, G. (2012a). Childhood experiences of professional comedians: Peer and parent relationships and humor use. *Humor: International Journal of Humor Research, 25*(4), 491–505. https://doi.org/10.1515/humor-2012-0026

Greengross, G., Martin, R. A., & Miller, G. (2012b). Personality traits, intelligence, humor styles, and humor production ability of professional stand-up comedians compared to college students. *Psychology of Aesthetics, Creativity, and the Arts, 6*(1), 74–82. https://doi.org/10.1037/a0025774

Greengross, G., & Miller, G. (2011). Humor ability reveals intelligence, predicts mating success, and is higher in males. *Intelligence, 39*(4), 188–192. https://doi.org/10.1016/j.intell.2011.03.006

Greengross, G., & Miller, G. F. (2008). Dissing oneself versus dissing rivals: Effects of status, personality, and sex on the short-term and long-term attractiveness of self-deprecating and other-deprecating humor. *Evolutionary Psychology, 6*(3), 393–408. https://doi.org/10.1177/147470490800600303

Greengross, G., & Miller, G. F. (2009). The Big Five personality traits of professional comedians compared to amateur comedians, comedy writers, and college students. *Personality and Individual Differences, 47*(2), 79–83. https://doi.org/10.1016/j.paid.2009.01.045

Greengross, G., Silvia, P. J., & Nusbaum, E. C. (2020). Sex differences in humor production ability: A meta-analysis. *Journal of Research in Personality, 84,* 103886. https://doi.org/10.1016/j.jrp.2019.103886

Greer, G. (2009, March 2). Women in comedy: Beaten to the punchline? *The Guardian.* https://www.theguardian.com/stage/2009/mar/02/germaine-greer-comedy-women

Griffin, R., Friedman, O., Ween, J., Winner, E., Happé, F., & Brownell, H. (2006). Theory of mind and the right cerebral hemisphere: Refining the scope of impairment. *Laterality, 11*(3), 195–225. https://doi.org/10.1080/13576500500450552

Grossman, P., Woods, A. J., Knotkova, H., & Bikson, M. (2019). Safety of transcranial direct current stimulation. In H. Knotkova, M. Nitsche, M. Bikson, & A. Woods (Eds.), *Practical guide to transcranial direct current stimulation* (pp. 165–195). Springer. https://doi.org/10.1007/978-3-319-95948-1_6

Gruner, C. R. (1978). *Understanding laughter: The working of wit and humor.* Nelson-Hall.

Guéguen, N. (2010). Men's sense of humor and women's responses to courtship solicitations: An experimental field study. *Psychological Reports, 107*(1), 145–156. https://doi.org/10.2466/07.17.PR0.107.4.145-156

Guillory, S. A., & Bujarski, K. A. (2014). Exploring emotions using invasive methods: Review of 60 years of human intracranial electrophysiology. *Social Cognitive and Affective Neuroscience, 9*(12), 1880–1889. https://doi.org/10.1093/scan/nsu002

Gunnery, S. D., & Ruben, M. A. (2016). Perceptions of Duchenne and non-Duchenne smiles: A meta-analysis. *Cognition and Emotion, 30*(3), 501–515. https://doi.org/10.1080/02699931.2015.1018817

Gutchess, A. (2019). *Cognitive and social neuroscience of aging.* Cambridge University Press.

Gutman, J., & Priest, R. F. (1969). When is aggression funny? *Journal of Personality and Social Psychology, 12*(1), 60–65. https://doi.org/10.1037/h0027357

Haase, C. M., Beermann, U., Saslow, L. R., Shiota, M. N., Saturn, S. R., Lwi, S. J., Casey, J. J., Nguyen, N. K., Whalen, P. K., Keltner, D., & Levenson, R. W. (2015). Short alleles, bigger smiles? The effect of 5-HTTLPR on positive emotional expressions. *Emotion, 15*(4), 438–448. https://doi.org/10.1037/emo0000074

Halberstadt, J., Ruffman, T., Murray, J., Taumoepeau, M., & Ryan, M. (2011). Emotion perception explains age-related differences in the perception of social gaffes. *Psychology and Aging, 26,* 133–136. https://doi.org/10.1037/a0021366

Hall, G., & Alliń, A. (1897). The psychology of tickling, laughing, and the comic. *The American Journal of Psychology, 9*(1), 1–41. https://doi.org/10.2307/1411471

Hall, G. B. (2011, September 8). *Precuneus.* Wikimedia Commons. https://commons.wikimedia.org/wiki/File:Precuneus.png

Haller, S., & Bartsch, A. J. (2009). Pitfalls in fMRI. *European Radiology, 19*(11), 2689–2706. https://doi.org/10.1007/s00330-009-1456-9

Halpern, C. H., Wolf, J. A., Bale, T. L., Stunkard, A. J., Danish, S. F., Grossman, M., Jaggi, J. L., Grady, M. S., & Baltuch, G. H. (2008). Deep brain stimulation in the treatment of obesity. *Journal of Neurosurgery, 109*(4), 625–634. https://doi.org/10.3171/JNS/2008/109/10/0625

Ham, A. T. (2018). Uncovering the fundamentals of polarity within the EEG: A closer look. *The Neurodiagnostic Journal, 58*(1), 40–68. https://doi.org/10.1080/21646821.2018.1428454

Hanna, J., Feinstein, A., & Morrow, S. A. (2016). The association of pathological laughing and crying and cognitive impairment in multiple sclerosis. *Journal of the Neurological Sciences, 361,* 200–203. https://doi.org/10.1016/j.jns.2016.01.002

Happé, E., Brownell, H., & Winner, E. (1999). Acquired "theory of mind" impairments following stroke. *Cognition, 70*(3), 211–240. https://doi.org/10.1016/S0010-0277(99)00005-0

Haq, I. U., Foote, K. D., Goodman, W. G., Wu, S. S., Sudhyadhom, A., Ricciuti, N., Siddiqui, M. S., Bowers, D., Jacobson, C. E., Ward, H., & Okun, M. S. (2011). Smile and laughter induction and intraoperative predictors of response to deep brain stimulation for obsessive-compulsive disorder. *NeuroImage, 54*(Suppl. 1), 247–255. https://doi.org/10.1016/j.neuroimage.2010.03.009

Harlow, J. M. (1848). Passage of an iron rod through the head. *Boston Medical and Surgical Journal, 39*(20), 389–393. https://doi.org/10.1056/NEJM184812130392001

Harris, G. J., Jaffin, S. K., Hodge, S. M., Kennedy, D., Caviness, V. S., Marinkovic, K., Papadimitriou, G. M., Makris, N., & Oscar-Berman, M. (2008). Frontal white matter and cingulum diffusion tensor imaging deficits in alcoholism. *Alcoholism, Clinical and Experimental Research, 32*(6), 1001–1013. https://doi.org/10.1111/j.1530-0277.2008.00661.x

Harrison, L. K., Carroll, D., Burns, V. E., Corkill, A. R., Harrison, C. M., Ring, C., & Drayson, M. (2000). Cardiovascular and secretory immunoglobulin A reactions to humorous, exciting, and didactic film presentations. *Biological Psychology*, *52*(2), 113–126. https://doi.org/10.1016/S0301-0511(99)00033-2

Hassler, R., & Riechert, T. (1961). Wirkungen der Reizungen und Koagulationen in den Stammganglien bei stereotaktischen Hirnoperationen [Effects of stimulations and coagulations in the basal ganglia in stereotactic brain surgery]. *Der Nervenarzt*, *32*, 97–109.

Hatzithomas, L., Zotos, Y., & Boutsouki, C. (2011). Humor and cultural values in print advertising: A cross-cultural study. *International Marketing Review*, *28*(1), 57–80. https://doi.org/10.1108/02651331111107107

Haug, M. C. (Ed.). (2013). *Philosophical methodology: The armchair or the laboratory?* Routledge. https://doi.org/10.4324/9780203798997

Havens, L. L., & Foote, W. E. (1963). The effect of competition on visual duration threshold and its independence of stimulus frequency. *Journal of Experimental Psychology*, *65*(1), 6–11. https://doi.org/10.1037/h0048690

Havranek, M. M., Volkart, F., Bolliger, B., Roos, S., Buschner, M., Mansour, R., Chmielewski, T., Gaudlitz, K., Hättenschwiler, J., Seifritz, E., & Ruch, W. (2017). The fear of being laughed at as additional diagnostic criterion in social anxiety disorder and avoidant personality disorder? *PLOS ONE*, *12*(11), e0188024. https://doi.org/10.1371/journal.pone.0188024

Hay, J. (2000). Functions of humor in the conversations of men and women. *Journal of Pragmatics*, *32*(6), 709–742. https://doi.org/10.1016/S0378-2166(99)00069-7

Hayashi, T., Urayama, O., Kawai, K., Hayashi, K., Iwanaga, S., Ohta, M., Saito, T., & Murakami, K. (2006). Laughter regulates gene expression in patients with Type 2 diabetes. *Psychotherapy and Psychosomatics*, *75*(1), 62–65. https://doi.org/10.1159/000089228

Head, H. (1926). *Aphasia and kindred disorders of speech*. Cambridge University Press.

Heath, R. L., & Blonder, L. X. (2005). Spontaneous humor among right hemisphere stroke survivors. *Brain and Language*, *93*(3), 267–276. https://doi.org/10.1016/j.bandl.2004.10.006

Heil, J. (2019). *Philosophy of mind: A contemporary introduction* (4th ed.). Routledge.

Heim, C., Ehlert, U., & Hellhammer, D. H. (2000). The potential role of hypocortisolism in the pathophysiology of stress-related bodily disorders. *Psychoneuroendocrinology*, *25*, 1–35. https://doi.org/10.1016/S0306-4530(99)00035-9

Heintz, S., & Ruch, W. (2015). An examination of the convergence between the conceptualization and the measurement of humor styles: A study of the construct validity of the Humor Styles Questionnaire. *Humor: International Journal of Humor Research*, *28*(4), 611–633. https://doi.org/10.1515/humor-2015-0095

Heintz, S., & Ruch, W. (2019). From four to nine styles: An update on individual differences in humor. *Personality and Individual Differences*, *141*, 7–12. https://doi.org/10.1016/j.paid.2018.12.008

Heintz, S., Ruch, W., Platt, T., Pang, D., Carretero-Dios, H., Dionigi, A., Argüello Gutiérrez, C., Brdar, I., Brzozowska, D., Chen, H. C., Chłopicki, W., Collins, M., Ďurka, R., Yahfoufi, N. Y. E., Quiroga-Garza, A., Isler, R. B., Mendiburo-Seguel, A., Ramis, T., Saglam, B., . . . Torres-Marín, J. (2018). Psychometric comparisons of benevolent and corrective humor across 22 countries: The virtue gap in humor goes international. *Frontiers in Psychology*, *9*, 92. https://doi.org/10.3389/fpsyg.2018.00092

Helmers, H. (1965). *Sprache und humor des kindes* [Language and humor of the child]. Ernst Klett Verlag.

Hendrie, C. A., & Brewer, G. (2012). Evidence to suggest that teeth act as human ornament displays signalling mate quality. *PLoS ONE, 7*(7), e42178. Advance online publication. https://doi.org/10.1371/journal.pone.0042178

Henry, J. D., Phillips, L. H., Ruffman, T., & Bailey, P. E. (2013). A meta-analytic review of age differences in theory of mind. *Psychology and Aging, 28*(3), 826–839. https://doi.org/10.1037/a0030677

Herbet, G., Lafargue, G., Bonnetblanc, F., Moritz-Gasser, S., & Duffau, H. (2013). Is the right frontal cortex really crucial in the mentalizing network? A longitudinal study in patients with a slow-growing lesion. *Cortex, 49*(10), 2711–2727. https://doi.org/10.1016/j.cortex.2013.08.003

Herold, R., Varga, E., Hajnal, A., Hamvas, E., Berecz, H., Tóth, B., & Tényi, T. (2018). Altered neural activity during irony comprehension in unaffected first-degree relatives of schizophrenia patients—An fMRI study. *Frontiers in Psychology, 8*, 2309. https://doi.org/10.3389/fpsyg.2017.02309

Herring, D. R., Burleson, M. H., Roberts, N. A., & Devine, M. J. (2011). Coherent with laughter: Subjective experience, behavior, and physiological responses during amusement and joy. *International Journal of Psychophysiology, 79*(2), 211–218. https://doi.org/10.1016/j.ijpsycho.2010.10.007

Herron, J. (Ed.). (2012). *Neuropsychology of left-handedness*. Elsevier.

Hickey, P., & Stacy, M. (2016). Deep brain stimulation: A paradigm shifting approach to treat Parkinson's disease. *Frontiers in Neuroscience, 10*(173), 1–11. https://doi.org/10.3389/fnins.2016.00173

Hill, R. A., & Dunbar, R. I. M. (2003). Social network size in humans. *Human Nature, 14*(1), 53–72. https://doi.org/10.1007/s12110-003-1016-y

Hinzen, W., & Rosselló, J. (2015). The linguistics of schizophrenia: Thought disturbance as language pathology across positive symptoms. *Frontiers in Psychology, 6*, 971. https://doi.org/10.3389/fpsyg.2015.00971

Hirosaki, M., Ohira, T., Kajiura, M., Kiyama, M., Kitamura, A., Sato, S., & Iso, H. (2013). Effects of a laughter and exercise program on physiological and psychological health among community-dwelling elderly in Japan: Randomized controlled trial. *Geriatrics & Gerontology International, 13*(1), 152–160. https://doi.org/10.1111/j.1447-0594.2012.00877.x

Hitchens, C. (2007, January). Why women aren't funny. *Vanity Fair*, 54–59.

Hodson, G., & MacInnis, C. C. (2016). Derogating humor as a delegitimization strategy in intergroup contexts. *Translational Issues in Psychological Science, 2*(1), 63–74. https://doi.org/10.1037/tps0000052

Hodson, G., Rush, J., & Macinnis, C. C. (2010). A joke is just a joke (except when it isn't): Cavalier humor beliefs facilitate the expression of group dominance motives. *Journal of Personality and Social Psychology, 99*(4), 660–682. https://doi.org/10.1037/a0019627

Hofmann, J., Carretero-Dios, H., & Carrell, A. (2018). Assessing the temperamental basis of the sense of humor: Adaptation of the English language version of the State-Trait Cheerfulness Inventory long and standard form. *Frontiers in Psychology, 9*, 2255. https://doi.org/10.3389/fpsyg.2018.02255

Hoicka, E. (2016). Parents and toddlers distinguish joke, pretend and literal intentional contexts through communicative and referential cues. *Journal of Pragmatics, 95*, 137–155. https://doi.org/10.1016/j.pragma.2015.10.010

Hoicka, E., & Akhtar, N. (2011). Preschoolers joke with jokers, but correct foreigners. *Developmental Science, 14*(4), 848–858. https://doi.org/10.1111/j.1467-7687.2010.01033.x

Hoicka, E., & Akhtar, N. (2012). Early humour production. *British Journal of Developmental Psychology, 30*(4), 586–603. https://doi.org/10.1111/j.2044-835X.2011.02075.x

Hoicka, E., & Butcher, J. (2016). Parents produce explicit cues that help toddlers distinguish joking and pretending. *Cognitive Science, 40*(4), 941–971. https://doi.org/10.1111/cogs.12264

Hoicka, E., Butcher, J., Malla, F., & Harris, P. L. (2017). Humor and preschoolers' trust: Sensitivity to changing intentions. *Journal of Experimental Child Psychology, 154*, 113–130. https://doi.org/10.1016/j.jecp.2016.10.006

Hoicka, E., & Gattis, M. (2008). Do the wrong thing: How toddlers tell a joke from a mistake. *Cognitive Development, 23*(1), 180–190. https://doi.org/10.1016/j.cogdev.2007.06.001

Hoicka, E., & Martin, C. (2016). Two-year-olds distinguish pretending and joking. *Child Development, 87*(3), 916–928. https://doi.org/10.1111/cdev.12526

Holmes, C. M., & Goldman, M. J. (2012). Seizures presenting as incessant laughter: A case of gelastic epilepsy. *The Journal of Emergency Medicine, 43*(6), e447–e449. https://doi.org/10.1016/j.jemermed.2012.02.068

Holstege, G., & Subramanian, H. H. (2016). Two different motor systems are needed to generate human speech. *The Journal of Comparative Neurology, 524*(8), 1558–1577. https://doi.org/10.1002/cne.23898

Holt-Lunstad, J., & Uchino, B. N. (2015). Social support and health. In K. Glanz, B. K. Rimer, & K. Viswanath (Eds.), *Health behavior: Theory, research, and practice* (5th ed., pp. 183–204). Jossey-Bass.

Hone, L. S., Hurwitz, W., & Lieberman, D. (2015). Sex differences in preferences for humor: A replication, modification, and extension. *Evolutionary Psychology, 13*(1), 167–181. https://doi.org/10.1177/147470491501300110

Hong, Y.-Y., Chiu, C.-Y., & Kung, T. M. (1997). Bringing culture out in front: Effects of cultural meaning system activation on social cognition. In K. Leung, Y. Kashima, U. Kim, & S. Yamaguchi (Eds.), *Progress in Asian social psychology* (Vol. 1, pp. 135–146). Wiley.

Hooper, J., Sharpe, D., & Roberts, S. B. (2016). Are men funnier than women, or do we just think they are? *Translational Issues in Psychological Science, 2*(1), 54–62. https://doi.org/10.1037/tps0000064

Hope, C. (2012, October 29). *EEG recording cap*. Wikimedia Commons. https://commons.wikimedia.org/wiki/File:EEG_Recording_Cap.jpg

Horvath, P., & Zuckerman, M. (1993). Sensation seeking, risk appraisal, and risky behavior. *Personality and Individual Differences, 14*(1), 41–52. https://doi.org/10.1016/0191-8869(93)90173-Z

Houston, D. M., McKee, K. J., Carroll, L., & Marsh, H. (1998). Using humour to promote psychological wellbeing in residential homes for older people. *Aging & Mental Health, 2*(4), 328–332. https://doi.org/10.1080/13607869856588

Howrigan, D. P., & MacDonald, K. B. (2008). Humor as a mental fitness indicator. *Evolutionary Psychology, 6*(4), 625–666. https://doi.org/10.1177/147470490800600411

Hsieh, C. J., Chang, C., Tsai, G., & Wu, H. F. (2015). Empirical study of the influence of a laughing Qigong program on long-term care residents. *Geriatrics & Gerontology International, 15*(2), 165–173. https://doi.org/10.1111/ggi.12244

Huang, L., Gino, F., & Galinsky, A. D. (2015). The highest form of intelligence: Sarcasm increases creativity for both expressers and recipients. *Organizational Behavior and Human Decision Processes, 131*, 162–177. https://doi.org/10.1016/j.obhdp.2015.07.001

Huber-Okrainec, J., Blaser, S. E., & Dennis, M. (2005). Idiom comprehension deficits in relation to corpus callosum agenesis and hypoplasia in children with spina bifida meningomyelocele. *Brain and Language, 93*(3), 349–368. https://doi.org/10.1016/j.bandl.2004.11.002

Hubert, W., & de Jong-Meyer, R. (1990). Psychophysiological response patterns to positive and negative film stimuli. *Biological Psychology, 31*(1), 73–93. https://doi.org/10.1016/0301-0511(90)90079-C

Hubert, W., & de Jong-Meyer, R. (1991). Autonomic, neuroendocrine, and subjective responses to emotion-inducing film stimuli. *International Journal of Psychophysiology, 11*(2), 131–140. https://doi.org/10.1016/0167-8760(91)90005-I

Hubert, W., Möller, M., & de Jong-Meyer, R. (1993). Film-induced amusement changes in saliva cortisol levels. *Psychoneuroendocrinology, 18*(4), 265–272. https://doi.org/10.1016/0306-4530(93)90023-E

Hucklebridge, F., Lambert, S., Clow, A., Warburton, D. M., Evans, P. D., & Sherwood, N. (2000). Modulation of secretory immunoglobulin A in saliva; Response to manipulation of mood. *Biological Psychology, 53*(1), 25–35. https://doi.org/10.1016/S0301-0511(00)00040-5

Hull, P. V. (1996). Bilingualism: Some personality and cultural issues. In D. I. Slobin, J. Gerhardt, A. Kyratzis, & J. Guo (Eds.), *Social interaction, social context, and language: Essays in honor of Susan Ervin-Tripp* (pp. 419–434). Lawrence Erlbaum.

Human, L. J., Whillans, A. V., Hoppmann, C. A., Klumb, P., Dickerson, S. S., & Dunn, E. W. (2015). Finding the middle ground: Curvilinear associations between positive affect variability and daily cortisol profiles. *Emotion, 15*(6), 705–720. https://doi.org/10.1037/emo0000071

Huster, R. J., Debener, S., Eichele, T., & Herrmann, C. S. (2012). Methods for simultaneous EEG–fMRI: An introductory review. *The Journal of Neuroscience, 32*(18), 6053–6060. https://doi.org/10.1523/JNEUROSCI.0447-12.2012

Ibrahim, C., Rubin-Kahana, D. S., Pushparaj, A., Musiol, M., Blumberger, D. M., Daskalakis, Z. J., Zangen, A., & Le Foll, B. (2019). The insula: A brain stimulation target for the treatment of addiction. *Frontiers in Pharmacology, 10*, 720. https://doi.org/10.3389/fphar.2019.00720

Im-Bolter, N., Agostino, A., & Owens-Jaffray, K. (2016). Theory of mind in middle childhood and early adolescence: Different from before? *Journal of Experimental Child Psychology, 149*, 98–115. https://doi.org/10.1016/j.jecp.2015.12.006

Irwin, K., Sexton, C., Daniel, T., Lawlor, B., & Naci, L. (2018). Healthy aging and dementia: Two roads diverging in midlife? *Frontiers in Aging Neuroscience, 10*, 275. https://doi.org/10.3389/fnagi.2018.00275

Isen, A. M., Daubman, K. A., & Nowicki, G. P. (1987). Positive affect facilitates creative problem solving. *Journal of Personality and Social Psychology, 52*, 1122–1131. https://doi.org/10.1037/0022-3514.52.6.1122

Isen, A. M., Johnson, M. M. S., Mertz, E., & Robinson, G. F. (1985). The influence of positive affect on the unusualness of word associations. *Journal of Personality and Social Psychology, 48*, 1413–1426. https://doi.org/10.1037/0022-3514.48.6.1413

Isserlin, M. (1936). Aphasie [Aphasia]. In O. Bumke & O. Foerster (Eds.), *Handbuch der Neurologie* [Handbook of neurology] (Vol. 10, pp. 626–806). Springer.

Itami, J., Nobori, M., & Texhima, H. (1994). Laughter and immunity. *Japanese Journal of Psychosomatic Medicine, 34*, 565–571.

Ivanova, A. M., Enikolopov, S. N., & Mitina, O. V. (2014). Sense of humor disorders in patients with schizophrenia and affective disorders. *Psychology in Russia: State of The Art, 7*(1), 146–157. https://doi.org/10.11621/pir.2014.0114

Jablensky, A. (2010). The diagnostic concept of schizophrenia: Its history, evolution, and future prospects. *Dialogues in Clinical Neuroscience, 12*(3), 271–287.

Janes, L., & Olson, J. (2015). Humor as an abrasive or a lubricant in social situations: Martineau revisited. *Humor: International Journal of Humor Research, 28*(2), 271–288. https://doi.org/10.1515/humor-2015-0021

Janes, L. M., & Olson, J. M. (2000). Jeer pressures: The behavioral effects of observing ridicule of others. *Personality and Social Psychology Bulletin, 26*(4), 474–485. https://doi.org/10.1177/0146167200266006

Janus, S. S. (1975). The great comedians: Personality and other factors. *American Journal of Psychoanalysis, 35*, 169–174. https://doi.org/10.1007/BF01358189

Janus, S. S., Bess, B. E., & Janus, B. R. (1978). The great comediennes: Personality and other factors. *American Journal of Psychoanalysis, 38*(4), 367–372. https://doi.org/10.1007/BF01253595

Jaroenkiatboworn, K. (2007). Compounding construction in Thai: Its contribution to humor. *Humor: International Journal of Humor Research, 20*(3), 261–275. https://doi.org/10.1515/HUMOR.2007.013

Jasper, H., & Penfield, W. (1954). *Epilepsy and the functional anatomy of the human brain* (2nd ed.). Little, Brown.

Jensen, A. R. (2006). *Clocking the mind: Mental chronometry and individual differences.* Elsevier.

Jiang, T., Li, H., & Hou, Y. (2019). Cultural differences in humor perception, usage, and implications. *Frontiers in Psychology, 10*, 123. https://doi.org/10.3389/fpsyg.2019.00123

Johnson, A. M. (1992). Language ability and sex affect humor appreciation. *Perceptual and Motor Skills, 75*(2), 571–581. https://doi.org/10.2466/pms.1992.75.2.571

Johnson, W., Onuma, O., Owolabi, M., & Sachdev, S. (2016). Stroke: A global response is needed. *Bulletin of the World Health Organization, 94*(9), 634. https://doi.org/10.2471/BLT.16.181636

Jones, J. M., & Harris, P. E. (1971). Psychophysiological correlates of cartoon humor appreciation. *Proceedings of the Annual Convention of the American Psychological Association, 6*, 381–382.

Jones, S. S., & Raag, T. (1989). Smile production in older infants: The importance of a social recipient for the facial signal. *Child Development, 60*(4), 811–818. https://doi.org/10.2307/1131021

Jung, W. E. (2003). The inner eye theory of laughter: Mindreader signals cooperator value. *Evolutionary Psychology, 1*, 214–253.

Kaas, J. H. (2013). The evolution of brains from early mammals to humans. *Wiley Interdisciplinary Reviews: Cognitive Science, 4*(1), 33–45. https://doi.org/10.1002/wcs.1206

Kalliny, M., Cruthirds, K. W., & Minor, M. S. (2006). Differences between American, Egyptian and Lebanese humor styles: Implications for international management. *International Journal of Cross Cultural Management, 6*, 121–134. https://doi.org/10.1177/1470595806062354

Kamble, S. V., Proyer, R. T., & Ruch, W. (2014). Gelotophobia in India: The assessment of the fear of being laughed at with the Kannada version of the

GELOPH<15>. *Psychological Studies, 59*(4), 337–344. https://doi.org/10.1007/s12646-014-0254-x

Kamei, T., Kumano, H., & Masumura, S. (1997). Changes of immunoregulatory cells associated with psychological stress and humor. *Perceptual and Motor Skills, 84*(3, Suppl.), 1296–1298. https://doi.org/10.2466/pms.1997.84.3c.1296

Kanai, R., & Rees, G. (2011). The structural basis of inter-individual differences in human behaviour and cognition. *Nature Reviews Neuroscience, 12*(4), 231–242. https://doi.org/10.1038/nrn3000

Kann, J. (1950). A translation of Broca's original article on the location of the speech center. *The Journal of Speech and Hearing Disorders, 15*(1), 16–20. https://doi.org/10.1044/jshd.1501.16

Kantrowitz, J. T., Hoptman, M. J., Leitman, D. I., Silipo, G., & Javitt, D. C. (2014). The 5% difference: Early sensory processing predicts sarcasm perception in schizophrenia and schizo-affective disorder. *Psychological Medicine, 44*(1), 25–36. https://doi.org/10.1017/S0033291713000834

Kanwisher, N. (2017). The quest for the FFA and where it led. *The Journal of Neuroscience, 37*(5), 1056–1061. https://doi.org/10.1523/JNEUROSCI.1706-16.2016

Kaplan, R. M., & Pascoe, G. C. (1977). Humorous lectures and humorous examples: Some effects upon comprehension and retention. *Journal of Educational Psychology, 69*(1), 61–65. https://doi.org/10.1037/0022-0663.69.1.61

Kappenman, E. S., & Luck, S. J. (2012). ERP components: The ups and downs of brainwave recordings. In S. J. Luck & E. S. Kappenman (Eds.), *The Oxford handbook of event-related potential components* (pp. 3–30). Oxford University Press.

Kashdan, T. B., Yarbro, J., McKnight, P. E., & Nezlek, J. B. (2014). Laughter with someone else leads to future social rewards: Temporal change using experience sampling methodology. *Personality and Individual Differences, 58*, 15–19. https://doi.org/10.1016/j.paid.2013.09.025

Kaufman, A. B., & Kaufman, J. C. (2018). *Pseudoscience: The conspiracy against science.* MIT Press.

Kaufman, S. B., Kozbelt, A., Bromley, M. L., & Miller, G. R. (2008). The role of creativity and humor in human mate selection. In G. Geher & G. Miller (Eds.), *Mating intelligence: Sex, relationships, and the mind's reproductive system* (pp. 227–262). Lawrence Erlbaum.

Kawakami, F., Kawakami, K., Tomonaga, M., & Takai-Kawakami, K. (2009). Can we observe spontaneous smiles in 1-year-olds? *Infant Behavior and Development, 32*(4), 416–421. https://doi.org/10.1016/j.infbeh.2009.07.005

Kawakami, F., & Yanaihara, T. (2012). Smiles in the fetal period. *Infant Behavior and Development, 35*(3), 466–471. https://doi.org/10.1016/j.infbeh.2012.04.002

Kawakami, K., Takai-Kawakami, K., Tomonaga, M., Suzuki, J., Kusaka, F., & Okai, T. (2007). Spontaneous smile and spontaneous laugh: An intensive longitudinal case study. *Infant Behavior and Development, 30*(1), 146–152. https://doi.org/10.1016/j.infbeh.2006.08.004

Kawakami, K., Takai-Kawakami, K., Tomonaga, M., Suzuki, J., Kusaka, T., & Okai, T. (2006). Origins of smile and laughter: A preliminary study. *Early Human Development, 82*(1), 61–66. https://doi.org/10.1016/j.earlhumdev.2005.07.011

Kazarian, S. S., Ruch, W., & Proyer, R. T. (2009). Gelotophobia in the Lebanon: The Arabic version of a questionnaire for the subjective assessment of the fear of being laughed at. *Arab Journal of Psychiatry, 20*(1), 42–56.

Kellaway, P. (1946). The part played by electric fish in the early history of bioelectricity and electrotherapy. *Bulletin of the History of Medicine, 20*, 112–137.

Kellner, R., & Benedek, M. (2017). The role of creative potential and intelligence for humor production. *Psychology of Aesthetics, Creativity, and the Arts, 11*(1), 52–58. https://doi.org/10.1037/aca0000065

Keltner, D., Young, R. C., Heerey, E. A., Oemig, C., & Monarch, N. D. (1998). Teasing in hierarchical and intimate relations. *Journal of Personality and Social Psychology, 75*(5), 1231–1247. https://doi.org/10.1037/0022-3514.75.5.1231

Kemmerer, D. (2015). *Cognitive neuroscience of language.* Psychology Press.

Kenderdine, M. (1931). Laughter in the pre-school child. *Child Development, 2*(3), 228–230. https://doi.org/10.2307/1125379

Kennison, S. (2019). *Psychology of language: Theories and applications.* Red Globe Press.

Kennison, S. M. (2014). *Introduction to language development.* Sage. https://doi.org/10.4135/9781506374499

Kennison, S. M., & Messer, R. H. (2019). Humor as social risk-taking: The relationships among humor styles, sensation-seeking, and use of curse words. *Humor, 32*(1), 1–21.

Kenny, A. (2012). *A new history of Western philosophy.* Oxford University Press.

Kerkkänen, P., Kuiper, N. A., & Martin, R. A. (2004). Sense of humor, physical health, and well-being at work: A three-year longitudinal study of Finnish police officers. *Humor, 17*(1–2), 21–35. https://doi.org/10.1515/humr.2004.006

Khadilkar, S., Menezes, K., Lele, V., & Katrak, S. (2001). Gelastic epilepsy—A case report with SPECT studies. *The Journal of the Association of Physicians of India, 49*, 581–583.

Kielar-Turska, M., & Białecka-Pikul, M. (2009). Generating and understanding jokes by five- and nine-year-olds as an expression of theory of mind. *Polish Psychological Bulletin, 40*(4), 8–14.

Kim, H. S., & Plester, B. A. (2019). Harmony and distress: Humor, culture, and psychological well-being in South Korean organizations. *Frontiers in Psychology, 9*, 2643. Advance online publication. https://doi.org/10.3389/fpsyg.2018.02643

Kim, S. H., Kim, Y. H., & Kim, H. J. (2015). Laughter and stress relief in cancer patients: A pilot study. *Evidence-Based Complementary and Alternative Medicine, 2015*, 1–6. https://doi.org/10.1155/2015/864739

Kimata, H. (2001). Effect of humor on allergen-induced wheal reactions. *JAMA, 285*(6), 738.

Kimata, H. (2004a). Differential effects of laughter on allergen-specific immunoglobulin and neurotrophin levels in tears. *Perceptual & Motor Skills, 98*(3), 901–908. https://doi.org/10.2466/pms.98.3.901-908

Kimata, H. (2004b). Effect of viewing a humorous vs. nonhumorous film on bronchial responsiveness in patients with bronchial asthma. *Physiology & Behavior, 81*(4), 681–684. https://doi.org/10.1016/j.physbeh.2004.03.010

Kipps, C. M., Nestor, P. J., Acosta-Cabronero, J., Arnold, R., & Hodges, J. R. (2009). Understanding social dysfunction in the behavioural variant of frontotemporal dementia: The role of emotion and sarcasm processing. *Brain: A Journal of Neurology, 132*(3), 592–603. https://doi.org/10.1093/brain/awn314

Kisko, T. M., Euston, D. R., & Pellis, S. M. (2015). Are 50-khz calls used as play signals in the playful interactions of rats? III. The effects of devocalization on play with unfamiliar partners as juveniles and as adults. *Behavioural Processes, 113*, 113–121. https://doi.org/10.1016/j.beproc.2015.01.016

Kline, L. W. (1907). The psychology of humor. *The American Journal of Psychology,* *18*(4), 421–441. https://doi.org/10.2307/1412574

Knotkova, H., Nitsche, M. A., Bikson, M., & Woods, A. J. (Eds.). (2019). *Practical guide to transcranial direct current stimulation: Principles, procedures and applications.* Springer. https://doi.org/10.1007/978-3-319-95948-1

Knutson, B., Burgdorf, J., & Panksepp, J. (1998). Anticipation of play elicits high-frequency ultrasonic vocalizations in young rats. *Journal of Comparative Psychology, 112,* 65–73. https://doi.org/10.1037/0735-7036.112.1.65

Ko, H.-J., & Youn, C.-H. (2011). Effects of laughter therapy on depression, cognition and sleep among the community-dwelling elderly. *Geriatrics & Gerontology International, 11*(3), 267–274. https://doi.org/10.1111/j.1447-0594.2010.00680.x

Koelsch, S., & Jentschke, S. (2008). Short-term effects of processing musical syntax: An ERP study. *Brain Research, 1212,* 55–62. https://doi.org/10.1016/j.brainres.2007.10.078

Koestler, A. (1964). *The act of creation.* Hutchinson.

Kohler, G., & Ruch, W. (1993). *The cartoon punchline production test—CPPT.* Dusseldorf.

Kohn, N., Kellermann, T., Gur, R. C., Schneider, F., & Habel, U. (2011). Gender differences in the neural correlates of humor processing: Implications for different processing modes. *Neuropsychologia, 49*(5), 888–897. https://doi.org/10.1016/j.neuropsychologia.2011.02.010

Kolb, B., Whishaw, I. Q., & Teskey, G. C. (2019). *An introduction to brain and behavior* (7th ed.). Macmillan.

Konradt, B., Hirsch, R. D., Jonitz, M. F., & Junglas, K. (2013). Evaluation of a standardized humor group in a clinical setting: A feasibility study for older patients with depression. *International Journal of Geriatric Psychiatry, 28*(8), 850–857. https://doi.org/10.1002/gps.3893

Kontos, P., Miller, K. L., Colobong, R., Palma Lazgare, L. I., Binns, M., Low, L. F., Surr, C., & Naglie, G. (2016). Elder-clowning in long-term dementia care: Results of a pilot study. *Journal of the American Geriatrics Society, 64*(2), 347–353. https://doi.org/10.1111/jgs.13941

Kornreich, C., Petit, G., Rolin, H., Ermer, E., Campanella, S., Verbanck, P., & Maurage, P. (2016). Decoding of nonverbal language in alcoholism: A perception or a labeling problem? *Psychology of Addictive Behaviors, 30*(2), 175–183. https://doi.org/10.1037/adb0000147

Kosslyn, S. M., & Andersen, R. A. (1992). *Frontiers in cognitive neuroscience.* MIT Press.

Kovarsky, D., Schiemer, C., & Murray, A. (2011). Humor, rapport, and uncomfortable moments in interactions with adults with traumatic brain injury. *Topics in Language Disorders, 31*(4), 325–335. https://doi.org/10.1097/TLD.0b013e3182358e98

Krack, P., Kumar, R., Ardouin, C., Dowsey, P. L., McVicker, J. M., Benabid, A. L., & Pollak, P. (2001). Mirthful laughter induced by subthalamic nucleus stimulation. *Movement Disorders, 16*(5), 867–875. https://doi.org/10.1002/mds.1174

Krolak-Salmon, P., Hénaff, M. A., Vighetto, A., Bauchet, F., Bertrand, O., Mauguière, F., & Isnard, J. (2006). Experiencing and detecting happiness in humans: The role of the supplementary motor area. *Annals of Neurology, 59,* 196–199. https://doi.org/10.1002/ana.20706

Krys, K., Melanie Vauclair, C., Capaldi, C. A., Lun, V. M., Bond, M. H., Domínguez-Espinosa, A., Torres, C., Lipp, O. V., Manickam, L. S., Xing, C., Antalíková, R.,

Pavlopoulos, V., Teyssier, J., Hur, T., Hansen, K., Szarota, P., Ahmed, R. A., Burtceva, E., Chkhaidze, A., . . . Yu, A. A. (2016). Be careful where you smile: Culture shapes judgments of intelligence and honesty of smiling individuals. *Journal of Nonverbal Behavior, 40*(2), 101–116. https://doi.org/10.1007/s10919-015-0226-4

Ku, L., Feng, Y., Chan, Y., Wu, C., & Chen, H. (2017). A re-visit of three-stage humor processing with readers' surprise, comprehension, and funniness ratings: An ERP study. *Journal of Neurolinguistics, 42*, 49–62. https://doi.org/10.1016/j.jneuroling.2016.11.008

Kuiper, N. A., Martin, R. A., & Olinger, L. J. (1993). Coping humour, stress, and cognitive appraisals. *Canadian Journal of Behavioural Science, 25*(1), 81–96. https://doi.org/10.1037/h0078791

Kuiper, N. A., Martin, R. A., Olinger, L. J., Kazarian, S. S., & Jette, J. L. (1998). Sense of humor, self-concept, and psychological well-being in psychiatric inpatients. *Humor, 11*(4), 357–381. https://doi.org/10.1515/humr.1998.11.4.357

Kumar, V., Croxson, P. L., & Simonyan, K. (2016). Structural organization of the laryngeal motor cortical network and its implication for evolution of speech production. *The Journal of Neuroscience, 36*(15), 4170–4181. https://doi.org/10.1523/JNEUROSCI.3914-15.2016

Kuperberg, G. R. (2010a). Language in schizophrenia Part 1: An introduction. *Language and Linguistics Compass, 4*(8), 576–589. https://doi.org/10.1111/j.1749-818X.2010.00216.x

Kuperberg, G. R. (2010b). Language in schizophrenia Part 2: What can psycholinguistics bring to the study of schizophrenia . . . and vice versa? *Language and Linguistics Compass, 4*(8), 590–604. https://doi.org/10.1111/j.1749-818X.2010.00217.x

Kurtz, M. M., Gagen, E., Rocha, N. B. F., Machado, S., & Penn, D. L. (2016). Comprehensive treatments for social cognitive deficits in schizophrenia: A critical review and effect-size analysis of controlled studies. *Clinical Psychology Review, 43*, 80–89. https://doi.org/10.1016/j.cpr.2015.09.003

Kuru, N., & Kublay, G. (2017). The effect of laughter therapy on the quality of life of nursing home residents. *Journal of Clinical Nursing, 26*(21-22), 3354–3362. https://doi.org/10.1111/jocn.13687

Kusnecov, A. W., & Anisman, H. (Eds.). (2014). *The Wiley-Blackwell handbook of psychoneuroimmunology*. Wiley-Blackwell.

Kutas, M., & Federmeier, K. D. (2000). Electrophysiology reveals semantic memory use in language comprehension. *Trends in Cognitive Sciences, 4*(12), 463–470. https://doi.org/10.1016/S1364-6613(00)01560-6

Kutas, M., & Federmeier, K. D. (2011). Thirty years and counting: Finding meaning in the N400 component of the event-related brain potential (ERP). *Annual Review of Psychology, 62*, 621–647. https://doi.org/10.1146/annurev.psych.093008.131123

Kuusimäki, T., Korpela, J., Pekkonen, E., Martikainen, M. H., Antonini, A., & Kaasinen, V. (2019). Deep brain stimulation for monogenic Parkinson's disease: A systematic review. *Journal of Neurology*. Advance online publication. https://doi.org/10.1007/s00415-019-09181-8

Lábadi, B., & Beke, A. M. (2017). Mental state understanding in children with agenesis of the corpus callosum. *Frontiers in Psychology, 8*, 94. https://doi.org/10.3389/fpsyg.2017.00094

Labott, S. M., Ahleman, S., Wolever, M. E., & Martin, R. B. (1990). The physiological and psychological effects of the expression and inhibition of emotion. *Behavioral Medicine, 16*(4), 182–189. https://doi.org/10.1080/08964289.1990.9934608

Lackner, H. K., Weiss, E. M., Hinghofer-Szalkay, H., & Papousek, I. (2014). Cardiovascular effects of acute positive emotional arousal. *Applied Psychophysiology and Biofeedback, 39*(1), 9–18. https://doi.org/10.1007/s10484-013-9235-4

Lackner, H. K., Weiss, E. M., Schulter, G., Hinghofer-Szalkay, H., Samson, A. C., & Papousek, I. (2013). I got it! Transient cardiovascular response to the perception of humor. *Biological Psychology, 93*(1), 33–40. https://doi.org/10.1016/j.biopsycho.2013.01.014

Lagravinese, G., Avanzino, L., Raffo De Ferrari, A., Marchese, R., Serrati, C., Mandich, P., Abbruzzese, G., & Pelosin, E. (2017). Theory of mind is impaired in mild to moderate Huntington's disease independently from global cognitive functioning. *Frontiers in Psychology, 8*, 80. https://doi.org/10.3389/fpsyg.2017.00080

Lai, J. C., Chong, A. M., Siu, O. T., Evans, P., Chan, C. L., & Ho, R. T. (2010). Humor attenuates the cortisol awakening response in healthy older men. *Biological Psychology, 84*(2), 375–380. https://doi.org/10.1016/j.biopsycho.2010.03.012

Lambert, R. B., & Lambert, N. K. (1995). The effects of humor on secretory immunoglobulin A levels in school-aged children. *Pediatric Nursing, 21*(1), 16–19.

Lamm, E., & Meeks, M. D. (2009). Workplace fun: The moderating effects of generational differences. *Employee Relations, 31*(6), 613–631. https://doi.org/10.1108/01425450910991767

Lampert, M. D. (1996). Studying gender differences in the conversational humor of adults and children. In D. I. Slobin & J. Gerhardt (Eds.), *Social interaction, social context, and language: Essays in honor of Susan Ervin-Tripp* (pp. 579–596). Lawrence Erlbaum.

Langevin, R., & Day, H. I. (1972). Physiological correlates of humor. In J. H. Goldstein & P. E. McGhee (Eds.), *The psychology of humor: Theoretical perspectives and empirical issues* (pp. 129–142). Academic Press. https://doi.org/10.1016/B978-0-12-288950-9.50012-2

Lapierre, S. S., Baker, B. D., & Tanaka, H. (2019). Effects of mirthful laughter on pain tolerance: A randomized controlled investigation. *Journal of Bodywork and Movement Therapies, 23*(4), 733–738. https://doi.org/10.1016/j.jbmt.2019.04.005

LaPointe, L. L., Katz, R. C., & Kraemer, I. (1985). The effects of stroke on appreciation of humor. *Cognitive Rehabilitation, 3*(6), 22–24.

Lashley, K. S. (1929). *Brain mechanisms and intelligence: A quantitative study of injuries to the brain.* University of Chicago Press. https://doi.org/10.1037/10017-000

Lau, C., Chiesi, F., Saklofske, D. H., & Yan, G. (2019). What is the temperamental basis of humour like in China? A cross-national examination and validation of the standard version of the state-trait cheerfulness inventory. *International Journal of Psychology.* Advance online publication. https://doi.org/10.1002/ijop.12582

Lau, Y. C., Hinkley, L. B., Bukshpun, P., Strominger, Z. A., Wakahiro, M. L., Baron-Cohen, S., Allison, C., Auyeung, B., Jeremy, R. J., Nagarajan, S. S., Sherr, E. H., & Marco, E. J. (2013). Autism traits in individuals with agenesis of the corpus callosum. *Journal of Autism and Developmental Disorders, 43*(5), 1106–1118. https://doi.org/10.1007/s10803-012-1653-2

Leacock, S. B. (1935). *Humor: Its theory and technique.* Dodd, Mead.

Lebowitz, K. R., Suh, S., Diaz, P. T., & Emery, C. F. (2011). Effects of humor and laughter on psychological functioning, quality of life, health status, and pulmonary functioning among patients with chronic obstructive pulmonary disease: A preliminary investigation. *Heart & Lung, 40*(4), 310–319. https://doi.org/10.1016/j.hrtlng.2010.07.010

Leckey, M., & Federmeier, K. D. (2019). The P3b and P600(s): Positive contributions to language comprehension. *Psychophysiology.* Advance online publication. https://doi.org/10.1111/psyp.13351

Lefcourt, H. M. (2001). *Humor: The psychology of living buoyantly.* Kluwer Academic. https://doi.org/10.1007/978-1-4615-4287-2

Lefcourt, H. M., Davidson, K., Prkachin, K. M., & Mills, D. E. (1997). Humor as a stress moderator in the prediction of blood pressure obtained during five stressful tasks. *Journal of Research in Personality, 31*(4), 523–542. https://doi.org/10.1006/jrpe.1997.2191

Lefcourt, H. M., Davidson-Katz, K., & Kueneman, K. (1990). Humor and immune system functioning. *Humor: International Journal of Humor Research, 3*(3), 305–322. https://doi.org/10.1515/humr.1990.3.3.305

Lehmann, W. P. (2013). *Historical linguistics: An introduction.* Routledge. https://doi.org/10.4324/9780203416433

Lei, X., Valdes-Sosa, P. A., & Yao, D. (2012). EEG/fMRI fusion based on independent component analysis: Integration of data-driven and model-driven methods. *Journal of Integrative Neuroscience, 11*(3), 313–337. https://doi.org/10.1142/S0219635212500203

Lerner, M. D., Mazefsky, C. A., White, S. W., & McPartland, J. C. (2018). Autism spectrum disorder. In J. N. Butcher & P. C. Kendall (Eds.), *APA handbook of psychopathology: Child and adolescent psychopathology* (Vol. 2, pp. 447–471). American Psychological Association. https://doi.org/10.1037/0000065-020

Leventhal, H., & Safer, M. A. (1977). Individual differences, personality, and humour appreciation: Introduction to symposium. In A. J. Chapman & H. C. Foot (Eds.), *It's a funny thing, humour* (pp. 335–349). Pergamon Press.

Lewis, D. A., & Levitt, P. (2002). Schizophrenia as a disorder of neurodevelopment. *Annual Review of Neuroscience, 25*, 409–432. https://doi.org/10.1146/annurev.neuro.25.112701.142754

Liederman, J., Merola, J., & Martinez, S. (1985). Interhemispheric collaboration in response to simultaneous bilateral input. *Neuropsychologia, 23*(5), 673–683. https://doi.org/10.1016/0028-3932(85)90068-5

Lippa, R. A. (2007). The preferred traits of mates in a cross-national study of heterosexual and homosexual men and women: An examination of biological and cultural influences. *Archives of Sexual Behavior, 36*(2), 193–208. https://doi.org/10.1007/s10508-006-9151-2.

Liu, C.-H., Huang, P.-S., Chang, J.-H., Lin, C.-Y., & Huang, C.-C. (2016). Helpful or unhelpful? Self-affirmation on challenge-confronting tendencies for students who fear being laughed at. *Learning and Individual Differences, 45*, 43–52. https://doi.org/10.1016/j.lindif.2015.11.023

Liu, X., Chen, Y., Ge, J., & Mao, L. (2019). Funny or angry? Neural correlates of individual differences in aggressive humor processing. *Frontiers in Psychology, 10*, 1849. https://doi.org/10.3389/fpsyg.2019.01849

Lloyd, E. L. (1938). The respiratory mechanism in laughter. *The Journal of General Psychology, 19*(1), 179–189. https://doi.org/10.1080/00221309.1938.9711194

Locke, S. E., Kraus, L., Leserman, J., Hurst, M. W., Heisel, J. S., & Williams, R. M. (1984). Life change stress, psychiatric symptoms, and natural killer cell activity. *Psychosomatic Medicine, 46*, 441–453. https://doi.org/10.1097/00006842-198409000-00005

Lockwood, N. L., & Yoshimura, S. M. (2014). The heart of the matter: The effects of humor on well-being during recovery from cardiovascular disease. *Health Communication, 29*(4), 410–420. https://doi.org/10.1080/10410236.2012.762748

Logothetis, N. K. (2008). What we can do and what we cannot do with fMRI. *Nature, 453*(7197), 869–878. https://doi.org/10.1038/nature06976

Loonen, A. J. M., & Ivanova, S. A. (2018). Circuits regulating pleasure and happiness: Evolution and role in mental disorders. *Acta Neuropsychiatrica, 30*(1), 29–42. https://doi.org/10.1017/neu.2017.8

López-Benítez, R., Acosta, A., Lupiáñez, J., & Carretero-Dios, H. (2017). High trait cheerfulness individuals are more sensitive to the emotional environment. *Journal of Happiness Studies, 19*, 1589–1612.

López-Benítez, R., Acosta, A., Lupiáñez, J., & Carretero-Dios, H. (2019). Are you ready to have fun? The Spanish state form of the State–Trait–Cheerfulness Inventory. *Journal of Personality Assessment, 101*(1), 84–95. https://doi.org/10.1080/00223891.2017.1368022

LoSchiavo, F. M., & Shatz, M. A. (2005). Enhancing online instruction with humor. *Teaching of Psychology, 32*, 246–248.

Lourey, E., & McLachlan, A. (2003). Elements of sensation seeking and their relationship with two aspects of humour appreciation-perceived funniness and overt expression. *Personality and Individual Differences, 35*(2), 277–287. https://doi.org/10.1016/S0191-8869(02)00188-5

Low, L.-F., Brodaty, H., Goodenough, B., Spitzer, P., Bell, J. P., Fleming, R., Casey, A. N., Liu, Z., & Chenoweth, L. (2013). The Sydney Multisite Intervention of LaughterBosses and ElderClowns (SMILE) study: Cluster randomised trial of humour therapy in nursing homes. *BMJ Open, 3*, e002072. https://doi.org/10.1136/bmjopen-2012-002072

Luce, P. A., Pisoni, D. B., & Goldinger, S. D. (1990). Similarity neighborhoods of spoken words. In G. Altmann (Ed.), *Cognitive models of speech processing* (pp. 122–147). MIT Press.

Luce, R. D. (1986). *Response times: Their role in inferring elementary mental organization.* Oxford University Press.

Luck, S. J. (2005). *An introduction to the event-related potential technique.* MIT Press.

Luck, S. J., & Gaspelin, N. (2017). How to get statistically significant effects in any ERP experiment (and why you shouldn't). *Psychophysiology, 54*(1), 146–157. https://doi.org/10.1111/psyp.12639

Luck, S. J., & Kappenman, E. S. (Eds.). (2012). *The Oxford handbook of event-related potential components.* Oxford University Press.

Ludovici, A. M. (1933). *The secret of laughter.* Viking Press.

Lundquist, L. (2014). Danish humor in cross-cultural professional settings: Linguistic and social aspects. *Humor: International Journal of Humor Research, 27*(1), 141–163. https://doi.org/10.1515/humor-2013-0044

Luria, A. R. (1970). *Traumatic aphasia: Its syndromes, psychology and treatment* (M. Critchley, Trans.). Mouton. https://doi.org/10.1515/9783110816297

Lyons, V., & Fitzgerald, M. (2004). Humor in autism and Asperger syndrome. *Journal of Autism and Developmental Disorders, 34*(5), 521–531. https://doi.org/10.1007/s10803-004-2547-8

MacCarron, P., Kaski, K., & Dunbar, R. (2016). Calling Dunbar's numbers. *Social Networks, 47*, 151–155. https://doi.org/10.1016/j.socnet.2016.06.003

MacDonald, N. E., & Silverman, I. W. (1978). Smiling and laughter in infants as a function of level of arousal and cognitive evaluation. *Developmental Psychology, 14*(3), 235–241. https://doi.org/10.1037/0012-1649.14.3.235

MacFarlane, B. (Director). (2014). *Women aren't funny* [Film]. Brainstorm Media.

Machts, J., Cardenas-Blanco, A., Acosta-Cabronero, J., Kaufmann, J., Loewe, K., Kasper, E., Schuster, C., Prudlo, J., Vielhaber, S., & Nestor, P. J. (2018). Prefrontal cortical thickness in motor neuron disease. *NeuroImage: Clinical, 18*, 648–655. https://doi.org/10.1016/j.nicl.2018.03.002

MacLachlan, C., Shipton, E. A., & Wells, J. E. (2016). The cold pressor test as a predictor of prolonged postoperative pain, a prospective cohort study. *Pain and Therapy, 5*(2), 203–213. https://doi.org/10.1007/s40122-016-0056-z

MacLean, P. D. (1990). *The triune brain in evolution: Role in paleocerebral functions.* Plenum Press.

MacMillan, M. (2002). *An odd kind of fame: Stories of Phineas Gage.* MIT Press.

MacPherson, S. E., & Della Sala, S. (Eds.). (2019). *Cases of amnesia: Contributions to understanding memory and the brain.* Routledge. https://doi.org/10.4324/9780429023880

MacPherson, S. E., Phillips, L. H., & Della Sala, S. (2002). Age, executive function, and social decision making: A dorsolateral prefrontal theory of cognitive aging. *Psychology and Aging, 17*(4), 598–609. https://doi.org/10.1037/0882-7974.17.4.598

Maiolino, N., & Kuiper, N. (2016). Examining the impact of a brief humor exercise on psychological well-being. *Translational Issues in Psychological Science, 2*(1), 4–13. https://doi.org/10.1037/tps0000065

Mak, W., & Carpenter, B. D. (2007). Humor comprehension in older adults. *Journal of the International Neuropsychological Society, 13*(4), 606–614. https://doi.org/10.1017/S1355617707070750

Mak, W., & Sörensen, S. (2018). Are humor styles of people with dementia linked to greater purpose in life? *The Gerontologist, 58*(5), 835–842. https://doi.org/10.1093/geront/gnx207

Mallett, R. K., Ford, T. E., & Woodzicka, J. A. (2016). What did he mean by that? Humor decreases attributions of sexism and confrontation of sexist jokes. *Sex Roles, 75*(5–6), 272–284. https://doi.org/10.1007/s11199-016-0605-2

Manfredi, M., Proverbio, A. M., Gonçalves Donate, A. P., Macarini Gonçalves Vieira, S., Comfort, W. E., De Araújo Andreoli, M., & Boggio, P. S. (2017). tDCS application over the STG improves the ability to recognize and appreciate elements involved in humor processing. *Experimental Brain Research, 235*(6), 1843–1852. https://doi.org/10.1007/s00221-017-4932-5

Manfredi, M., Proverbio, A. M., Marques, L. M., Ribeiro, B., Morello, L. Y. M., & Boggio, P. S. (2019). Anodal transcranial direct current stimulation of MPFC enhances humor processing. *Social Neuroscience.* Advance online publication. https://doi.org/10.1080/17470919.2019.1674687

Manke, B. (1998). Genetic and environmental contributions to children's interpersonal humor. In W. Ruch (Ed.), *The sense of humor: Explorations of a personality characteristic* (pp. 361–384). Walter de Gruyter. https://doi.org/10.1515/9783110804607.361

Manninen, S., Tuominen, L., Dunbar, R. I., Karjalainen, T., Hirvonen, J., Arponen, E., Hari, R., Jääskeläinen, I. P., Sams, M., & Nummenmaa, L. (2017). Social laughter triggers endogenous opioid release in humans. *The Journal of Neuroscience, 37*(25), 6125–6131. https://doi.org/10.1523/JNEUROSCI.0688-16.2017

Mapes, D. (2015, August 4). Tough room: As the saying goes, dying is easy, it's comedy that's hard—Particularly when it's a sensitive subject. *Fred Hutchison Cancer Center News.* https://www.fredhutch.org/en/news/center-news/2015/08/cancer-humor-eases-stress.html

Marci, C. D., Moran, E. K., & Orr, S. P. (2004). Physiologic evidence for the interpersonal role of laughter during psychotherapy. *Journal of Nervous and Mental Disease, 192*(10), 689–695. https://doi.org/10.1097/01.nmd.0000142032.04196.63

Marco, E. J., Harrell, K. M., Brown, W. S., Hill, S. S., Jeremy, R. J., Kramer, J. H., Sherr, E. H., & Paul, L. K. (2012). Processing speed delays contribute to executive function deficits in individuals with agenesis of the corpus callosum. *Journal of the International Neuropsychological Society, 18*(3), 521–529. https://doi.org/10.1017/S1355617712000045

Marjoram, D., Job, D. E., Whalley, H. C., Gountouna, V.-E., McIntosh, A. M., Simonotto, E., Cunningham-Owens, D., Johnstone, E. C., & Lawrie, S. (2006). A visual joke fMRI investigation into theory of mind and enhanced risk of schizophrenia. *NeuroImage, 31*(4), 1850–1858. https://doi.org/10.1016/j.neuroimage.2006.02.011

Marneweck, M., Palermo, R., & Hammond, G. (2014). Discrimination and recognition of facial expressions of emotion and their links with voluntary control of facial musculature in Parkinson's disease. *Neuropsychology, 28*(6), 917.

Martin, G. N., & Sullivan, E. (2013). Sense of humor across cultures: A comparison of British, Australian and American respondents. *North American Journal of Psychology, 15*(2), 375–384.

Martin, I., & McDonald, S. (2006). That can't be right! What causes pragmatic language impairment following right hemisphere damage? *Brain Impairment, 7*(3), 202–211. https://doi.org/10.1375/brim.7.3.202

Martin, J., Rychlowska, M., Wood, A., & Niedenthal, P. (2017). Smiles as multipurpose social signals. *Trends in Cognitive Sciences, 21*(11), 864–877.

Martin, L. R., Friedman, H. S., Tucker, J. S., Tomlinson-Keasey, C., Criqui, M. H., & Schwartz, J. E. (2002). A life course perspective on childhood cheerfulness and its relation to mortality risk. *Personality and Social Psychology Bulletin, 28*(9), 1155–1165. https://doi.org/10.1177/01461672022812001

Martin, R., & Ford, T. (2018). *The psychology of humor: An integrative approach* (2nd ed.). Elsevier.

Martin, R. A. (2014). Humor and gender: An overview of psychological research. In D. Chiaro & R. Baccolini (Eds.), *Gender and humor* (pp. 137–160). Routledge.

Martin, R. A. (2015). On the challenges of measuring humor styles: Response to Heintz and Ruch. *Humor: International Journal of Humor Research, 28*(4), 635–639. https://doi.org/10.1515/humor-2015-0096

Martin, R. A., & Dobbin, J. P. (1989). Sense of humor, hassles, and immunoglobulin A: Evidence for a stress-moderating effect of humor. *International Journal of Psychiatry in Medicine, 18*, 93–105. https://doi.org/10.2190/724B-3V06-QC5N-6587

Martin, R. A., & Kuiper, N. A. (1999). Daily occurrence of laughter: Relationships with age, gender, and Type A personality. *Humor: International Journal of Humor Research, 12*(4), 355–384. https://doi.org/10.1515/humr.1999.12.4.355

Martin, R. A., Kuiper, N. A., Olinger, L. J., & Dance, K. A. (1993). Humor, coping with stress, self-concept, and psychological well-being. *Humor: International Journal of Humor Research, 6*(1), 89–104. https://doi.org/10.1515/humr.1993.6.1.89

Martin, R. A., Lastuk, J. M., Jeffery, J., Vernon, P. A., & Veselka, L. (2012). Relationships between the Dark Triad and humor styles: A replication and extension. *Personality and Individual Differences, 52*(2), 178–182. https://doi.org/10.1016/j.paid.2011.10.010

Martin, R. A., & Lefcourt, H. M. (1983). Sense of humor as a moderator of the relation between stressors and moods. *Journal of Personality and Social Psychology, 45*(6), 1313–1324. https://doi.org/10.1037/0022-3514.45.6.1313

Martin, R. A., & Lefcourt, H. M. (1984). Situational Humor Response Question-naire: Quantitative measure of sense of humor. *Journal of Personality and Social Psychology, 47*(1), 145–155. https://doi.org/10.1037/0022-3514.47.1.145

Martin, R. A., Puhlik-Doris, P., Larsen, G., Gray, J., & Weir, K. (2003). Individual differences in uses of humor and their relation to psychological well-being: Development of the humor styles questionnaire. *Journal of Research in Personality, 37*(1), 48–75. https://doi.org/10.1016/S0092-6566(02)00534-2

Marziali, E., McDonald, L., & Donahue, P. (2008). The role of coping humor in the physical and mental health of older adults. *Aging & Mental Health, 12*(6), 713–718. https://doi.org/10.1080/13607860802154374

Marzouk, T., Winkelbeiner, S., Azizi, H., Malhotra, A. K., & Homan, P. (2019). Transcranial magnetic stimulation for positive symptoms in schizophrenia: A Systematic Review. *Neuropsychobiology.* Advance online publication. https://doi.org/10.1159/000502148

Maslow, A. H. (1954). *Motivation and personality.* Harper.

Mason, O., Linney, Y., & Claridge, G. (2005). Short scales for measuring schizotypy. *Schizophrenia Research, 78*(2–3), 293–296. https://doi.org/10.1016/j.schres.2005.06.020

Mathieu, S. I. (2008). Happiness and humor group promotes life satisfaction for senior center participants. *Activities, Adaptation and Aging, 32*(2), 134–148. https://doi.org/10.1080/01924780802143089

Matsusaka, T. (2004). When does play panting occur during social play in wild chimpanzees? *Primates, 45,* 221–229. https://doi.org/10.1007/s10329-004-0090-z

Mauss, I. B., & Robinson, M. D. (2010). Measures of emotion: A review. In J. De Houwer & D. Hermans (Eds.), *Cognition and emotion: Reviews of current research and theories* (pp. 99–127). Psychology Press.

Mayerhofer, B., & Schacht, A. (2015). From incoherence to mirth: Neuro-cognitive processing of garden-path jokes. *Frontiers in Psychology, 6,* 550. https://doi.org/10.3389/fpsyg.2015.00550

McCauley, C., Woods, K., Coolidge, C., & Kulick, W. (1983). More aggressive cartoons are funnier. *Journal of Personality & Social Psychology, 44*(4), 817–823.

McClelland, D. C., & Cheriff, A. D. (1997). The immunoenhancing effects of humor on secretory IgA and resistance to respiratory infections. *Psychology & Health, 12*(3), 329–344. https://doi.org/10.1080/08870449708406711

McCrae, R. R., & John, O. P. (1992). An introduction to the five-factor model and its applications. *Journal of Personality, 60*(2), 175–215. https://doi.org/10.1111/j.1467-6494.1992.tb00970.x

McGettigan, C., Walsh, E., Jessop, R., Agnew, Z. K., Sauter, D. A., Warren, J. E., & Scott, S. K. (2015). Individual differences in laughter perception reveal roles for mentalizing and sensorimotor systems in the evaluation of emotional authenticity. *Cerebral Cortex, 25,* 246–257. https://doi.org/10.1093/cercor/bht227

McGhee, P. E. (1974). Moral development and children's appreciation of humor. *Developmental Psychology, 10*(4), 514–525. https://doi.org/10.1037/h0036597

McGhee, P. E. (1979). *Humor: Its origin and development.* W. H. Freeman.

McGhee, P. E. (1999). *Health, healing, and the amuse system: Humor as survival training.* Kendall Hunt.

McGhee, P. E. (2010). *Humor: The lighter path to resilience and health.* AuthorHouse.

McGhee, P. E. (2014). *Humor and children's development.* Routledge.

McGhee, P. E. (2018). Chimpanzee and gorilla humor: Progressive emergence from origins in the wild to captivity to sign language learning. *Humor: International Journal of Humor Research, 31*(2), 405–449. https://doi.org/10.1515/humor-2018-0017

McGrath, J., Saha, S., Chant, D., & Welham, J. (2008). Schizophrenia: A concise overview of incidence, prevalence, and mortality. *Epidemiologic Reviews, 30*(1), 67–76. https://doi.org/10.1093/epirev/mxn001

McLeod, S. A., Lam, A., Spencer, A., Wei, X., & Gnanakumar, V. (2019). A case report of aphonogelia following recovery from severe traumatic brain injury. *PM&R: Journal of Injury, Function, and Rehabilitation, 11*(1), 94–97. https://doi.org/10.1016/j.pmrj.2018.05.018

Mecklinger, A. (1998). On the modularity of recognition memory for object form and spatial location: A topographic ERP analysis. *Neuropsychologia, 36*(5), 441–460. https://doi.org/10.1016/S0028-3932(97)00128-0

Mednick, S. A. (1962). The associative basis of the creative process. *Psychological Review, 69*(3), 220–232. https://doi.org/10.1037/h0048850

Mednick, S. A. (1968). The Remote Associates Test. *The Journal of Creative Behavior, 2*(3), 213–214. https://doi.org/10.1002/j.2162-6057.1968.tb00104.x

Meier, S. L., Charleston, A. J., & Tippett, L. J. (2010). Cognitive and behavioural deficits associated with the orbitomedial prefrontal cortex in amyotrophic lateral sclerosis. *Brain: A Journal of Neurology, 133,* 3444–3457. https://doi.org/10.1093/brain/awq254

Meinhardt, J., Kühn-Popp, N., Sommer, M., & Sodian, B. (2012). Distinct neural correlates underlying pretense and false belief reasoning: Evidence from ERPs. *NeuroImage, 63*(2), 623–631. https://doi.org/10.1016/j.neuroimage.2012.07.019

Meinhardt, J., Sodian, B., Thoermer, C., Döhnel, K., & Sommer, M. (2011). True- and false-belief reasoning in children and adults: An event-related potential study of theory of mind. *Developmental Cognitive Neuroscience, 1*(1), 67–76. https://doi.org/10.1016/j.dcn.2010.08.001

Mendiburo-Seguel, A., Páez, D., & Martínez-Sánchez, F. (2015). Humor styles and personality: A meta-analysis of the relation between humor styles and the Big Five personality traits. *Scandinavian Journal of Psychology, 56*(3), 335–340. https://doi.org/10.1111/sjop.12209

Mengelberg, A., & Siegert, R. J. (2003). Is theory-of-mind impaired in Parkinson's disease? *Cognitive Neuropsychiatry, 8,* 191–209. https://doi.org/10.1080/13546800244000292

Merz, E. L., Malcarne, V. L., Hansdottir, I., Furst, D. E., Clements, P. J., & Weisman, M. H. (2009). A longitudinal analysis of humor coping and quality of life in systemic sclerosis. *Psychology, Health & Medicine, 14*(5), 553–566. https://doi.org/10.1080/13548500903111798

Mettler, F. A., & Guiberteau, M. J. (2012). *Essentials of nuclear medicine imaging* (6th ed.). Saunders.

Meyer, D. E., Osman, A. M., Irwin, D. E., & Yantis, S. (1988). Modern mental chronometry. *Biological Psychology, 26*(1–3), 3–67. https://doi.org/10.1016/0301-0511(88)90013-0

Meyer, D. E., & Schvaneveldt, R. W. (1971). Facilitation in recognizing pairs of words: Evidence of a dependence between retrieval operations. *Journal of Experimental Psychology, 90,* 227–234. https://doi.org/10.1037/h0031564

Meyer, D. E., Schvaneveldt, R. W., & Ruddy, M. G. (1975). Loci of contextual effects on visual word recognition. In P. Rabbitt & S. Dornic (Eds.), *Attention and performance V* (pp. 98–118). Academic Press.

Meyer, M. C., Scheeringa, R., Webb, A. G., Petridou, N., Kraff, O., & Norris, D. G. (2020). Adapted cabling of an EEG cap improves simultaneous measurement of EEG and fMRI at 7T. *Journal of Neuroscience Methods, 331,* 108518.

Michel, C. M., & Brunet, D. (2019). EEG source imaging: A practical review of the analysis steps. *Frontiers in Neurology, 10,* 325. https://doi.org/10.3389/fneur.2019.00325

Mickes, L., Walker, D. E., Parris, J. L., Mankoff, R., & Christenfeld, N. J. (2012). Who's funny: Gender stereotypes, humor production, and memory bias. *Psychonomic Bulletin & Review, 19*(1), 108–112. https://doi.org/10.3758/s13423-011-0161-2

Miettunen, J., Immonen, J., McGrath, J. J., Isohanni, M., & Jääskeläinen, E. (2019). The age of onset of schizophrenia spectrum disorders. In G. de Girolamo, P. McGorry, & N. Sartorius (Eds.), *Age of onset of mental disorders: Etiopathogenetic and treatment implications* (pp. 55–73). Springer.

Miller, A. (2006). Pseudobulbar affect in multiple sclerosis: Toward the development of innovative therapeutic strategies. *Journal of the Neurological Sciences, 245*(1–2), 153–159. https://doi.org/10.1016/j.jns.2005.09.018

Miller, G. F. (1997). Protean primates: The evolution of adaptive unpredictability in competition and courtship. In A. Whiten & R. W. Byrne (Eds.), *Machiavellian intelligence II: Extensions and evaluations* (pp. 312–340). Cambridge University Press. https://doi.org/10.1017/CBO9780511525636.013

Miller, G. F. (2000). *The mating mind: How sexual choice shaped the evolution of human nature.* Doubleday.

Miller, P. M., & Commons, M. L. (2007). Stages of infant development, as illustrated by responses to the peek-a-boo game. *Behavioral Development Bulletin, 13*(1), 18–23. https://doi.org/10.1037/h0100496

Miller, S. A. (2012). *Theory of mind: Beyond the preschool years.* Psychology Press. https://doi.org/10.4324/9780203122730

Milligan, K., Astington, J. W., & Dack, L. A. (2007). Language and theory of mind: Meta-analysis of the relation between language ability and false-belief understanding. *Child Development, 78*(2), 622–646. https://doi.org/10.1111/j.1467-8624.2007.01018.x

Milton, K. (2003). The critical role played by animal source foods in human (*Homo*) evolution. *The Journal of Nutrition, 133*(2), 3886S–3892S. https://doi.org/10.1093/jn/133.11.3886S

Minagar, A., Ragheb, J., & Kelley, R. E. (2003). The Edwin Smith surgical papyrus: Description and analysis of the earliest case of aphasia. *Journal of Medical Biography, 11*(2), 114–117. https://doi.org/10.1177/096777200301100214

Miocinovic, S., Somayajula, S., Chitnis, S., & Vitek, J. L. (2013). History, applications, and mechanisms of deep brain stimulation. *JAMA Neurology*, *70*(2), 163–171. https://doi.org/10.1001/2013.jamaneurol.45

Mireault, G., Poutre, M., Sargent-Hier, M., Dias, C., Perdue, B., & Myrick, A. (2012). Humour perception and creation between parents and 3- to 6-month-old infants. *Infant and Child Development*, *21*(4), 338–347. https://doi.org/10.1002/icd.757

Mireault, G., Sparrow, J., Poutre, M., Perdue, B., & Macke, L. (2012). Infant humor perception from 3- to 6-months and attachment at one year. *Infant Behavior and Development*, *35*(4), 797–802. https://doi.org/10.1016/j.infbeh.2012.07.018

Mireault, G. C., Crockenberg, S. C., Heilman, K., Sparrow, J. E., Cousineau, K., & Rainville, B. (2018). Social, cognitive, and physiological aspects of humour perception from 4 to 8 months: Two longitudinal studies. *British Journal of Developmental Psychology*, *36*(1), 98–109. https://doi.org/10.1111/bjdp.12216

Mireault, G. C., Crockenberg, S. C., Sparrow, J. E., Cousineau, K., Pettinato, C., & Woodard, K. (2015). Laughing matters: Infant humor in the context of parental affect. *Journal of Experimental Child Psychology*, *13*, 630–641. https://doi.org/10.1016/j.jecp.2015.03.012

Mireault, G. C., Crockenberg, S. C., Sparrow, J. E., Pettinato, C. A., Woodard, K. C., & Malzac, K. (2014). Social looking, social referencing and humor perception in 6- and 12-month-old infants. *Infant Behavior and Development*, *37*(4), 536–545. https://doi.org/10.1016/j.infbeh.2014.06.004

Mireault, G. C., & Reddy, V. (2016). *Humor in infants: Developmental and psychological perspectives.* Springer Science + Business Media. https://doi.org/10.1007/978-3-319-38963-9

Miron-Spektor, E., Efrat-Treister, D., Rafaeli, A., & Schwarz-Cohen, O. (2011). Others' anger makes people work harder not smarter: The effect of observing anger and sarcasm on creative and analytic thinking. *Journal of Applied Psychology*, *96*(5), 1065–1075. https://doi.org/10.1037/a0023593

Mitchell, L. A., MacDonald, R. A., & Brodie, E. E. (2006). A comparison of the effects of preferred music, arithmetic and humour on cold pressor pain. *European Journal of Pain*, *10*(4), 343–351. https://doi.org/10.1016/j.ejpain.2005.03.005

Mittwoch-Jaffe, T., Shalit, F., Srendi, B., & Yehuda, S. (1995). Modification of cytokine secretion following mild emotional stimuli. *NeuroReport*, *6*(5), 789–792. https://doi.org/10.1097/00001756-199503270-00021

Miyake, K., Hirasawa, T., Koide, T., & Kubota, T. (2012). Epigenetics in autism and other neurodevelopmental diseases. In S. I. Ahmad (Ed.), *Advances in experimental medicine and biology* (pp. 91–98). Springer. https://doi.org/10.1007/978-1-4614-0653-2_7

Mobbs, D., Greicius, M. D., Abdel-Azim, E., Menon, V., & Reiss, A. L. (2003). Humor modulates the mesolimbic reward centers. *Neuron*, *40*(5), 1041–1048. https://doi.org/10.1016/S0896-6273(03)00751-7

Mobbs, D., Hagan, C. C., Azim, E., Menon, V., & Reiss, A. L. (2005). Personality predicts activity in reward and emotional regions associated with humor. *PNAS: Proceedings of the National Academy of Sciences of the United States of America*, *102*(45), 16502–16506. https://doi.org/10.1073/pnas.0408457102

Mondino, M., Bennabi, D., Poulet, E., Galvao, F., Brunelin, J., & Haffen, E. (2014). Can transcranial direct current stimulation (tDCS) alleviate symptoms and improve cognition in psychiatric disorders? *The World Journal of Biological Psychiatry, 15*(4), 261–275. https://doi.org/10.3109/15622975.2013.876514

Monetta, L., Grindrod, C. M., & Pell, M. D. (2009). Irony comprehension and theory of mind deficits in patients with Parkinson's disease. *Cortex, 45*(8), 972–981.

Moran, J. M. (2013). Lifespan development: The effects of typical aging on theory of mind. *Behavioural Brain Research, 23*, 732–740. https://doi.org/10.1016/j.bbr.2012.09.020

Moran, J. M., Wig, G. S., Adams, R. B., Jr., Janata, P., & Kelley, W. M. (2004). Neural correlates of humor detection and appreciation. *NeuroImage, 21*(3), 1055–1060. https://doi.org/10.1016/j.neuroimage.2003.10.017

Morishita, T., Foote, K. D., Archer, D. B., Coombes, S. A., Vaillancourt, D. E., Hassan, A., Haq, I. U., Wolf, J., & Okun, M. S. (2015). Smile without euphoria induced by deep brain stimulation: A case report. *Neurocase, 21*(6), 674–678. https://doi.org/10.1080/13554794.2014.973883

Morisseau, T., Mermillod, M., Eymond, C., Van Der Henst, J., & Noveck, I. A. (2017). You can laugh at everything, but not with everyone: What jokes can tell us about group affiliations. *Interaction Studies: Social Behaviour and Communication in Biological and Artificial Systems, 18*(1), 116–141. https://doi.org/10.1075/is.18.1.06mor

Morreall, J. (Ed.). (1987). *The philosophy of laughter and humor.* State University of New York Press.

Morse, L. A., Xiong, L., Ramirez-Zohfeld, V., Anne, S., Barish, B., & Lindquist, L. A. (2018). Humor doesn't retire: Improvisation as a health-promoting intervention for older adults. *Archives of Gerontology and Geriatrics, 75*, 1–5. https://doi.org/10.1016/j.archger.2017.10.013

Moselhy, H. F., Georgiou, G., & Kahn, A. (2001). Frontal lobe changes in alcoholism: A review of the literature. *Alcohol and Alcoholism, 36*(5), 357–368. https://doi.org/10.1093/alcalc/36.5.357

Mothersill, O., Knee-Zaska, C., & Donohoe, G. (2016). Emotion and theory of mind in schizophrenia—Investigating the role of the cerebellum. *Cerebellum, 15*(3), 357–368. https://doi.org/10.1007/s12311-015-0696-2

Motulsky, H. J. (2015). Common misconceptions about data analysis and statistics. *Pharmacology Research & Perspectives, 3*(1), e00093. https://doi.org/10.1002/prp2.93

Mozaffarian, D., Benjamin, E. J., Go, A. S., Arnett, D. K., Blaha, M. J., Cushman, M., Das, S. R., de Ferranti, S., Després, J. P., Fullerton, H. J., Howard, V. J., Huffman, M. D., Isasi, C. R., Jiménez, M. C., Judd, S. E., Kissela, B. M., Lichtman, J. H., Lisabeth, L. D., Liu, S., . . . Turner, M. B. (2016). Heart disease and stroke statistics–2016 update: A report from the American Heart Association. *Circulation, 133*(4), e38–e360. https://doi.org/10.1161/CIR.0000000000000350

Muris, P., Merckelbach, H., Otgaar, H., & Meijer, E. (2017). The malevolent side of human nature: A meta-analysis and critical review of the literature on the dark triad (narcissism, Machiavellianism, and psychopathy). *Perspectives on Psychological Science, 12*(2), 183–204. https://doi.org/10.1177/1745691616666070

Murray, M. M., Brunet, D., & Michel, C. M. (2008). Topographic ERP analyses: A step-by-step tutorial review. *Brain Topography, 20*(4), 249–264. https://doi.org/10.1007/s10548-008-0054-5

Mutz, J., Vipulananthan, V., Carter, B., Hurlemann, R., Fu, C. H. Y., & Young, A. H. (2019). Comparative efficacy and acceptability of nonsurgical brain stimulation for the acute treatment of major depressive episodes in adults: Systematic review and network meta-analysis. *BMJ, 364,* l1079. https://doi.org/10.1136/bmj.l1079

Myers, S., Ropog, B., & Rodgers, R. (1997). Sex differences in humor. *Psychological Reports, 81*(1), 221–222. https://doi.org/10.2466/pr0.1997.81.1.221

Nachev, P., Kennard, C., & Husain, M. (2008). Functional role of the supplementary and pre-supplementary motor areas. *Nature Reviews Neuroscience, 9,* 856–869. https://doi.org/10.1038/nrn2478

Nagase, K., & Tanaka, M. (2015). Cognitive processes in humor appreciation among individuals with autism spectrum disorder: Causal inference and stimulus elaboration. *Japanese Journal of Developmental Psychology, 26*(2), 123–134.

Nakamura, T., Matsui, T., Utsumi, A., Yamazaki, M., Makita, K., Harada, T., Tanabe, H. C., & Sadato, N. (2018). The role of the amygdala in incongruity resolution: The case of humor comprehension. *Social Neuroscience, 13*(5), 553–565. https://doi.org/10.1080/17470919.2017.1365760

National Cancer Institute. (n.d.). *SEER Training Modules: Anatomical terminology.* https://training.seer.cancer.gov/anatomy/body/terminology.html

National Institute of Mental Health. (n.d.). *Schizophrenia.* https://www.nimh.nih.gov/health/topics/schizophrenia/index.shtml

National Institute of Neurological Disorders and Stroke. (n.d.). *Huntington's disease information page.* https://www.ninds.nih.gov/Disorders/All-Disorders/Huntingtons-Disease-Information-Page

National Stroke Association. (n.d.-a). *Pseudobulbar affect (PBA).* https://www.stroke.org/we-can-help/survivors/stroke-recovery/post-stroke-conditions/emotional/pseudobulbar-affect-pba/

National Stroke Association. (n.d.-b). *Stroke risk factors not within your control.* https://www.stroke.org/en/about-stroke/stroke-risk-factors/stroke-risk-factors-not-within-your-control

Neale, J. M., & Stone, A. A. (1989). Stress, illness, and secretory immunity. In L. L. Carstensen & J. M. Neale (Eds.), *Mechanisms of psychological influence on physical health: With special attention to the elderly* (pp. 81–104). Plenum Press. https://doi.org/10.1007/978-1-4613-0775-4_5

Neely, M. N., Walter, E., Black, J. M., & Reiss, A. L. (2012). Neural correlates of humor detection and appreciation in children. *The Journal of Neuroscience, 32*(5), 1784–1790. https://doi.org/10.1523/JNEUROSCI.4172-11.2012

Negishi, M., Abildgaard, M., Laufer, I., Nixon, T., & Constable, R. T. (2008). An EEG recording system with carbon wire electrodes for simultaneous EEG-fMRI recording. *Journal of Neuroscience Methods, 173*(1), 99–107. https://doi.org/10.1016/j.jneumeth.2008.05.024

Nerhardt, G. (1970). Humor and inclination to laugh: Emotional reactions to stimuli of different divergence from a range of expectancy. *Scandinavian Journal of Psychology, 11*(1), 185–195. https://doi.org/10.1111/j.1467-9450.1970.tb00734.x

Nerhardt, G. (1976). Incongruity and funniness: Towards a new descriptive model. In A. J. Chapman & H. C. Foot (Eds.), *Humor and laughter: Theory, research, and applications* (pp. 55–62). John Wiley & Sons.

Netter, P., Hennig, J., & Roed, I. S. (1996). Serotonin and dopamine as mediators of sensation seeking behavior. *Neuropsychobiology, 34*(3), 155–165. https://doi.org/10.1159/000119318

Neuhoff, C. C., & Schaefer, C. (2002). Effects of laughing, smiling, and howling on mood. *Psychological Reports, 91*(7), 1079–1080. https://doi.org/10.2466/PR0.2002.91.3f.1079

Nevo, O. (1984). Appreciation and production of humor as an expression of aggression: A study of Jews and Arabs in Israel. *Journal of Cross-Cultural Psychology, 15*(2), 181–198. https://doi.org/10.1177/0022002184015002006

Nevo, O. (1985). Does one ever really laugh at one's own expense? The case of Jews and Arabs in Israel. *Journal of Personality and Social Psychology, 49*(3), 799–807. https://doi.org/10.1037/0022-3514.49.3.799

Nevo, O. (1986). Humor diaries of Israeli Jews and Arabs. *The Journal of Social Psychology, 126*(3), 411–413. https://doi.org/10.1080/00224545.1986.9713605

Nevo, O., Keinan, G., & Teshimovsky-Arditi, M. (1993). Humor and pain tolerance. *Humor: International Journal of Humor Research, 6*(1), 71–88.

Nevo, O., Nevo, B., & Yin, J. L. (2001). Singaporean humor: A cross-cultural, cross-gender comparison. *The Journal of General Psychology, 128*(2), 143–156. https://doi.org/10.1080/00221300109598904

Newman, A. (2019). *Research methods for cognitive neuroscience.* Sage.

Nezu, A. M., Nezu, C. M., & Blissett, S. E. (1988). Sense of humor as a moderator of the relation between stressful events and psychological distress: A prospective analysis. *Journal of Personality and Social Psychology, 54*(3), 520–525. https://doi.org/10.1037/0022-3514.54.3.520

Nias, D. K., & Wilson, G. D. (1977). A genetic analysis of humour preferences. In A. J. Chapman & H. C. Foot (Eds.), *It's a funny thing, humour* (pp. 371–373). Pergamon Press. https://doi.org/10.1016/B978-0-08-021376-7.50072-3

Nicholson, A., Whalen, J. M., & Pexman, P. M. (2013). Children's processing of emotion in ironic language. *Frontiers in Psychology, 4,* 691. https://doi.org/10.3389/fpsyg.2013.00691

Nir, N., & Halperin, E. (2018). Effects of humor on intergroup communication in intractable conflicts: Using humor in an intergroup appeal facilitates stronger agreement between groups and a greater willingness to compromise. *Political Psychology.* Advance online publication. https://doi.org/10.1111/pops.12535

Niwa, S., & Maruno, S. (2009). Self-denigrating humor for constructing relationships and regional cultural differences in Japan: A focus on blunder-telling behavior. *Journal of Social, Evolutionary, & Cultural Psychology, 3*(2), 133–154. https://doi.org/10.1037/h0099325

Njus, D. M., Nitschke, W., & Bryant, F. B. (1996). Positive affect, negative affect, and the moderating effect of writing on sIgA antibody levels. *Psychology & Health, 12*(1), 135–148. https://doi.org/10.1080/08870449608406927

Noordewier, M. K., & Breugelmans, S. M. (2013). On the valence of surprise. *Cognition and Emotion, 27*(7), 1326–1334. https://doi.org/10.1080/02699931.2013.777660

Norrick, N. R., & Spitz, A. (2008). Humor as a resource for mitigating conflict in interaction. *Journal of Pragmatics, 40*(10), 1661–1686. https://doi.org/10.1016/j.pragma.2007.12.001

Nusbaum, E. C., Silvia, P. J., & Beaty, R. E. (2017). Ha ha? Assessing individual differences in humor production ability. *Psychology of Aesthetics, Creativity, and the Arts, 11*(2), 231–241. https://doi.org/10.1037/aca0000086

Nwokah, E. E., Davies, P., Islam, A., Hsu, H.-C., & Fogel, A. (1993). Vocal affect in three-year-olds: A quantitative acoustic analysis of child laughter. *The Journal of the Acoustical Society of America, 94*(6), 3076–3090. https://doi.org/10.1121/1.407242

Nwokah, E. E., & Fogel, A. (1993). Laughter in mother–infant emotional communication. *Humor: International Journal of Humor Research, 6*(2), 137–161. https://doi.org/10.1515/humr.1993.6.2.137

Nwokah, E. E., Hsu, H.-C., Davies, P., & Fogel, A. (1999). The integration of laughter and speech in vocal communication: A dynamic systems perspective. *Journal of Speech, Language, and Hearing Research, 42*(4), 880–894. https://doi.org/10.1044/jslhr.4204.880

Nwokah, E. E., Hsu, H.-C., Dobrowolska, O., & Fogel, A. (1994). The development of laughter in mother–infant communication: Timing parameters and temporal sequences. *Infant Behavior and Development, 17*(1), 23–35. https://doi.org/10.1016/0163-6383(94)90019-1

Oakley, B. F. M., Brewer, R., Bird, G., & Catmur, C. (2016). Theory of mind is not theory of emotion: A cautionary note on the Reading the Mind in the Eyes Test. *Journal of Abnormal Psychology, 125*(6), 818–823. https://doi.org/10.1037/abn0000182

Obrdlik, A. (1942). "Gallows humor"—A sociological phenomenon. *American Journal of Sociology, 47*(5), 709–716. https://doi.org/10.1086/219002

O'Brien, G. (1994). The behavioral and developmental consequences of callosal agenesis. In M. Lassonde & M. A. Jeeves (Eds.), *Callosal agenesis: A natural split brain?* (pp. 235–246). Plenum Press. https://doi.org/10.1007/978-1-4613-0487-6_24

O'Connell, W. E. (1960). The adaptive functions of wit and humor. *Journal of Abnormal and Social Psychology, 61*, 263–270. https://doi.org/10.1037/h0047766

O'Connell, W. E. (1976). Freudian humour: The eupsychia of everyday life. In A. J. Chapman & H. C. Foot (Eds.), *Humor and laughter: Theory, research, and applications* (pp. 313–329). John Wiley & Sons.

O'Connor, E. C., Ford, T. E., & Banos, N. C. (2017). Restoring threatened masculinity: The appeal of sexist and anti-gay humor. *Sex Roles, 77*(9–10), 567–580. https://doi.org/10.1007/s11199-017-0761-z

Oh, K., Kim, H. J., Kim, B. J., Park, K. W., & Lee, D. H. (2008). Pathological laughter as an unusual manifestation of acute stroke. *European Neurology, 59*, 83–84. https://doi.org/10.1159/000109573

OpenStax College. (2013, June 19). *Anatomy & physiology*. Connexions. http://cnx.org/content/col11496/1.6/

Osaka, M., Yaoi, K., Minamoto, T., & Osaka, N. (2015). Serial changes of humor comprehension for four-frame comic Manga: An fMRI study. *Scientific Reports, 4*, 5828. https://doi.org/10.1038/srep05828

Osterhout, L., & Holcomb, P. J. (1992). Event-related brain potentials elicited by syntactic anomaly. *Journal of Memory and Language, 31*(6), 785–806. https://doi.org/10.1016/0749-596X(92)90039-Z

Oveis, C., Spectre, A., Smith, P. K., Liu, M. Y., & Keltner, D. (2016). Laughter conveys status. *Journal of Experimental Social Psychology, 65*, 109–115. https://doi.org/10.1016/j.jesp.2016.04.005

Overeem, S., Lammers, G. J., & van Dijk, J. G. (1999). Weak with laughter. *The Lancet, 354*(9181), 838. https://doi.org/10.1016/S0140-6736(99)80023-3

Overeem, S., Taal, W., Ocal Gezici, E., Lammers, G. J., & van Dijk, J. G. (2004). Is motor inhibition during laughter due to emotional or respiratory influences? *Psychophysiology, 41*(2), 254–258. https://doi.org/10.1111/j.1469-8986.2003.00145.x

Overholser, J. C. (1992). Sense of humor when coping with life stress. *Personality and Individual Differences*, *13*(7), 799–804. https://doi.org/10.1016/0191-8869(92)90053-R

Palagi, E. (2008). Sharing the motivation to play: The use of signals in adult bonobos. *Animal Behaviour*, *75*(3), 887–896. https://doi.org/10.1016/j.anbehav.2007.07.016

Palagi, E., Antonacci, D., & Cordoni, G. (2007). Fine-tuning of social play in juvenile lowland gorillas (*Gorilla gorilla gorilla*). *Developmental Psychobiology*, *49*(4), 433–445. https://doi.org/10.1002/dev.20219

Palagi, E., Norscia, I., & Spada, G. (2014). Relaxed open mouth as a playful signal in wild ring-tailed lemurs. *American Journal of Primatology*, *76*(11), 1074–1083. https://doi.org/10.1002/ajp.22294

Palaniyappan, L., Crow, T. J., Hough, M., Voets, N. L., Liddle, P. F., James, S., Winmill, L., & James, A. C. (2013). Gyrification of Broca's region is anomalously lateralized at onset of schizophrenia in adolescence and regresses at 2-year follow-up. *Schizophrenia Research*, *147*, 39–45. https://doi.org/10.1016/j.schres.2013.03.028

Paller, K. A., Kutas, M., & McIsaac, H. K. (1995). Monitoring conscious recollection via the electrical activity of the brain. *Psychological Science*, *6*(2), 107–111. https://doi.org/10.1111/j.1467-9280.1995.tb00315.x

Palmer, C. T. (1993). Anger, aggression, and humor in Newfoundland floor hockey: An evolutionary analysis. *Aggressive Behavior*, *19*(3), 167–173. https://doi.org/10.1002/1098-2337(1993)19:3<167::AID-AB2480190302>3.0.CO;2-V

Panksepp, J. (1993). Neurochemical control of moods and emotions: Amino acids to neuropeptides. In M. Lewis & J. M. Haviland (Eds.), *Handbook of emotions* (pp. 87–107). Guilford Press.

Panksepp, J. (1998). *Affective neuroscience: The foundations of human and animal emotions*. Oxford University Press.

Panksepp, J. (2000). The riddle of laughter: Neural and psychoevolutionary underpinnings of joy. *Current Directions in Psychological Science*, *9*(6), 183–186. https://doi.org/10.1111/1467-8721.00090

Panksepp, J. (2005). Psychology. Beyond a joke: From animal laughter to human joy? *Science*, *308*(5718), 62–63. https://doi.org/10.1126/science.1112066

Panksepp, J. (2007). Neuroevolutionary sources of laughter and social joy: Modeling primal human laughter in laboratory rats. *Behavioural Brain Research*, *182*(2), 231–244. https://doi.org/10.1016/j.bbr.2007.02.015

Panksepp, J., & Burgdorf, J. (2000). 50-kHz chirping (laughter?) in response to conditioned and unconditioned tickle-induced reward in rats: Effects of social housing and genetic variables. *Behavioural Brain Research*, *115*(1), 25–38. https://doi.org/10.1016/S0166-4328(00)00238-2

Panksepp, J., & Burgdorf, J. (2003). "Laughing" rats and the evolutionary antecedents of human joy? *Physiology & Behavior*, *79*(3), 533–547. https://doi.org/10.1016/S0031-9384(03)00159-8

Papousek, I., Aydin, N., Lackner, H. K., Weiss, E. M., Bühner, M., Schulter, G., Charlesworth, C., & Freudenthaler, H. H. (2014). Laughter as a social rejection cue: Gelotophobia and transient cardiac responses to other persons' laughter and insult. *Psychophysiology*, *51*(11), 1112–1121. https://doi.org/10.1111/psyp.12259

Parent, A. (2004). Giovanni Aldini: From animal electricity to human brain stimulation. *The Canadian Journal of Neurological Sciences*, *31*(4), 576–584. https://doi.org/10.1017/S0317167100003851

Parkinson's Foundation. (n.d.). *Deep-brain stimulation*. https://www.parkinson.org/ Understanding-Parkinsons/Treatment/Surgical-Treatment-Options/Deep-Brain-Stimulation

Parrott, W. G., & Gleitman, H. (1989). Infants' expectations in play: The joy of peek-a-boo. *Cognition and Emotion, 3*(4), 291–311. https://doi.org/10.1080/02699938908412710

Parssinen, T. M. (1974). Popular science and society: The phrenology movement in early Victorian Britain. *Journal of Social History, 8*(1), 1–20. https://doi.org/10.1353/jsh/8.1.1

Parvizi, J., Coburn, K. L., Shillcutt, S. D., Coffey, C. E., Lauterbach, E. C., & Mendez, M. F. (2009). Neuroanatomy of pathological laughing and crying: A report of the American Neuropsychiatric Association Committee on Research. *The Journal of Neuropsychiatry and Clinical Neurosciences, 21*(1), 75–87. https://doi.org/10.1176/jnp.2009.21.1.75

Pascual-Leone, A., Walsh, V., & Rothwell, J. (2000). Transcranial magnetic stimulation in cognitive neuroscience—Virtual lesion, chronometry, and functional connectivity. *Current Opinion in Neurobiology, 10*(2), 232–237. https://doi.org/10.1016/S0959-4388(00)00081-7

Paskind, H. S. (1932). The effect of laughter on muscle tone. *Archives of Neurology and Psychiatry, 28*(3), 623–628. https://doi.org/10.1001/archneurpsyc.1932.02240030143007

Patanwala, A. E., Norwood, C., Steiner, H., Morrison, D., Li, M., Walsh, K., Martinez, M., Baker, S. E., Snyder, E. M., & Karnes, J. H. (2019). Psychological and genetic predictors of pain tolerance. *Clinical and Translational Science, 12*(2), 189–195. https://doi.org/10.1111/cts.12605

Patel, A. D., Gibson, E., Ratner, J., Besson, M., & Holcomb, P. J. (1998). Processing syntactic relations in language and music: An event-related potential study. *Journal of Cognitive Neuroscience, 10*(6), 717–733. https://doi.org/10.1162/089892998563121

Patel, N., Combs, H., York, M., Phan, C., & Jimenez-Shahed, J. (2018). Pseudo-bulbar affect correlates with mood symptoms in Parkinsonian disorders but not amyotrophic lateral sclerosis. *The Journal of Neuropsychiatry and Clinical Neurosciences, 30*(3), 214–219. https://doi.org/10.1176/appi.neuropsych.17070131

Paul, L. K., Corsello, C., Kennedy, D. P., & Adolphs, R. (2014). Agenesis of the corpus callosum and autism: A comprehensive comparison. *Brain: A Journal of Neurology, 137*(6), 1813–1829. https://doi.org/10.1093/brain/awu070

Paul, L. K., Erickson, R. L., Hartman, J. A., & Brown, W. S. (2016). Learning and memory in individuals with agenesis of the corpus callosum. *Neuropsychologia, 86*, 183–192. https://doi.org/10.1016/j.neuropsychologia.2016.04.013

Paul, L. K., Van Lancker-Sidtis, D., Schieffer, B., Dietrich, R., & Brown, W. S. (2003). Communicative deficits in agenesis of the corpus callosum: Nonliteral language and affective prosody. *Brain and Language, 85*(2), 313–324. https://doi.org/10.1016/S0093-934X(03)00062-2

Pawełczyk, A., Kotlicka-Antczak, M., Łojek, E., Ruszpel, A., & Pawełczyk, T. (2018). Schizophrenia patients have higher-order language and extralinguistic impairments. *Schizophrenia Research, 192*, 274–280. https://doi.org/10.1016/j.schres.2017.04.030

Paxton, P., & Hughes, M. M. (2017). *Women, politics, and power: A global perspective* (3rd ed.). Sage.

Pell, M. D., Rothermich, K., Liu, P., Paulmann, S., Sethi, S., & Rigoulot, S. (2015). Preferential decoding of emotion from human nonlinguistic vocalizations

versus speech prosody. *Biological Psychology, 111,* 14–25. https://doi.org/10.1016/
j.biopsycho.2015.08.008

Pellis, S. M., Pellis, V. C., Reinhart, C. J., & Thierry, B. (2011). The use of the
bared-teeth display during play fighting in Tonkean macaques (*Macaca tonkeana*):
Sometimes it is all about oneself. *Journal of Comparative Psychology, 125*(4),
393–403. https://doi.org/10.1037/a0024514

Penfield, W. (1952). Memory mechanisms. *Archives of Neurology and Psychiatry,
67*(2), 178–198. https://doi.org/10.1001/archneurpsyc.1952.02320140046005

Penfield, W. (1958). Some mechanisms of consciousness discovered during
electrical stimulation of the brain. *PNAS: Proceedings of the National Academy of
Sciences of the United States of America, 44*(2), 51–66. https://doi.org/10.1073/
pnas.44.2.51

Penfield, W., & Roberts, L. (2014). *Speech and brain mechanisms.* Princeton University Press. (Original work published 1959)

Penfield, W., & Welch, K. (1951). The supplementary motor area of the cerebral
cortex: A clinical and experimental study. *A.M.A. Archives of Neurology and
Psychiatry, 66*(3), 289–317. https://doi.org/10.1001/archneurpsyc.1951.
02320090038004

Penny, S. M. (2006). Agenesis of the corpus callosum: Neonatal sonographic
detection. *Radiologic Technology, 78*(1), 14–18.

Perera, S., Sabin, E., Nelson, P., & Lowe, D. (1998). Increases in salivary lysozyme
and IgA concentrations and secretory rates independent of salivary flow rates
following viewing of humorous videotape. *International Journal of Behavioral
Medicine, 5*(2), 118–128. https://doi.org/10.1207/s15327558ijbm0502_3

Peters, R. (2006). Ageing and the brain. *Postgraduate Medical Journal, 82*(964),
84–88. https://doi.org/10.1136/pgmj.2005.036665

Peterson, C. (2014). Theory of mind understanding and empathic behavior in
children with autism spectrum disorders. *International Journal of Developmental
Neuroscience, 39,* 16–21. https://doi.org/10.1016/j.ijdevneu.2014.05.002

Peterson, C., Ruch, W., Beermann, U., Park, N., & Seligman, M. E. P. (2007). Strengths
of character, orientations to happiness, and life satisfaction. *The Journal of Positive
Psychology, 2*(3), 149–156. https://doi.org/10.1080/17439760701228938

Pexman, P. M., Rostad, K. R., McMorris, C. A., Climie, E. A., Stowkowy, J., &
Glenwright, M. R. (2011). Processing of ironic language in children with
high-functioning autism spectrum disorder. *Journal of Autism and Developmental
Disorders, 41*(8), 1097–1112. https://doi.org/10.1007/s10803-010-1131-7

Phillips, L. H., Allen, R., Bull, R., Hering, A., Kliegel, M., & Channon, S. (2015).
Older adults have difficulty in decoding sarcasm. *Developmental Psychology,
51*(12), 1840–1852. https://doi.org/10.1037/dev0000063

Phillips, L. H., Bull, R., Allen, R., Insch, P., Burr, K., & Ogg, W. (2011). Lifespan
aging and belief reasoning: Influences of executive function and social cue
decoding. *Cognition, 120*(2), 236–247. https://doi.org/10.1016/j.cognition.
2011.05.003

Phillips, L. H., Slessor, G., Bailey, P. E., & Henry, J. D. (2014). Older adults' perception of social and emotional cues. In P. Verhaeghen & C. Hertzog (Eds.),
The Oxford handbook of emotion, social cognition, and problem solving in adulthood
(pp. 9–25). Oxford University Press.

Picci, G., Gotts, S. J., & Scherf, K. S. (2016). A theoretical rut: Revisiting and critically evaluating the generalized under/over-connectivity hypothesis of autism.
Developmental Science, 19(4), 524–549. https://doi.org/10.1111/desc.12467

Pien, D., & Rothbart, M. K. (1976). Incongruity and resolution in children's humor: A reexamination. *Child Development, 47*(4), 966–971. https://doi.org/10.2307/1128432

Pinker, S. (2003). *The language instinct: How the mind creates language*. Penguin UK.

Pitcher, D., Walsh, V., & Duchaine, B. (2011). Transcranial magnetic stimulation studies of face processing. In A. Calder, G. Rhodes, M. Johnson, & J. Haxby (Eds.), *Oxford handbook of face perception* (pp. 362–378). Oxford University Press. https://doi.org/10.1093/oxfordhb/9780199559053.013.0019

Platt, T., Ruch, W., & Proyer, R. T. (2010). A lifetime of fear of being laughed at: An aged perspective. *Zeitschrift für Gerontologie und Geriatrie, 43*(1), 36–41. https://doi.org/10.1007/s00391-009-0083-z

Plessen, C. Y., Franken, F. R., Ster, C., Schmid, R. R., Wolfmayr, C., Mayer, A.-M., Sobisch, M., Kathofer, M., Rattner, K., Kotlyar, E., Maierwieser, R. J., & Tran, U. S. (2020). Humor styles and personality: A systematic review and meta-analysis on the relations between humor styles and the Big Five personality traits. *Personality and Individual Differences, 154*, 109676. https://doi.org/10.1016/j.paid.2019.109676

Plomin, R., DeFries, J. C., & Loehlin, J. C. (1977). Genotype-environment interaction and correlation in the analysis of human behavior. *Psychological Bulletin, 84*(2), 309–322. https://doi.org/10.1037/0033-2909.84.2.309

Poeck, K. (1985). Pathological laughter and crying. In P. J. Vmken, G. W. Bruyn & H. L. Klawans (Eds.), *Handbook of clinical neurology* (Vol. 45, pp. 219–225). Elsevier Science.

Poletti, M., Enrici, I., Bonuccelli, U., & Adenzato, M. (2011). Theory of mind in Parkinson's disease. *Behavioural Brain Research, 219*, 342–350. https://doi.org/10.1016/j.bbr.2011.01.010

Polich, J. (2003). Overview of P3a and P3b. In J. Polich (Ed.), *Detection of change: Event-related potential and fMRI findings* (pp. 83–98). Kluwer Academic Press.

Polich, J., & Kok, A. (1995). Cognitive and biological determinants of P300: An integrative review. *Biological Psychology, 41*(2), 103–146. https://doi.org/10.1016/0301-0511(95)05130-9

Polimeni, J., & Reiss, J. P. (2006). The first joke: Exploring the evolutionary origins of humor. *Evolutionary Psychology, 4*(1), 347–366. https://doi.org/10.1177/147470490600400129

Polimeni, J. O., Campbell, D. W., Gill, D., Sawatzky, B. L., & Reiss, J. P. (2010). Diminished humour perception in schizophrenia: Relationship to social and cognitive functioning. *Journal of Psychiatric Research, 44*(7), 434–440. https://doi.org/10.1016/j.jpsychires.2009.10.003

Pollio, H. R., & Mers, R. W. (1974). Predictability and the appreciation of comedy. *Bulletin of the Psychonomic Society, 4*(4-A), 229–232. https://doi.org/10.3758/BF03336718

Popik, P., Potasiewicz, A., Pluta, H., & Zieniewicz, A. (2012). High-frequency ultrasonic vocalizations in rats in response to tickling: The effects of restraint stress. *Behavioural Brain Research, 234*(2), 223–227. https://doi.org/10.1016/j.bbr.2012.06.028

Porterfield, A. L. (1987). Does sense of humor moderate the impact of life stress on psychological and physical well-being? *Journal of Research in Personality, 21*(3), 306–317. https://doi.org/10.1016/0092-6566(87)90013-4

Premack, D., & Woodruff, G. (1978). Does the chimpanzee have a theory of mind? *Behavioral and Brain Sciences, 1*(4), 515–526. https://doi.org/10.1017/S0140525X00076512

Prerost, F. J. (1993). A strategy to enhance humor production among elderly persons: Assisting in the management of stress. *Activities, Adaptation and Aging, 17*(4), 17–24. https://doi.org/10.1300/J016v17n04_03

Prerost, F. J., & Ruma, C. (1987). Exposure to humorous stimuli as an adjunct to muscle relaxation training. *Psychology: A Journal of Human Behavior, 24*(4), 70–74.

Pressman, S. D., & Cohen, S. (2005). Does positive affect influence health? *Psychological Bulletin, 131*(6), 925–971. https://doi.org/10.1037/0033-2909.131.6.925

Preuschoft, S., & Van-Hooff, J. A. (1997). The social function of "smile" and "laughter": Variations across primate species and societies. In U. Segerstrale & P. Molnar (Eds.), *Nonverbal communication: Where nature meets culture* (pp. 171–190). Lawrence Erlbaum.

Prodan, C. I., Orbelo, D. M., & Ross, E. D. (2007). Processing of facial blends of emotion: Support for right hemisphere cognitive aging. *Cortex, 43*(2), 196–206. https://doi.org/10.1016/S0010-9452(08)70475-1

Provine, R. R. (2000). *Laughter: A scientific investigation.* Viking.

Provine, R. R. (2004). Laughing, tickling, and the evolution of speech and self. *Current Directions in Psychological Science, 13*(6), 215–218.

Provine, R. R. (2016). Laughter as a scientific problem: An adventure in sidewalk neuroscience. *The Journal of Comparative Neurology, 524*(8), 1532–1539. https://doi.org/10.1002/cne.23845

Provine, R. R. (2017). Laughter as an approach to vocal evolution: The bipedal theory. *Psychonomic Bulletin & Review, 24*(1), 238–244. https://doi.org/10.3758/s13423-016-1089-3

Provine, R. R., & Yong, Y. L. (1991). Laughter: A stereotyped human vocalization. *Ethology, 89*(2), 115–124. https://doi.org/10.1111/j.1439-0310.1991.tb00298.x

Proyer, R. T., Ruch, W., Ali, N. S., Al-Olimat, H. S., Amemiya, T., Adal, T. A., Ansari, S. A., Arhar, Š., Asem, G., Baudin, N., Bawab, S., Bergen, D., Brdar, I., Brites, R., Brunner-Sciarra, M., Carrell, A., Dios, H. C., Celik, M., Ceschi, G., . . . Yeun, E. J. (2009). Breaking ground in cross-cultural research on the fear of being laughed at (gelotophobia): A multi-national study involving 73 countries. *Humor: International Journal of Humor Research, 22*(1), 253–279. https://doi.org/10.1515/HUMR.2009.012

Proyer, R. T., Ruch, W., & Buschor, C. (2013). Testing strengths-based interventions: A preliminary study on the effectiveness of a program targeting curiosity, gratitude, hope, humor, and zest for enhancing life satisfaction. *Journal of Happiness Studies: An Interdisciplinary Forum on Subjective Well-Being, 14*(1), 275–292. https://doi.org/10.1007/s10902-012-9331-9

Proyer, R. T., Ruch, W., & Chen, G.-H. (2012). Gelotophobia: Life satisfaction and happiness across cultures. *Humor: International Journal of Humor Research, 25*(1), 23–40. https://doi.org/10.1515/humor-2012-0002

Pryor, J. B. (1995a). The phenomenology of sexual harassment: Why does sexual behavior bother people in the workplace? *Consulting Psychology Journal, 47*(3), 160–168. https://doi.org/10.1037/1061-4087.47.3.160

Pryor, J. B. (1995b). The psychological impact of sexual harassment on women in the U.S. military. *Basic and Applied Social Psychology, 17*(4), 581–603. https://doi.org/10.1207/s15324834basp1704_9

Puche-Navarro, R. (2004). Graphic jokes and children's mind: An unusual way to approach children's representational activity. *Scandinavian Journal of Psychology, 45*(4), 343–355. https://doi.org/10.1111/j.1467-9450.2004.00414.x

Puche-Navarro, R. (2009). From implicit to explicit representation in children's response to pictorial humor. *International Journal of Behavioral Development, 33*(6), 543–555. https://doi.org/10.1177/0165025409343755

Raichle, M. E. (2009). A brief history of human brain mapping. *Trends in Neurosciences, 32*(2), 118–126. https://doi.org/10.1016/j.tins.2008.11.001

Rajji, T. K. (2019). Transcranial magnetic and electrical stimulation in Alzheimer's disease and mild cognitive impairment: A review of randomized controlled trials. *Clinical Pharmacology and Therapeutics, 106*(4), 776–780. https://doi.org/10.1002/cpt.1574

Rakoczy, H., Harder-Kasten, A., & Sturm, L. (2012). The decline of theory of mind in old age is (partly) mediated by developmental changes in domain-general abilities. *British Journal of Psychology, 103*(1), 58–72. https://doi.org/10.1111/j.2044-8295.2011.02040.x

Ramachandran, V. S. (1998). The neurology and evolution of humor, laughter, and smiling: The false alarm theory. *Medical Hypotheses, 51*(4), 351–354. https://doi.org/10.1016/S0306-9877(98)90061-5

Ramírez-Esparza, N., Gosling, S. D., Benet-Martínez, V., Potter, J. P., & Pennebaker, J. W. (2006). Do bilinguals have two personalities? A special case of cultural frame switching. *Journal of Research in Personality, 40*(2), 99–120. https://doi.org/10.1016/j.jrp.2004.09.001

Rapinesi, C., Kotzalidis, G. D., Ferracuti, S., Sani, G., Girardi, P., & Del Casale, A. (2019). Brain stimulation in obsessive-compulsive disorder (OCD): A systematic review. *Current Neuropharmacology, 17*(8), 787–807. https://doi.org/10.2174/1570159X17666190409142555

Rapp, A. (1951). *The origins of wit and humor*. Dutton.

Rapp, A. M., Langohr, K., Mutschler, D. E., & Wild, B. (2014). Irony and proverb comprehension in schizophrenia: Do female patients "dislike" ironic remarks? *Schizophrenia Research and Treatment, 84*, 1086. https://doi.org/10.1155/2014/841086

Rapp, A. M., Mutschler, D. E., Wild, B., Erb, M., Lengsfeld, I., Saur, R., & Grodd, W. (2010). Neural correlates of irony comprehension: The role of schizotypal personality traits. *Brain and Language, 113*(1), 1–12. https://doi.org/10.1016/j.bandl.2009.11.007

Rayner, K., Pollatsek, A., Ashby, J., & Clifton, C. (2012). *The psychology of reading* (2nd ed.). Psychology Press. https://doi.org/10.4324/9780203155158

Renton, A. E., Chiò, A., & Traynor, B. J. (2014). State of play in amyotrophic lateral sclerosis genetics. *Nature Neuroscience, 17*(1), 17–23. https://doi.org/10.1038/nn.3584

Rieber, R. (Ed.). (2013). *Wilhelm Wundt and the making of a scientific psychology*. Springer Science & Business Media.

Roaldsen, B. L., Sørlie, T., & Lorem, G. F. (2015). Cancer survivors' experiences of humour while navigating through challenging landscapes—A socio-narrative approach. *Scandinavian Journal of Caring Sciences, 29*(4), 724–733. https://doi.org/10.1111/scs.12203

Robinson, D. T., & Smith-Lovin, L. (2001). Getting a laugh: Gender, status, and humor in task discussions. *Social Forces, 80*(1), 123–158. https://doi.org/10.1353/sof.2001.0085

Roesch, S. C., Wee, C., & Vaughn, A. A. (2006). Relations between the Big Five personality traits and dispositional coping in Korean Americans: Acculturation as a moderating factor. *International Journal of Psychology, 41*(2), 85–96. https://doi.org/10.1080/00207590544000112

Rogers, L. J., & Vallortigara, G. (Eds.). (2017). *Lateralized brain functions: Methods in human and nonhuman species.* Springer SBM. https://doi.org/10.1007/978-1-4939-6725-4

Rogers, M. H., & Anderson, P. B. (2009). *Deep brain stimulation: Applications, complications and side effects.* Nova Biomedical Books.

Romaniello, R., Marelli, S., Giorda, R., Bedeschi, M. F., Bonaglia, M. C., Arrigoni, F., Triulzi, F., Bassi, M. T., & Borgatti, R. (2017). Clinical characterization, genetics, and long-term follow-up of a large cohort of patients with agenesis of the corpus callosum. *Journal of Child Neurology, 32*(1), 60–71. https://doi.org/10.1177/0883073816664668

Romanova, A. L. (2014). Age specifics of perceptions of funny and scary things in animated films. *Cultural-Historical Psychology, 10*(4), 47–56.

Romundstad, S., Svebak, S., Holen, A., & Holmen, J. (2016). A 15-year follow-up study of sense of humor and causes of mortality: The Nord-Trøndelag health study. *Psychosomatic Medicine, 78*(3), 345–353. https://doi.org/10.1097/PSY.0000000000000275

Rosen, B. R., Buckner, R. L., & Dale, A. M. (1998). Event-related functional MRI: Past, present, and future. *PNAS: Proceedings of the National Academy of Sciences of the United States of America, 95*(3), 773–780. https://doi.org/10.1073/pnas.95.3.773

Rosenbaum, R. S., Gilboa, A., & Moscovitch, M. (2014). Case studies continue to illuminate the cognitive neuroscience of memory. *Annals of the New York Academy of Sciences, 1316*(1), 105–133. https://doi.org/10.1111/nyas.12467

Rosenheim, E., & Golan, G. (1986). Patients' reactions to humorous interventions in psychotherapy. *American Journal of Psychotherapy, 40*(1), 110–124. https://doi.org/10.1176/appi.psychotherapy.1986.40.1.110

Rosenheim, E., Tecucianu, E., & Dimitrovsky, L. (1989). Schizophrenics' appreciation of humorous therapeutic interventions. *Humor: International Journal of Humor Research, 2*(2), 141–152. https://doi.org/10.1515/humr.1989.2.2.141

Rothbart, M. K. (1973). Laughter in young children. *Psychological Bulletin, 80,* 247–256. https://doi.org/10.1037/h0034846

Rotton, J. (1992). Trait humor and longevity: Do comics have the last laugh? *Health Psychology, 11*(4), 262–266. https://doi.org/10.1037/0278-6133.11.4.262

Rotton, J., & Shats, M. (1996). Effects of state humor, expectancies, and choice on postsurgical mood and self-medication: A field experiment. *Journal of Applied Social Psychology, 26*(20), 1775–1794. https://doi.org/10.1111/j.1559-1816.1996.tb00097.x

Roy, D., McCann, U., Han, D., & Rao, V. (2015). Pathological laughter and crying and psychiatric comorbidity after traumatic brain injury. *The Journal of Neuropsychiatry and Clinical Neurosciences, 27*(4), 299–303. https://doi.org/10.1176/appi.neuropsych.15030045

Ruch, W. (1988). Sensation seeking and the enjoyment of structure and content of humor: Stability of findings across four samples. *Personality and Individual Differences, 9*(5), 861–871. https://doi.org/10.1016/0191-8869(88)90004-9

Ruch, W. (2012, November 2–4). *Towards a new structural model of the sense of humor: Preliminary findings* [Paper presentation]. Association for the Advancement of Artificial Intelligence Fall Symposium, Arlington, VA, United States.

Ruch, W., & Carrell, A. (1998). Trait cheerfulness and the sense of humour. *Personality and Individual Differences, 24*(4), 551–558. https://doi.org/10.1016/S0191-8869(97)00221-3

Ruch, W., & Ekman, P. (2001). The expressive pattern of laughter. In A. Kasziak (Ed.), *Emotion, qualia, and consciousness* (pp. 426–443). World Scientific. https://doi.org/10.1142/9789812810687_0033

Ruch, W., Hofmann, J., & Platt, T. (2015). Individual differences in gelotophobia and responses to laughter-eliciting emotions. *Personality and Individual Differences, 72*, 117–121. https://doi.org/10.1016/j.paid.2014.08.034

Ruch, W., & Köhler, G. (1999). The measurement of state and trait cheerfulness. In I. Mervielde, I. J. Deary, F. De Fruyt, & F. Ostendorf (Eds.), *Personality psychology in Europe* (pp. 67–83). Tilburg University Press.

Ruch, W., Köhler, G., & van Thriel, C. (1996). Assessing the "humorous temperament": Construction of the facet and standard trait forms of the State-Trait-Cheerfulness-Inventory—STCI. *Humor: International Journal of Humor Research, 9*(3–4), 303–339. https://doi.org/10.1515/humr.1996.9.3-4.303

Ruch, W., McGhee, P. E., & Hehl, F.-J. (1990). Age differences in the enjoyment of incongruity-resolution and nonsense humor during adulthood. *Psychology and Aging, 5*(3), 348–355. https://doi.org/10.1037/0882-7974.5.3.348

Ruch, W., Ott, C., Accoce, J., & Bariaud, F. (1991). Cross-national comparison of humor categories: France and Germany. *Humor: International Journal of Humor Research, 4*(1), 391–414. https://doi.org/10.1515/humr.1991.4.3-4.391

Ruch, W., Platt, T., Proyer, R. T., & Chen, H. C. (2019). Humor and laughter, playfulness and cheerfulness: Upsides and downsides to a life of lightness. *Frontiers in Psychology, 10*, 730. https://doi.org/10.3389/fpsyg.2019.00730

Ruch, W., Proyer, R. T., Harzer, C., Park, N., Peterson, C., & Seligman, M. E. P. (2010). Values in action inventory of strengths (VIA-IS): Adaptation and validation of the German version and the development of a peer-rating form. *Journal of Individual Differences, 31*(3), 138–149. https://doi.org/10.1027/1614-0001/a000022

Ruch, W., & Titze, M. (1998). *GELOPH 46* [Unpublished questionnaire]. University of Düsseldorf.

Rudnick, A., Kohn, P. M., Edwards, K. R., Podnar, D., Caird, S., & Martin, R. (2014). Humour-related interventions for people with mental illness: A randomized controlled pilot study. *Community Mental Health Journal, 50*(6), 737–742. https://doi.org/10.1007/s10597-013-9685-4

Rugg, M. D., & Curran, T. (2007). Event-related potentials and recognition memory. *Trends in Cognitive Sciences, 11*(6), 251–257. https://doi.org/10.1016/j.tics.2007.04.004

Rushton, J. P., Bons, T. A., Ando, J., Hur, Y. M., Irwing, P., Vernon, P. A., Petrides, K. V., & Barbaranelli, C. (2009). A general factor of personality from multitrait-multimethod data and cross-national twins. *Twin Research and Human Genetics, 12*(4), 356–365. https://doi.org/10.1375/twin.12.4.356

Russell, J. A. (2003). Core affect and the psychological construction of emotion. *Psychological Review, 110*(1), 145–172. https://doi.org/10.1037/0033-295X.110.1.145

Ryu, K. H., Shin, H. S., & Yang, E. Y. (2015). Effects of laughter therapy on immune responses in postpartum women. *Journal of Alternative and Complementary Medicine, 21*(12), 781–788. https://doi.org/10.1089/acm.2015.0053

Sabbagh, M. A., & Flynn, J. (2006). Mid-frontal EEG alpha asymmetries predict individual differences in one aspect of theory of mind: Mental state decoding. *Social Neuroscience, 1*(3–4), 299–308. https://doi.org/10.1080/17470910601029163

Sabbagh, M. A., Moulson, M. C., & Harkness, K. L. (2004). Neural correlates of mental state decoding in human adults: An event-related potential study. *Journal of Cognitive Neuroscience, 16*(3), 415–426. https://doi.org/10.1162/089892904322926755

Safranek, R., & Schill, T. (1982). Coping with stress: Does humor help? *Psychological Reports, 51*(1), 222. https://doi.org/10.2466/pr0.1982.51.1.222

Salameh, W. A., & Fry, W. F. (Eds.). (2001). *Humor and wellness in clinical interventions.* Praeger.

Saltzman, J., Strauss, E., Hunter, M., & Archibald, S. (2000). Theory of mind and executive functions in normal human aging and Parkinson's disease. *Journal of the International Neuropsychological Society, 6*(7), 781–788. https://doi.org/10.1017/S1355617700677056

Samson, A. C. (2012). The influence of empathizing and systemizing on humor processing: Theory of mind and humor. *Humor: International Journal of Humor Research, 25*(1), 75–98. https://doi.org/10.1515/humor-2012-0005

Samson, A. C., & Antonelli, Y. (2013). Humor as character strength and its relation to life satisfaction and happiness in autism spectrum disorders. *Humor: International Journal of Humor Research, 26*(3), 477–491. https://doi.org/10.1515/humor-2013-0031

Samson, A. C., & Hegenloh, M. (2010). Stimulus characteristics affect humor processing in individuals with Asperger syndrome. *Journal of Autism and Developmental Disorders, 40*(4), 438–447. https://doi.org/10.1007/s10803-009-0885-2

Samson, A. C., Huber, O., & Ruch, W. (2013). Seven decades after Hans Asperger's observations: A comprehensive study of humor in individuals with autism spectrum disorders. *Humor: International Journal of Humor Research, 26*(3), 441–460. https://doi.org/10.1515/humor-2013-0026

Samson, A. C., Lackner, H. K., Weiss, E. M., & Papousek, I. (2012). Perception of other people's mental states affects humor in social anxiety. *Journal of Behavior Therapy and Experimental Psychiatry, 43*, 625–631. https://doi.org/10.1016/j.jbtep.2011.08.007

Samson, A. C., Zysset, S., & Huber, O. (2008). Cognitive humor processing: Different logical mechanisms in nonverbal cartoons—An fMRI study. *Social Neuroscience, 3*(2), 125–140. https://doi.org/10.1080/17470910701745858

Samson, A. M., & Waller, B. M. (2010). Not growling but smiling: New interpretations of the bared-teeth motif in the pre-Columbian Caribbean. *Current Anthropology, 51*(3), 425–433. https://doi.org/10.1086/651090

Sánchez, J. C., Echeverri, L. F., Londoño, M. J., Ochoa, S. A., Quiroz, A. F., Romero, C. R., & Ruiz, J. O. (2017). Effects of a humor therapy program on stress levels in pediatric inpatients. *Hospital Pediatrics, 7*(1), 46–53. https://doi.org/10.1542/hpeds.2016-0128

Santangelo, G., Vitale, C., Trojano, L., Errico, D., Amboni, M., Barbarulo, A. M., Grossi, D., & Barone, P. (2012). Neuropsychological correlates of theory of mind in patients with early Parkinson's disease. *Movement Disorders, 27*(1), 98–105. https://doi.org/10.1002/mds.23949

Sapolsky, R. M. (1994). *Why zebras don't get ulcers.* W. H. Freeman.

Satow, T., Usui, K., Matsuhashi, M., Yamamoto, J., Begum, T., Shibasaki, H., Ikeda, A., Miyamoto, S., & Hashimoto, H. (2003). Mirth and laughter arising from human temporal cortex. *Journal of Neurology, Neurosurgery & Psychiatry, 74*(7), 1004–1005. https://doi.org/10.1136/jnnp.74.7.1004

Saucier, D. A., O'Dea, C. J., & Strain, M. L. (2016). The bad, the good, the misunderstood: The social effects of racial humor. *Translational Issues in Psychological Science, 2*(1), 75–85. https://doi.org/10.1037/tps0000059

Sauerwein, H. C., Nolin, P., & Lassonde, M. (1994). Cognitive functioning in callosal agenesis. In M. Lassonde & M. A. Jeeves (Eds.), *Callosal agenesis: A natural split brain?* Springer. https://doi.org/10.1007/978-1-4613-0487-6_23

Schaier, A. H., & Cicirelli, V. G. (1976). Age differences in humor comprehension and appreciation in old age. *Journal of Gerontology, 31*(5), 577–582. https://doi.org/10.1093/geronj/31.5.577

Scherg, M., Berg, P., Nakasato, N., & Beniczky, S. (2019). Taking the EEG back into the brain: The power of multiple discrete sources. *Frontiers in Neurology, 10,* 855. https://doi.org/10.3389/fneur.2019.00855

Schermer, J. A., Kfrerer, M. L., & Lynskey, M. T. (2019). Alcohol dependence and humor styles. *Current Psychology.* Advance online publication. https://www.researchgate.net/publication/337953092_Alcohol_dependence_and_humor_styles

Schermer, J. A., Martin, R. A., Martin, N. G., Lynskey, M., & Vernon, P. (2013). The general factor of personality and humor styles. *Personality and Individual Differences, 54*(8), 890–893. https://doi.org/10.1016/j.paid.2012.12.026

Schmidt, H. E., & Williams, D. I. (1971). The evolution of theories of humour. *Journal of Behavioural Sciences, 1*(3), 95–106.

Schmidt, S. R. (1994). Effects of humor on sentence memory. *Journal of Experimental Psychology, 20*(4), 953–967. https://doi.org/10.1037/0278-7393.20.4.953

Schmidt, S. R. (2002). The humour effect: Differential processing and privileged retrieval. *Memory, 10*(2), 127–138. https://doi.org/10.1080/09658210143000263

Schmidt, S. R., & Williams, A. R. (2001). Memory for humorous cartoons. *Memory & Cognition, 29*(2), 305–311. https://doi.org/10.3758/BF03194924

Schmitt, J. J., Janszky, J., Woermann, F., Tuxhorn, I., & Ebner, A. (2006). Laughter and the mesial and lateral premotor cortex. *Epilepsy & Behavior, 8,* 773–775. https://doi.org/10.1016/j.yebeh.2006.03.003

Schneider, M., Voracek, M., & Tran, U. S. (2018). "A joke a day keeps the doctor away?" Meta-analytical evidence of differential associations of habitual humor styles with mental health. *Scandinavian Journal of Psychology, 59*(3), 289–300. https://doi.org/10.1111/sjop.12432

Schneider, M. A., & Schneider, M. D. (2017). Pseudobulbar affect: What nurses, stroke survivors, and caregivers need to know. *The Journal of Neuroscience Nursing, 49*(2), 114–117. https://doi.org/10.1097/JNN.0000000000000264

Schretlen, D. J. (2010). *Modified Wisconsin Card Sorting Test (M-WCST).* PAR.

Schwehm, A. J., McDermut, W., & Thorpe, K. (2015). A gender study of personality and humor in comedians. *Humor: International Journal of Humor Research, 28*(3), 427–448. https://doi.org/10.1515/humor-2015-0069

Scott, S. K., Lavan, N., Chen, S., & McGettigan, C. (2014). The social life of laughter. *Trends in Cognitive Sciences, 18*(12), 618–620. https://doi.org/10.1016/j.tics.2014.09.002

Seligman, M. E. P., & Csikszentmihalyi, M. (2000). Positive psychology. An introduction. *American Psychologist, 55*(1), 5–14. https://doi.org/10.1037/0003-066X.55.1.5

Sem-Jacobsen, C. W. (1968). *Depth-electrographic stimulation of the human brain and behavior: From fourteen years of studies and treatment of Parkinson's disease and mental disorders with implanted electrodes.* Charles C Thomas.

Shadyac, T. (Director). (1999). *Patch Adams* [film]. Universal Studios.

Shamay, S. G., Tomer, R., & Aharon-Peretz, J. (2002). Deficit in understanding sarcasm in patients with prefrontal lesion is related to impaired empathic ability. *Brain and Cognition, 48*(2–3), 558–563. https://doi.org/10.1006/brcg.2001.1417

Shamay-Tsoory, S. G., Tomer, R., Berger, B. D., Goldsher, D., & Aharon-Peretz, J. (2005). Impaired "affective theory of mind" is associated with right ventro-medial prefrontal damage. *Cognitive and Behavioral Neurology, 18*, 55–67. https://doi.org/10.1097/01.wnn.0000152228.90129.99

Shammi, P., & Stuss, D. T. (1999). Humour appreciation: A role of the right frontal lobe. *Brain: A Journal of Neurology, 122*(4), 657–666. https://doi.org/10.1093/brain/122.4.657

Shammi, P., & Stuss, D. T. (2003). The effects of normal aging on humor appreciation. *Journal of the International Neuropsychological Society, 9*(6), 855–863. https://doi.org/10.1017/S135561770396005X

Shany-Ur, T., Poorzand, P., Grossman, S. N., Growdon, M. E., Jang, J. Y., Ketelle, R. S., Miller, B. L., & Rankin, K. P. (2012). Comprehension of insincere communication in neurodegenerative disease: Lies, sarcasm, and theory of mind. *Cortex, 48*(10), 1329–1341. https://doi.org/10.1016/j.cortex.2011.08.003

Sheldrick, R. C., Maye, M. P., & Carter, A. S. (2017). Age at first identification of autism spectrum disorder: An analysis of two US surveys. *Journal of the American Academy of Child & Adolescent Psychiatry, 56*(4), 313–320. https://doi.org/10.1016/j.jaac.2017.01.012

Sher, P. K., & Brown, S. B. (1976). Gelastic epilepsy. Onset in neonatal period. *American Journal of Diseases of Children, 130*(10), 1126–1131. https://doi.org/10.1001/archpedi.1976.02120110088013

Sherman, L. W. (1975). An ecological study of glee in small groups of preschool children. *Child Development, 46*(1), 53–61. https://doi.org/10.2307/1128833

Shibata, M., Terasawa, Y., & Umeda, S. (2014). Integration of cognitive and affective networks in humor comprehension. *Neuropsychologia, 65*, 137–145. https://doi.org/10.1016/j.neuropsychologia.2014.10.025

Shin, H. Y., Hong, S. B., Joo, E. Y., Tae, W. S., Han, S. J., Cho, J. W., Seo, D. W., Kim, S. H., Lee, J. M., & Kim, S. I. (2006). Gelastic seizures involving the right parietal lobe. *Epileptic Disorders, 8*(3), 209–212.

Shlesinger, I. (2017). *Girl logic: The genius and the absurdity.* Hachette Books.

Shultz, T. (1976). A cognitive–developmental analysis of humor. In T. Chapman & H. Foot (Eds.), *Humor and laughter: Theory, research and applications* (pp. 12–13). Wiley.

Shultz, T. R. (1972). The role of incongruity and resolution in children's appreciation of cartoon humor. *Journal of Experimental Child Psychology, 13*(3), 456–477. https://doi.org/10.1016/0022-0965(72)90074-4

Shultz, T. R. (1974a). Development of the appreciation of riddles. *Child Development, 45*(1), 100–105. https://doi.org/10.2307/1127755

Shultz, T. R. (1974b). Order of cognitive processing in humour appreciation. *Canadian Journal of Psychology, 28*(4), 409–420. https://doi.org/10.1037/h0082006

Shultz, T. R., & Horibe, F. (1974). Development of the appreciation of verbal jokes. *Developmental Psychobiology, 10*(1), 13–20. https://doi.org/10.1037/h0035549

Shultz, T. R., & Robillard, J. (1980). The development of linguistic humour in children: Incongruity through rule violation. In P. E. McGhee & A. J. Chapman (Eds.), *Children's humour* (pp. 59–90). John Wiley & Sons.

Shultz, T. R., & Scott, M. B. (1974). The creation of verbal humour. *Canadian Journal of Psychology, 28*(4), 421–425. https://doi.org/10.1037/h0082007

Shuster, S. (2012). The evolution of humor from male aggression. *Psychology Research and Behavior Management, 5,* 19–23. https://doi.org/10.2147/PRBM.S29126

Silva, C., Da Fonseca, D., Esteves, F., & Deruelle, C. (2017). Seeing the funny side of things: Humour processing in autism spectrum disorders. *Research in Autism Spectrum Disorders, 43–44,* 8–17. https://doi.org/10.1016/j.rasd.2017.09.001

Simon, J. M. (1990). Humor and its relationship to perceived health, life satisfaction, and morale in older adults. *Issues in Mental Health Nursing, 11*(1), 17–31. https://doi.org/10.3109/01612849009014542

Simonet, P. R. (2004). Laughter in animals. In M. Bekoff (Ed.), *Encyclopedia of animal behavior* (Vol. 2, pp. 561–563). Greenwood Press.

Singer, D. L., Gollob, H. F., & Levine, J. (1967). Mobilization of inhibitions and the enjoyment of aggressive humor. *Journal of Personality, 35*(4), 562–569. https://doi.org/10.1111/j.1467-6494.1967.tb01448.x

Sinkeviciute, V., & Dynel, M. (2017). Approaching conversational humour culturally: A survey of the emerging area of investigation. *Language & Communication, 55,* 1–9. https://doi.org/10.1016/j.langcom.2016.12.001

Sinnott, J. D., & Ross, B. M. (1976). Comparison of aggression and incongruity as factors in children's judgments of humor. *The Journal of Genetic Psychology, 128*(2), 241–249. https://doi.org/10.1080/00221325.1976.10533994

Sirigatti, S., Penzo, I., Giannetti, E., Casale, S., & Stefanile, C. (2016). Relationships between humorism profiles and psychological well-being. *Personality and Individual Differences, 90,* 219–224. https://doi.org/10.1016/j.paid.2015.11.011

Sironi, V. A. (2011). Origin and evolution of deep brain stimulation. *Frontiers in Integrative Neuroscience, 5,* 42. https://doi.org/10.3389/fnint.2011.00042

Siviy, S. M., & Panksepp, J. (2011). In search of the neurobiological substrates for social playfulness in mammalian brains. *Neuroscience and Biobehavioral Reviews, 35*(9), 1821–1830. https://doi.org/10.1016/j.neubiorev.2011.03.006

Slaby, I., Holmes, A., Moran, J. M., Eddy, M. D., Mahoney, C. R., Taylor, H. A., & Brunyé, T. T. (2015). Direct current stimulation of the left temporoparietal junction modulates dynamic humor appreciation. *NeuroReport, 26*(16), 988–993. https://doi.org/10.1097/WNR.0000000000000456

Slobodchikoff, C. N., Perla, B. S., & Verdolin, J. L. (2009). *Prairie dogs: Communication and community in an animal society.* Harvard University Press.

Smith, P. K. (1982). Does play matter? Functional and evolutionary aspects of animal and human play. *Behavioral & Brain Sciences, 5*(1), 139–184. https://doi.org/10.1017/S0140525X0001092X

Smith, P. K., & Pelligrini, A. D. (2005). Play in great apes and humans. In A. D. Pellegrini & P. K. Smith (Eds.), *The nature of play: Great apes and humans* (pp. 285–298). Guilford Press.

Smoski, M., & Bachorowski, J.-A. (2003). Antiphonal laughter between friends and strangers. *Cognition and Emotion, 17,* 327–340. https://doi.org/10.1080/02699930302296

Snow, C. E. (1989). Imitativeness: A trait or a skill? In G. Speidel & K. Nelson (Eds.), *The many faces of imitation* (pp. 73–90). Springer Verlag.

Spencer, H. (1911). On the physiology of laughter. *Essays on education*. Dent.

Sperli, F., Spinelli, L., Pollo, C., & Seeck, M. (2006). Contralateral smile and laughter, but no mirth, induced by electrical stimulation of the cingulate cortex. *Epilepsia, 47*(2), 440–443. https://doi.org/10.1111/j.1528-1167.2006.00442.x

Sporns, O. (2016). *Networks of the brain*. MIT Press.

Sporns, O., & Betzel, R. F. (2016). Modular brain networks. *Annual Review of Psychology, 67*, 613–640. https://doi.org/10.1146/annurev-psych-122414-033634

Squire, L. R. (2009). The legacy of patient H.M. for neuroscience. *Neuron, 61*(1), 6–9. https://doi.org/10.1016/j.neuron.2008.12.023

Sroufe, L. A., & Waters, E. (1976). The ontogenesis of smiling and laughter: A perspective on the organization of development in infancy. *Psychological Review, 83*, 173–189. https://doi.org/10.1037/0033-295X.83.3.173

Sroufe, L. A., & Wunsch, J. P. (1972). The development of laughter in the first year of life. *Child Development, 43*(4), 1326–1344. https://doi.org/10.2307/1127519

Staios, M., Fisher, F., Lindell, A. K., Ong, B., Howe, J., & Reardon, K. (2013). Exploring sarcasm detection in amyotrophic lateral sclerosis using ecologically valid measures. *Frontiers in Human Neuroscience, 7*, 178. https://doi.org/10.3389/fnhum.2013.00178

Stanley, J. T., Lohani, M., & Isaacowitz, D. M. (2014). Age-related differences in judgments of inappropriate behavior are related to humor style preferences. *Psychology and Aging, 29*(3), 528–541. https://doi.org/10.1037/a0036666

Stewart, S., & Thompson, D. R. (2015). Does comedy kill? A retrospective, longitudinal cohort, nested case-control study of humour and longevity in 53 British comedians. *International Journal of Cardiology, 180*, 258–261. https://doi.org/10.1016/j.ijcard.2014.11.152

St. James, P. J., & Tager-Flusberg, H. (1994). An observational study of humor in autism and Down syndrome. *Journal of Autism and Developmental Disorders, 24*(5), 603–617. https://doi.org/10.1007/BF02172141

Stoel, R. D., De Geus, E. J. C., & Boomsma, D. I. (2006). Genetic analysis of sensation seeking with an extended twin design. *Behavior Genetics, 36*(2), 229–237. https://doi.org/10.1007/s10519-005-9028-5

Storey, R. (2003). Humor and sexual selection. *Human Nature, 14*(4), 319–336. https://doi.org/10.1007/s12110-003-1009-x

Strauss, W., & Howe, N. (1991). *Generations: The history of America's future, 1584 to 2069*. Morrow.

Striano, S., Meo, R., Bilo, L., Cirillo, S., Nocerino, C., Ruosi, P., Striano, P., & Estraneo, A. (1999). Gelastic epilepsy: Symptomatic and cryptogenic cases. *Epilepsia, 40*(3), 294–302. https://doi.org/10.1111/j.1528-1157.1999.tb00707.x

Striedter, G. F. (2006). Précis of principles of brain evolution. *Behavioral and Brain Sciences, 29*(1), 1–12. https://doi.org/10.1017/S0140525X06009010

Substance Abuse and Mental Health Services Administration. (2013). *National survey on drug use and health*. Center for Behavioral Health Statistics and Quality. https://www.samhsa.gov/data/data-we-collect/nsduh-national-survey-drug-use-and-health

Sullivan, K., Winner, E., & Hopfield, N. (1995). How children tell a lie from a joke: The role of second-order mental state attributions. *British Journal of Develop-*

mental Psychology, 13(2), 191–204. https://doi.org/10.1111/j.2044-835X.1995. tb00673.x

Suls, J. M. (1972). A two-stage model for the appreciation of jokes and cartoons: An information-processing analysis. In J. H. Goldstein & P. E. McGhee (Eds.), *The psychology of humor: Theoretical perspectives and empirical issues* (pp. 81–100). Academic Press. https://doi.org/10.1016/B978-0-12-288950-9.50010-9

Suls, J. M. (1983). Cognitive processes in humor appreciation. In P. E. McGhee & J. H. Goldstein (Eds.), *Handbook of humor research* (Vol. 1, pp. 39–57). Springer-Verlag. https://doi.org/10.1007/978-1-4612-5572-7_3

Summerfelt, H., Lippman, L., & Hyman, I. E., Jr. (2010). The effect of humor on memory: Constrained by the pun. *The Journal of General Psychology, 137*(4), 376–394. https://doi.org/10.1080/00221309.2010.499398

Sutton, J. (2017). "Many fairy tales about the brain still propagate through our field." Interview with Lisa Feldman Barrett. *The Psychologist, 30*, 54–57.

Svebak, S. (1975). Respiratory patterns as predictors of laughter. *Psychophysiology, 12*(1), 62–65. https://doi.org/10.1111/j.1469-8986.1975.tb03062.x

Svebak, S. (1982). The effect of mirthfulness upon the amount of discordant right-left occipital EEG alpha. *Motivation and Emotion, 6*, 133–147. https://doi.org/10.1007/BF00992460

Svebak, S., Kristoffersen, B., & Aasarød, K. (2006). Sense of humor and survival among a county cohort of patients with end-stage renal failure: A two-year prospective study. *International Journal of Psychiatry in Medicine, 36*(3), 269–281. https://doi.org/10.2190/EFDR-CMDW-X8MH-WKUD

Svebak, S., Martin, R. A., & Holmen, J. (2004). The prevalence of sense of humor in a large, unselected county population in Norway: Relations with age, sex, and some health indicators. *Humor: International Journal of Humor Research, 17*(1–2), 121–134. https://doi.org/10.1515/humr.2004.001

Svebak, S., Romundstad, S., & Holmen, J. (2010). A 7-year prospective study of sense of humor and mortality in an adult county population: The HUNT-2 study. *International Journal of Psychiatry in Medicine, 40*(2), 125–146. https://doi.org/10.2190/PM.40.2.a

Swaab, T. Y., Ledoux, K., Camblin, C. C., & Boudewyn, M. A. (2012). Language-related ERP components. In S. J. Luck & E. S. Kappenman (Eds.), *The Oxford handbook of event-related potential components* (pp. 397–439). Oxford University Press.

Swani, K., Weinberger, M. G., & Gulas, C. S. (2013). The impact of violent humor on advertising success: A gender perspective. *Journal of Advertising, 42*(4), 308–319. https://doi.org/10.1080/00913367.2013.795121

Swartz, B. E. (1998). The advantages of digital over analog recording techniques. *Electroencephalography and Clinical Neurophysiology, 106*(2), 113–117. https://doi.org/10.1016/S0013-4694(97)00113-2

Symington, S. H., Paul, L. K., Symington, M. F., Ono, M., & Brown, W. S. (2010). Social cognition in individuals with agenesis of the corpus callosum. *Social Neuroscience, 5*(3), 296–308. https://doi.org/10.1080/17470910903462419

Szabo, A. (2003). The acute effects of humor and exercise on mood and anxiety. *Journal of Leisure Research, 35*(2), 152–162. https://doi.org/10.1080/00222216.2003.11949988

Szabo, A., Ainsworth, S. E., & Danks, P. K. (2005). Experimental comparison of the psychological benefits of aerobic exercise, humor, and music. *Humor: International Journal of Humor Research, 18*(3), 235–246. https://doi.org/10.1515/humr.2005.18.3.235

Takanashi, H. (2007). Orthographic puns: The case of Japanese kyoka. *Humor: International Journal of Humor Research, 20*(3), 235–259. https://doi.org/10.1515/HUMOR.2007.012

Takeda, M., Hashimoto, R., Kudo, T., Okochi, M., Tagami, S., Morihara, T., Sadick, G., & Tanaka, T. (2010). Laughter and humor as complementary and alternative medicines for dementia patients. *BMC Complementary & Alternative Medicine, 10*(28), 1–7. https://doi.org/10.1186/1472-6882-10-28

Tasch, E., Cendes, F., Li, L. M., Dubeau, F., Montes, J., Rosenblatt, B., Andermann, F., & Arnold, D. (1998). Hypothalamic hamartomas and gelastic epilepsy: A spectroscopic study. *Neurology, 51*(4), 1046–1050. https://doi.org/10.1212/WNL.51.4.1046

Taylor, S. E., Klein, L. C., Lewis, B. P., Gruenewald, T. L., Gurung, R. A. R., & Updegraff, J. A. (2000). Biobehavioral responses to stress in females: Tend-and-befriend, not fight-or-flight. *Psychological Review, 107*(3), 411–429. https://doi.org/10.1037/0033-295X.107.3.411

Temple, C. M., Jeeves, M. A., & Vilarroya, O. (1989). Ten pen men: Rhyming skills in two children with callosal agenesis. *Brain and Language, 37*(4), 548–564. https://doi.org/10.1016/0093-934X(89)90111-9

Temple, C. M., Jeeves, M. A., & Vilarroya, O. O. (1990). Reading in callosal agenesis. *Brain and Language, 39*, 235–253. https://doi.org/10.1016/0093-934X(90)90013-7

Thakore, N. J., & Pioro, E. P. (2017). Laughter, crying and sadness in ALS. *Journal of Neurology, Neurosurgery, and Psychiatry, 88*(10), 825–831. https://doi.org/10.1136/jnnp-2017-315622

Thaler, A., Posen, J., Giladi, N., Manor, Y., Mayanz, C., Mirelman, A., & Gurevich, T. (2012). Appreciation of humor is decreased among patients with Parkinson's disease. *Parkinsonism & Related Disorders, 18*(2), 144–148. https://doi.org/10.1016/j.parkreldis.2011.09.004

Thermenos, H. W., Whitfield-Gabrieli, S., Seidman, L. J., Kuperberg, G., Juelich, R. J., Divatia, S., Riley, C., Jabbar, G. A., Shenton, M. E., Kubicki, M., Manschreck, T., Keshavan, M. S., & DeLisi, L. E. (2013). Altered language network activity in young people at familial high-risk for schizophrenia. *Schizophrenia Research, 151*(1–3), 229–237. https://doi.org/10.1016/j.schres.2013.09.023

Thomae, M., & Pina, A. (2015). Sexist humor and social identity: The role of sexist humor in men's in-group cohesion, sexual harassment, rape proclivity, and victim blame. *Humor: International Journal of Humor Research, 28*(2), 187–204. https://doi.org/10.1515/humor-2015-0023

Thomas, C. A., & Esses, V. M. (2004). Individual differences in reactions to sexist humor. *Group Processes & Intergroup Relations, 7*(1), 89–100. https://doi.org/10.1177/1368430204039975

Thorson, J. A., & Powell, F. C. (1994). Depression and sense of humor. *Psychological Reports, 75*(3), 1473–1474. https://doi.org/10.2466/pr0.1994.75.3f.1473

Thorson, J. A., & Powell, F. C. (1996). Women, aging, and sense of humor. *Humor: International Journal of Humor Research, 9*(2), 169–186. https://doi.org/10.1515/humr.1996.9.2.169

Thorson, J. A., Powell, F. C., Sarmany-Schuller, I., & Hampes, W. P. (1997). Psychological health and sense of humor. *Journal of Clinical Psychology, 53*(6), 605–619. https://doi.org/10.1002/(SICI)1097-4679(199710)53:6<605::AID-JCLP9>3.0.CO;2-I

Tian, F., Hou, Y., Zhu, W., Dietrich, A., Zhang, Q., Yang, W., Chen, Q., Sun, J., Jiang, Q., & Cao, G. (2017). Getting the joke: Insight during humor comprehension–Evidence from an fMRI study. *Frontiers in Psychology, 8,* 1835. https://doi.org/10.1016/j.neuroimage.2006.09.049

Tie, Y., Suarez, R. O., Whalen, S., Radmanesh, A., Norton, I. H., & Golby, A. J. (2009). Comparison of blocked and event-related fMRI designs for pre-surgical language mapping. *NeuroImage, 47*(Suppl. 2), T107–T115. https://doi.org/10.1016/j.neuroimage.2008.11.020

Titze, M. (2009). Gelotophobia: The fear of being laughed at. *Humor: International Journal of Humor Research, 22*(1–2), 27–48. https://doi.org/10.1515/HUMR.2009.002

Todt, D., & Vettin, J. (2005). Human laughter, social play, and play vocalizations of non-human primates: An evolutionary approach. *Behaviour, 142*(2), 217–240. https://doi.org/10.1163/1568539053627640

Tosun, S., Faghihi, N., & Vaid, J. (2018). Is an ideal sense of humor gendered? A cross-national study. *Frontiers in Psychology, 9,* 199. https://doi.org/10.3389/fpsyg.2018.00199

Tran, T. P. Y., Truong, V. T., Wilk, M., Tayah, T., Bouthillier, A., Mohamed, I., & Nguyen, D. K. (2014). Different localizations underlying cortical gelastic epilepsy: Case series and review of literature. *Epilepsy & Behavior, 35,* 34–41. https://doi.org/10.1016/j.yebeh.2014.03.024

Treger, S., Sprecher, S., & Erber, R. (2013). Laughing and liking: Exploring the interpersonal effects of humor use in initial social interactions. *European Journal of Social Psychology, 43*(6), 532–543. https://doi.org/10.1002/ejsp.1962

Tse, M. M. Y., Lo, A. P. K., Cheng, T. L. Y., Chan, E. K. K., Chan, A. H. Y., & Chung, H. S. W. (2010). Humor therapy: Relieving chronic pain and enhancing happiness for older adults. *Journal of Aging Research, 2010,* 343574. https://doi.org/10.4061/2010/343574

Tsoi, D. T., Lee, K. H., Gee, K. A., Holden, K. L., Parks, R. W., & Woodruff, P. W. (2008). Humour experience in schizophrenia: Relationship with executive dysfunction and psychosocial impairment. *Psychological Medicine, 38*(6), 801–810. https://doi.org/10.1017/S0033291707002528

Tu, S., Cao, X. J., Yun, X. J., Wang, K. C., Zhao, G., & Qiu, J. (2014). A new association evaluation stage in cartoon apprehension: Evidence from an ERP study. *Journal of Behavioral and Brain Science, 4*(2), 75–83. https://doi.org/10.4236/jbbs.2014.42010

Tucker, R. P., Judah, M. R., O'Keefe, V. M., Mills, A. C., Lechner, W. V., Davidson, C. L., Grant, D. M. M., & Wingate, L. R. (2013). Humor styles impact the relationship between symptoms of social anxiety and depression. *Personality and Individual Differences, 55*(7), 823–827. https://doi.org/10.1016/j.paid.2013.07.008

Tucker, R. P., Wingate, L. R., O'Keefe, V. M., Slish, M. L., Judah, M. R., & Rhoades-Kerswill, S. (2013). The moderating effect of humor style on the relationship between interpersonal predictors of suicide and suicidal ideation. *Personality and Individual Differences, 54*(5), 610–615. https://doi.org/10.1016/j.paid.2012.11.023

Turk, A. A., Brown, W. S., Symington, M., & Paul, L. K. (2010). Social narratives in agenesis of the corpus callosum: Linguistic analysis of the Thematic Apperception Test. *Neuropsychologia, 48,* 43–50. https://doi.org/10.1016/j.neuropsychologia.2009.08.009

Turkeltaub, P. E. (2019). A taxonomy of brain–behavior relationships after stroke. *Journal of Speech, Language, and Hearing Research, 62*(11), 3907–3922. https://doi.org/10.1044/2019_JSLHR-L-RSNP-19-0032

Turkstra, L. S., Norman, R. S., Mutlu, B., & Duff, M. C. (2018). Impaired theory of mind in adults with traumatic brain injury: A replication and extension of findings. *Neuropsychologia, 111*, 117–122. https://doi.org/10.1016/j.neuropsychologia.2018.01.016

Twenge, J. M. (2014). *Generation me: Why today's young Americans are more confident, assertive, entitled—and more miserable than ever before.* Simon and Schuster.

Twenge, J. M., & Campbell, S. M. (2008). Generational differences in psychological traits and their impact on the workplace. *Journal of Managerial Psychology, 23*(8), 862–877. https://doi.org/10.1108/02683940810904367

Tzovara, A., Murray, M. M., Michel, C. M., & De Lucia, M. (2012). A tutorial review of electrical neuroimaging from group-average to single-trial event-related potentials. *Developmental Neuropsychology, 37*(6), 518–544. https://doi.org/10.1080/87565641.2011.636851

Uekermann, J., Channon, S., & Daum, I. (2006). Humor processing, mentalizing, and executive function in normal aging. *Journal of the International Neuropsychological Society, 12*, 184–191. https://doi.org/10.1017/S1355617706060280

Uekermann, J., Channon, S., Winkel, K., Schlebusch, P., & Daum, I. (2007). Theory of mind, humour processing and executive functioning in alcoholism. *Addiction, 102*(2), 232–240. https://doi.org/10.1111/j.1360-0443.2006.01656.x

Uekermann, J., Daum, I., & Channon, S. (2007). Toward a cognitive and social neuroscience of humor processing. *Social Cognition, 25*(4), 553–572. https://doi.org/10.1521/soco.2007.25.4.553

Uekermann, J., Thoma, P., & Daum, I. (2008). Proverb interpretation changes in aging. *Brain and Cognition, 67*(1), 51–57. https://doi.org/10.1016/j.bandc.2007.11.003

Ulrich-Lai, Y. M., & Herman, J. P. (2009). Neural regulation of endocrine and autonomic stress responses. *Nature Reviews Neuroscience, 10*(6), 397–409. https://doi.org/10.1038/nrn2647

Vacas, S. M., Stella, F., Loureiro, J. C., Simões do Couto, F., Oliveira-Maia, A. J., & Forlenza, O. V. (2019). Noninvasive brain stimulation for behavioural and psychological symptoms of dementia: A systematic review and meta-analysis. *International Journal of Geriatric Psychiatry, 34*(9), 1336–1345. https://doi.org/10.1002/gps.5003

Vaid, J. (2006). Joking across languages: Perspectives on humor, emotion, and bilingualism. A. Pavlenko (Ed.), *Bilingual minds: Emotional experience, expression and representation* (pp. 152–182). Multilingual Matters.

van den Heuvel, M. P., Bullmore, E. T., & Sporns, O. (2016). Comparative connectomics. *Trends in Cognitive Sciences, 20*(5), 345–361. https://doi.org/10.1016/j.tics.2016.03.001

van Os, J., & Kapur, S. (2009). Schizophrenia. *The Lancet, 374*(9690), 635–645. https://doi.org/10.1016/S0140-6736(09)60995-8

Varga, E., Simon, M., Tényi, T., Schnell, Z., Hajnal, A., Orsi, G., Dóczi, T., Komoly, S., Janszky, J., Füredi, R., Hamvas, E., Fekete, S., & Herold, R. (2013). Irony comprehension and context processing in schizophrenia during remission—A functional MRI study. *Brain and Language, 126*(3), 231–242. https://doi.org/10.1016/j.bandl.2013.05.017

Vasey, G. (1877). *The philosophy of laughter and smiling* (2nd ed.). https://doi.org/10.1037/12373-000

Vaudano, A. E., Pizza, F., Talami, F., Plazzi, G., & Meletti, S. (2019). The neuronal network of laughing in young patients with untreated narcolepsy. *Neurology, 92*(5), e504–e515. https://doi.org/10.1212/WNL.0000000000006853

Vernon, P. A., Martin, R. A., Schermer, J. A., Cherkas, L. F., & Spector, T. D. (2008). Genetic and environmental contributions to humor styles: A replication study. *Twin Research and Human Genetics, 11*(1), 44–47. https://doi.org/10.1375/twin.11.1.44

Vernon, P. A., Martin, R. A., Schermer, J. A., & Mackie, A. (2008). A behavioral genetic investigation of humor styles and their correlations with the Big Five personality dimensions. *Personality and Individual Differences, 44*(5), 1116–1125. https://doi.org/10.1016/j.paid.2007.11.003

Vernon, P. A., Villani, V. C., Schermer, J. A., Kirilovic, S., Martin, R. A., Petrides, K. V., Spector, T. D., & Cherkas, L. F. (2009). Genetic and environmental correlations between trait emotional intelligence and humor styles. *Journal of Individual Differences, 30*(3), 130–137. https://doi.org/10.1027/1614-0001.30.3.130

Veselka, L., Schermer, J. A., Martin, R. A., & Vernon, P. A. (2010). Relations between humor styles and the Dark Triad traits of personality. *Personality and Individual Differences, 48*(6), 772–774. https://doi.org/10.1016/j.paid.2010.01.017

Viana, A. (2017). Humour and laughter as vestiges of evolution. *The European Journal of Humour Research, 5*(1), 1–18. https://doi.org/10.7592/EJHR2017.5.1.viana

Visalberghi, E., Valenzano, D. R., & Preuschoft, S. (2006). Facial displays in *Cebus apella. International Journal of Primatology, 27*(6), 1689–1707. https://doi.org/10.1007/s10764-006-9084-6

Vogan, V. M., Morgan, B. R., Leung, R. C., Anagnostou, E., Doyle-Thomas, K., & Taylor, M. J. (2016). Widespread white matter differences in children and adolescents with autism spectrum disorder. *Journal of Autism and Developmental Disorders, 46*(6), 2138–2147. https://doi.org/10.1007/s10803-016-2744-2

Vrticka, P., Black, J. M., Neely, M., Walter Shelly, E., & Reiss, A. L. (2013). Humor processing in children: Influence of temperament, age and IQ. *Neuropsychologia, 51*(13), 2799–2811. https://doi.org/10.1016/j.neuropsychologia.2013.09.028

Vrticka, P., Black, J. M., & Reiss, A. L. (2013). The neural basis of humour processing. *Nature Reviews Neuroscience, 14*, 860–868. https://doi.org/10.1038/nrn3566

Wada, J. (1949). A new method for determination of the side of cerebral speech dominance: A preliminary report on the intracarotid injection of sodium amytal in man. *Medicine and Biology, 4*, 221–222.

Wada, J., & Rasmussen, T. (2007). Intracarotid injection of sodium amytal for the lateralization of cerebral speech dominance: Experimental and clinical observations. *Journal of Neurosurgery, 106*(6), 1117–1133. Original work published 1960. https://doi.org/10.3171/jns.2007.106.6.1117

Wada, J. A. (1997). Clinical experimental observations of carotid artery injections of sodium amytal. *Brain and Cognition, 33*(1), 11–13. https://doi.org/10.1006/brcg.1997.0880

Wagenbreth, C., Wattenberg, L., Heinze, H.-J., & Zaehle, T. (2016). Implicit and explicit processing of emotional facial expressions in Parkinson's disease. *Behavioural Brain Research, 303*, 182–190. https://doi.org/10.1016/j.bbr.2016.01.059

Wagner, H., Rehmes, U., Kohle, D., & Puta, C. (2014). Laughing: A demanding exercise for trunk muscles. *Journal of Motor Behavior, 46*(1), 33–37. https://doi.org/10.1080/00222895.2013.844091

Waller, B. M., Bard, K. A., Vick, S. J., & Smith Pasqualini, M. C. (2007). Perceived differences between chimpanzee (*Pan troglodytes*) and human (*Homo sapiens*) facial expressions are related to emotional interpretation. *Journal of Comparative Psychology, 121*(4), 398–404. https://doi.org/10.1037/0735-7036.121.4.398

Waller, B. M., & Cherry, L. (2012). Facilitating play through communication: Significance of teeth exposure in the gorilla play face. *American Journal of Primatology, 74*(2), 157–164. https://doi.org/10.1002/ajp.21018

Waller, B. M., & Dunbar, R. I. M. (2005). Differential behavioural effects of silent bared teeth display and relaxed open mouth display in chimpanzees (*Pan troglodytes*). *Ethology, 111*(2), 129–142. https://doi.org/10.1111/j.1439-0310.2004.01045.x

Walsh, J. D. (1928). *Laughter and health.* Appleton. https://doi.org/10.1001/jama.1928.02690420065030

Walter, M., Hänni, B., Haug, M., Amrhein, I., Krebs-Roubicek, E., Müller-Spahn, F., & Savaskan, E. (2007). Humour therapy in patients with late-life depression or Alzheimer's disease: A pilot study. *International Journal of Geriatric Psychiatry, 22*(1), 77–83. https://doi.org/10.1002/gps.1658

Wang, Y., & Su, Y. (2006). Theory of mind in old adults: The performance on Happé's stories and faux pas stories. *Psychologia, 49*(4), 228–237. https://doi.org/10.2117/psysoc.2006.228

Wapner, W., Hamby, S., & Gardner, H. (1981). The role of the right hemisphere in the apprehension of complex linguistic materials. *Brain and Language, 14*(1), 15–33. https://doi.org/10.1016/0093-934X(81)90061-4

Watson, K. K., Matthews, B. J., & Allman, J. M. (2007). Brain activation during sight gags and language-dependent humor. *Cerebral Cortex, 17*(2), 314–324. https://doi.org/10.1093/cercor/bhj149

Weaver, J., & Zillmann, D. (1994). Effect of humor and tragedy on discomfort tolerance. *Perceptual and Motor Skills, 78*(2), 632–634. https://doi.org/10.2466/pms.1994.78.2.632

Weber, M., Ruch, W., Riemann, R., Spinath, F. M., & Angleitner, A. (2014). A twin study on humor appreciation: The importance of separating structure and content. *Journal of Individual Differences, 35*(3), 130–136. https://doi.org/10.1027/1614-0001/a000136

Weed, E., McGregor, W., Feldbaek Nielsen, J., Roepstorff, A., & Frith, U. (2010). Theory of Mind in adults with right hemisphere damage: What's the story? *Brain and Language, 113*(2), 65–72. https://doi.org/10.1016/j.bandl.2010.01.009

Weems, S. (2014). *Ha! The science of when we laugh and why.* Basic Books.

Weinstein, N., Hodgins, H. S., & Ostvik-White, E. (2011). Humor as aggression: Effects of motivation on hostility expressed in humor appreciation. *Journal of Personality and Social Psychology, 100*(6), 1043–1055. https://doi.org/10.1037/a0022495

Weisenberg, M., Tepper, I., & Schwarzwald, J. (1995). Humor as a cognitive technique for increasing pain tolerance. *Pain, 63*(2), 207–212. https://doi.org/10.1016/0304-3959(95)00046-U

Weisfeld, G. E. (1993). The adaptive value of humor and laughter. *Ethology and Sociobiology, 14*(2), 141–169. https://doi.org/10.1016/0162-3095(93)90012-7

Weisfeld, G. E. (2006). Humor appreciation as an adaptive esthetic emotion. *Humor: International Journal of Humor Research, 19*(1), 1–26. https://doi.org/10.1515/HUMOR.2006.001

Weisfeld, G. E., Nowak, N. T., Lucas, T., Weisfeld, C. C., Imamoğlu, E. O., Butovskaya, M., Shen, J., & Parkhill, M. R. (2011). Do women seek humorousness in men because it signals intelligence? A cross-cultural test. *Humor: International Journal of Humor Research, 24*(4), 435–462. https://doi.org/10.1515/humr.2011.025

Weiss, E. M., Gschaidbauer, B. C., Samson, A. C., Steinbäcker, K., Fink, A., & Papousek, I. (2013). From Ice Age to Madagascar: Appreciation of slapstick humor in children with Asperger's syndrome. *Humor: International Journal of Humor Research, 26*(3), 423–440. https://doi.org/10.1515/humor-2013-0029

Weisskopf, M. G., Kioumourtzoglou, M. A., & Roberts, A. L. (2015). Air pollution and autism spectrum disorders: Causal or confounded? *Current Environmental Health Reports, 2*, 430–439. https://doi.org/10.1007/s40572-015-0073-9

Wellcome Library. (n.d.). *Phrenological head* [Illustration]. Wellcome Collection. https://wellcomecollection.org/

Wellenzohn, S., Proyer, R. T., & Ruch, W. (2016a). How do positive psychology interventions work? A short-term placebo-controlled humor-based study on the role of the time focus. *Personality and Individual Differences, 96*, 1–6. https://doi.org/10.1016/j.paid.2016.02.056

Wellenzohn, S., Proyer, R. T., & Ruch, W. (2016b). Humor-based online positive psychology interventions: A randomized placebo-controlled long-term trial. *The Journal of Positive Psychology, 11*(6), 584–594. https://doi.org/10.1080/17439760.2015.1137624

Wernicke, C. (1874). *Der aphasische Symptomencomplex. Eine psychologische Studie auf anatomischer Basis* [The aphasic complex of symptoms. An anatomical psychological study]. M. Crohn und Weigert.

Westbury, C., & Titone, D. (2011). Idiom literality judgments in younger and older adults: Age-related effects in resolving semantic interference. *Psychology and Aging, 26*(2), 467–474. https://doi.org/10.1037/a0022438

White, S., & Camarena, P. (1989). Laughter as a stress reducer in small groups. *Humor: International Journal of Humor Research, 2*(1), 73–79. https://doi.org/10.1515/humr.1989.2.1.73

Whitt, J. K., & Prentice, N. M. (1977). Cognitive processes in the development of children's enjoyment and comprehension of joking riddles. *Developmental Psychology, 13*(2), 129–136. https://doi.org/10.1037/0012-1649.13.2.129

Wickberg, D. (1998). *The senses of humor: Self and laughter in modern America.* Cornell University Press.

Widiger, T. A. (Ed.). (2017). *The Oxford handbook of the five factor model.* Oxford University Press.

Wilbur, C. J., & Campbell, L. (2011). Humor in romantic contexts: Do men participate and women evaluate? *Personality and Social Psychology Bulletin, 37*(7), 918–929. https://doi.org/10.1177/0146167211405343

Wild, B., Rodden, F. A., Rapp, A., Erb, M., Grodd, W., & Ruch, W. (2006). Humor and smiling: Cortical regions selective for cognitive, affective, and volitional components. *Neurology, 66*, 887–893. https://doi.org/10.1212/01.wnl.0000203123.68747.02

Willems, R. M., Van der Haegen, L., Fisher, S. E., & Francks, C. (2014). On the other hand: Including left-handers in cognitive neuroscience and neurogenetics. *Nature Reviews Neuroscience, 15*(3), 193–201. https://doi.org/10.1038/nrn3679

Wilson, G. D., Rust, J., & Kasriel, J. (1977). Genetic and family origins of humor preferences: A twin study. *Psychological Reports, 41*(2), 659–660. https://doi.org/10.2466/pr0.1977.41.2.659

Winner, E. (1997). *The point of words: Children's understanding of metaphor and irony.* Harvard University Press.

Winner, E., Brownell, H., Happé, F., Blum, A., & Pincus, D. (1998). Distinguishing lies from jokes: Theory of mind deficits and discourse interpretation in right hemisphere brain-damaged patients. *Brain and Language, 62*(1), 89–106. https://doi.org/10.1006/brln.1997.1889

Witztum, E., Briskin, S., & Lerner, V. (1999). The use of humor with chronic schizophrenic patients. *Journal of Contemporary Psychotherapy, 29*(3), 223–234. https://doi.org/10.1023/A:1021921202183

Wolfenstein, M. (1954). *Children's humor: A psychological analysis.* Free Press.

Wood, A., Martin, J., & Niedenthal, P. (2017). Towards a social functional account of laughter: Acoustic features convey reward, affiliation, and dominance. *PLOS ONE, 12*(8), e0183811. https://doi.org/10.1371/journal.pone.0183811

Wood, E. E., Kennison, S. M., & Bray, M. (2019, February 7–9). *To catch a (potential) predator: The relationship between verbal behavior and the dark triad* [Poster presentation]. SPSP Convention, Portland, OR, United States.

Wood, E. M. (2015). Amyotrophic lateral sclerosis. In J. S. Goldman (Ed.), *Genetic counseling for adult neurogenetic disease: A casebook for clinicians* (pp. 163–182). Springer Science + Business Media.

World Health Organization. (2017). *Dementia fact sheet.* https://www.who.int/mediacentre/factsheets/fs362/en/

Wortzel, H. S., Oster, T. J., Anderson, C. A., & Arciniegas, D. B. (2008). Pathological laughing and crying: Epidemiology, pathophysiology and treatment. *CNS Drugs, 22*(7), 531–545. https://doi.org/10.2165/00023210-200822070-00001

Wrangham, R. W. (2009). *Catching fire: How cooking made us human.* Basic Books.

Wu, C., Lin, H., & Chen, H. (2016). Gender differences in humour styles of young adolescents: Empathy as a mediator. *Personality and Individual Differences, 99,* 139–143. https://doi.org/10.1016/j.paid.2016.05.018

Wyer, R. S., Jr., & Collins, J. E., II. (1992). A theory of humor elicitation. *Psychological Review, 99*(4), 663–688. https://doi.org/10.1037/0033-295X.99.4.663

Xi, C., Zhu, Y., Mu, Y., Chen, B., Dong, B., Cheng, H., Hu, P., Zhu, C., & Wang, K. (2015). Theory of mind and decision-making processes are impaired in Parkinson's disease. *Behavioural Brain Research, 279,* 226–233. https://doi.org/10.1016/j.bbr.2014.11.035

Xi, C., Zhu, Y., Zhu, C., Song, D., Wang, Y., & Wang, K. (2013). Deficit of theory of mind after temporal lobe cerebral infarction. *Behavioral and Brain Functions, 9,* 15. https://doi.org/10.1186/1744-9081-9-15

Xie, Y., & Dorsky, R. I. (2017). Development of the hypothalamus: Conservation, modification and innovation. *Development, 144,* 1588–1599. https://doi.org/10.1242/dev.139055

Yalisove, D. (1978). The effect of riddle structure on children's comprehension of riddles. *Developmental Psychology, 14*(2), 173–180. https://doi.org/10.1037/0012-1649.14.2.173

Yalisove, M. (1954). *Children's humor: A psychological analysis.* The Free Press.

Yamao, Y., Matsumoto, R., Kunieda, T., Shibata, S., Shimotake, A., Kikuchi, T., Satow, T., Mikuni, N., Fukuyama, H., Ikeda, A., & Miyamoto, S. (2015). Neural correlates of mirth and laughter: A direct electrical cortical stimulation study. *Cortex, 66*, 134–140. https://doi.org/10.1016/j.cortex.2014.11.008

Yao, Z., Hu, B., Xie, Y., Moore, P., & Zheng, J. (2015). A review of structural and functional brain networks: Small world and atlas. *Brain Informatics, 2*(1), 45–52. https://doi.org/10.1007/s40708-015-0009-z

Yeh, Z.-T., & Tsai, C. F. (2014). Impairment on theory of mind and empathy in patients with stroke. *Psychiatry and Clinical Neurosciences, 68*(8), 612–620. https://doi.org/10.1111/pcn.12173

Yeh, Z.-T., Lo, C.-Y., Tsai, M.-D., & Tsai, M.-C. (2015). Mentalizing ability in patients with prefrontal cortex damage. *Journal of Clinical and Experimental Neuropsychology, 37*(2), 128–139. https://doi.org/10.1080/13803395.2014.992864

Yip, J. A., & Martin, R. A. (2006). Sense of humor, emotional intelligence, and social competence. *Journal of Research in Personality, 40*(6), 1202–1208. https://doi.org/10.1016/j.jrp.2005.08.005

York, G. K., III, & Steinberg, D. A. (2011). Hughlings Jackson's neurological ideas. *Brain: A Journal of Neurology, 134*(10), 3106–3113. https://doi.org/10.1093/brain/awr219

Yoshikawa, Y., Ohmaki, E., Kawahata, H., Maekawa, Y., Ogihara, T., Morishita, R., & Aoki, M. (2019). Beneficial effect of laughter therapy on physiological and psychological function in elders. *Nursing Open, 6*, 93–99. https://doi.org/10.1002/nop2.190

Yoshino, S., Fujimori, J., & Kohda, M. (1996). Effects of mirthful laughter on neuroendocrine and immune systems in patients with rheumatoid arthritis. *The Journal of Rheumatology, 23*(4), 793–794.

Yue, X. (2018). *Humor and Chinese culture: A psychological perspective*. Routledge/Taylor & Francis.

Yue, X., Jiang, F., Lu, S., & Hiranandani, N. (2016). To be or not to be humorous? Cross cultural perspectives on humor. *Frontiers in Psychology, 7*, 1495. https://doi.org/10.3389/fpsyg.2016.01495

Yue, X. D. (2011). The Chinese ambivalence to humor: Views from undergraduates in Hong Kong and China. *Humor: International Journal of Humor Research, 24*(4), 463–480. https://doi.org/10.1515/humr.2011.026

Yue, X. D., Wong, A. Y. M., & Hiranandani, N. A. (2014). Humor styles and loneliness: A study among Hong Kong and Hangzhou undergraduates. *Psychological Reports, 115*(1), 65–74. https://doi.org/10.2466/20.21.PR0.115c11z1

Zahr, N. M., & Pfefferbaum, A. (2017). Alcohol's effects on the brain: Neuroimaging results in humans and animal models. *Alcohol Research: Current Reviews, 38*(2), 183–206.

Zeilig, G., Drubach, D. A., Katz-Zeilig, M., & Karatinos, J. (1996). Pathological laughter and crying in patients with closed traumatic brain injury. *Brain Injury, 10*(8), 591–598. https://doi.org/10.1080/026990596124160

Zhen, Z., Fang, H., & Liu, J. (2013). The hierarchical brain network for face recognition. *PLOS ONE, 8*(3), e59886. https://doi.org/10.1371/journal.pone.0059886

Ziegler, M., Danay, E., Heene, M., Asendorpf, J., & Buhner, M. (2012). Openness, fluid intelligence, and crystallized intelligence: Toward an integrative model. *Journal of Research in Personality, 46*(2), 173–183. https://doi.org/10.1016/j.jrp.2012.01.002

Zigler, E., Levine, J., & Gould, L. (1966). Cognitive processes in the development of children's appreciation of humor. *Child Development, 37*(3), 507–518. https://doi.org/10.2307/1126675

Zigler, E., Levine, J., & Gould, L. (1967). Cognitive challenge as a factor in children's humor appreciation. *Journal of Personality and Social Psychology, 6*(3), 332–336. https://doi.org/10.1037/h0024729

Zilles, K. (2018). Brodmann: A pioneer of human brain mapping—his impact on concepts of cortical organization. *Brain: A Journal of Neurology, 141*(11), 3262–3278. https://doi.org/10.1093/brain/awy273

Zillmann, D., de Wied, M., King-Jablonski, C., & Jenzowsky, S. (1996). Drama-induced affect and pain sensitivity. *Psychosomatic Medicine, 58*(4), 333–341. https://doi.org/10.1097/00006842-199607000-00006

Zillmann, D., Rockwell, S., Schweitzer, K., & Sundar, S. S. (1993). Does humor facilitate coping with physical discomfort? *Motivation and Emotion, 17*(1), 1–21. https://doi.org/10.1007/BF00995204

Zink, K. D., & Lieberman, D. E. (2016). Impact of meat and lower Palaeolithic food processing techniques on chewing in humans. *Nature, 531*, 500–503. https://doi.org/10.1038/nature16990

Ziv, A. (1976). Facilitating effects of humor on creativity. *Journal of Educational Psychology, 68*(3), 318–322. https://doi.org/10.1037/0022-0663.68.3.318

Ziv, A. (1983). The influence of humorous atmosphere on divergent thinking. *Contemporary Educational Psychology, 8*(1), 68–75. https://doi.org/10.1016/0361-476X(83)90035-8

Ziv, A. (1988). Teaching and learning with humor: Experiment and replication. *Journal of Experimental Education, 57*(1), 4–15. https://doi.org/10.1080/00220973.1988.10806492

Zola-Morgan, S., Squire, L. R., & Amaral, D. G. (1986). Human amnesia and the medial temporal region: Enduring memory impairment following a bilateral lesion limited to field CA1 of the hippocampus. *The Journal of Neuroscience, 6*(10), 2950–2967. https://doi.org/10.1523/JNEUROSCI.06-10-02950.1986

Zuckerman, M. (1983). Sensation seeking: The initial motive for drug abuse. In E. Gotheil, K. A. Druley, T. E. Skoloda, & H. M. Waxman (Eds.), *Etiological aspects of alcohol and drug abuse* (pp. 202–220). Thomas.

Zuckerman, M. (1984). Sensation seeking: A comparative approach to a human trait. *Behavioral and Brain Sciences, 7*(3), 413–434. https://doi.org/10.1017/S0140525X00018938

Zuckerman, M. (1985). Sensation seeking, mania, and monoamines. *Neuropsychobiology, 13*(3), 121–128. https://doi.org/10.1159/000118174

Zuckerman, M. (1987). Is sensation seeking a predisposing trait for alcoholism? In E. Gottheil, K. A. Druley, S. Pashkey, & S. P. Weinstein (Eds.), *Stress and addiction* (pp. 283–301). Bruner/Mazel.

Zuckerman, M. (1994). *Behavioural expressions and biosocial bases of sensation-seeking.* Cambridge University Press.

Zuckerman, M., Ball, S., & Black, J. (1990). Influences of sensation seeking, gender, risk appraisal, and situational motivation on smoking. *Addictive Behaviors, 15*(3), 209–220. https://doi.org/10.1016/0306-4603(90)90064-5

Zuckerman, M., Eysenck, S., & Eysenck, H. J. (1978). Sensation seeking in England and America: Cross-cultural, age, and sex comparisons. *Journal of Consulting and Clinical Psychology, 46*(1), 139–149. https://doi.org/10.1037/0022-006X.46.1.139

Zuckerman, M., Kolin, E. A., Price, L., & Zoob, I. (1964). Development of a sensation-seeking scale. *Journal of Consulting Psychology, 28*(6), 477–482. https://doi.org/10.1037/h0040995

Zuckerman, M., Tushup, R., & Finner, S. (1976). Sexual attitudes and experience: Attitude and personality correlates and changes produced by a course in sexuality. *Journal of Consulting and Clinical Psychology, 44*(1), 7–19. https://doi.org/10.1037/0022-006X.44.1.7

Zweyer, K., Velker, B., & Ruch, W. (2004). Do cheerfulness, exhilaration, and humor production moderate pain tolerance? A FACS study. *Humor: International Journal of Humor Research, 17*(1–2), 85–119. https://doi.org/10.1515/humr.2004.009

INDEX

pain after, 77, 78
pathological laughter after, 38
theory of mind processing after, 31
transcranial direct current stimulation
treatment of, 78
Structural anomaly detection, ERP
component for, 46
Stuss, D. T., 27
Substantia nigra, 33, 34, 152
Subthalamic nucleus, 34, 77, 78
Subtraction paradigm, 57
Suicidal ideation, 111
Sulcus, 152. *See also specific locations*
Sullivan, E., 138–139
Suls, J. M., 20–22, 47, 50, 59
Summerfelt, H., 20, 143
Superior (term), 44, 152
Superior frontal gyrus, 58, 152
activation of, in fMRI studies, 66, 67
electrical stimulation of, 73, 75
in humor appreciation, 67
for individuals with schizophrenia, 92
during resolution stage, 64, 65
Superiority, conveying, 16
Superior occipital gyrus, 58
Superior parietal lobule, 58
Superior temporal gyrus
activation of, in fMRI studies, 60,
64, 66
for individuals with schizophrenia, 92
transcranial direct current stimulation of,
79
Superior temporal sulcus, 61
Supplementary motor area, 36, 152
activation of, in fMRI studies, 59
bridging-inference jokes and activation
of, 68
electrical stimulation of, 73
laughter and activation of, 74
Supplementary sensorimotor area,
73, 75
Surprise, laughter and, 126
Surprise stage, 47
Survival, humor for, 123, 126, 133
Svebak, S., 46, 47, 110
Swani, K., 96
Sydney Multisite Intervention of
LaughterBosses and ElderClowns
study, 121
Sylvan fissure, 152
Sympathetic nervous system, 112–114,
122, 152
Syntactic ambiguity, 45

T

Tager-Flusberg, H., 89
Teasing, 98–99, 127

Television comedies, studies using, 27,
59–60, 64
Temporal cortex, 74, 75
Temporal lobe, 12, 14, 152
activation of, in EEG studies, 51
activation of, in fMRI studies, 57,
59, 63
cognitive processing of humor in,
60, 64
during detection stage, 51
electrical stimulation of, 72, 73
ERP components and activation of,
45, 46
humor ability and activation of, 68
in humor comprehension, 60, 63, 64
humor processing and degeneration of,
32, 39
for individuals with schizophrenia, 92,
93
for individuals with schizotypal
personality traits, 93
medial, 52
mirth and activation of, 74
personality and activation of, 63
in theory of mind processing, 31
Temporal–occipital junction, 59, 62, 64,
153
Temporal–occipital–parietal junction, 60,
153
Temporal pole, 58, 62, 64, 152
Temporoparietal junction, 153
activation of, in fMRI studies, 59, 61, 64,
65, 67
bridging-inference jokes and activation
of, 68
in humor processing by children, 87
during resolution stage, 67
transcranial stimulation of, 79
Tension release, humor for, 16–17
Thalamus, 18, 77, 153
Thaler, A., 34–35
Theory of mind, 132, 153
Theory of mind processing
and agenesis of corpus callosum,
90–91
and autism spectrum disorder, 88–90
by children, 94
and dementia, 33
development of, 86
EEG studies of, 41, 51–53
and executive function, 31–32
fMRI studies of, 61
and Huntington's disease, 35–36
by individuals with brain damage,
30–32
by older adults, 26–28
and Parkinson's disease, 34–35
and schizophrenia spectrum disorder,
91–92

ABOUT THE AUTHOR

Shelia M. Kennison, PhD, is a professor of psychology at Oklahoma State University. She earned her doctorate in cognitive psychology from the University of Massachusetts at Amherst and her bachelor's degree in psychology and linguistics from Harvard University. She is a fellow of the American Psychological Association and the Psychonomic Society. Her research interests include humor, language processing in monolinguals and bilinguals, and individual differences in verbal and physical risk-taking. She has published research articles in numerous journals, including *Cognition*; *Journal of Experimental Psychology: Learning, Memory, and Cognition*; *Journal of Memory and Language*; and *Discourse Processes*. Her research has received financial support from the National Science Foundation and the Fulbright Foundation. Her previous books include *An Introduction to Language Development* (2013) and *Psychology of Language: Theory and Applications* (2018). She has been a lifelong fan of humor but came to rely on it heavily when she was diagnosed with thyroid cancer at the age of 24. In the decades since, she has followed the research showing that experiencing humor can positively influence our mental and physical health. For the past 5 years, Dr. Kennison has taught a course on the psychology of humor in which she can share her interest in humor research.